London
2013

A SELECTION
OF **RESTAURANTS** & **HOTELS**

Commitments

*S*ince our first edition in 1900, our ambition has remained the same: to accompany you on your journeys and to help you choose the best establishments in which to stay or eat, whether that's an intimate townhouse or a grand hotel, a local gastropub or a fine dining restaurant.

→ Anonymous inspections

Our inspectors make regular and anonymous visits to hotels and restaurants to gauge the quality of products and services offered to an ordinary customer. They settle their own bill and may then introduce themselves and ask for more information about the establishment. Our readers' comments are also a valuable source of information, which we can then follow up with another visit of our own.

→ Independence

Our choice of establishments is a completely independent one, made for the benefit of our readers alone. The decisions to be taken are discussed around the table by the inspectors and the editor. The most important awards are decided at a European level. Inclusion in the Guide is completely free of charge.

→ Selection & choice

The Guide offers a selection of the best hotels and restaurants in every category of comfort and price. This is only possible because all the inspectors rigorously apply the same methods.

→ Annual updates

All the practical information, the classifications and awards are revised and updated every single year to give the most reliable information possible.

→ Consistency

The criteria for the classifications are the same in every country covered by the Michelin Guide.

→ And our aim...

...to do everything possible to make travel, holidays and eating out a pleasure, as part of Michelin's ongoing commitment to improving travel and mobility.

Dear reader

We are delighted to present the 2013 edition of the Michelin Guide for London.

All the restaurants within this guide have been chosen first and foremost for the quality of their cooking. You'll find comprehensive information on over 500 dining establishments, ranging from gastropubs and neighbourhood brasseries to internationally renowned restaurants. The diverse and varied selection also bears testament to the rich and buoyant dining scene in London, with the city now enjoying a worldwide reputation for the quality and range of its restaurants.

You'll see that Michelin Stars are not our only awards – look out also for the Bib Gourmands. These are restaurants where the cooking is still carefully prepared but in a simpler style and, priced at under £28 for three courses, they represent excellent value for money.

To complement the selection of restaurants, our team of independent, full-time inspectors have also chosen 50 hotels. These carefully selected hotels represent the best that London has to offer, from the small and intimate to the grand and luxurious. All have been chosen for their individuality and personality.

We are committed to remaining at the forefront of the culinary world and to meeting the demands of our readers. As such, we are always very interested to hear your opinions on any of the establishments listed in our guide. Please don't hesitate to contact us as your contributions are invaluable in directing our work and improving the quality of the information we provide.

Thank you for your support and happy travelling with the 2013 edition of the Michelin Guide for London.

Consult the Michelin Guide at www.viamichelin.com
and write to us at themichelinguide-gbirl@uk.michelin.com

Contents

● Where to **eat**

CENTRAL LONDON   30

Where to stay

Maps & plans

How to use this guide

Restaurant classified according to comfort (particularly pleasant if in red)	✗ Quite comfortable	✗✗ Very comfortable	✗✗✗✗ Luxury in the traditional style
	✗✗ Comfortable	✗✗✗ Top class comfort	🍺 Pubs severing good food

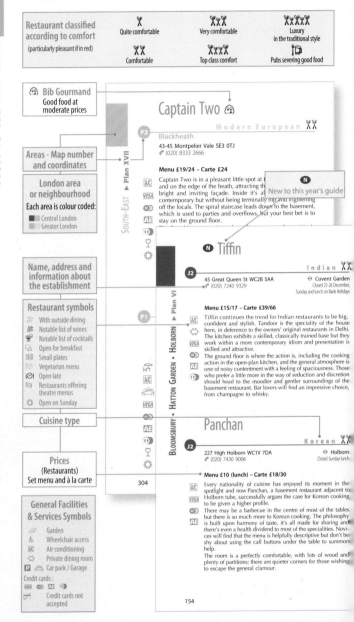

Bib Gourmand
Good food at moderate prices

Areas - Map number and coordinates

London area or neighbourhood
Each area is colour coded:
■ Central London
■ Greater London

Name, address and information about the establishment

Restaurant symbols
- 🌳 With outside dining
- 🍷 Notable list of wines
- 🍸 Notable list of cocktails
- Open for breakfast
- Small plates
- Vegetarian menu
- Open late
- Restaurants offering theatre menus
- Open on Sunday

Cuisine type

Prices
(Restaurants)
Set menu and à la carte

General Facilities & Services Symbols
- Garden
- Wheelchair access
- Air conditioning
- Private dining room
- 🅿 Car park / Garage

Credit cards :
VISA ⬤ AE ⬤
Credit cards not accepted

Captain Two 😊

Modern European ✗✗

P2 Blackheath

43-45 Montpelier Vale SE3 0TJ
📞 (020) 8333 2666

Menu £19/24 – Carte £24

AE
VISA
⬤
AE
⬤
🍷

Captain Two is in a pleasant little spot at t
and on the edge of the heath, attracting th
bright and inviting façade. Inside it's a
contemporary but without being terminally hip and frightening
off the locals. The spiral staircase leads down to the basement,
which is used to parties and overflows, but your best bet is to
stay on the ground floor.

N New to this year's guide

Tiffin

Indian ✗✗

J2

45 Great Queen St WC2B 5AA
📞 (020) 7240 9329

⊖ Covent Garden
Closed 25-26 December,
Sunday and lunch on Bank Holidays

Menu £15/17 – Carte £39/66

AE
VISA
⬤
AE
⬤

Tiffin continues the trend for Indian restaurants to be big,
confident and stylish. Tandoor is the speciality of the house
here, in reference to the owners' original restaurants in Delhi.
The kitchen exhibits a skilled, classically trained base but they
work within a more contemporary idiom and presentation is
skilled and attractive.
The ground floor is where the action is, including the cooking
action in the open-plan kitchen, and the general atmosphere is
one of noisy contentment with a feeling of spaciousness. Those
who prefer a little more in the way of seduction and discretion
should head to the moodier and gentler surroundings of the
basement restaurant. Bar lovers will find an impressive choice,
from champagne to whisky.

Panchan

Korean ✗✗

J2

227 High Holborn WC1V 7DA
📞 (020) 7430 9006

⊖ Holborn
Closed Sunday lunch

Menu £10 (lunch) – Carte £18/30

AE
VISA
⬤
AE

Every nationality of cuisine has enjoyed its moment in the
spotlight and now Panchan, a basement restaurant adjacent to
Holborn tube, successfully argues the case for Korean cooking
to be given a higher profile.
There may be a barbecue in the centre of most of the tables
but there is so much more to Korean cooking. The philosophy
is built upon harmony of taste, it's all made for sharing and
there's even a health dividend to most of the specialities. Novi-
ces will find that the menu is helpfully descriptive but don't be
shy about using the call buttons under the table to summon
help.
The room is a perfectly comfortable, with lots of wood and
plenty of partitions; there are quieter corners for those wishing
to escape the general clamour.

(side text, vertical:) SOUTH-EAST ▶ Plan XVII   BLOOMSBURY • HATTON GARDEN • HOLBORN ▶ Plan VI

304

154

Hotel classification according to comfort
(particularly pleasant if in red)

- 🏠 Quite comfortable
- 🏠🏠 Comfortable
- 🏠🏠🏠 Very comfortable
- 🏠🏠🏠🏠 Top class comfort
- 🏠🏠🏠🏠🏠 Luxury in the traditional style

Hotel symbols

- **39 rm** Number of rooms
- ☕ Breakfast included (or not)
- 👤/👥 Prices for a single/double room
- 🐌 Quiet hotel
- 🍴 With restaurant
- ▧ Swimming pool
- ● Spa
- ♨ Sauna
- ✂ Tennis
- 🏋 Exercise room
- ⇅ Lift
- ☎ Broadband connection
- ≋ Wireless
- 🪑 Equipped conference room

Map coordinates

⊖ Underground station

Agatha's

I2 🏠🏠🏠

15 Charlotte St W1T 1RJ ⊖ Goodge Street
☎ (020) 7806 2000

44 rm – 👤£247/282 👥£347, ☕ £19 – 8 suites
🍴 **Hercule** *(See restaurant listing)*

🍴 🏋 ⇅ ♿ A/C 🪑 VISA

Charlotte Street

...ion, within strolling distance of Soho, or ... own private screening room that attract ...n industry sorts and arty souls who have ... own, but the stimulating way in which it ...and the prevailing vibe.
... warehouse has been deftly transformed ...l and proves that comfort and design can ... and that something good has come from ...ng a combination of abstract art, sculpture ...rtists of the neighbouring Bloomsbury set, ... be also quite English in tone. The drawing ...ress-free areas, in contrast to the bustle of ...restaurant.
...bedrooms are one-off pieces of furniture ...rawer fabrics and fittings, all supported by ...amme of virtually constant refurbishment. ... enthusiastic and confident. The loft and ...l stir emotions of envy and desire or, if

WESTMINSTER ▶ Plan V

373

Le Petit François ✿✿

French ✕✕✕✕

G3

43 Upper Brook St W1K 7QR ⊖ Marble Arch
☎ (020) 7408 0881

Closed Christmas-New Year, Sunday, Saturday lunch and Bank Holidays – booking essential

Menu £48 – Carte £60/130

A/C VISA ⦾ AE ◐ ✿

Le Gavroche

In today's rush for the new and the novel, we sometimes forget about the jewels we already have. Le Petit François is guaranteed its own chapter when the history of British gastronomy is written and today, over forty years after it first opened in Chelsea, it's still maintaining its own high standards and respect for tradition. The service is unerringly professional: this is where any budding restaurateur should come if they want to learn how things are done 'properly' and one can observe the hierarchical structure from one's chair. The room retains a clubby and masculine feel but it also offers a palpable sense of history; those new to the restaurant are guided gently through its customs and politely reminded of its traditions.

The menu represents classic French cuisine and not just an English idea of French cuisine; a style of food which is becoming rarer by the day. A Soufflé Suissesse is rich enough to live on for days and the use of luxury items, from lobster to foie gras, would make Epicurus blanch. Those who prefer a lighter style, however, are not ignored.

First Course	*Main Course*	*Dessert*
• Hot foie gras and crispy duck pancake flavoured with cinnamon.	• Roast saddle of rabbit with crispy potatoes and parmesan.	• Bitter chocolate and praline 'indulgence'.
• Lobster mousse with caviar and champagne butter sauce.	• Whole roast John Dory with artichokes, olive oil mashed potato.	• Iced amaretto nougat with cherries cooked in red wine syrup.

MAYFAIR • SOHO • ST JAMES'S ▶ Plan II

41

Area - Map number

✿ **Starred restaurant**
Stars for good cooking
✿ to ✿✿✿

Sample menu for starred restaurant

A culinary history of London

London, influenced by worldwide produce arriving via the Thames, has always enjoyed a close association with its food, though most of the time the vast majority of its people have looked much closer to home for their sustenance.

Even as far back as the 2nd century AD, meat was on the menu: the profusion of wildlife in the woods and forests around London turned it into a carnivore's paradise, thereby setting the tone and the template. Large stoves were employed to cook everything from pork and beef to goose and deer. The Saxons added the likes of garlic, leeks, radishes and turnips to the pot, while eels became a popular staple in later years.

WHAT A LARK!

By the 13th century, the taste for fish had evolved to the more exotic porpoise, lamprey and sturgeon, with saffron and spices perking up the common-or-garden meat dish. Not that medieval tastes would have been considered mundane to the average 21st century diner: Londoners of the time would think nothing about devouring roasted thrush or lark from the cook's stalls dotted around the city streets. And you'd have been unlikely to hear the cry "Eat your greens!" In the 15th century, the vegetable diet, such as it was, seemed to run mainly to herbs such as rosemary, fennel, borage and thyme.

As commercial and maritime success burgeoned in the age of the Tudors, so tables began to groan under the weight of London's penchant for feasting. No excess was spared, as oxen, sheep, boars and pigs were put to the griddle; these would have been accompanied by newly arrived yams and sweet potatoes from America and 'washed down' with rhubarb from Asia. People on the streets could 'feast-lite': by the 17th century hawkers were offering all sorts of goodies on the hoof.

FULL OF BEANS

All of this eating was of course accompanied by a lot of drinking. Though much of it took place in the alehouses and taverns - which ran into the thousands - by the 18th century coffee houses had become extraordinarily popular. These were places to do business as well as being convenient 'for passing evenings socially at a very small charge'.

Perhaps the biggest re-volution in eating habits came midway through the 19ᵗʰ century when the first cavernous dining halls and restaurants appeared. These 'freed' diners from the communal benches of the cook-house and gave them, for the first time, the chance for a bit of seclusion at separate tables. This private dining experience was an egalitarian movement: plutocrats may have had their posh hotels, but the less well-off were buttering teacakes and scones served by 'nippies' at the local Lyons Corner House.

Influenced by post World War II flavours brought in by immigrants from Asia, the Caribbean and Africa – and, most recently, from Eastern Bloc Countries – Londoners now enjoy an unparalleled cuisine alive with global flavours. Perhaps the Queen's Jubilee and the Olympics have made us more confident about waving the flag for Britain as we are also rediscovering and celebrating our own culinary heritage.

S.Vidler / Prisma/Age Fotostock

9

Practical London

ARRIVAL/DEPARTURE

If you're coming to London from abroad, it's worth bearing in mind that the capital's airports are (with one exception) a long way from the city itself. Better news is that they're all well served by speedy express train services; even better news is that if you travel by Eurostar you can go by train direct from the heart of Europe to the heart of London without having to worry about luggage limits, carousels and carbon footprints...

By air

Most people coming to London from overseas arrive via Heathrow (the UK's busiest) and Gatwick airports (more on both at www.baa.com). You can catch the Heathrow Express rail service (www.heathrowexpress.com) to Paddington (just west of the centre) every 15 minutes, and that's just about how long the journey takes. Another alternative is to board the Piccadilly line tube train from Heathrow: it's cheaper, but

the drawn-out travelling time can make it seem as if you've spent most of your holiday just getting into the centre. Gatwick is further out, south of London's M25 ring road, and the quickest way into the city is via the Gatwick Express rail service (www.gatwickexpress. com), which takes half an hour to reach Victoria station. There are also frequent train services run by Southern (www.southernrailway.com) between Gatwick and Victoria, and Thameslink (www.first-capitalconnect.co.uk), which connect with a host of central London stations, including London Bridge and King's Cross. The capital has three other airports: Stansted (www. stanstedairport.com), 35 miles northeast of the city; Luton (www.london-luton.com), 30 miles to the north, and London City Airport (www. londoncityairport.com), which is nine miles to the east, and connects to the centre via the Docklands Light Railway.

By train

The days of having to fly into London from abroad are long gone. Smart travellers from the Continent now jump on the Eurostar (www.eurostar. com) from Paris, Brussels or Lille, zip along at 186mph, and step onto the platform at St Pancras International in the time it takes to devour a coffee and a croissant (a big coffee, admittedly). From there, three tube lines from the adjoining King's Cross station whisk you into town. Book Eurostar far enough in advance (which isn't very far, by any means) and you can get tickets for just £69 return.

GETTING AROUND
By tube

First, the bad news: the tube can get hot and overcrowded; engineering works can close lines at weekends and the escalators are sometimes out of action. But the good news? Generally speaking, the tube is by far the quickest way to get around town. There are 12 lines, plus the Docklands Light Railway; these cover pretty much the whole city and are all clearly shown on the free map you can pick up at any tube station or London Travel Information Centre. Trains run from 5am to just past midnight Monday-Saturday, with a reduced timetable on Sundays. For details about the line you wish to use, check the Transport for London website www.tfl. gov.uk or phone the 24-hour Travel Information Service on + 44(0) 843 222 1234.

By bus

They might move a bit slower than tubes, but when you ride on the top of a double-decker bus, you get the added bonus of an absorbing, tourist-friendly view to take in on the way. The world-famous Routemasters were all but phased out in 2005; their low-floored replacements much more accessible to wheelchair-users and passengers with buggies. The iconic Routemaster made a comeback in 2012, however, with a newly designed bus which runs between Victoria Station and Hackney – and there are more on the way. There's a handy central London bus map which you can pick up at transport information centres at larger tube stations. Or you can plan your bus trip online by checking out the useful 'Journey Planner' to be found on the Transport for London website. Most Central London routes require that you buy tickets before you board; you can get these from machines by the bus stop. The flat fare is £2.30 and this includes travel across all zones (see also 'The Pearl that is Oyster', below).

By car

The best advice is not to drive in central London, not if you want your sanity preserved anyway. Roadworks and parking can be the stuff of nightmares, and that's before the Congestion Charge Zone, albeit now reduced in size, is even taken into consideration. This zone covers the central area and is clearly marked by the red 'C' signs painted on the road. It's in operation Monday-Friday 7am-6pm (weekends and holidays are free) and you'll need to register the car's number plate on a database (go to www.cclondon.com for details). If it all sounds a bit too much of a headache, you always have the option of hailing a black cab – just stick out your hand when you see one with its taxi light illuminated.

By bike

A greener alternative to the taxi for short journeys is the humble bike – and those aged 14 and above can hire a so-called 'Boris Bike' from one of the many Barclays Cycle Hire docking points spread over the capital. There's no need to book ahead and they're available 24 hours a day, 7 days a week. Simply pay an access fee (£1 for 24 hours/£5 for 7 days) with a credit or debit card, either at a docking station terminal, by phone (0845 026 3630), or online (www.tfl.gov.uk). You are then charged for your usage, but the good news is that, as the scheme is designed to be used for short journeys, the first 30 minutes are free and it's only £1 for the second 30 minutes. Simply return the bike any docking station when you're done.

By boat

'Taking to the water' has become increasingly popular over the last few years: the Thames offers some little-seen views of London, and cutting through the open expanse of river can certainly lay claim to being your most relaxing travel option. Most river services operate every 20 minutes to one hour, and there are piers all over the central area where you can jump on board, from Chelsea Harbour in the west to Woolwich Arsenal in the east. For more details go to www.tfl.gov.uk

The pearl that is oyster

Londoners on the move make sure they don't leave home

without their Oyster. It's an electronic smartcard and it's the fastest and easiest way to pay for single journeys around town. You don't even have to take it out of your purse or wallet: you just zap it over a yellow reader to let you through tube gates or onto a bus. Oysters are charged with a pre-paid amount of credit and can cover a set period of time or be used to pay-as-you-go. You'll always pay less for a journey than on the equivalent Day Travelcard or Bus Pass. To check out the whole deal, visit www.tfl.gov.uk/oyster

LIVING LONDON LIFE

It almost goes without saying that visitors to the capital are spoilt for choice when it comes to having a good time. For instance, you could visit one of the city's 300 museums or galleries, many of which are free, or you could see for yourself why London's theatre scene is considered the best in the world. Come nightfall, choose from the vast number of restaurants, offering cuisines from all parts of the world, or from one of 5,000 pubs and bars. At the weekend, an interesting alternative to shopping or sports events is to browse one of the farmers' markets that have sprung up in recent years. On a Saturday, the best of the bunch can be found at Ealing, Notting Hill, Pimlico, Wimbledon and Twickenham. On Sundays, two of the favourites are in Marylebone and Blackheath, while, on the same day, the Columbia Road flower market, in the East End, is a wonderful place to spend time comparing flora while chomping on a bagel from a local café.

The more mainstream shopper might do well to steer clear of frenetic Oxford Street. Regent Street is a more alluring thoroughfare with its mid-priced fashion stores and hallowed names. If you're after a destination with a real touch of class, then nearby Jermyn Street is the place for bespoke men's clothing, but if your taste is for more outré threads, then Notting Hill or Camden are good bets. Back in the centre of town, Covent Garden is packed with speciality stores, quirky alleyways, and – if you choose the wrong time to go – an awful lot of people!

Escape can always be found in the relative quiet of a good bookshop, and London is full of them. Still in Covent Garden, Stanford's is the city's number one travel bookshop, while not far away in Charing Cross Road, the legendary Foyles has thrown over its fusty image with a stylish makeover. But for the marriage of real elegance with a good read, head to Daunt Books in Marylebone High Street, which is set in an Edwardian building with long oak galleries and skylights; the bustle of London's streets will seem a million miles away.

Where to **eat**

Stephanie Guillaume/Fotolia.com

Starred restaurants

Within this selection, we have highlighted a number of restaurants for their particularly good cooking. When awarding one, two or three Michelin Stars there are a number of factors we consider: the quality and compatibility of the ingredients, the technical skill and flair that goes into their preparation, the clarity and combination of flavours, the value for money and, above all, the taste. Equally important is the ability to produce excellent cooking not once but time and time again. Our inspectors make as many visits as necessary, so that you can be sure of the quality and consistency.

A two or three star restaurant has to offer something very special in its cuisine; a real element of creativity, originality or personality that sets it apart from the rest. Three stars – our highest award – are given to the very best.

Cuisines in any style and of any nationality are eligible for a star. The decoration, service and comfort have no bearing on the award.

For every restaurant awarded a star we include six specialities that are typical of their cooking style.

These specific dishes may not always be available.

Let us know what you think; not just about the stars but about all the restaurants in this guide.

The awarding of a star is based solely on the quality of the cuisine.

N : highlights those establishments newly promoted to one, two or three stars.

Exceptional cuisine, worth a special journey.
One always eats here extremely well, sometimes superbly. Distinctive dishes are precisely executed, using superlative ingredients.

Alain Ducasse at The Dorchester	XxXxX 38	Gordon Ramsay	XxxX 272

Excellent cooking, worth a detour.
Skillfully and carefully crafted dishes of outstanding quality.

L'Atelier de Joël Robuchon	X 113	Marcus Wareing at The Berkeley	XxxX 137
Le Gavroche	XxxX 64	Sketch (The Lecture Room and Library) N	XxxX 97
Hélène Darroze at The Connaught	XxxX 69	Square	XxxX 99
Hibiscus	XxX 70		
Ledbury	XxX 296		

A very good restaurant in its category.
A place offering cuisine prepared to a consistently high standard.

Alyn Williams at the Westbury N	XxxX 40	Nobu	XX 83
Amaya	XxX 130	Nobu Berkeley St	XX 84
Apsleys	XxxX 131	North Road	XX 233
Arbutus	X 43	Petersham Nurseries Café	X 398
L'Autre Pied	XX 152	Pétrus	XxX 142
Benares	XxX 50	Pied à Terre	XxX 187
Chez Bruce	XX 404	Pollen Street Social	XX 86
Club Gascon	XX 220	Quilon	XxX 143
Dabbous N	X 180	Rasoi	XX 280
Dinner by Heston Blumenthal	XxX 266	Rhodes Twenty Four	XxX 238
Galvin at Windows	XxxX 63	Rhodes W1 (Restaurant)	XxxX 165
Galvin La Chapelle	XxxX 355	River Café	XX 393
The Glasshouse	XX 394	St John (Clerkenwell)	X 240
Greenhouse	XxX 66	St John (Soho) N	X 92
Hakkasan Hanway Place	XX 183	Semplice	XX 94
Hakkasan Mayfair	XX 68	Seven Park Place	XxX 95
Harwood Arms	🍴 386	Tamarind	XxX 100
Hedone N	XX 377	Texture	XX 169
Kai	XxX 75	Tom Aikens N	XxX 282
Kitchen W8	XX 294	Trishna N	X 170
Launceston Place N	XxX 295	La Trompette	XxX 379
Locanda Locatelli	XxX 160	Umu	XX 104
Maze	XX 78	Viajante	XX 346
Medlar N	XX 276	Wild Honey	XX 106
Murano	XxX 81	Yauatcha	XX 108

17

Bib Gourmand

Restaurants offering good quality cooking for less than £28 (price of a 3 course meal excluding drinks)

Anchor and Hope	🍴🏠 208	Hereford Road	✗ 196
Azou	✗ 389	José	✗ 225
Barrafina	✗ 46	Kateh	✗ 197
Barrica **N**	✗ 178	Koya	✗ 76
Benja Bangkok Table	✗ 49	Made in Camden **N**	✗ 310
Bistro Union **N**	✗ 380	Mango and Silk	✗ 384
Bocca di Lupo	✗ 52	Market	✗ 311
Bradley's	✗✗ 319	Medcalf	✗ 229
Brasserie Zédel **N**	✗✗ 53	Morito	✗ 231
Brawn	✗ 344	Opera Tavern	✗✗ 121
Cafe Spice Namaste	✗✗ 359	Polpo Covent Garden	✗ 122
Canton Arms	🍴🏠 358	Polpo Soho	✗ 87
Comptoir Gascon	✗ 219	Princess of Shoreditch **N**	🍴🏠 338
Copita **N**	✗ 58	St John Bread and Wine	✗ 357
Corner Room **N**	✗ 345	Salt Yard	✗ 188
Drapers Arms	🍴🏠 334	Simply Thai	✗ 402
Elliot's **N**	✗ 222	Soif **N**	✗ 374
Empress **N**	🍴🏠 329	Sushi-Say	✗ 321
500	✗ 308	Terroirs	✗ 125
Fox and Grapes	🍴🏠 406	Triphal	✗ 400
Galvin Café a Vin	✗ 354	Trullo	✗ 328
Giaconda Dining Room	✗ 181	Zucca	✗ 247
Great Queen Street	✗ 182		

Restaurants by Cuisine Type

eat ▶ Cuisine Type

Argentinian

Casa Malevo	✗	195

Asian

Asia de Cuba	✗✗	114
Cicada	✗	217
E and O	✗✗	291
Eight over Eight	✗✗	267
Goldfish	✗	315
Great Eastern Dining Room	✗✗	332
Singapore Garden	✗✗	320
Spice Market	✗✗	96
XO	✗✗	310

Asian influences

Kopapa	✗	182
Suka	✗✗	168

Basque

Donostia	✗	156

British modern

Anchor and Hope	🍴 ⊛	208
Bistro Union	✗ ⊛	380
Bluebird	✗✗	257
Brown Dog	🍴	369
Canton Arms	🍴 ⊛	358
Chelsea Ram	🍴	264
Chiswell Street Dining Rooms	✗✗	217
Corrigan's Mayfair	✗✗✗	59
Dean Street Townhouse Restaurant	✗✗	60
Dinner by Heston Blumenthal	✗✗✗ ✿	266
Drapers Arms	🍴 ⊛	334
Fox and Grapes	🍴 ⊛	406
Georgina's	✗	369
Great Queen Street	✗ ⊛	182
Hampshire Hog	🍴	390
Harwood Arms	🍴 ✿	386
Hereford Road	✗ ⊛	196
Inn the Park	✗	73
Magdalen	✗✗	228
Market	✗ ⊛	311
Narrow	🍴	354
The National Dining Rooms	✗	82
Northall	✗✗✗	138
Pantechnicon	🍴	141
Paradise by way of Kensal Green	🍴	316
Peasant	🍴	235
Prince Arthur	🍴	330
Prince of Wales	🍴	396
Quo Vadis	✗✗✗	89
Ransome's Dock	✗	373
Restaurant at St Paul's Cathedral	✗	237
Rhodes Twenty Four	✗✗✗ ✿	238
Rivington Grill (Greenwich)	✗	352
Rivington Grill (Shoreditch)	✗	339
Roast	✗✗	239
Sands End	🍴	387
Tate Modern (Restaurant)	✗	242
Victoria	🍴	385
Well	🍴	245
Wells	🍴	316

British traditional

Albion	🍴	333
Angel & Crown	🍴	114
Anglesea Arms	🍴	388
Avalon	🍴	367
Barnsbury	🍴	334
Bedford and Strand	✗	115
Bentley's (Grill)	✗✗✗	51
Bob Bob Ricard	✗✗	52
Builders Arms	🍴	259
Bull and Last	🍴	313
Bumpkin (North Kensington)	✗	288
Bumpkin (South Kensington)	✗	259
Butlers Wharf Chop House	✗	213
Cadogan Arms	🍴	260
Cat and Mutton	🍴	329
Foxtrot Oscar	✗	269

19

Chinese

French

Japanese

Korean

Lebanese

Mediterranean

innovative

meats and grills

modern

Ledbury	XxX❀❀	296
Lutyens	XxX	227
Magdala	�🍴	315
Medlar	XX❀	276
The Mercer	XX	229
Mews of Mayfair	XX	79
Michael Nadra	XX	378
North Road	XX❀	233
Odette's	XX	317
Orange	⍔	140
Orrery	XxX	161
Oxo Tower	XxX	234
Oxo Tower Brasserie	X	234
Paramount	X	186
Pétrus	XxX❀	142
Phoenix	⍔	278
Plateau	XX	349
Portman	⍔	163
Portrait	X	87
Prince Alfred and Formosa		
Dining Room	⍔	199
Quaglino's	XX	88
Refuel	XX	90
Rhodes W1 (Brasserie)	XX	164
Riding House Café	X	164
River Restaurant	XxX	122
St John's Tavern	⍔	308
Seven Park Place	XxX❀	95
Sketch (The Gallery)	XX	96
Skylon	XxX	241
Sonny's Kitchen	XX	371
10 Greek Street	X	102
Thomas Cubitt	⍔	145
Tom Aikens	XxX❀	282
Tramshed	X	339
La Trompette	XxX❀	379

28°-50° Marylebone	X	168
Upstairs	XX	375
Verru	XX	171
Village East	X	243
Vinoteca (Soho)	X	105
Vinoteca (Clerkenwell)	X	244
Vinoteca (Regent's Park and Marylebone)	X	171
Wapping Food	X	359
Waterway	⍔	199
The White Swan	XX	246
Wild Honey	XX❀	106
The Wolseley	XxX	107
York and Albany	⍔	311

other world kitchens

Baku	XxX	255
Baltic	XX	209
Caravan	X	215
Ceviche	X	57
Colchis	XX	196
Floridita	XX	62
Kateh	X⍟	197
Made in Camden	X⍟	310
The Modern Pantry	X	230
Shrimpy's	X	319
Tandis	X	309
Tom Ilić	X	374
Vivat Bacchus	X	244
Vivat Bacchus London Bridge	X	245

regional

Boisdale	XX	132
Boisdale of Bishopsgate	XX	212
Boisdale of Canary Wharf	XX	347

Restaurants with outside dining

Where to **eat** ▶ **Outside dining**

Open Late

Time of last orders in brackets

Amaya (23.30)	𝕏𝕩𝕏✾ 130	Imperial China (23.30)	𝕏𝕩𝕏 73
Asia de Cuba (23.30)	𝕏𝕏 114	The Ivy (23.15)	𝕏𝕩𝕏 119
Automat (23.45)	𝕏 44	J. Sheekey (00.00)	𝕏𝕏 119
Bentley's (Oyster Bar) (23.30)	𝕏 51	J. Sheekey	
Bob Bob Ricard (23.30)	𝕏𝕏 52	Oyster Bar (00.00)	𝕏 120
Boisdale (01.00)	𝕏𝕏 132	Kenza (23.30)	𝕏𝕏 226
Boisdale of Canary		Kyashii (23.15)	𝕏𝕏 120
Bombay Brasserie (23.30)	𝕏𝕩𝕩𝕏 258	Malabar (23.30)	𝕏𝕏 293
Brasserie Max (00.00)	𝕏𝕏 179	Mao Tai (23.15)	𝕏𝕏 387
Brasserie Zédel (00.00)	𝕏𝕏 53	Momo (23.30)	𝕏𝕏 80
Le Caprice (00.00)	𝕏𝕏 55	Mishkin's (23.30)	𝕏 121
Cecconi's (23.15)	𝕏𝕩𝕏 56	Mr Chow (00.00)	𝕏𝕏 275
China Tang (23.30)	𝕏𝕩𝕩𝕏 57	Nobu (23.15)	𝕏𝕏✾ 83
Chutney Mary (23.30)	𝕏𝕩𝕏 264	Nobu Berkeley St (00.00)	𝕏𝕏✾ 84
Clos Maggiore (23.30)	𝕏𝕏 116	One Blenheim	
Daphne's (23.30)	𝕏𝕏 265	Paramount (23.15)	𝕏 186
Dean Street Townhouse		Plum Valley (23.15)	𝕏𝕏 85
Restaurant (23.45)	𝕏𝕏 60	Poissonnerie de	
Le Deuxième (00.00)	𝕏𝕏 117	l'Avenue (23.30)	𝕏𝕏 279
Eighty-Six (00.00)	𝕏𝕏 267	Refuel (00.00)	𝕏𝕏 90
Eleven Park Walk (23.45)	𝕏𝕩𝕏 268	St John (Soho) (00.00)	𝕏✾ 92
Fakhreldine (23.30)	𝕏𝕏 61	Sketch (The Gallery) (00.00)	𝕏𝕏 96
Hakkasan Hanway		Spuntino (00.00)	𝕏 98
Place (23.30)	𝕏𝕏✾ 183	Tendido Cero (23.30)	𝕏 281
Hakkasan Mayfair (23.30)	𝕏𝕏✾ 68	The Wolseley (00.00)	𝕏𝕩𝕏 107
Haozhan (02.00)	𝕏𝕏 67	Yauatcha (23.30)	𝕏𝕏✾ 108

Open for Breakfast

Central London

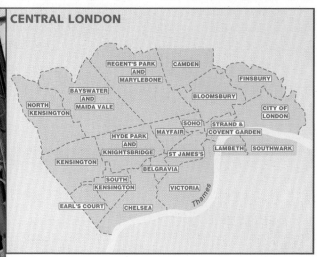

CENTRAL LONDON

REGENT'S PARK AND MARYLEBONE · CAMDEN · FINSBURY · BAYSWATER AND MAIDA VALE · NORTH KENSINGTON · BLOOMSBURY · CITY OF LONDON · SOHO · STRAND & COVENT GARDEN · HYDE PARK AND KNIGHTSBRIDGE · MAYFAIR · LAMBETH · SOUTHWARK · KENSINGTON · ST JAMES'S · BELGRAVIA · SOUTH KENSINGTON · VICTORIA · Thames · EARL'S COURT · CHELSEA

Robert Haidinger/Agentur Anzenberger/Photononstop

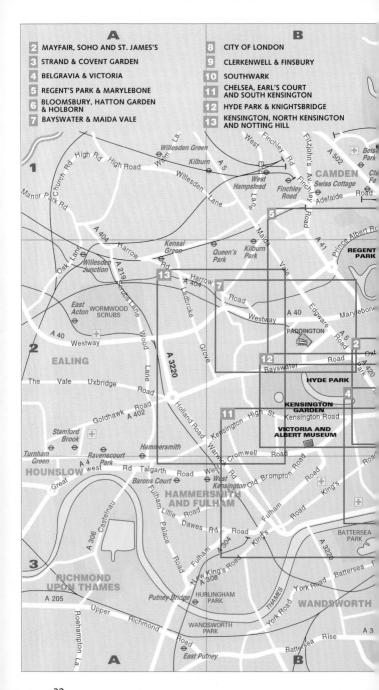

A

2	MAYFAIR, SOHO AND ST. JAMES'S
3	STRAND & COVENT GARDEN
4	BELGRAVIA & VICTORIA
5	REGENT'S PARK & MARYLEBONE
6	BLOOMSBURY, HATTON GARDEN & HOLBORN
7	BAYSWATER & MAIDA VALE

B

8	CITY OF LONDON
9	CLERKENWELL & FINSBURY
10	SOUTHWARK
11	CHELSEA, EARL'S COURT AND SOUTH KENSINGTON
12	HYDE PARK & KNIGHTSBRIDGE
13	KENSINGTON, NORTH KENSINGTON AND NOTTING HILL

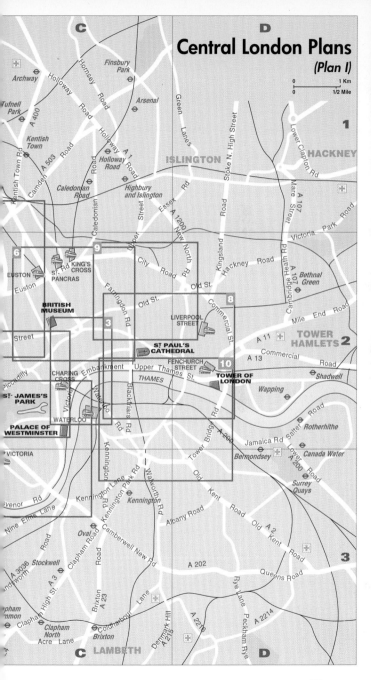

Central London Plans
(Plan I)

C **D**

0 — 1 Km
0 — 1/2 Mile

1

Archway

Tufnell Park

Kentish Town

Finsbury Park

Arsenal

ISLINGTON

HACKNEY

Holloway Road

Hornsey Road

Caledonian Road

Highbury and Islington

Green Lanes

Stoke N. High Street

Lower Clapton Rd

Mare Street

A 107

Victoria Park Road

Camden Rd

Kentish Town Rd

A 503

A 400

A 1

Holloway Road

Essex Rd

New North Rd

A 1200

City Road

Kingsland Road

Hackney Road

Bethnal Green

A 107

Cambridge Heath Rd

6

9

Euston

Euston

St PANCRAS

KING'S CROSS

St Rd

BRITISH MUSEUM

Street

Old St.

Old St.

Farringdon Rd

3

8

LIVERPOOL STREET

Commercial St.

Mile End Road

TOWER HAMLETS

2

A 11

A 13 Commercial Road

St PAUL'S CATHEDRAL

FENCHURCH STREET

10

TOWER OF LONDON

Shadwell

CHARING CROSS

St JAMES'S PARK

Piccadilly

Upper Thames St.

THAMES

Wapping

Salter Road

Rotherhithe

Victoria Embankment

Waterloo Rd

Blackfriars Rd

Tower Bridge Rd A 100

Lower Road

Canada Water

A 200

WATERLOO

PALACE OF WESTMINSTER

VICTORIA

Jamaica Rd

Bermondsey

Surrey Quays

venor Rd

Kennington Lane

Kennington Rd

Kennington Park Rd

Walworth Rd

Old Kent Road

A 2

Kent Road

Nine Elms Lane

Kennington

Oval

Camberwell New Rd

Albany Road

3

Stockwell

Clapham Road

Brixton Road

A 202

Queens Road

A 3036

andsworth

pham mmon

Clapham High St.

A 3

Clapham North

Acre Lane

Brixton

A 23

Coldharbour Lane

Denmark Hill

A 215

Rye Lane

Peckham Rye

A 2216

A 2214

LAMBETH

C **D**

Mayfair · Soho · St James's

There's one elegant dividing line between Mayfair and Soho - the broad and imposing sweep of **Regent Street** - but mindsets and price tags keep them a world apart. It's usual to think of easterly Soho as the wild and sleazy half of these ill-matched twins, with Mayfair to the west the more sedate and sophisticated of the two. Sometimes, though, the natural order of things runs awry: why was rock's legendary wild man Jimi Hendrix, the embodiment of Soho decadence, living in the rarefied air of Mayfair's smart 23 Brook Street? And what induced Vivienne Westwood, punk queen and fashionista to the edgy, to settle her sewing machine in the uber-smart Conduit Street?

Mayfair has been synonymous with elegance for three and a half centuries, ever since the Berkeley and Grosvenor families bought up the local fields and turned them into posh real estate. The area is named after the annual May fair introduced in 1686, but suffice it to say that a raucous street celebration would be frowned upon big time by twenty-first century inhabitants. The grand residential boulevards can seem frosty and imposing, and even induce feelings of inadequacy to the humble passer-by but should he become the proud owner of a glistening gold card, then hey ho, doors will open wide. Claridge's is an art deco wonder, while **New Bond Street** is London's number one thoroughfare for the most chi-chi names in retailing. **Savile Row** may sound a little 'passé' these days, but it's still the place to go for the sharpest cut in town, before sashaying over to compact **Cork Street** to indulge in the purchase of a piece of art at one of its superb galleries. Science and music can also be found here, and at a relatively cheap price: the Faraday Museum in **Albemarle Street** has had a sparkling refurbishment, and the Handel House Museum in Brook Street boasts an impressive two-for-one offer: you can visit the beautifully presented home of the German composer and view his musical scores… before looking at pictures of Hendrix, his 'future' next door neighbour.

Soho challenges the City as London's most famous square mile. It may not have the money of its brash easterly rival, but it sure has the buzz. It's always been fast and loose, since the days when hunters charged through with their cries of 'So-ho!' Its narrow jumbled streets throng with humanity, from the tourist to the tipsy, the libertine to the louche. A lot of the fun is centred round the streets just south of **Soho Square,** where area legends like The Coach & Horses ('Norman's Bar'), Ronnie Scott's and Bar Italia cluster in close proximity. There's 80s favourite, the Groucho Club, too, though some of its lustre may have waned since a corporate takeover. The tightest t-shirts in town are found in **Old Compton Street,** where the pink pound jangles the registers in a

C. Barrely / MICHELIN

swathe of gay-friendly bars and restaurants. To get a feel of the 'real' Soho, where old engraved signs enliven the shop fronts and the market stall cries echo back to the 1700s, a jaunt along **Berwick Street** is always in vogue, taking in a pint at the eternally popular Blue Posts, an unchanging street corner stalwart that still announces 'Watney's Ales' on its stencilled windows.

Not a lot of Watney's ale was ever drunk in **St James's;** not a lot of ale of any kind for that matter. Champagne and port is more the style here, in the hushed and reverential gentlemen's clubs where discretion is the key, and change is measured in centuries rather than years. The sheer class of the area is typified by **Pall Mall's** Reform Club, where Phileas Fogg wagered that he could zip round the world in eighty days, and the adjacent **St James's Square,** which was the most fashionable address in London in the late seventeenth century, when dukes and earls aplenty got their satin shoes under the silver bedecked tables.

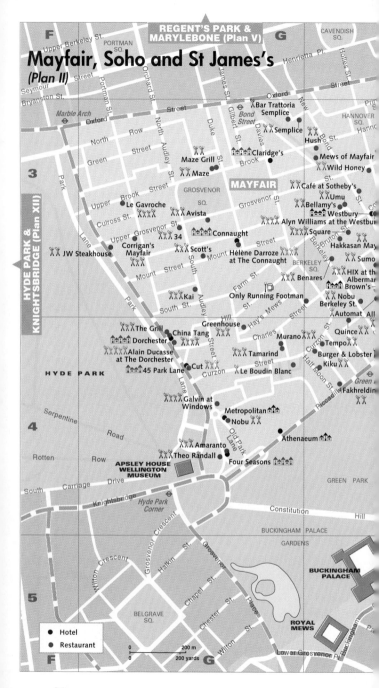

Mayfair, Soho and St James's
(Plan II)

REGENT'S PARK & MARYLEBONE (Plan V)

HYDE PARK & KNIGHTSBRIDGE (Plan XII)

MAYFAIR

Bar Trattoria Semplice
Semplice
Hush
Mews of Mayfair
Wild Honey
Claridge's
Maze Grill
Maze
GROSVENOR SQ.
Café at Sotheby's
Umu
Le Gavroche
Avista
Bellamy's
Westbury
Alyn Williams at the Westbury
Connaught
34
Hakkasan Mayfair
Corrigan's Mayfair
Scott's
JW Steakhouse
Hélène Darroze at The Connaught
Sumo
HIX at the Albemarle
Benares
Brown's
Kai
Only Running Footman
Nobu Berkeley St.
Automat
Greenhouse
Quince
Murano
The Grill
China Tang
Tempo
Dorchester
Tamarind
Burger & Lobster
Alain Ducasse at The Dorchester
Kiku
Cut
Le Boudin Blanc
45 Park Lane
Fakhreldine
Galvin at Windows
Metropolitan
Nobu
Athenaeum
Amaranto
Theo Randall
Four Seasons

HYDE PARK

APSLEY HOUSE
WELLINGTON MUSEUM

Hyde Park Corner

BUCKINGHAM PALACE GARDENS

BELGRAVE SQ.

BUCKINGHAM PALACE

ROYAL MEWS

● Hotel
● Restaurant

0   200 m
0   200 yards

36

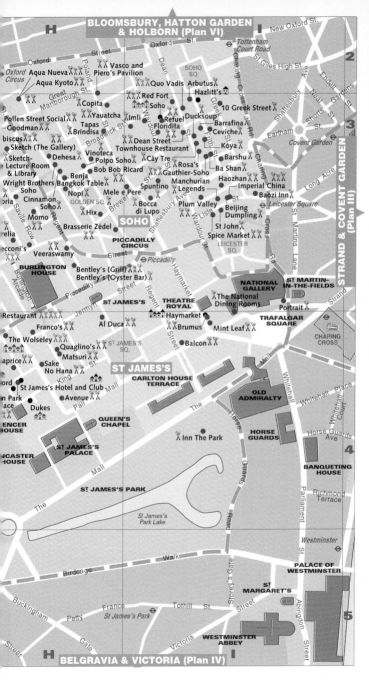

New Oxford St.

Oxford Street
Oxford St.

Tottenham Court Road

Oxford Circus

Aqua Nueva
Aqua Kyoto

Poland St.

Dean St.

SOHO SQ.

Vasco and Piero's Pavilion

St Giles High St.

Endell St.

Quo Vadis
Arbutus
Hazlitt's

Great Marlborough St.

Copita
Yauatcha
Tapas
Brindisa

Red Fort
Soho
Imli
Refuel
Floridita

Ducksoup

10 Greek Street

Shaftesbury Ave.

Neal St.

Shorts Gardens

Pollen Street Social
Goodman
hibiscus

Wardour St.

Barrafina
Ceviche

Earlham St.

Covent Garden

Sketch (The Gallery)

Dehesa
Vinoteca
Polpo Soho

Dean Street
Townhouse Restaurant

Cây Tre

Koya

Barshu

Long Acre

STRAND & COVENT GARDEN (Plan III)

Sketch – Lecture Room & Library

Wright Brothers Soho

Benja
Bangkok Table

Nopi
Cinnamon Soho

Berwick St.

Rosa's
Gauthier-Soho

Ba Shan

Haozhan

Imperial China

Baozi Inn

Mele e Pere

Spuntino

Manchurian Legends

Leicester Square

victoria

GOLDEN SQ.

Hix

Bocca di Lupo

Plum Valley

Beijing Dumpling

St Martins Lane

Momo

Brewer St.

Lisle St.

St John

Savile Row

Brasserie Zédel

Wardour St.

Spice Market

ecconi's

SOHO

PICCADILLY CIRCUS

LEICESTER SQ.

Veeraswamy

Piccadilly

Charing Cross Rd.

relia

BURLINGTON HOUSE

Bentley's (Grill)
Bentley's (Oyster Bar)

NATIONAL GALLERY

ST MARTIN-IN-THE-FIELDS

Restaurant

Burlington Arcade

Piccadilly

Regent Street

Haymarket

ST JAMES'S

THEATRE ROYAL

Haymarket

The National Dining Rooms

Portrait

TRAFALGAR SQUARE

Strand

Franco's

Jermyn Street

Al Duca

Brumus

Mint Leaf

CHARING CROSS

The Wolseley

Quaglino's
Matsuri

ST JAMES'S SQ.

King St.

Balcon

aprice

Sake No Hana

 St James's Hotel and Club

Avenue

n Park ace

Dukes

Pall Mall

The Mall

ST JAMES'S

CARLTON HOUSE TERRACE

OLD ADMIRALTY

Whitehall

Whitehall Place

Whitehall Court

Horse Guards Ave.

ENCER OUSE

NCASTER OUSE

ST JAMES'S PALACE

QUEEN'S CHAPEL

Inn The Park

HORSE GUARDS

BANQUETING HOUSE

Mall

ST JAMES'S PARK

Horse Guards Road

St James's Park Lake

Westminster St.

Richmond Terrace

Birdcage Walk

Buckingham

Petty France

St James's Park

Tothill

Storey's Gate

Victoria Street

PALACE OF WESTMINSTER

ST MARGARET'S

Abingdon St.

Street

WESTMINSTER ABBEY

Alain Ducasse at The Dorchester ✿✿✿

French XXXXX

G4

Dorchester Hotel,
Park Ln ✉ W1K 1QA
✆ (020) 7629 8866
www.alainducasse-dorchester.com

⊖ Hyde Park Corner
Closed 13 August-5 September, 26-30
December, Saturday lunch,
Sunday and Monday

Menu £55/85

A/C

VISA
M/C
AE

Alain Ducasse

Alain Ducasse is one of France's greatest post-war chefs and his London team display a confidence in their ability and maturity in their attitude that does justice to his reputation. The service is assured and the meal perfectly paced; the settled, experienced team know when to engage with guests and when to stand back. The room has a serene and luxurious feel, its tables immaculately set, but try to avoid the raised section by the windows as, although you may have a partial view of the park, you do end up feeling somewhat disengaged from the rest of the room. The kitchen team have steadily lightened the classical French dishes but they remain superbly crafted, with wonderfully complementary flavours and textures. The menu uses the best of British and French produce, from Dorset crab and Scottish lobster to Limousin veal and Anjou pigeon, and some of the dishes will remain long in the memory. The wine list is exemplary, with a particularly impressive selection of Domaine de la Romanée Conti and Château d'Yquem.

First Course

- Sauté of lobster, truffled chicken quenelles and pasta.
- Dorset crab two ways.

Main Course

- Fillet of beef Rossini with Périgueux sauce.
- Baked halibut, celeriac, shellfish and squid.

Dessert

- 'Baba like in Monte-Carlo'.
- Chocolate soufflé with vanilla ice cream.

Al Duca

4-5 Duke of York St
✉ SW1Y 6LA
✆ (020) 7839 3090
www.alduca-restaurant.co.uk

⊖ Piccadilly Circus
Closed Easter, 25 December,
Sunday and bank holidays

Menu £20/28

Al Duca has become as much a part of the fabric of St James's as many of the shirt makers who have made neighbouring Jermyn Street home over the years. It is also one of the those restaurants that manage the trick of appearing quiet one minute and full to the rafters the next without anyone noticing and this ensures that the atmosphere is never less than spirited. The serving team are a young, confident bunch and the manager knows who his regulars are. The menu is priced per course; there is plenty of choice and the cooking is crisp and confident, with plenty of well-priced bottles to match. The rib-eye with porcini mushrooms is a highlight. Prices are also pretty keen, especially for a restaurant in this neck of the woods.

Alloro

19-20 Dover St
✉ W1S 4LU
✆ (020) 7495 4768
www.atozrestaurants.com/alloro

⊖ Green Park
Closed 25 December, Saturday lunch
and Sunday – booking essential

Menu £35, £39/45

Alloro opened at the turn of the century and this comparative longevity owes much to its sensible prices, confident service and easy-to-eat Italian food. The current chef has been here for nearly half the restaurant's life; he comes from Piedmont and manages to sneak in a few specialties from his home region. The menu offers an appealing choice and nicely balanced selection, from a crisp chicory salad with bottarga to slow-cooked lamb shoulder, with all breads and pastas being made in-house. It's priced per number of courses taken; having all four represents the best value. Noise drifts in from the adjacent, boisterous baretto and so ensures that the atmosphere in the comfortable and urbane restaurant is always lively.

N Alyn Williams at the Westbury ✿

H3

modern XXXX

Westbury Hotel,
Bond St ⊠ W1S 2YF
☎ (020) 7078 9579
www.westburymayfair.com

⊖ Bond Street
Closed Saturday lunch and Sunday

Menu £24/45

Alyn Williams at The Westbury

Over recent years, a small fortune has been spent putting back some of the style for which The Westbury was known when it opened back in the 1950s. But decoration is nothing without the right personnel and in 2012 the owners enticed Alyn Williams away from Marcus Wareing and put his name above the door of the restaurant. It's notoriously difficult to lend personality to hotel restaurants – and this one has the added disadvantage of being windowless – but the rosewood panelling, judicious lighting and a striking wine display more than compensate. The confident and cheery service team also ensure that the atmosphere never strays into the terminal seriousness that afflicts restaurants with ambition. In contrast to the fairly terse menu descriptions, Alyn Williams' cooking is creative and even at times quite playful— but however technically adept and elaborately constructed the dish, the combinations of flavours and textures always work. Vegetarians are well looked after; the breads are terrific and the wine list comprehensive.

First Course

- Veal sweetbreads with artichokes, celery and sherry.
- Langoustine, morcilla, cider apple and chestnut.

Main Course

- Cotswold chicken with girolles, smoked egg and charred leek.
- Grilled plaice, squid ink, cuttlefish, puntarella and smoked lardo.

Dessert

- 'Walnut whip'.
- Tiramisu and Nutella brioche.

Amaranto

G4

Italian XX X

Four Seasons Hotel,
Hamilton Pl, Park Ln ✉ W1J 7DR
✆ (020) 7499 0888
www.fourseasons.com/london/

⊖ Hyde Park Corner

Menu £22 (lunch) – Carte £32/55

The Four Seasons hotel emerged from its huge refurbishment programme with a restaurant that's all about flexibility. Amaranto is a bar, a lounge and a dining room, and the idea is that you can have what you want, where you want it, from a largely Italian inspired menu that covers all bases. That means you can enjoy some crab cakes with your drink in the smart bar, share a plate of charcuterie with friends in the comfortable lounge or order a full 3 course meal with business clients in the handsome dining room. No expense was spared on the decoration – the space is full of the colours of the plant after which it is named and there's lots of lacquered wood. Unusually for hotels on Park Lane, there is also a fine terrace attached.

Aqua Kyoto

H3

Japanese XX

240 Regent St. (entrance on Argyll St.)
✉ W1F 7EB
✆ (020) 7478 0540
www.aqua-london.com

⊖ Oxford Circus
Closed 25 December
and 1 January

Menu £20 (weekday lunch) – Carte £23/61 s

Aqua London occupies all 17,000 square foot of the 5th floor of the former Dickins & Jones department store and boasts, along with a big bar and terrific terraces, two large restaurants. Aqua Kyoto is the more boisterous of the two, although getting to the table can be a drawn out affair, as you first give your name at the Argyll Street entrance, do so again when you get out of the lift, and only then are you handed over to the restaurant reception. However, Aqua Kyoto offers a fun night out, more so if you've come in a group – not just so you can compete with the noise, but also because the contemporary Japanese food is designed for sharing. Highlights include the eel teriyaki and the noodle dishes. Service means well but lacks direction.

Aqua Nueva

H3

S p a n i s h ✗✗✗

240 Regent St. (entrance on Argyll St.)   ⊖ Oxford Circus
✉ W1B 3BR   Closed 25 December
✆ (020) 7478 0540   and 1 January
www.aqua-london.com

Menu £23 (weekday lunch) – Carte £22/60

To reach the relative tranquillity of this Spanish restaurant, one first has to fight through the crowds enjoying a drink and a sense of exclusivity in Aqua Spirit, another part of this huge operation. Aqua Nueva feels more sophisticated than Aqua Kyoto with which its shares the 5th floor. It comes divided into two; the main room is more elegant and comfortable, but the tapas bar area, with its ceiling feature of 15,000 wooden beads, has more buzz and character and fills up first. The food comes in a stylised fashion that delivers the classic combinations of Spanish cuisine in original ways, although some subtle balances can get lost in the interpretation. The tapas, however, is more traditional and often features regional specialities.

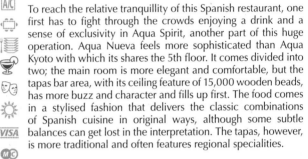 Aurelia

H3

M e d i t e r r a n e a n ✗✗

13-14 Cork St   ⊖ Green Park
✉ W1S 3NS   Closed Sunday
✆ (020) 7409 1370
www.aurelialondon.co.uk

Carte £26/93

The Roman road that stretched from Rome through southern France and into Spain not only provides the inspiration for the kitchen but, it would appear, is also the favoured location for the holiday homes of many of the customers here. All dishes on this culinary journey around the Med are advertised as being ideal for sharing but this works better when it's the impressive charcuterie board in front of you rather than a plate of linguine. The dishes that everyone will expect to go around the table are those from the charcoal grill or the rotisserie, such as the tender leg of lamb with anchovies, the corn-fed baby chicken or the veal cutlet. Those in the know sit downstairs where the aromas are enticing and the atmosphere more animated.

Arbutus ✤

63-64 Frith St.
✉ W1D 3JW
✆ (020) 7734 4545
www.arbutusrestaurant.co.uk

⊖ Tottenham Court Road
Closed 25-26 December and 1 January
– booking advisable

Menu £19 (lunch) – Carte £29/40

A/C
🎭
☼
VISA
MC
AE

Arbutus

When a restaurant makes it look as easy as this, you know that an enormous amount of work and experience have actually gone into it. Arbutus has proved an enormous success because all its components dovetail together just so: the decoration is relaxed and contemporary but seems to work in harmony with the food; service is prompt and efficient but also bubbly and affable; the cooking is intelligent and honest and the prices are realistic and accessible. Despite the apparent simplicity of the food on the plate, this is highly accomplished cooking which demonstrates an inherent understanding of ingredients, textures and flavours. Dishes are dictated by the seasonal availability of their component parts and the skilled use of cheaper cuts like tripe, tongue and trotters rather than luxury ingredients highlights the kitchen's level of ability and also keeps prices down-to-earth. Factor in a wine list that makes experimenting with some serious wines an affordable practice and you have a restaurant that deserves its success.

First Course	Main Course	Dessert
• Squid and mackerel burger.	• Saddle of rabbit, shoulder cottage pie.	• Classic English custard tart, golden sultanas.
• Chicken and smoked eel terrine.	• Cod with crispy chicken wings and ginger and honey preserve.	• Panna cotta scented with barley, sugared almonds and mango.

Automat

H3

33 Dover St.
✉ W1S 4NF
☎ (020) 7499 3033
www.automat-london.com

⊖ Green Park
Closed 25 December and 1 January

Carte £27/47

An antidote to Mayfair's inherent formality and overwhelming sense of Englishness can be found in the form of this American brasserie. Open from breakfast until late, it offers an appealingly accessible menu full of recognisable words that could have come straight out of NYC: crab cakes for starters, cheesecakes for dessert, with burgers, 'mac and cheese' or Nebraskan corn-fed beef in between. There are pasta dishes and more ambitious main courses too but it's best to stick to the classics, with a side order of fries. They'll try to palm you off with a table in the first section but don't have it – ask to sit in the mid-section, decked out in the style of a railway carriage, or the fun part at the back with the open kitchen.

Avenue

H4

7-9 St James's St.
✉ SW1A 1EE
☎ (020) 7321 2111
www.avenue-restaurant.co.uk

⊖ Green Park
Closed Saturday lunch,
Sunday dinner and bank Holidays

Menu £24 (lunch) – Carte dinner £25/48

Such is The Avenue's longevity — due, in part, to an ability to subtly reinvent itself every now and again – that it risks becoming as much a part of the fabric of St James's as some of the gentlemen's clubs at which it once cocked a snook. A generous application of burgundy paint and some large canvases have left this large room looking a lot more colourful and there's greater warmth too from the service team. The menu roams predatorily around the globe looking for influences but the ingredients and particularly the main component, be it venison or salmon, come from these shores. The kitchen displays a greater degree of care and complexity than one expects, while the pre/post menus offer adequate choice and appealing prices.

Avista

G3

Italian 🍴🍴🍴

Millennium Mayfair Hotel, 39 Grosvenor Sq
✉ W1K 2HP
☎ (020) 7596 3399
www.avistarestaurant.com

⊖ Bond Street
Closed Saturday lunch
and Sunday

Carte £25/57

AC
📺
🎭
VISA
MC
AE
DC

Avista occupies the generous space within the Millennium Hotel that was previously farmed out to Brian Turner. Not only did they soften the room but they also added a separate street entrance which helps in establishing the restaurant's identity, despite the best efforts of the intrusively anodyne music. Veneto born Chef Michele Granziera, a Zafferano alumnus, has created a menu that traverses Italy and marries the rustic with the more refined. There are dishes designed for sharing as well as pre-starter 'snacks' if you really can't wait. The homemade pastas are a particular highlight, while the kitchen's creativity is given full rein on the 'Surprise' seven course menu which is available at dinner.

 Balcon

I4

French 🍴🍴

Sofitel London St James Hotel,
8 Pall Mall. ✉ SW1Y 5NG
☎ (020) 7968 2900
www.thebalconlondon.com

⊖ Piccadilly Circus

Menu £15/30 – Carte £21/49

AC
🍷
☀
VISA
MC
AE
DC

The increasingly ubiquitous Russell Sage was the designer charged with revamping this striking former banking hall and he's wrestled control of the room by installing vast chandeliers, upping the glamour and creating a balcony to house their impressive champagne 'cellar'. The room certainly has a grandeur that raises one's expectations but it needs to be near capacity to create an atmosphere. It's open from breakfast onwards and the classic brasserie menu is designed to appeal at any time of day. Dishes are rooted in French cuisine but most ingredients are British: snails are from Herefordshire, pork for the cassoulet is from Berkshire and their charcuterie, which is a feature, comes from Wales and France. A good value set menu changes weekly.

Baozi Inn

I3

25 Newport Court
✉ WC2H 7JS
✆ (020) 7287 6877

⊖ Leicester Square
Closed 24-25 December –
bookings not accepted

Carte approx. £16

Further proof that Chinatown is shaking off its tired, touristy image comes in the shape of Baozi Inn. Granted, there's nothing particularly noteworthy about the predictable surroundings of red lanterns and chunky tables but the friendly staff are welcoming and eager to please and the food is generously sized. It's also hard to blow your budget, which is especially significant as they only take cash. The eponymous baozi, or steamed filled buns, are a good way to start, although one is certainly enough; dishes have a fiery Sichuan slant and you'll feel the force in the noodle soup. The peanut and rolled tofu skin salad makes a perfect, calming side dish. Only Chinese beer is served but that's the ideal accompaniment anyway.

Barrafina

I3

54 Frith St.
✉ W1D 3SL
✆ (020) 7813 8016
www.barrafina.co.uk

⊖ Tottenham Court Road
Closed 24 December and 1 January
– bookings not accepted

Carte £20/30

London was once a bit iffy about restaurants that didn't take reservations but Barrafina was one of the first to show how it could be done. This is the younger sibling to the Hart brothers' Fino restaurant and its success is down to its mix of satisfyingly unfussy and authentic tapas and a buzzy atmosphere. Seafood is a speciality and the fish displays an exhilarating freshness; the Jabugo ham is also well worth trying. Four dishes per person is about par and the choice varies from razor clams a la plancha and tuna tartar to grilled chorizo and lamb sweetbreads with capers. It all centres around a counter, with seating for 20, so be prepared to talk to your neighbour - another thing that's slowly catching on in the capital. Be sure to try one of the sherries.

Barshu

28 Frith St.
✉ W1D 5LF
✆ (020) 7287 8822
www.bar-shu.co.uk

⊖ Leicester Square
Closed 24-25 December –
booking advisable

Carte £20/50

Those who like their food with a kick won't be disappointed by Bar Shu as it features the fiery flavours of China's Sichuan Province. The menu, which looks more like a brochure, features a photo of each dish along with a chilli rating – a useful aid, as the staff can be a little reluctant to engage with customers. But it's not all mouth-numbingly hot and some of the dishes do display a more subtle balance of flavours. The legendary chillies and pepper are imported directly from China and, with the chef coming from the province too, authenticity is assured, particularly with the 'Five colour appetiser platter', which includes duck tongues and pig intestines. Lots of carved wood and lanterns decorate the place; larger groups should head downstairs.

Bar Trattoria Semplice

22 Woodstock St.
✉ W1C 2AR
✆ (020) 7491 8638
www.bartrattoriasemplice.com

⊖ Bond Street

Menu £20/25 – Carte £27/42

In contrast to the more adventurous and ambitious cooking at Semplice a few doors down, here at Bar Trattoria Semplice it's all about recognisable Italian dishes and straightforward preparation. Fritto misto, bresaola, lasagne, tiramisu – all the favourites are here and done just how you remember them. If you're popping in for a glass of wine and a plate of pasta at the bar the place doesn't seem so pricey, but if you're after something more substantial – sea bass and a few side dishes, for example – then the bill can mount up quite quickly; but do stay for espresso – you'll be hard pressed to find a better one. The exclusively Italian wine list has something from most main regions. The service is reassuring and efficient.

Ba Shan

13

24 Romilly St.
✉ W1D 5AH
✆ (020) 7287 3266

⊖ Leicester Square
Closed 24-25 December –
booking advisable

Carte £19/45

A/C
⊡
☼
VISA
M/C
AE

Ba Shan is the third enterprise from the team who brought you Bar Shu and Baozi Inn. While this cosy place still has some Sichuan leanings, it mainly focuses on traditional styles from Northern areas and Henan province. Somewhat confusingly, there are two menus: one 'snack', the other 'home-style' - but just pick from both. Dry-wok dishes are plentiful and the guotie dumplings are their own take on a classic. Shaanxi flatbread 'sandwiches' or pork Chaoshou are a good way to start; noodles and vegetables come dressed with a provocative amount of chilli. Decoratively, it treads a fine line between cute and kitsch. There are three or four tables in each of the five rooms and service copes well with the constant influx of customers.

Beijing Dumpling

13

23 Lisle St.
✉ WC2H 7BA
✆ (0207) 2876 888

⊖ Leicester Square
Closed 24-25 December

Menu £15/20 – Carte £10/39

A/C
☼
VISA
M/C
AE

Flashing neon or hanging roast ducks in the window appear to be the popular Chinatown method of attracting passers-by; this little restaurant catches their attention by showing its chefs hard at work preparing dumplings. It's also a lot less frenzied than many of its more excitable neighbours and a cut above the norm with its food. It serves freshly prepared dumplings of both Beijing and Shanghai styles and, although the range is not quite as comprehensive as the restaurant's name would suggest, they are still the highlight, especially varieties of the famed Siu Lung Bao. The rest of the menu has a wide base but its worth exploring the specials which include the occasional Taiwanese offering like spicy chicken.

Bellamy's

H3

French 🍴🍴

18 Bruton Pl.
✉ W1J 6LY
☎ (020) 7491 2727
www.bellamysrestaurant.co.uk

⊖ Bond Street
Closed Saturday lunch,
Sunday and bank holidays

Menu £25/30 – Carte £32/53

A/C
VISA
MC
AE

If Audrey Tautou ever opened a shop it would probably look a little like Bellamy's: it's sweet, petite and pretty. The counter doubles as the oyster bar but turn left and you'll find yourself in a roomy, ersatz French brasserie, complete with assorted Gallic posters and accented waiters. The menu covers all bases, from foie gras and caviar to duck rillettes and entrecôtes and the kitchen keeps to the classic techniques and combinations. The good value little set menu offers some financial sanctuary from the more robust prices on the à la carte, although the cover charge is an unwelcome anachronism. The lunchtime crowd are mostly male, suited and serious but dinner is more relaxed, while the mews location adds to the feeling of exclusivity.

Benja Bangkok Table

H3

Thai 🍴

17 Beak St.
✉ W1F 9RW
☎ (020) 7287 0555
www.benja-bangkoktable.com

⊖ Oxford Circus

Menu £10/20 – Carte £18/26

A/C
☼
VISA
MC
AE
①

The last makeover left this Thai restaurant on the edge of Soho with a new name and a simpler look – and it is all the better for it. Styled on a typical Bangkok eatery, the interior is bright and well-lit and offers intimate – or, depending on your view, slightly cramped – surroundings, which are spread over three floors. The food offers true tastes of Thailand and the menu is suitably wide-ranging, from their signature Pad Thai to crisp salads, assorted snacks, punchy soups and nicely balanced curries. Those looking for the best value for money should head straight for the set menus, which are named after Bangkok streets familiar to every backpacker. Staff have that endearing charm and easy confidence so typical of Thailand.

Benares ❀

H3

12a Berkeley Square House
✉ W1J 6BS
✆ (020) 7629 8886
www.benaresrestaurant.com

⊖ **Green Park**
Closed 24- 26 December
and 1 January

Menu £32 (lunch)/85 – Carte £50/90

A/C

◻

¶♥

☼

VISA

MC

AE

Benares

When Benares was re-launched a few years ago after an extended hiatus caused by a kitchen fire, it seemed that not a great deal had changed in its appearance although, apparently, much work did take place behind the scenes. One terrific addition, however, was the Chef's Table with its floor to ceiling windows looking directly into the kitchen; the Sommelier's Table doesn't quite have the same cachet. Another difference came in the subtle evolution of Atul Kochhar's cooking. His dishes appear a little simpler on the plate; the main ingredient takes centre stage, with the Indian spices adding interesting and complementary flavours but without being the dominant force. Those who want to experience as much of the cooking as they can are able to do so thanks to the Grazing menu, although those who don't care for too much modernity with their Indian food will find enough recognisable dishes to satisfy them. Much thought has also gone into the wine list and in choosing the right pairings for the food.

First Course	*Main Course*	*Dessert*
• Fennel lamb chop, chicken and king prawn platter.	• Seared duck breast, Goan style spiced savoy cabbage.	• Star anise apple tart with fennel, vanilla ice cream and salted butter caramel.
• Scallop with broccoli purée and lentils.	• Lobster with fricassé of okra and mango, moilee sauce and couscous.	• Betel leaf baba, tropical fruit and passion fruit yoghurt.

Bentley's (Grill)

British traditional XXX

11-15 Swallow St.
⊠ W1B 4DG
✆ (020) 7734 4756
www.bentleys.org

⊖ Piccadilly Circus
Closed 25-26 December
and 1 January

Menu £25 (weekdays) – Carte £37/67

A/C

The green neon sign may still be outside but these days the upstairs dining room at Bentley's has a contemporary look, with leather chairs, fabric covered walls and paintings of boats and fish for those who haven't twigged that seafood is the draw here. One thing that will probably never change is the clubby feel and the preponderance of suited male customers, many of whom don't seem to mind paying the anachronistic cover charge. Much of the produce comes from St Ives and Looe in Cornwall and the freshness is palpable. Fish on the bone dissected at the table remains something of a speciality. Dover and Lemon soles feature strongly, as do oysters and soups, whilst the breads and beef remind you that owner Richard Corrigan is Irish.

VISA
MC
AE

Bentley's (Oyster Bar)

fish and seafood X

11-15 Swallow St
⊠ W1B 4DG
✆ (020) 7734 4756
www.bentleys.org

⊖ Piccadilly Circus
Closed 25-26 December
and 1 January

Menu £25 (lunch) – Carte £37/60

There's something about Swallow Street that always seems to get the taste buds going. Bentley's small reception area acts for both the upstairs restaurant and the ground floor Oyster Bar so be patient; dining on the ground floor means you'll be ushered through the curtain into a dimly lit bar with marbled-topped tables, banquette seating and places laid up at the counter. Oysters are naturally one of the main features, and the fish pie is a popular choice, but there are usually lots of daily specials and these often represent the most appealing option. The restaurant's illustrious past is almost tangible and the atmosphere is chummy and clubby, helped along with noise from the bar on the other side and the evening pianist.

A/C
VISA
MC
AE

Bob Bob Ricard

British traditional 🍴🍴

H3

1 Upper James St
✉ W1F 9DF
✆ (020) 3145 1000
www.bobbobricard.com

⊖ Oxford Circus
Closed 25-26 December,
1 January, Sunday and Monday

Carte £23/95

A/C
🕐
VISA
MC
AE
⊙

"Taste is the enemy of creativeness" said Pablo Picasso. The creatively decorated Bob Bob Ricard was set up to compete with the traditional grand cafés and diners by serving anything to anyone at anytime. Your table could be getting stuck into beef Wellington while your neighbours are spooning an evening bowl of cornflakes – and no one raises an eyebrow. If your doctor has prescribed a diet of caviar and jelly then this place is ideal. Each table even has a button to press if you want more champagne. Don't get palmed off with a table by the entrance: to get the full, flamboyant effect of all the smoked glass and marble you need to be in the body of the restaurant. But spare a thought for the waiters in those bubblegum-pink waistcoats.

Bocca di Lupo 😊

Italian 🍴

I3

12 Archer St
✉ W1D 7BB
✆ (020) 7734 2223
www.boccadilupo.com

⊖ Piccadilly Circus
Closed 24 December-3 January
– booking essential

Carte £21/35

A/C

VISA
MC
AE
⊙

Deservedly busy from the day it opened, Bocca di Lupo is one of the best things to have arrived in Soho since the espresso bar. But be sure to sit at the marble counter in front of the chefs rather than at one of the faux-distressed tables at the back – not only is the atmosphere here more fun but the food is often better as it hasn't hung around the waiters' station waiting to be delivered. Each item has its region of origin within Italy noted on the menu and is available in a large or smaller size. The flavours don't hang back and over-ordering in all the excitement is very hard to resist. Highlights include the veal and pork agnolotti, the poussin in bread, and tripe; leave room for dessert or visit their Gelato shop opposite.

Le Boudin Blanc

5 Trebeck St
✉ W1J 7LT
✆ (020) 7499 3292
www.boudinblanc.co.uk

⊖ Green Park
Closed 24-26 December

Menu £15/45 – Carte £27/55

Cries of "Bonjour!" and "Bon appétit!" will soon alert even the most limited linguist that they've wandered into a little bit of France here in Shepherd Market. The terrific atmosphere hits you as soon as you sit down – it's warm, lively and contagious, thanks largely to the ebullient service team, and is also helped by the closeness of the tables – but do ask for the ground floor rather than upstairs. The large menu is unapologetically classical and very comforting; French onion soup, steak frites and of course boudin blanc are omnipresent, while daily fish or game specials are chalked up on the blackboard. Even the most nationalistic of customers will find it hard not to be swept along by the very Frenchness of it all.

N Brasserie Zédel 😊

20 Sherwood St
✉ W1F 7ED
✆ (020) 7734 4888
www.brasseriezedel.com

⊖ Piccadilly Circus
Closed 25 December – booking advisable

Menu £12/20 – Carte £16/29

After bedding in their Delaunay restaurant, Chris Corbin and Jeremy King then opened this grand French brasserie, which is far more about inclusivity and accessibility. Those mourning the old Atlantic Bar and Grill will be pleased to see this big, bustling subterranean space restored to its original art deco glory and this time it also comes with a small café, a bar and a cabaret theatre. The menu is a gloriously unapologetic roll-call of classic French dishes – from escargots to confit de canard – but what is most striking is the exceptionally fair pricing when one considers the location, the glamour, the service and the quality of the cooking. Plenty of tables are kept back for 'walk-ins' so it's always worth trying your luck.

Brumus

I4

Haymarket Hotel,　　　　　　　　　　⊖ Piccadilly Circus
1 Suffolk Pl ✉ SW1Y 4HX
℘ (020) 7470 4000
www.haymarkethotel.com

Menu £20 – Carte £25/50

Being moments away from a number of theatres – and next door to the Theatre Royal – means than dinner at Brumus before curtain-up doesn't get spoiled by worry over the time. It's part of the Haymarket hotel although, with its own street entrance and personality, it feels more like a stand-alone restaurant. Named after the owners' much loved cocker spaniel, the room is warmly lit and brightly decorated and comes with a busy bar attached. The kitchen's influences are largely European, offering everything from pasta to pork belly; lighter dishes like salads and grilled fish are done well. However, your best bet is to stick with the good value, monthly changing set menu which offers a choice of three dishes per course.

ⓝ Burger & Lobster

H4

29 Clarges St　　　　　　　　　　⊖ Green Park.
✉ W1J 7EF　　　　　　　　Bookings not accepted
℘ (020) 7409 1699
www.burgerandlobster.com

Menu £24

Around the corner from the Curzon cinema, in what was a pub called the Field, is a 'concept' so simple it borders on genius. The choice, if you didn't get the clue in the name, is between a burger, a lobster or a lobster roll, served with chips, salad and sauces, with either chocolate or lime mousse for dessert - that's it. You're given a numbered luggage tag if you want a tab at the bar; there are no menus to read through and no side dishes to choose. There's a small, well-chosen wine and cocktail list under headings B or L (work it out). The lobsters are Canadian; the burgers 10oz and the customers mostly men. Bookings aren't taken so get your name down on the list as soon as you arrive - it may well be a bunfight, but it's a very well organised one.

Cafe at Sotheby's

H3

modern ✗✗

34-35 New Bond St.
✉ W1A 2AA
✆ (020) 7293 5077
www.sothebys.com/cafe

⊖ Bond Street
Closed 3 weeks August, Christmas
and New Year, Saturday, Sunday
and bank holidays – booking essential
– (lunch only)

Carte £26/37 s

VISA
MC
AE
DC

It's usually the seasons that inform the menu of most restaurants but here at Sotheby's they change the style of the dishes according to the art being sold. For instance, experience has shown that modern and Impressionist artists attract a diet-conscious crowd who like their salads, while the Old Masters appeal to those who favour a more substantial, well-lubricated lunch which ends with a proper pudding. The lobster sandwich is a perennial feature and the wine list is brief but appealingly eclectic. Occupying a cosy space just off the lobby of the auction house, this is a little gem of a restaurant which is smarter than the 'café' moniker would suggest. Service is well-judged and the many regulars are discreetly acknowledged.

Le Caprice

H4

modern ✗✗

Arlington House, Arlington St.
✉ SW1A 1RJ
✆ (020) 7629 2239
www.le-caprice.co.uk

⊖ Green Park
Closed 25-26 December

Menu £22 – Carte £29/46

A/C

VISA
MC
AE

There are two types of customer at Le Caprice: those who are regulars and others who wish they were. This is one of those glamorous restaurants where the atmosphere is effortlessly sophisticated and the clientele confident and urbane; even first-timers feel in safe hands from the moment they enter. The menu offers something for everyone, whether that's a salad or pasta, their famous and very rich salmon fishcake with sorrel sauce, a burger or a more ambitious offering like well-judged game dishes or Asian spiced fish; the kitchen is well-practised and capable. Le Caprice celebrated its 30th anniversary in 2011 by having a little makeover which left it better lit and feeling a little warmer with its different sections more connected.

Cây Tre

I3

42-43 Dean St
✉ W1D 4PZ
☏ (020) 7739 6686
www.caytresoho.co.uk

⊖ Tottenham Court Road
Booking advisable

Menu £23/29 – Carte £17/28

The West End could do with having plenty more Vietnamese restaurants, so hopefully others will follow the lead of Cây Tre. The bright and sleek surroundings of this Soho branch are smarter than the original in Hoxton and the bustling environment provides plenty of atmosphere. Staff know their menu and go about their business with determined efficiency. Dishes are made for sharing and influences cover all points from north to south. Standouts include Cha La lot (spicy ground pork wrapped in betel leaves) and the fragrant slow-cooked Mekong catfish, with its well-judged sweet and spicy sauce. Pho (noodle soup) is available in six different versions and represents good value; the set menu is a great starting point for neophytes.

Cecconi's

H3

5a Burlington Gdns
✉ W1S 3EP
☏ (020) 7434 1500
www.cecconis.com

⊖ Green Park
Booking essential

Carte £30/44

It's obviously a winning formula because Cecconi's are now popping up in various appropriately fashionable cities around the world. One can certainly see the appeal as they do feel like a private members club and even have a roped off VIP area to induce envy amongst those who find themselves insufficiently famous. The bar is the place to sit if you want to give the impression you're a regular who's often in for a quick bite; and if you are one such regular then you'll be assured of good service. The all-day menu offers a good selection of cicchetti, or small Italian tapas; prosciutto is sliced to order; the salads are popular at lunch and the classic, no-nonsense main courses are clearly prepared with care.

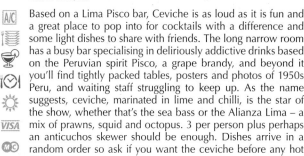

N Ceviche

13

17 Frith St
✉ W1D 4RG
☎ (020) 7292 2040
www.cevicheuk.com

⊖ Tottenham Court Road

Carte £13/26

Based on a Lima Pisco bar, Ceviche is as loud as it is fun and a great place to pop into for cocktails with a difference and some light dishes to share with friends. The long narrow room has a busy bar specialising in deliriously addictive drinks based on the Peruvian spirit Pisco, a grape brandy, and beyond it you'll find tightly packed tables, posters and photos of 1950s Peru, and waiting staff struggling to keep up. As the name suggests, ceviche, marinated in lime and chilli, is the star of the show, whether that's the sea bass or the Alianza Lima – a mix of prawns, squid and octopus. 3 per person plus perhaps an anticuchos skewer should be enough. Dishes arrive in a random order so ask if you want the ceviche before any hot dish.

China Tang

G4

Chinese ✗✗✗✗

Dorchester Hotel,
Park Ln ✉ W1K 1QA
☎ (020) 7629 9988
www.thedorchester.com

⊖ Hyde Park Corner
Closed 24-25 December

Menu £23 (lunch) – Carte £26/79

Sir David Tang's atmospheric, art deco inspired Chinese restaurant at The Dorchester Hotel is always a blur of activity, with noise spilling out from the large tables in the centre; regulars head for the library side, from where one can take in the whole room. In contrast to the sleek and decorative surroundings, the kitchen is a model of conservatism and rightly sticks to what it does best, namely classic Cantonese cooking. Peking duck and roasted meats are the highlights, but check out the chef's recommendations at the back of the menu too. The standard is good considering the numbers of customers and you can have dim sum in the striking bar for lunch or dinner. Apart from the set lunch menu, it isn't cheap – but it is fun.

MAYFAIR, SOHO & ST JAMES'S ▶ PLAN II

Cinnamon Soho

H3

5 Kingly St
✉ W1B 5PF
℘ (020) 7437 1664
www.cinnamonsoho.com

⊖ Oxford Circus

Menu £18/24 – Carte £17/29

Its logo is 'Joho Soho', Hindi for 'whatever happens' and this Cinnamon outpost is altogether more fun than its two older siblings. Taking our love of Indian food to its logical conclusion, it blends Indian flavours with traditional British dishes, so you can order Rogan Josh shepherd's pie, curried Cullen Skink or Cumbrian lamb biryani. It's hard to miss the signature dish as the menu is emblazoned with the word 'Balls': these include crab cakes, potato bondas and even Scotch eggs – and all are served with different pickles. Don't be afraid to ask about relative spiciness, do have one of their fun cocktails and sit on the ground floor rather than in the soulless basement. It's open all day and also has a terrace front and back.

 Copita

H3

27 d'Arblay St
✉ W1F 8EP
℘ (020) 7436 9448
www.barrica.co.uk

⊖ Oxford Circus
Closed bank holidays –
bookings not accepted

Carte £11/21

It may not occupy a prime Soho spot but that hasn't stopped this tapas bar, a sister to Barrica, from being packed most nights. A no bookings policy means your best bet is to come before 7pm or else try your luck at lunch when there are fewer drinkers; then simply perch yourself on one of the high stools or stay standing and get stuck in. The daily menu offers a colourful array of diminutive dishes like pea and cheese croquettes, crab and spinach tart, and pumpkin and sage ravioli and you'll find it hard to stop ordering – even the delicate custard tart is delightfully moreish. Staff add to the lively atmosphere and everything on the thoughtfully compiled Spanish wine list is available by the glass or copita.

Corrigan's Mayfair

British modern ✕✕✕

G3

28 Upper Grosvenor St.
✉ W1K 7EH
✆ (020) 7499 9943
www.corrigansmayfair.com

⊖ Marble Arch
Closed 25-26 December, 1 January and
Saturday lunch

Menu £27 (lunch) – Carte £39/78

Richard Corrigan's flagship restaurant feels as though it has been part of the London scene for years. It's comfortable, clubby yet quite glamorous and Martin Brudnizki's design includes some playful features, such as the feather-covered lamps that give a nod to the restaurant's forte, which is game. The menu is lengthy and the food largely a celebration of British and Irish cooking. It is also fiercely seasonal, which makes having the day's special always a worthwhile choice. This relatively straightforward style of cooking still requires care and precise timing but sometimes the kitchen takes its eye off the ball. Service is smooth and well organised but the anachronistic cover charge is an unwelcome sight.

ⓝ Cut

meats and grills ✕✕✕

G4

45 Park Lane Hotel,
45 Park Ln ✉ W1K 1PN
✆ (020) 7493 4554
www.45parklane.com

⊖ Hyde Park Corner
Booking essential

Menu £55 (weekday lunch) – Carte £40/119

Cut is the first European venture from Wolfgang Puck, the US-based Austrian chef whose level of celebrity makes our lot look positively anonymous. Teaming up with the Dorchester's 45 Park Lane hotel, he has created a slick, stylish and sexy room where glamorous people come to eat meat. The steaks – from Kansas, Chile, Australia and Devon— are first presented raw with a few words about their heritage and then cooked over hardwood and charcoal and finished off in a broiler. Sides are as good as the steaks, especially the fries and the macaroni cheese. Artery hardening continues with dessert which eschews the much-needed citrus in favour of lots of cream. You'll leave eminently satisfied, if slightly heavier in weight and lighter in pocket.

Dean Street Townhouse Restaurant

I3

British modern ✗✗

69-71 Dean St.
✉ W1D 3SE
✆ (020) 7434 1775
www.deanstreettownhouse.com

⊖ Tottenham Court Road
Booking essential

Menu £20 (early dinner) – Carte £27/50

A restaurant for every occasion – even shouty ones, as you're hit by a cacophony of sound as soon as you open the heavy door of this attractive Georgian house. It's also a place to be seen, or perhaps not — a ban on flash photography means it's ideal for illicit trysts too. The classic brasserie aesthetic makes it look like it's been here for years and the heart-warming British comfort food fits these surroundings well. Prices for some of the fish and steak dishes can get pretty exclusive but there's plenty more proletariat fare on offer, like faggots with cabbage or mince and potatoes. The salads such as trout with truffled potato or smoked pigeon with Scotch egg are noteworthy and who can resist kipper pâté for afternoon tea?

Dehesa

H3

Mediterranean ✗

25 Ganton St
✉ W1F 9BP
✆ (020) 7494 4170
www.dehesa.co.uk

⊖ Oxford Circus
Closed Sunday dinner

Carte £22/34

Dehesa does now take bookings, except for lunch on Saturday, so there's no longer a need to get here quite so early. It's a few streets away from its sister restaurant, Salt Yard, and repeats the format of offering delicious Spanish and Italian tapas. The menu is not an exact copy but the bestsellers all feature: the pork belly with cannellini beans; courgette flowers with Monte Enebro and honey; and the soft chocolate cake with Frangelico ice cream. They recommend 2-3 plates per person. Between 3pm and 5pm the kitchen takes a breather so the choice becomes ham on or off the bone, charcuterie and cheese. The drinks list is worthy of a visit in itself. Dehesa is a wooded area of Spain and home to Ibérico pigs who produce such great ham.

Ⓝ Ducksoup

I3

41 Dean St
✉ W1D 4PY
✆ (020) 7287 4599
www.ducksoupsoho.co.uk

⊖ **Leicester Square**
Closed bank holidays and Sunday dinner

Carte £22/31

It's compact, with seating at the bar; decoratively it's knowingly underwhelming; and the menu, which includes small plates, is handwritten each day – yes, every 'on-trend' box is ticked here at Ducksoup. There's even a little retro thrown in courtesy of a turntable – for younger readers, those are 'records' being played. The chef-owner describes his food as "ambient" which translates as being as natural and seasonal as possible and the dishes, such as fried lamb chops with lemon and salt, are confidently unadorned; they do a good Brillat Savarin cheesecake. Wines are also 'natural' and biodynamic and from small producers. There is a somewhat nebulous reservation system but this place is more about just dropping in for a quick bite.

Fakhreldine

H4

85 Piccadilly
✉ W1J 7NB
✆ (020) 7493 3424
www.fakhreldine.co.uk

⊖ **Green Park**

Menu £14/47 – Carte £29/41

Climbing the stairs with candlelit lanterns lighting the way adds an exotic charge to one's expectations; once in the restaurant you'll be grateful you asked for a window table because these offer great views across Green Park. A large, copper-topped bar, reds, golds and wood panelling, plus lights that gradually dim as the evening progresses, add to the sophisticated feel. Start with a hoppy Almaza beer, share some meze such as grilled halloumi cheese or baby aubergines filled with walnuts, then order one of the tasty lamb dishes, like the minced lamb skewer with either a chickpea dip or a spicy tomato sauce. If you can still manage dessert then your appetite is impressive; Bouza Daa ice cream provides a suitably refreshing finish.

Floridita

other world kitchens ✗✗

I3

100 Wardour St.
✉ W1F 0TN
☎ (020) 7314 4000
www.floriditalondon.com

⊖ Tottenham Court Road
Closed Sunday, Monday and bank holidays
– (dinner only and lunch in December for
groups of 12 or more)

Menu £28 (weekdays) – Carte £23/54

A/C

VISA

M/C

AE

It's Salsa all the way, from the spicy food to the live music and dancing. If you think the ground floor with its Mediterranean tapas is busy, try downstairs for size. Here you'll find yourself in a huge nightclub-style space boasting an impressive cocktail list and a variety of Latin American dishes, from Cuban classics like ropa vieja to a whole-roast suckling pig and a large selection of assorted cuts of Argentinean beef aged for 28 days. It's not cheap but then again everything is done very well and everyone is here for a Big Night Out. The bands are flown in from Cuba, the music starts at 7.30pm and the party atmosphere never lets up. Those whose pace is more Cohiba than Mojito can nip next door to La Casa del Habano.

Franco's

Italian ✗✗

H4

61 Jermyn St
✉ SW1Y 6LX
☎ (020) 7499 2211
www.francoslondon.com

⊖ Green Park
Closed Sunday and bank holidays
– booking essential

Menu £20/26 – Carte £29/59

A/C

VISA

M/C

AE

There can be few things more English than afternoon tea or the sound of Alan Bennett reading from The Wind in the Willows and, surprisingly enough, both can be enjoyed here at Franco's, one of London's oldest Italian restaurants that was relaunched in the mid-noughties. Open from breakfast onwards, it attracts a largely well-groomed clientele as befits its Jermyn Street address and boasts a clubby feel. Indeed, if you're not a regular visitor, you may find yourself with time to admire the service being enjoyed by other tables. The chef hails from Northern Italy but his menu covers all parts. There is a popular grill section, along with classics like Beef Rossini – ideal accompaniment for one of those big Tuscan reds on the wine list.

Galvin at Windows ✿

French XXXX

London Hilton Hotel,
22 Park Ln (28th floor)
✉ W1K 1BE
✆ (020) 7208 4021
www.galvinatwindows.com

⊖ Hyde Park Corner
Closed 25 December, Saturday lunch
and Sunday dinner

Menu £29/65

VISA
MC
AE

Galvin at Windows

There have never been any doubts about the magnificence of the views from this restaurant on the 28th floor of the Hilton Hotel, nor about the capabilities of the well-drilled serving brigade who are attentive without being over-solicitous; but now many of the customers come for the quality of the cooking, which displays similarly lofty ambitions. André Garrett and his team have great confidence in their own abilities and so know when to allow the ingredients to speak for themselves, whether that's a tender fillet of Scottish beef with foie gras or a braised fillet of halibut with crab and lemon oil. Flavours are adeptly balanced and complementary, while presentation, notwithstanding some crowd-pleasing use of gold leaf, is measured and appetising. The menus are nicely balanced in content but also vary in price so that eating here does not need to end in bankruptcy. The best tables for lunch are those on the near side looking down over Buckingham Palace; the far side gazing north over twinkling lights is the better option for dinner.

First Course

- Cured salmon, Cornish crab, avocado purée and fennel.
- Spiced ballotine of foie gras with raisin and port purée.

Main Course

- Saddle of venison with watercress, red cabbage and pancetta.
- Brill with pomme purée, white onion, lime and verjus butter sauce.

Dessert

- Tarte Tatin, vanilla ice cream and caramel sauce.
- Peanut butter parfait with caramel and popcorn ice cream.

Le Gavroche ✿ ✿

French XXXX

G3

43 Upper Brook St
✉ W1K 7QR
✆ (020) 7408 0881
www.le-gavroche.co.uk

⊖ Marble Arch
Closed Christmas-New Year,
Saturday lunch, Sunday
and bank holidays – booking essential

Menu £52 (lunch)/110 – Carte £62/148

A/C
🍇
VISA
MC
AE
⓪

A little indulgence never did anyone any harm and Le Gavroche is all about indulgence. Michel Roux and head chef Rachel Humphrey's unapologetically extravagant French dishes are an exhilarating riposte to all those hectoring health-conscious calorie-counters. The menu is a roll-call of luxury ingredients, the sauces are sublime and the cooking is accompanied by one of London's best wine lists. There are oohs and aahs as trolleys are brought forward and carving knives sharpened; regulars mingle with newcomers and the atmosphere is refreshingly unstuffy, helped along by there being more of a female presence to the service these days. Anyone with an interest in Britain's post-war culinary adventures should be aware of Le Gavroche's significance, not just because of its celebration of, and dedication to, the art of French cuisine but also because of all those chefs who have benefitted from passing through its kitchen. Just avoid sitting too close to the stairs by asking for a table in the main body of this historic restaurant.

First Course

- Soufflé Suissesse.
- Coquilles St Jacques grillés et minestrone de palourdes.

Main Course

- Râble de lapin et galette au parmesan.
- Homard sauté et son jus à la citronelle et coco.

Dessert

- Palet au chocolat amer et praliné croustillant.
- Millefeuille aux framboises et Gianduja.

64

Gauthier - Soho

French $\times\!\!\times\!\!\times$

21 Romilly St
✉ W1D 5AF
✆ (020) 7494 3111
www.gauthiersoho.co.uk

⊖ Leicester Square
Closed Saturday lunch,
Sunday and bank holidays

Menu £25, £40/40

A/C

Tucked away from the mischief and mayhem of Soho is this charming Georgian townhouse. Dining is spread over three floors, with the ground floor often the busiest, the first floor used more for the special occasion diner and the top floor consisting of two private dining rooms. There are a few other menus running alongside the à la carte and that includes a Vegetarian menu – the very charming Alex Gauthier has always been a chef who regards fruit and vegetables as more than mere addendums to a dish. While the standard of the cooking remains accomplished, it is, however, missing some of its previous vitality. Wine is still taken seriously and, when asked, the sommeliers come up with some refreshingly original recommendations.

VISA

AE

Goodman

meats and grills $\times\!\!\times$

26 Maddox St
✉ W1S 1QH
✆ (020) 7499 3776
www.goodmanrestaurants.com

⊖ Oxford Circus
Closed Sunday and bank holidays
– booking essential

Carte £25/68

A/C

Goodman is a Russian-owned New York steakhouse in Mayfair, which sounds like a sketch from the UN's Christmas party. Wood and leather give it an authentic feel and it has captured that macho swagger that often seems to accompany the eating of red meat. Tables are usually full of guffawing men, with their jackets thrown over the back of their chairs and their sleeves rolled up. The American and Irish beef is mostly grain-fed and either dry or wet aged in-house – Australian beef is an option at lunch. It is cooked in a Josper oven using a blend of three types of charcoal and offered with a choice of four sauces. While the steaks, especially the rib-eye, are certainly worth coming for, side dishes tend to be more variable in quality.

AE

Greenhouse ✿

innovative XXX

27a Hay's Mews
✉ W1J 5NY
☎ (020) 7499 3331
www.greenhouserestaurant.co.uk

⊖ Hyde Park Corner
Closed Saturday lunch, Sunday and
bank holidays

Menu £29/75 – Carte £87/106

A/C

🍴🍷

VISA

MC

AE

The Greenhouse

In 2012 a new head chef arrived at The Greenhouse in the form of Arnaud Bignon, who joined from Spondi restaurant in Athens. Before choosing your dishes, you have to decide on your menu and there's a plethora of them: a 6 course tasting menu, a set menu, an à la carte and a separate lunch menu, as well as a 6 course vegetable-inspired dinner menu. Whatever you go for, you'll find the food modern, innovative, technically impressive and well-balanced. The chef demonstrates his confidence and understanding of flavour combinations in dishes where coffee, morels and liquorice are matched with a veal chop, and calamansi and citrus powder are coupled with langoustines. His cooking comes with an invigorating freshness and ingredients are sourced from Europe's larder: there's Limousin veal, Dorset lamb, Cornish crab and Challans duck. The breadth of the wine list is astounding and includes vintages of Château Lafite back to 1870, Château Latour to 1900, Château Haut-Brion to 1945 and 14 vintages of La Tâche; the New World is not forgotten – there are 38 vintages of Penfolds Grange.

First Course	Main Course	Dessert
• Smoked potato with oysters and shallots.	• Cod with quinoa, lemongrass, shiitake and coriander.	• Lemon 'textures'.
• Crab with mint jelly, cauliflower, apple and curry.	• Lamb with aubergine, ras el hanout, sweetbreads and red pepper.	• Raspberry with granola, white chocolate and cheesecake foam.

The Grill

G4

B r i t i s h   t r a d i t i o n a l   🍴🍴🍴

Dorchester Hotel,
Park Ln. ✉ W1K 1QA
☎ (020) 7629 8888
www.thedorchester.com

⊖ Hyde Park Corner

Menu £27/35 – Carte £48/91

A/C
☼
🚗
VISA
MC
AE
①

The Grill is a bastion of Britishness that celebrates our own culinary heritage and appeals to those for whom modern life can seem at times just a little too shouty and shambolic. Granted, there are more than a few nods on the menu to contemporary mores but if you stick to the classics – smoked salmon carved at your table, kedgeree, grilled Dover sole, assorted game and Black Angus beef – you'll leave feeling infinitely better about the world, although your bank manager may not be quite so jubilant. The colourful room, on the ground floor of the Dorchester hotel, is extravagantly kitted out in acres of tartan and dancing Highlanders look down at you from the walls as you tuck into your Barnsley chop.

Haozhan

I3

C h i n e s e   🍴🍴

8 Gerrard St
✉ W1D 5PJ
☎ (020) 7434 3838
www.haozhan.co.uk

⊖ Leicester Square
Closed 24-25December

Menu £15/48 – Carte £20/78

A/C
🍴⊘
☼
VISA
MC
AE

A plethora of Chinatown restaurants vie for your attention by offering special deals or just brightening their neon. Haozhan adopts the more worthy policy of serving food that's a cut above the norm. Inside the somewhat garish looking menu is not the usual vast list but rather an interesting collection of dishes that owe more to a fusion style, with mostly Cantonese but other Asian influences too; head straight for the specialities, such as jasmine ribs or wasabi prawns. You'll find there's a freshness to the ingredients that also marks this restaurant out – for example, try the Tom Yum prawns in their pancake cones and leave room for the egg custard buns. Appropriately enough, the name Haozhan translates as "a good place to eat".

Hakkasan Mayfair ✿

Chinese 🍴🍴

17 Bruton St · ⊖ Green Park
✉ W1J 6QB · Closed 25 December – booking
℘ (020) 7907 1888 · essential
www.hakkasan.com

Menu £50 – Carte £32/96 s

A/C

iⓋ

i◔i

☼

VISA

M/C

AE

This is less a copy, more a sister to the original Hakkasan; a sister who's just as fun and glamorous but simply lives in a far nicer part of town. As with many of the best addresses, it doesn't draw attention to itself – you could easily walk past the entrance without knowing, and that adds to the appeal. The biggest difference is that this Hakkasan has a funky, more casual ground floor to go with the downstairs dining room; but it's still worth booking for the lower level, as a walk down the stairs will heighten the sense of occasion and add a little mystery. The menu of Cantonese treats is an appealing tome; dim sum must surely be the only way to go at lunch, while the signature dishes, such as silver cod with champagne and honey, and Jasmine tea smoked chicken, can be saved for dinner. Desserts are unashamedly tailored towards European tastes but there's a fine range of speciality teas, as well as an impressive selection of cocktails. The staff, dressed in black – what else? – know their menu backwards, so are more than willing to help those seeking guidance.

First Course

- Crispy duck salad.
- Golden-fried soft shell crab.

Main Course

- Roasted silver cod with champagne and Chinese honey.
- Pan-fried Wagyu beef in spicy Szechuan sauce.

Dessert

- Jivara hazelnut bombe and hot chocolate sauce.
- Coconut brûlée.

Hélène Darroze
at The Connaught ✿✿

French 🍴🍴🍴🍴

Connaught Hotel,
Carlos Pl. ✉ W1K 2AL
📞 (020) 3147 7200
www.the-connaught.co.uk

⊖ **Bond Street**
Closed Sunday and Monday
– booking essential

Menu £35/80

Connaught Hotel

London's diverse and vibrant dining scene has had quite an influence on Hélène Darroze and although she insists it is France and her native region of Landes that informs her cooking, she also uses interesting flavours of a more international persuasion. In essence, the dishes appear relatively simple on the plate, even though their descriptions on the menu can be quite florid. She is keen to champion the high quality produce they use, much more of which now comes from within the UK. Bayonne ham sliced on their gleaming Berkel machine heralds the start of one's meal and delightful mignardises round things off. Dishes can be surprisingly robust and the presentation is often exquisite. Service is courteous and professional, and the staff also manage to inject personality into the proceedings. Meanwhile, the room itself is warm and elegant, thanks to India Mahdavi's clever softening of all that mahogany wall panelling. A small private dining room has been added adjacent to the wine cellar, two floors below.

First Course

- Duck foie gras with mild spices and dried fruit chutney.
- Salmon carpaccio, lemon caviar, capers and smoked haddock cream.

Main Course

- Line-caught sea bass with celeriac purée and salmis sauce.
- Rack of lamb, grilled chuletilla, confit shoulder and smoked aubergine.

Dessert

- Exotic fruits with bourbon vanilla and mascarpone cream.
- Morello cherry jelly, speculoos biscuit and tonka bean cream.

Hibiscus ❀ ❀

innovative 💥💥💥

29 Maddox St
✉ **W1S 2PA**
☏ (020) 7629 2999
www.hibiscusrestaurant.co.uk

⊖ Oxford Circus
Closed 23 December-3
January, Sunday and bank holidays

Menu £35/80

Nothing dampens the ardour like a restaurant failing to live up to the promise of its great setting or grand façade. Fortunately for Hibiscus, neither its location on dreary old Maddox Street nor its featureless façade will set too many pulses racing. Inside, though, you'll find an immaculately dressed room with warm wood panelling, a discreet backdrop to chef-owner Claude Bosi's creative cooking. He offers 3, 6 or 9 courses and lets customers create their own menus from a list of around 20 seasonal ingredients. Alternatively you can let the 14-strong kitchen team choose for you, which works well as it gets everyone talking. Even if your table decide on 3 courses, you'll find that everyone gets different dishes. The cooking is inventive without being overly intricate and everything on the plate has a reason for being there; it's French influenced but unafraid of incorporating ingredients from around the world. Wine flights are available – if you've decided to go blind on the food front then leave the selection to the sommelier.

First Course

- Ravioli of white onion and lime, broad bean and mint purée.
- Smoked potato and hens' egg ravioli with truffle purée and Comté.

Main Course

- Roast suckling pig, carrot and orange purée, and cumin.
- Skate wing with fennel purée and clementine sauce.

Dessert

- Chocolate tart with basil ice cream.
- Oat ice cream, burnt caramel cream, artichoke purée and meringue.

Hix

British traditional ✕

66-70 Brewer St.
✉ WlF 9UP
✆ (020) 7292 3518
www.hixsoho.co.uk

⊖ Piccadilly Circus
Closed 25-26 December

Menu £18 (lunch) – Carte £26/61

AC
⟨·⟩
⟨♥⟩
☼
VISA
MC
AE

Leaded, frosted windows similar to The Ivy hint at exclusivity within, as does the huge wooden door and the discreet name plaque. Once entry has been secured, one finds oneself in an enormous space with specially commissioned artwork from Damien Hirst, Sue Webster and Sarah Lucas, reflecting Mark Hix's close relationship with London's artists. Meanwhile, his menu reflects his passion for British recipes and ingredients, which translates as plenty of game in season, unusual cuts of meat, rediscovered classics and proper puddings. Portions aren't over-generous – side dishes are required which makes the bill rise quickly – and sometimes a dish may not quite deliver the promise of the menu, but it's a fun, inclusive place.

HIX at The Albemarle

British traditional ✕✕✕

Brown's Hotel,
Albemarle St ✉ W1S 4BP
✆ (020) 7518 4004
www.roccofortecollection.com

⊖ Green Park

Menu £33 – Carte £30/61

AC
⟨♥⟩
☼
VISA
MC
AE
⓪

Brown's is a thoroughly British hotel with a long history so it makes sense for its restaurant to celebrate Britain's own culinary traditions. Mark Hix – surely one of London's busiest restaurateurs at the moment – was the man entrusted with the task and he has put together an appealing looking menu that's big on seasonality and provenance. Good use is made of ingredients from across the UK, such as Portland crab, Morecambe Bay shrimps and Aberdeenshire beef and there's also a daily roast for lunch, served from the trolley. The traditional feel of the wood panelled dining room is enlivened by the works from leading contemporary British artists, which ensure that the atmosphere never gets too solemn.

Hush

modern XX

8 Lancashire Ct., Brook St.
✉ W1S 1EY
☎ (020) 7659 1500
www.hush.co.uk

⊖ Bond Street
Closed Easter, 25-26 December,
1 January and Sunday – booking essential

Carte £25/54

Any time the mercury nudges past 16° Londoners feel the need to eat outside, even if that means battling with passers-by for a few feet of pavement space. There's no such indignity at Hush as you'll find in this courtyard once used to store materials and cloth for Savile Row a large and appealing terrace. Its occupants are usually here for the long haul and it's easy to understand why: the menu is a likeable, all-purpose affair which skips merrily around Europe so that you have duck confit, a risotto or a schnitzel; if you want to stay closer to home then order one of their terrific homemade pies. You can also just pop in for cocktails and share some small plates and if you're in no hurry you can simply stay put for afternoon tea.

Imli

Indian X

167-169 Wardour St
✉ W1F 8WR
☎ (020) 7287 4243
www.imli.co.uk

⊖ Tottenham Court Road
Closed 25-26 December and 1 January

Menu £20 (dinner) – Carte £20/26

'Relatively timely food' may not sound quite as snappy as 'fast food' but Imli proves that, if you don't want to linger long over a meal, there are alternatives to multinationals. It may be an Indian restaurant but 'tapas' is the shorthand for dishes that are diminutive and involve sharing. The menu is short, well-priced and to the point; three dishes per person should suffice, although the hungry should go for the 'Taste of Imli'. The cooking is a combination of street food and some regional, particularly Northern Indian, influences; vegetarians will find themselves with plenty of choice. Where Imli has borrowed from the 'experts' is in its use of bright lighting and vivid colours to encourage a rapid turnover.

Imperial China

Chinese XXX

I3

White Bear Yard, 25a Lisle St
✉ WC2H 7BA
✆ (020) 7734 3388
www.imperial-china.co.uk

⊖ Leicester Square
Closed 24-25 December –
booking advisable

Menu £18/35 – Carte £14/77

Heave open the heavy smoked-glass double doors, cross the bamboo bridge and you'll be transported to a calm oasis that seems a world away from the bustle outside. Sharp, well-organised service and comfortable surroundings are not the only things that set this restaurant apart: the Cantonese cooking exudes freshness and vitality, whether that's the steamed dumplings or the XO minced pork with fine beans. Indeed, they pride themselves on seafood and their 'lobster feasts' are very popular - the personable staff are also more than happy to offer recommendations. There are eight private rooms of various sizes available upstairs and these are often in full swing. The owners also run Beijing Dumpling a few doors down.

Inn the Park

British modern X

I4

St James's Park
✉ SW1A 2BJ
✆ (020) 7451 9999
www.innthepark.com

⊖ Charing Cross
Closed 25 December –
booking essential at dinner

Carte £25/35

When the sun has a little spring warmth and the season's first asparagus has appeared, few restaurants can compete with Oliver Peyton's place in the park. Its eco-friendly credentials are such that it resembles a camouflaged bunker; approach from the east and you won't see it. The entrance can be a little confusing: to avoid the self-service section, head for the 'waiter service' reception. The terrace is terrific and quickly fills in summer. The menu makes much of its Britishness and uses many small suppliers. The kitchen does have a somewhat heavy hand that lessens the impact and service can also lack a little humour but, despite these shortcomings, the restaurant is worthy without being pious and the setting is glorious.

JW Steakhouse

m e a t s   a n d   g r i l l s ✕✕

Grosvenor House Hotel,
Park Ln ✉ W1K 7TN
☎ (020) 7399 8460
www.londongrosvenorhouse.co.uk

⊖ Marble Arch

Carte £23/92

It's all about beer, bourbon and beef here— things couldn't get more macho if they handed out hunting rifles and Stetsons. This large restaurant at the Grosvenor House hotel has enjoyed various incarnations over the years but being an American steakhouse seems to suit it very well. Your eyes are instantly drawn to the blackboards on the far wall which advertise the steaks and their sizes. Corn-fed, dry-aged USDA cuts along with Aberdeen Angus are the stars of the show and are cooked in a special broiler at 650°C. As well as the perennially popular burger, you'll find a roll-call of American steakhouse classics like short ribs and crab cakes. If you make it to dessert then a cheesecake or peanut parfait will certainly finish you off.

Kiku

J a p a n e s e ✕✕

17 Half Moon St.
✉ W1J 7BE
☎ (020) 7499 4208
www.kikurestaurant.co.uk

⊖ Green Park
Closed 25-27 December, 1 January,
Sunday and lunch on bank holidays

Menu £22/25 – Carte £20/83

Kiku is a traditional Japanese restaurant, which makes it something of a rarity these days. The menus are numerous and varied, offering sushi to assorted kaiseki, a selection of soba noodle dishes, salads and casseroles; the lunch time menus are very popular locally. Apart from the kaiseki set menus, the prices are not unreasonable when one considers the Mayfair location, the crisp and understated décor and the endearingly charming staff, who can swiftly soothe the most cantankerous of diner, and who are also on hand to offer sensible advice. The best place to sit is in the raised section at the back with its own sushi counter; here it's never quite so busy and you get to really appreciate the skills of the chefs.

Kai ✿

Chinese XXX

G3

65 South Audley St   ⊖ Hyde Park Corner
✉ W1K 2QU   Closed 25-26 December and 1 January
✆ (020) 7493 8988   – booking essential
www.kaimayfair.co.uk

Menu £27 (lunch) – Carte £39/90

Kai

A warm and sincere welcome and elegant, opulent and intimate surroundings tell you immediately that Kai is a different kind of Chinese restaurant, although what the incongruously funky music is telling you is anyone's guess. Beg the indulgence of your date or dining companions by taking time to read the menu fully because the descriptions of exotically named dishes like 'A nest of imperial jewels' and 'Mermaids of the mist' will have a Pavlovian effect on your appetite, although the prices may also have the reverse effect on your wallet. The cooking uses influences from across China; some dishes are re-workings of popular classics – the Szechuan chicken cashew nuts being a sophisticated Kung Pao. The best ones are those created by Chef Alex Chow such as the wasabi prawns and oriental lamb shank but do also order the superb Peking duck. The kitchen can adapt the spiciness of certain dishes but it's dangerous to say you like it hot if you don't really. Charming staff are on hand to offer friendly advice; and ask for the ground floor, not the basement.

First Course

- Scallop with spicy XO sauce, lotus root crisp and stir-fried vegetables.
- 'Little Shanghai' spare ribs.

Main Course

- Spiced pork belly in ginger, rice wine, cinnamon and soy.
- Sea bass with ginger and spring onions.

Dessert

- Mango mousse with dragonfruit, agar and coconut jelly.
- 6 textures of chocolate and peanuts.

Koya 🐶

I3

49 Frith St
✉ W1D 4SG
℘ (020) 7434 4463
www.koya.co.uk

⊖ Tottenham Court Road
Closed Christmas – bookings not accepted

Carte £12/27

🅰/🅲
▦
☼
VISA
🅜🅒
🅐🅔
Ⓓ

Authenticity is the key to Koya's success: the Japanese wheat is kneaded by foot, while the dashi base stock is freshly made every day. Do your bit by slurping unselfconsciously to get the full benefit of these delicious noodles with their wonderful chewiness or 'koshi'. They come in three styles: hot in a hot broth, cold with a hot broth or cold with a cold dipping sauce, and arrive on a bamboo mat and with a sprinkling of nori (seaweed). Be sure to order some small plates too, such as the onsen tamago, a delicate poached egg, or crisp tempura. A small selection of sake, shochu, beer and wine is also available. The decoration is modest, service is sweet and if you aren't here before the noren curtain is put out then be prepared to queue.

Ⓝ Manchurian Legends

I3

16 Lisle St
✉ WC2H 7BE
℘ (020) 7287 6606
www.manchurianlegends.com

⊖ Leicester Square
Closed Christmas

Carte £20/30

🅰/🅲
⟨⊡⟩
☼
VISA
🅜🅒

China's cuisine is one of enormous diversity, with each region having its own style and specialities. With Manchurian Legends, Londoners now have the chance to try dishes from a less familiar part of the country: Dongbei, which means 'northeast'. As winters here are long, stews and bbq dishes are popular and so are pickled ingredients; try the delicious Xin-Jian-style fried lamb or the juicy duck with pickled vegetables. The cooking is certainly robust of flavour yet also delivers on richness –but ignore the chilli scale next to each dish at your peril! Further warmth comes from the sweet natured service. The restaurant moved to new premises at the address listed above just as we went to print.

Matsuri

Japanese ✗✗

15 Bury St.
✉ SW1Y 6AL
☎ (020) 7839 1101
www.matsuri-restaurant.com

⊖ Green Park
Closed 25 December

Menu £35 (dinner) – Carte £18/119

One of the capital's longest running Japanese restaurants remains refreshingly impervious to the contemporary trend towards 'reinterpretation' and instead focuses on traditional dishes and combinations. You're whisked downstairs past the drums, fans and masks by gracious and traditionally costumed ladies where you can choose between teppan-yaki or a seat at the sushi counter. You'll be assailed by a plethora of menus ranging from a chef's special to a Wagyu beef menu as well as a monthly changing list of seasonal specials such as crab marinated in rice vinegar or pork shabu-shabu. Once decided, you need do nothing except sit and appreciate a bit of knife juggling while enjoying fresh ingredients that taste of what they should.

Maze Grill

meats and grills ✗✗

London Marriott Hotel Grosvenor Square,
10-13 Grosvenor Sq. ✉ W1K 6JP
☎ (020) 7495 2211
www.gordonramsay.com

⊖ Bond Street

Menu £21/24 – Carte £24/111

Use the Grosvenor Square entrance as it offers a little more charm than if one wanders in from the adjacent Marriott Hotel, for which this restaurant also acts as the breakfast room. But then again, this is less about glamour, more about just enjoying good quality beef. The assorted cuts, from Casterbridge grain-fed and Hereford grass-fed through to Creekstone prime USDA corn-fed and Wagyu, are brought to your table in their raw state for you to hear about their differing personalities. Your preferred steak is then given a blast in the super-hot broiler before being served on a wooden board. The sides and sauces are numerous, varied and individually priced so your wallet can also end up feeling a little tender.

Maze ⁣⁣⁣❀

innovative XX

10-13 Grosvenor Sq   ⊖ Bond Street
✉ W1K 6JP
✆ (020) 7107 0000
www.gordonramsay.com/maze

Menu £25, £25/70 – Carte £27/41

A/C
VISA
M/C
AE

Gordon Ramsay Holdings

Standing still should never be an option for any restaurant – however successful – and at Gordon Ramsay's Maze there has been a little tinkering taking place. A cocktail 'mixologist' has arrived to draw in more customers to the bar and there is now a greater element of Asian influence to the cooking. The hallmark precision is evident in all the dishes; combinations are not overworked and flavours and textures have been intelligently thought out. There's a deceptive simplicity here and a playful element too; the Asian tones enhance rather than overpower the ingredients. Four dishes per person should be about right, and the set lunch and early evening menus are bargains. The iPad wine list is more than just a gimmick – it's a great way of running through the list, which may be light on mature vintages but has strength in depth across all regions. The David Rockwell designed room looks as good as ever and the restaurant continues to attract an appealingly mixed crowd, from the romantically inclined to the corporately minded.

First Course

- Lobster, langoustine and salmon dumpling with aromatic broth.
- Crispy veal sweetbread, lemongrass and star anise.

Main Course

- Braised featherblade beef, pomme purée and togarashi spice.
- Scallops, salsify, cauliflower and basil velouté.

Dessert

- Frozen yoghurt and granola sandwich, daiquiri sorbet.
- Apple terrine, rhubarb and custard ice cream.

Mele e Pere

Italian ✗

46 Brewer St
✉ W1F 9TF
✆ (020) 7096 2096
www.meleepere.co.uk

⊖ **Piccadilly Circus**
Closed 25-26 December,
1 January and Sunday

Menu £13/18 – Carte £18/39

A/C
😊
VISA
⓪
AE

Faced with a wall of Murano glass apples and pears as colourful as the street you're standing in, you'd be forgiven for thinking this is a gallery. But head downstairs – the 'apple and pears'? – and you'll find yourself in a vaulted, if somewhat hard-edged room with an appealing Vermouth bar. The owner-chef has worked in some decent London kitchens over a few years but hails from Verona so expect a selection of gutsy Italian dishes, like rabbit with olives, shoulder of lamb, and tripe with grated Parmigiano. Main courses come with a side dish that you get to choose and puds are excellent, especially the panna cotta. The weekly changing pre-theatre menu should be enough in itself for this newcomer to make its mark in Soho.

Mews of Mayfair

modern ✗✗

10-11 Lancashire Ct, Brook St (1st floor)
✉ W1S 1EY
✆ (020) 7518 9388
www.mewsofmayfair.com

⊖ **Bond Street**
Closed 25 December

Menu £19 – Carte £26/48

🍽
🍸
☀
VISA
⓪
AE
⓪

Mews manages that trick of being cool and bright in summer and warm and inviting in winter. The relative serenity of the pretty restaurant is in sharp contrast to the crowds in the narrow lane and busy cocktail bar below, while the private dining room on the next floor up is a very pleasant space. The menu is very appealing and sufficiently sensitive to the changing seasons, so expect venison in winter, spring lamb and summer fruit. Simpler dishes are also pepped up, so burgers come with an optional foie gras topping and fish and chips arrive with a wasabi tartare. Flavours are sometimes compromised by an over-eagerness to make dishes look pretty but prices are generally sensible and the atmosphere thoroughly civilised.

Mint Leaf

I4

Indian ✕✕

Suffolk Pl.　　　　　　　　　⊖ Piccadilly Circus
✉ SW1Y 4HX　　　　Closed lunch Saturday and Sunday
✆ (020) 7930 9020
www.mintleafrestaurant.com

Menu £14/20 – Carte £28/49

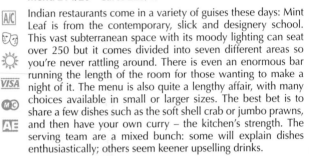

Indian restaurants come in a variety of guises these days: Mint Leaf is from the contemporary, slick and designery school. This vast subterranean space with its moody lighting can seat over 250 but it comes divided into seven different areas so you're never rattling around. There is even an enormous bar running the length of the room for those wanting to make a night of it. The menu is also quite a lengthy affair, with many choices available in small or larger sizes. The best bet is to share a few dishes such as the soft shell crab or jumbo prawns, and then have your own curry – the kitchen's strength. The serving team are a mixed bunch: some will explain dishes enthusiastically; others seem keener upselling drinks.

Momo

H3

Moroccan ✕✕

25 Heddon St.　　　　　　　　⊖ Oxford Circus
✉ W1B 4BH　　　　　　　　　Closed 25 December,
✆ (020) 743 4404 0　　　1 January and Sunday lunch
www.momoresto.com

Menu £20 (lunch) – Carte £32/49

Lanterns, rugs, trinkets and music all contribute to the authentic Moroccan atmosphere that makes Momo such a fun night out. That being said, it's even more fun if you come with friends as tables of two can get somewhat overawed. The menu is divided into three: a somewhat expensive set menu, traditional dishes and Momo specialities. The traditional section is the best as here you'll find the classics from pastilla to tagines; the Momo specialities are more contemporary in their make-up. Whatever you order, you'll end up with a pile of couscous and enough good food to last the week. The wine list lacks affordable bottles but there's a great bar downstairs. If it weren't for the absence of cigarette smoke, you could be in Marrakech.

Murano ✿

20 Queen St
W1J 5PP
(020) 7495 1127
www.angela-hartnett.com

⊖ **Green Park**
Closed Christmas and Sunday

Menu £25/85

AC
VISA
MC
AE

MAYFAIR, SOHO & ST JAMES'S ▶ PLAN II

Murano

Chef owner Angela Hartnett is clearly immeasurably proud of her stylish Mayfair restaurant and it's easy to understand why. The cooking exhibits an appealing lightness of touch borne out of greater confidence in her ingredients, which come from Italy and the British Isles, but also in her own abilities and those of Diego Cardoso, her head chef. Her passion for Italian food is palpable. The food uses a blend of classical techniques so that flavours are refined, defined and balanced. The fish dishes, such as sea bass with mussels, are particularly delicious and stand out for their clarity and freshness. The service has also become a little more relaxed these days which suits the place more than the somewhat overly formal style previously adopted; it helps too when you have plenty of regulars who have got to know the staff well. Named after the famous glassware from the Venetian island of Murano, the restaurant is stylish and elegant and comes with an appealing freshness and vitality.

First Course	*Main Course*	*Dessert*
• Octopus with apple purée, white bean and clam ragout. • Breast of quail, tortellini and date purée.	• John Dory, hand-rolled macaroni and morels. • Venison with grilled foie gras, parsnip, pancetta and pearl barley.	• Lemon parfait, sesame meringue and thyme crumble. • Caramel soufflé with fresh mint Chantilly.

The National Dining Rooms

British modern 🍴

I3/4

Sainsbury Wing, The National Gallery,
Trafalgar Sq ✉ WC2N 5DN
☎ (020) 7747 2525
www.peytonandbyrne.co.uk

⊖ Charing Cross
Closed 24-26 December –
(lunch only and Friday dinner)

Carte £26/40

There's usually a queue but don't panic – it's either those wanting the bakery section or others realising they should have booked. Oliver Peyton's restaurant on the first floor of the National Gallery's Sainsbury Wing is a bright, open affair, enriched by Paula Rego's complex mural 'Crivelli's Garden'. Ask for a table by the window, not just for the views of Trafalgar Square but also because the other half of the room is darker and under the eaves of the early Renaissance on the floor above. The menu champions British cooking and produce; fish and cheeses are the highlight – pies and puds will write-off the afternoon. The set menu represents decent value and is popular with the customers, who resemble a bridge club up from Winchester for the day.

Nopi

Mediterranean 🍴

H3

21-22 Warwick St.
✉ W1B 5NE
☎ (020) 7494 9584
www.nopi-restaurant.com

⊖ Piccadilly Circus
Closed 25-26 December,
1 January and Sunday dinner

Carte £27/47

After relishing his delis and devouring his cookbooks, fans of Yotam Ottolenghi are now flocking to his first 'proper' restaurant. It's an enthusiastically run and luminous affair and is spread over two floors, all whitewashed walls, tiles, marble and brass. The communally minded can ask to share one of the two large tables downstairs which face the open kitchen and are surrounded by the chefs' supplies. Flavours take in the Mediterranean, the Middle East and various parts of Asia, and the menu is subdivided under the headings of Veg, Fish or Meat; one of each per person should suffice. The veggie dishes are best, such as burrata with coriander seeds, but the fish creations like grilled mackerel with a pea and mint salad are also refreshing.

Nobu ⇔

G4

Metropolitan Hotel,
19 Old Park Ln
✉ W1Y 1LB
✆ (020) 7447 4747
www.noburestaurants.com

⊖ Hyde Park Corner
Closed 25-26 December –
booking essential

Menu £60/95 – Carte £37/68

Nobu

Nobu restaurants now number over twenty and are spread around the world, but this one was the first to open in Europe, back in 1997, and came not long after the original in Manhattan. The two London branches can be considered the pick of the bunch and much of the credit is down to the long-standing executive chef, Mark Edwards. He has also been responsible for introducing the Osusume menu, which is exclusive to London and is aimed at offering neophytes the opportunity to discover what makes the food – Japanese with South American influences – quite so interesting. The reason is that the flavours are unique, the combinations wholly complementary and the ingredients top-notch – it's little wonder the dishes have been plagiarised across the city. The enthusiasm of the staff is undimmed and while the restaurant is perhaps less obviously glitzy than its younger sibling, that does mean that the fashionable crowd here are a little less excitable. Those who don't have the time to visit can now simply pick up a lunch or pre-theatre bento box.

First Course	*Main Course*	*Dessert*
• Yellowtail jalapeño. • Matsuhisa shrimp with caviar.	• Black cod with miso. • Anticucho Peruvian style tea-smoked lamb.	• Chocolate bento box with green tea ice cream. • Suntory whisky cappuccino.

Nobu Berkeley St ✿

H3

15 Berkeley St.   ⊖ **Green Park**
✉ W1J 8DY   Closed 25-26 December, Saturday
✆ (020) 7290 9222   and Sunday lunch and bank holiday
www.noburestaurants.com/berkeley   Mondays – booking essential

Menu £27, £33/90 – Carte £34/73

AC
VISA
MC
AE

Nobu

As a general rule, if there are paparazzi outside a restaurant, then the talent inside is unlikely to be in the kitchen. But there are exceptions and Nobu Berkeley St is one of them. This is a restaurant that still does things properly, despite serving around 900 people each day. There are 45 chefs in the kitchen, 60% of whom are Japanese, and considerable care is taken with the food. Nobu tacos are a good way of getting things started and staff are well-informed if you need help. Greatest hits like yellowtail sashimi, black cod with miso and shrimp tempura remain on the menu but each Nobu has some unique element and at Nobu Berkeley St it is the wood oven. The cabbage steak with truffles and lamb anti cucho miso are top sellers, and the chocolate tart is catching the chocolate bento box in popularity. Lunch sees regular or deluxe bento boxes with organic juices. Anyone whose fame does not extend beyond their own home needs to book well in advance to get their desired time; although, if you're prepared to wait in the busy bar, it may be worth just pitching up.

First Course
- Tuna sashimi salad with Matsuhisa dressing.
- Octopus carpaccio with bottarga.

Main Course
- Black cod with miso.
- Duck breast with wasabi salsa.

Dessert
- Chocolate bento box with green tea ice cream.
- Cheesecake with ginger ice cream and raspberry foam.

Only Running Footman

GH3

5 Charles St   ⊖ Green Park.
✉ W1J 5DF
☎ (020) 7499 2988
www.therunningfootmanmayfair.com

Menu £30/40 – Carte £22/39

Apparently the owners added 'only' to the title when they found out that theirs was the only pub in the land called 'The Running Footman'. Spread over several levels, it offers cookery demonstrations and private dinners along with its two floors of dining. Downstairs is where the action usually is, with its menu offering pub classics from steak sandwiches to fishcakes, but you can't book here and it's always packed. Upstairs is where you'll find a surprisingly formal dining room and here they do take reservations. Its menu is far more ambitious and European in its influence but the best dishes are still the simpler ones, with desserts a strength. You can't help feeling that you would be having a lot more fun below stairs, though.

VISA

MC

AE

Plum Valley

I3

20 Gerrard St.   ⊖ Leicester Square
✉ W1D 6JQ   Closed 23-24 December
☎ (020) 7494 4366

Menu £38 – Carte £19/37

Is Chinatown finally casting off its tourist-trap reputation? Plum Valley is the latest venture with genuine aspirations to open in Gerrard Street and its contemporary styling gives the street a much-needed boost. The striking black façade makes it easy to notice, while flattering lighting and layered walls give the interior a dash of sophistication. The chef is from Chiu Chow, a region near Guangdong, and his menu is largely based on Cantonese cooking, with occasional forays into Vietnam and Thailand as well as the odd nod towards contemporary presentation. Dim sum is his kitchen's main strength which fits nicely with the all-day opening of the restaurant. If only those doing the service could muster the same levels of enthusiasm.

VISA

MC

AE

Pollen Street Social ✿

innovative ✗✗

H3

8-10 Pollen St
✉ W1S 1NQ
✆ (020) 7290 7600
www.pollenstreetsocial.com

⊖ Oxford Circus
Closed Christmas, Sunday and bank
holidays – booking essential

Menu £26 (lunch) – Carte £42/60

Pollen Street Social

Regardless of how experienced the team, it is not until a restaurant has been up and running for a while that it becomes clear what works and what doesn't. Here at Pollen Street Social there was a little tinkering done in year two – Jason Atherton ceased with the 'small plates' concept and reverted back to the more traditional starter-main course-dessert format. The other change concerned the bar which, owing to the popularity of the place, no longer offers its own menu but instead has been seconded into acting as an overflow dining area. As such, it's certainly worth asking for the main room with its 'dessert' bar and glass-fronted kitchen, because this is where the action is. What hasn't altered is the cooking which marries innovation and imagination with sound culinary techniques and an innate appreciation of good ingredients. Dishes are elaborately constructed but there are never too many flavours or any discordant notes. There's also a great cocktail list which includes their terrific version of a negroni.

First Course

- 'Full English breakfast'.
- Scallop ceviche with cucumber and radish.

Main Course

- Roasted sea bass, celeriac and truffle sauce.
- Black Angus rib-eye, oxtail, charred eggplant and smoked potatoes.

Dessert

- Peanut butter parfait, cherry jam, creamed rice puffs.
- White chocolate and coconut panna cotta.

Polpo Soho

H3

41 Beak St.
✉ W1F 9SB
✆ (020) 7734 4479
www.polpo.co.uk

⊖ Oxford Circus
Closed 25 December-1 January,
Sunday and dinner bank holidays
– (bookings not taken at dinner)

Carte £17/28

Opening a Venetian bacaro in an 18C townhouse where Canaletto once lodged does seem providential and Polpo has indeed been packing them in since day one. The stripped-down faux-industrial look is more New York's SoHo than London's Soho, as is the no-reservation policy which means you'll probably have to wait. But the fun atmosphere and the appealing prices of the small plates will assuage any impatience you feel in waiting your turn. Order a couple of cicheti, like arancini or prosciutto, a plate of fritto misto, ham and pea risotto or Cotechino sausage along with a vegetable dish per person and you should leave satisfied; if you do over-order, it's not going to break the bank. Venetian wines, available by the carafe, complete the picture.

Portrait

modern ✕

I3

National Portrait Gallery, (3rd floor),
St Martin's Pl. ✉ WC2H 0HE
✆ (020) 7312 2490
www.searcys.co.uk

⊖ Charing Cross
Closed 24-26 December –
booking essential –
(lunch only and dinner Thursday-Saturday)

Menu £18/35

Portrait is on the third floor of the Ondaatje wing of the National Portrait Gallery and is run by the catering company Searcy's. You needn't ask for a window seat because the views, of recognisable rooftops and Nelson in Trafalgar Square, are just as good from any of the tables. Although open for breakfast and tea, this is principally a lunchtime operation, with dinner limited to Thursday, Friday and Saturday - the nights of the gallery's extended opening hours. The à la carte menu keeps things relatively light and the influences mostly from Europe; there is a good value set menu at weekends. This is a useful spot, not only for gallery visitors but also for those attending matinee performances at various nearby theatres.

MAYFAIR, SOHO & ST JAMES'S ▶ PLAN II

Quaglino's

H4

modern ✗✗

16 Bury St
✉ SW1Y 6AJ
☏ (020) 7930 6767
www.quaglinos.co.uk

⊖ **Green Park**
Closed 24-27 December and Sunday

Menu £20 (lunch) – Carte £30/55

A/C

Few London restaurants are as synonymous with the early '90s as Quaglino's when, for a time, securing a table at this vast, glamorous, colourful and glitzy restaurant was the overriding ambition of many. The in-crowd may have since moved on – to other bustling, design-led restaurants which owe a debt to the trail blazed by 'Quag's' – but the old girl can still shake it on a weekend for those wanting a fun night out. The kitchen also feels invigorated and successfully delivers on the promise of the appealing, brasserie-style menu. Classics like pork belly, duck confit and chargrilled steaks are done well, along with shellfish from the 'Crustacea Counter'; look out too for the 'dish of the day'; perhaps a smoked haddock fishcake.

VISA
MC
AE
DC

Quince

H4

Turkish ✗✗

Stratton St
✉ W1J 8LT
☏ (020) 7915 3892
www.quincelondon.com

⊖ **Green Park**
Closed Saturday lunch

A/C

Menu £20/25 – Carte £28/40

As a hotel known mostly for attracting youthful celebrity guests, it's perhaps appropriate that The Mayfair turned to a celebrity TV chef to run its restaurant. Bulgarian born Silvena Rowe has brought along her inimitable Eastern Mediterranean cooking and her personality is evident throughout, from the personal references on the menu – "a homage to my grandfather Mehmed" – to the Ottoman-influenced style of the room. The menu kicks off with a selection of small plates – 'mezze' by any other name – although these can quickly crank up the bill. The best bet is to head straight for the main courses, whether they're grilled, like the sea bass with fennel tzatziki or roasted in the stone oven, as with the slow-cooked shoulder of lamb.

VISA
MC
AE

Quo Vadis

13

26-29 Dean St
✉ W1D 3LL
✆ (020) 7437 9585
www.quovadissoho.co.uk

⊖ Tottenham Court Road
Closed Sunday and bank holidays

Menu £20 – Carte £26/40

The neon sign and stained glass windows have long been familiar Dean Street landmarks and the building is inextricably linked with Soho's colourful past – it was once home to Karl Marx and opened as a restaurant in 1926. The current owners, the Hart brothers, recruited the services of Jeremy Lee in 2012 to rejuvenate the kitchen and his menu is a celebration of all things British. Start with some bites like delicious baked salsify or potted pork before enjoying excellent crab or grilled mackerel. There's a daily pie and a braised dish, and the grill dishes are flavoursome and filling. The pre-theatre menu is a steal. The room is stylish and elegant and while service is quite formally structured, it does need the occasional nudge.

Red Fort

13

77 Dean St.
✉ W1D 3SH
✆ (020) 7437 2525
www.redfort.co.uk

⊖ Tottenham Court Road
Closed 25 December, lunch Saturday,
Sunday and bank holidays –
bookings advisable at dinner

Menu £14/49 – Carte £21/53

Red Fort has been in Soho since 1983, although anyone who hasn't visited for a while will be surprised to see how up-to-date this Indian restaurant now is in the looks department. It's still quite a sizeable place but neatly broken up; the far end even boasts a little waterfall. Service isn't quite so memorable and staff could do with being a little more willing to engage with their customers but the menu does impress. It is not overlong and comes divided between starters, grills and main courses. Much of the produce comes from within the UK, such as Herdwick lamb, and there are also more unusual ingredients like rabbit used. Cooking is nicely balanced but the final bill can be a little high, especially when one has added breads, rice and vegetables.

Refuel

I3

modern ✕✕

Soho Hotel,
4 Richmond Mews ✉ W1D 3DH
☎ (020) 7559 3007
www.sohohotel.com

⊖ Tottenham Court Road

Carte £26/50

It comes as no surprise that a hotel as fashionable as The Soho has a restaurant as cool as Refuel. A large part of the room is given over to a slick cocktail bar and the lively atmosphere here tends to seep through into the restaurant through osmosis. Service in the hotel is one of its great strengths and the serving team here are a bright and enthusiastic bunch who are always ready with a smile. The menu is all about ease of eating and includes a popular section of grilled dishes, which could range from Dover sole to a burger, as well as assorted pasta dishes and salads for the image-conscious. Side dishes are needed but can leave you with a sizeable bill so it's worth considering the better value set menu.

Ritz Restaurant

H4

British traditional ✕✕✕✕✕

Ritz Hotel,
150 Piccadilly ✉ W1J 9BR
☎ (020) 7493 8181
www.theritzlondon.com

⊖ Green Park

Menu £45/50 s – Carte £73/95 s

Dining at The Ritz is not just a mightily grand occasion but also provides a lesson in how things used to be done. The room is certainly unmatched in the sheer lavishness of its Louis XVI decoration; the table settings positively gleam thanks to all that polishing and there are probably more ranks to the serving team than in a ship's company. Little wonder they insist on jackets and ties. There's a plethora of menus: Ritz Classics could be saddle of Kentish lamb or roast sirloin; Ritz Traditions might include smoked salmon carved at your table or Dover sole filleted in front of you. For the full experience, have the six-course Sonata Menu, go at a weekend for a dinner dance and don't tell your bank manager.

N Rosa's

Thai ✕

48 Dean St
✉ W1D 5BF
✆ (020) 7494 1638
www.rosaslondon.com

⊖ **Leicester Square**
Closed Easter and Christmas –
booking advisable

Carte £18/30

☀   Those instinctively suspicious of anywhere too shiny and
flashy will find Rosa's worn-in appearance suitably reassuring.
VISA   The simple, pared down look of this authentic Thai café also
adds to its intimate feel; the waitresses, in bright red T-shirts
to match the colour of the façade, provide cheerful and swift
service. The menu is appealing and wide ranging and the
relative heat levels of each dish are indicated. The chef may
be from Chiang Mai but his cooking is influenced by all parts
of the country. Signature dishes include warm minced chicken
salad and a sweet pumpkin red curry; while squid, prawns,
mussels and scallops all go into their seafood Pad Cha. The
refreshing Tom Yam soup comes with lovely balance of sweet,
sour and spice.

Sake No Hana

Japanese ✕✕

23 St James's St
✉ SW1A 1HA
✆ (020) 7925 8988
www.sakenohana.com

⊖ **Green Park**
Closed Sunday

Carte £31/75

A/C   As with most restaurants, things look a little different now
from when the place opened. At Sake No Hana the idea of not
VISA   offering wine along with the shochu and sake lasted about six
months. The menu is also now shorter and less adventurous. It
is dominated by sashimi and sushi, after which one is expected
to order a grilled dish and perhaps one of their 'special plates'-
which could be fried tofu with bonito flakes – then end with
some miso soup. Service can be hit and miss and whilst all that
cedar wood goes some way towards hiding the ugliness of this
stangely iconic '60s building, one does get the impression that
this isn't yet the finished article, as the overall experience can
be a little lacklustre and quite expensive.

MAYFAIR, SOHO & ST JAMES'S ▶ PLAN II

St John ✿

British traditional ✗

1 Leicester St
✉ WC2H 7BL
✆ (020) 3301 8069
www.stjohnhotellondon.com

⊖ Leicester Square
Booking advisable

Menu £23 (lunch and early dinner) – Carte £22/52

St John

The last time food this good was on show in Leicester Square was when 'Babette's Feast' was being screened at the Odeon. St John Hotel opened in 2011 and its ground floor restaurant is the heart of the operation. It shares the same features as the Clerkenwell original – so that means an eminently appealing, daily-changing menu and fiercely seasonal, no-nonsense "nose to tail" British-inspired food. It's no mean feat making cooking look this easy and when the plates arrive you instinctively want to roll up your sleeves. The square room, with an open kitchen at one end, also shares the unadorned, mildly municipal look, while the young service team know the food inside and out and are more than willing to elaborate on the somewhat terse menu descriptions. For decades this was Manzi's and, in a nice touch, they've not only kept the signs outside proclaiming "Langouste, Huîtres and Moules" but also ensure that they feature on the menu when in season. Be sure to order the warm madeleines for the journey home.

First Course
- Salt hake and tartare sauce.
- Snails, duck hearts and watercress.

Main Course
- Ox cheek, celeriac and pickled walnuts.
- Middle White chop, squash and sage.

Dessert
- Rhubarb and sherry trifle.
- Treacle toffee ice cream.

Sartoria

Italian XXX

H3

20 Savile Row
✉ W1S 3PR
☎ (020) 7534 7000
www.sartoria-restaurant.co.uk

⊖ **Green Park**
Closed 25 December, Saturday lunch,
Sunday and bank holidays

Menu £26 – Carte £23/64

A/C

If you're going to have any restaurant occupying a prime site in Savile Row then it might as well be Italian as they know one or two things about tailoring themselves. Sartoria is an elegant, smartly dressed restaurant that always seems to exude a certain poise and self-assurance, along with a little charm. There are subtle allusions to tailoring in the decoration and the sofa-style seating in the middle of the room is very appealing. The à la carte menu is an extensive number and prices can quickly add up, but the cooking, which covers all parts of the country, is undertaken with care and it's apparent that the ingredients are top-notch. Service is also not lacking in confidence and is overseen by assorted suited managers.

VISA

MC

AE

Scott's

fish and seafood XXX

G3

20 Mount St
✉ W1K 2HE
☎ (020) 7495 7309
www.scotts-restaurant.com

⊖ **Bond Street**
Closed 25-26 December

Carte £35/66

A/C

VISA

MC

AE

Scott's is one of those rare restaurants which is both fashionable and also has a palpable sense of history. As soon as you're through the door, you'll find the aroma and the bustle an enticing draw. Purportedly Ian Fleming's favourite restaurant, it still appeals to those whose faces we recognise and everyone looks as though they've dressed up for the occasion. The wood panelling is juxtaposed with modern art and the bar forms a striking centrepiece. The menu offers an enticing and varied choice, from caviar to razor clams, oysters to spider crabs and sea bass and turbot. The fish is cooked with skill and innate understanding. If only the taciturn staff could crack the occasional smile and add some personality to their efficiency.

Semplice ❀

Italian XX

G3

9-10 Blenheim St
✉ W1S 1LJ
✆ (020) 7495 1509
www.ristorantesemplice.com

⊖ Bond Street
Closed 2 weeks
Christmas, Easter, Sunday and bank
holidays – booking essential at dinner

Menu £28 (lunch) – Carte £33/63

A/C

VISA

MC

AE

Semplice

The young owners' enthusiasm for their restaurant and their
determination to uphold its reputation is palpable. As such,
the chef is intent on instilling in his brigade the importance of
using good produce and the respect one should show it. Along
with many ingredients imported directly from small, specialist
suppliers in Italy, fresh fish arrives each day from Cornwall.
The kitchen remains loyal to its North Italian roots and the
main ingredient of each dish is allowed to shine. The Fassone
carpaccio and the Milanese risotto with bone marrow are
two choices that keep the many regulars particularly content,
but those who are more trusting leave the decisions about
what they'll eat to the kitchen. The gold waves on the walls,
leather and lacquered ebony panels add a hint of luxury to the
room, which takes on a more intimate feel in the evening. The
lunch set menu allows newcomers the chance to experience
Semplice without breaking the bank. Bar Trattoria Semplice is
the simpler sibling a few yards away.

First Course	*Main Course*	*Dessert*
• Risotto Milanese with saffron and bone marrow. • Carpaccio of Fassone beef.	• Rabbit with glazed carrots and artichoke sauce. • Gnocchi of buffalo ricotta with asparagus and langoustines.	• Tiramisu with Giovanni Erbisti coffee and ice cream. • Dark chocolate mousse, brownie and cassata ice cream.

Seven Park Place ✿

H4

modern XXX

St James's Hotel and Club,
7-8 Park Pl
✉ SW1A 1LS
✆ (020) 7316 1614
www.stjameshotelandclub.com

⊖ Green Park
Closed Sunday and Monday
– booking essential

Menu £25/69

St James's Hotel and Club

The problem facing the owners of the St James's Hotel when they converted it from a private club, was in operating within the limited amount of space available. Accordingly, this small restaurant is somewhat concealed at the end of a bar through which one has to navigate. It's divided between two very contrasting rooms: the plush back room is the place to sit, as it holds just three large tables in its gilded setting; the outer room is not quite so intimate. The restaurant does, however, have a grown-up feel to it and the professional serving team make everyone feel suitably relaxed. The hotel has also got the right chef, cooking the right food. William Drabble made his name at Michael's Nook in Grasmere and Aubergine in Chelsea and his food has always displayed a sense of clarity, offering clean, unadulterated flavours. It is French at its base but the ingredients are decidedly British and mostly from more northerly parts, so expect lamb from the Lune Valley, game from Cumbria and shellfish from the west coast of Scotland.

First Course

- Tortellini of lobster with lobster butter sauce.
- Warm salad of quail with sweetbreads and foie gras.

Main Course

- Saddle of lamb with garlic purée and rosemary jus.
- Fillet of turbot with apple, mussels, celeriac and chives.

Dessert

- Dark chocolate mousse cake with raspberries.
- Tarte Tatin of banana with rum and raisin ice cream.

Sketch (The Gallery)

modern ✗✗

H3

9 Conduit St
☒ W1S 2XG
✆ (020) 7659 4500
www.sketch.uk.com

⊖ Oxford Circus
Closed 25-26 December, Sunday and bank
holidays – booking essential – (dinner only)

Carte £30/67

Martin Creed was the artist charged with changing the look of The Gallery restaurant on the ground floor of Sketch and he's turned it into a vibrant, witty and provocative space, where every piece of furniture and cutlery is different. The room is awash with collages of colour and is a cross between a restaurant and an art installation. The menus have also been updated and are now a blend of influences; some dishes are re-workings of brasserie classics, some are dishes with some added luxury, others are more original. So you can order steak tartare, a burger where the beef comes with foie gras, or scallops poached in a mussel jus with added galangal. The place is certainly fun, although the prices are not always particularly friendly.

Spice Market

Asian ✗✗

I3

W London Hotel,
10 Wardour St ☒ W1D 6QF
✆ (020) 7758 1082
www.spicemarketlondon.co.uk

⊖ Leicester Square

Carte £32/46

Leicester Square might not be as hip as Manhattan's Meatpacking district but this offshoot of Jean-Georges Vongerichten's New York original may just start to change things around here. This London branch certainly learnt about service from its American cousin because staff are all very confident, keen and clued-up. The restaurant is spread over two floors, linked by a spiral staircase, with eye-catching screens of gold mesh, walls of spices and ceilings of upturned woks. The kitchen traverses various Asian countries for influences and dishes are designed for sharing; ingredients are good and curries are a highlight. 'Street food' is how they describe their cooking, although the street in question is clearly a well-to-do one.

Sketch (The Lecture Room & Library) ✿✿

French XXXX

H3

9 Conduit St (1st floor) ✉ W1S 2XG
℘ (020) 7659 4500
www.sketch.uk.com

Menu £35 (lunch) – Carte £70/129

⊖ Oxford Circus
Closed last 2 weeks August,
Saturday lunch, Sunday and Monday
– booking essential

A/C
✿
VISA
MC
AE

Sketch

Stroll up Conduit Street and the only hint that something intriguing may be happening in this 18C townhouse is the presence of a bowler-hatted doorman and some flickering flames. Celebrated chef Pierre Gagnaire's glamorous London lair comes with various quirky design touches and eye-catching elements and that's even before you get to the beautifully decorated first floor Library and Lecture Room. The room is split in two, with the front section being the place to sit, although the chairs are so comfortable, sitting can easily become slumping. The menu may initially appear quite limited but the number of elements that make up each dish are certainly not. Gagnaire's style is highly individual, with the main 'plate' surrounded by its accompaniments; the quality of the produce is second to none and the kitchen's skill is evident. The wine list is impressive but with such elaborate constructions it's worth enlisting the sommelier's help to find a suitable match. The front of house team provides detailed service but does so with genuine warmth.

First Course	Main Course	Dessert
• 'Perfume of the Earth'. • 'Sea Garden N° 10'.	• Saddle of Quercy Lamb. • Sea bass and Gillardeau oyster.	• Pierre Gagnaire's 'Grand Dessert'. • Manjari chocolate soufflé.

Spuntino

61 Rupert St.
✉ W1D 7PW
www.spuntino.co.uk

⊖ Piccadilly Circus
Closed 24-26 December –
bookings not accepted

Carte £15/25

A/C · VISA · MC · AE

Despite its Italian name – meaning 'snack'– Spuntino draws its influences from Downtown New York and is so convincing you feel you could be on Clinton Street. It has the so-discreet-you-walk-straight-past-it entrance, a no-reservations policy (not even a phone number) and an interior that more than hints at a former industrial life – this was once a dairy. Just grab, or wait for, space at the counter and, from the brown paper menu, go for the more American dishes such as Mac 'n' Cheese, soft-shell crab, farmhouse cheddar grits or 'sliders', which are mini burgers. The peanut butter and jelly sandwiches for dessert will be always on your mind. The staff, who look like they could also fix your car, really add to the fun.

Sumosan

26 Albemarle St.
✉ W1S 4HY
℘ (020) 7495 5999
www.sumosan.com

⊖ Green Park
Closed lunch Saturday-Sunday
and bank holidays

Menu £25 (weekday lunch) – Carte £19/103

Sumosan isn't the only restaurant serving this kind of contemporary Japanese food in London, or indeed in Mayfair, but what it does do is offer a greater degree of sophistication. The lighting is seductive, the booths discreet and the design chic; it still appeals to a young and prosperous crowd but one that is a little less shouty. Deciding what and how much to order is a little confusing, and assistance from the staff isn't always forthcoming, but the kitchen is sufficiently flexible to allow for ordering as you go along. Its understanding of flavour combinations is showcased in dishes like duck with lingonberry sauce and turbot with wasabi risotto. Those who prefer things more traditional should head straight for the sushi bar.

Square ✿✿

French 🍴🍴🍴🍴

6-10 Bruton St.
✉ W1J 6PU
☎ (020) 7495 7100
www.squarerestaurant.com

⊖ **Green Park**
Closed 24-26 December
and Sunday lunch

Menu £35/80

The Square

Fame rather than acclaim appear to drive many chefs in this age of celebrity. By contrast, and despite being much in demand and having interests in other restaurants, Philip Howard is a chef who is nearly always to be found in his own kitchen – and this is one of the reasons The Square has been one of London's leading restaurants for two decades. His sophisticated food has its roots in classic French cooking but he isn't put off by new techniques if he thinks they will improve the dish. His menu is one of those that is so appealing it's hard to choose; it changes seasonally but there are some dishes like the crab lasagne that his regulars wouldn't allow him to take off. The dishes are visually appealing and come with a lightness of touch and finesse that few can match and the tasting menu, with its matching wines, provides a memorable experience. The wine list has an Old World bias and is strong on burgundies. The room is comfortable and understated and the service discreet and detailed.

First Course

- Lasagne of crab with shellfish cappuccino and champagne foam.
- Quail, white asparagus and morels with roast onion jelly.

Main Course

- Assiette of Pyrenean lamb with ewe's curd ravioli and pine nuts.
- John Dory with turnip tops, snails, morels, peas and parmesan.

Dessert

- Crème caramel with candied fruit and blood orange brioche roulade.
- Vanilla soufflé with rhubarb ripple ice cream.

99

Tamarind ✿

Indian 🏛🏛🏛

20 Queen St.
✉ W1J 5PR
✆ (020) 7629 3561
www.tamarindrestaurant.com

⊖ Green Park
Closed 25-26 December, 1 January
and Saturday lunch

Menu £19/68 – Carte £30/54

Tamarind

A constant re-laying of tables is required to keep up with the demand for Alfred Prasad's cooking and this, combined with the sometimes slightly hectic service, adds a reassuring buzz to proceedings at Tamarind. It is easy to see the appeal of the cooking: the flavours really shine through and the spicing is so deft that you can taste each component, whether that's the crushed peppercorns on the Jhinga Kalimirch tiger prawns, the green chillies with the Gilafi Reshmi kebab of ground chicken, or the cumin flavouring the side dish of seasonal green vegetables. Tamarind's dishes are mostly influenced by traditional Moghul cuisine so the tandoor oven is used to great effect – the breads and kebabs are terrific and the tandoori pineapple is a refreshing way to end the meal. Those seated closer to the kitchen get to see the chefs at work with the ovens, under Alfred's watchful eye. The basement location adds to the sense of exclusivity and the smoked mirrors and gilded columns lend a dash of Mayfair gloss.

First Course

- Mushrooms with pickled onions in a curry leaf dressing.
- Kebab of chicken with ginger, chillies, cheese and spices.

Main Course

- Tandoor-grilled lamb chops with papaya, chilli and garlic.
- Tiger prawns with tomatoes, spices and peppercorns.

Dessert

- Stewed pears with fennel and ginger ice cream.
- Pistachio kheer.

Tapas Brindisa

H3

Spanish ✗

46 Broadwick St.
✉ W1F 7AF
✆ (020) 7534 1690
www.brindisa.com

⊖ Oxford Circus
Closed dinner 24-27 December –
(bookings not accepted at dinner)

Carte £19/43

The owners didn't quite get it right when they first opened this sister to their successful operation in Borough Market, but it didn't take them long before they made the necessary changes – and the place has been packed ever since. In true tapas style, bookings are not taken – they want people to simply stroll in, have a drink and get something to eat and there are now plenty of other places in Soho doing the same thing. Look out for the specialities marked out in bold, such as Basque salt cod with spicy tomato sauce. The owners' expertise in importing Spanish produce is evident; although it's amazing how quickly the bill mounts up. Service is obliging and there's no 'push' to move you off, despite the clamour in the bar.

Tempo

H4

Italian ✗✗

54 Curzon St.
✉ W1J 8PG
✆ (020) 7629 2742
www.tempomayfair.co.uk

⊖ Green Park
Closed 25-27 December, Saturday lunch,
Sunday and bank holidays

Menu £22/25 – Carte £30/47

What we wouldn't all give for the reassuring presence of the owner when we're dining, especially when they're as affable and urbane as Henry Togna. His successful and rather sweet place fills with an eclectic mix of locals and tourists who come for the honestly priced, unfussy Italian cooking and the contagious conviviality. Start with a drink and some of the very good cicchetti, or small plates, on the terrace or in the funky first floor bar. The accessible menu ambles amiably around Italy; breads are excellent as is the homemade pasta which comes in a choice of two sizes; the regulars appear understandably partial to the lobster linguine. The pleasing buzz is helped along by the quiet efficiency of the friendly staff.

Ⓝ 10 Greek Street

modern 🍴

I3

10 Greek St
✉ W1D 4DH
℘ (020) 7734 4677
www.10greekstreet.com

⊖ **Tottenham Court Road**
Closed Christmas, Easter and Sunday

Carte £19/34

AC
⌀
🍷
🐝
VISA
MC
AE

With just 28 seats and a dozen more at the counter, the first challenge is getting a table at this modishly sparse-looking bistro – you can book at lunch but dinner is first-come-first-served. You'll then worry that those at the next table are too close for comfort but soon you'll find yourself caught up with the general bonhomie and start relaxing. The chef-owner's menu is chalked up on a couple of blackboards each day and his cooking comes with Anglo, Med and Middle Eastern elements. Start with some small plates – maybe burrata or sand eels – then try crab rigatoni or Cornish hake with dates; and it's worth choosing a dish for two, like leg of lamb. Wine is the passion of the other owner and the list is constantly evolving.

Theo Randall

Italian 🍴🍴🍴

G4

Intercontinental Hotel,
1 Hamilton Pl, Park Ln ✉ W1J 7QY
℘ (020) 7318 8747
www.theorandall.com

⊖ **Hyde Park Corner**
Closed 25-26 December,
1 January, Saturday lunch,
Sunday and bank holidays

Menu £27/60 – Carte £45/76

AC
⌀
🎭
VISA
MC
AE
⓪

It's no surprise that Theo Randall's menu is so heavily influenced by the River Café, as he spent 17 years there, many of these as Head Chef. It features influences and ingredients from across Italy – including Puglia, his favourite region – as well as produce from the British Isles. The veal chop is a perennial favourite but otherwise it's about what's in season– and when cooking appears this simple there's no room for error. If any dish sums up his philosophy it's his Amalfi lemon tart: he not only uses lemons from Amalfi but eggs too, from chickens fed on corn and carrots, which gives the tart a slight orange tinge. The pleasingly rustic nature of the food is a little at odds with the formal service and the corporate feel of the room.

G3

meats and grills XXX

34 Grosvenor Sq
(entrance on South Audley St)
✉ W1K 2HD
📞 (020) 3350 3434 – **www**.34-restaurant.co.uk

⊖ Marble Arch
Closed 25 December

Carte £29/61

A/C

Caprice Holdings' restaurants are all about glamour and exclusivity and 34 is no exception. Both its main culinary influences and intended customer base are announced by the flying of the Union Flag and the Stars and Stripes above the door, while inside is a wonderful mix of art deco style and Edwardian warmth – it feels like a classic brasserie that's been around for years. The star is the parrilla, an Argentinian charcoal grill used for the cooking of Dover sole and brochettes as well as the meat, which is a mix of Scottish dry-aged, US prime, organic Argentinian and Australian Wagyu. Game also features, along with short ribs which are becoming more popular over here. It may not come cheap but then glitz never does.

VISA
MC
AE
⓪

Vasco and Piero's Pavilion

H2/3

Italian XX

15 Poland St
✉ W1F 8QE
📞 (020) 7437 8774
www.vascosfood.com

⊖ Oxford Circus
Closed Saturday lunch, Sunday and bank holidays – booking essential at lunch

Menu £15/20 – Carte £27/44

A/C

This Soho institution celebrated its fortieth anniversary in 2011; if you ask them for the secret of their success the reply will be, "we just do what we believe in". That means a menu that changes twice a day, ingredients and influences from Umbria and simple but effective cooking, with homemade pasta a highlight. Service can sometimes lack a little enthusiasm but it does get the job done – it is not as if they don't care, more that their customers are often regulars who know the score, so why over-egg the pudding? The owners' confidence in their operation and their honest endeavours add to the grown-up feel. The restaurant, which was originally located in Oxford Street, remains fresh and bright.

VISA
MC
AE

Umu ⁣⁣❀

H3

14-16 Bruton Pl.
✉ W1J 6LX
✆ (020) 7499 8881
www.umurestaurant.com

⊖ Bond Street
Closed Saturday lunch,
Sunday and bank holidays

Menu £25 (lunch) – Carte £32/119

A/C
❀
VISA
MC
AE

Allowing the natural flavours of the ingredients to shine through is a fundamental element of Japanese cuisine. Accordingly, the search for the best produce is an integral part of any chef's responsibilities. Here at Umu the head chef has been working directly with select Cornish fisherman to ensure that his fish arrives at the restaurant in as fresh a state as possible and, as the quality improves, he plans to make his menus a little less Westernised and a little more authentic. At the moment the menu choice is extensive, but for the best overall experience head to the one of the seasonally changing, multi-course kaiseki menus, where the dishes are both flavoursome and visually appealing. The perfect accompaniment, especially for the sashimi, is sake; not only is the list impressive in its depth and range but the sommelier also offers thoughtful advice. The mostly French wine list is equally extensive in its scope. Warm wood, natural materials and judicious lighting make the restaurant feels as discreet as ever.

First Course

- 'Fuwa-fuwa' foie gras and dashi soufflé.
- Abalone with seaweed, cucumber and tosazu.

Main Course

- Grade 6 Wagyu, hoba leaf and seasonal vegetables.
- Black cod 'Kinome-yaki'.

Dessert

- Wild berry and black sesame panna cotta.
- Watermelon shiso granité, ice cream and cucumber sorbet.

Veeraswamy

Indian ✗✗

Victory House, 99 Regent St
(entrance on Swallow St.)
✉ W1B 4RS
✆ (020) 7734 1401 – www.realindianfood.com

⊖ Piccadilly Circus

Menu £18/24 – Carte £35/56

The manager here knows not to come between a regular and their favourite table: some were first brought here by their grandparents and are now, in turn, introducing their own grandchildren to London's oldest surviving Indian restaurant, which dates from 1926. You'd be excused for thinking it might be a tad old-fashioned but Veeraswamy is anything but: it is awash with vibrant colours and always full of bustle. The Hyderabad lamb biryani may have been on the original menu but there are plenty of other dishes with a more contemporary edge. The meaty Madagascar prawns are a good way of kicking things off; slow-cooked lamb dishes are also done very well. There's a tasting menu available and desserts, prepared with a flourish, shouldn't be ignored.

Vinoteca

modern ✗

53-55 Beak St
✉ W1F 9SH
✆ (020) 3544 7411
www.vinoteca.co.uk

⊖ Oxford Circus
Closed 24-26 December, 31 December and
1 January. – booking advisable

Carte £20/33

London is the wine capital of the world – largely because we're not allied to any particular wine producing region – so we should have many more wine bars than we do. This is the third Vinoteca and it's easy to see their appeal. Based on the wine bars and shops of Spain and Italy, the list of wines is terrific and mixes the classic with the esoteric; prices are fair and there's plenty of choice – even under £30. There are biodynamic and organic wines but there's no bandwagon-jumping going on here – emerging markets are also covered and if anything on the shelves catches your eye they all priced for take away. The food isn't forgotten – cured meats and cheeses are a highlight and European dishes like bavette and risotto also hit the spot.

Wild Honey ✿

H3

12 St George St.
✉ W1S 2FB
☎ (020) 7758 9160
www.wildhoneyrestaurant.co.uk

⊖ Oxford Circus
Closed 25-26 December and 1 January

Menu £22 (weekday lunch) – Carte £38/45

A/C

VISA
MC
AE

Wild Honey is all about relaxed and comfortable dining; the highly skilled cooking is a model of resourcefulness and the prices – when one considers the postcode and the quality of the food – are laudable. The kitchen proves that good – but not necessarily expensive – ingredients mean good food. The menus are hugely appealing and the seasonal ingredients are used at their peak; plates are never overcrowded and each component serves a purpose – there is nothing ostentatious here. The bouillabaisse and the wild honey ice cream are constants and the wine list is as magnanimous in its pricing as the menu, with all bottles available by the carafe. Like a talented sportsman, a lot of hard work and experience goes into making all this seem so easy. The fixed menu is a steal and there's now a short 'sweet and savoury' menu on offer for those who want an afternoon bite. Service is personable and unobtrusive and the atmosphere is far more animated than one would expect in a wood-panelled room that was once a private members club.

First Course

- Crab with sweet Italian leaves and avocado.
- Rabbit, pork and apricot terrine.

Main Course

- Bouillabaisse 'traditional Marseille style'.
- Breast of Limousin veal, caramelised onion and anchovy.

Dessert

- Wild honey ice cream with crushed honeycomb.
- Warm chocolate soup with milk sorbet.

The Wolseley

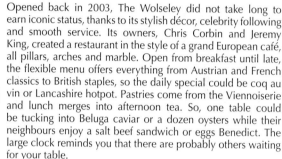

modern

160 Piccadilly
W1J 9EB
(020) 7499 6996
www.thewolseley.com

Carte £24/58

⊖ Green Park
Closed 25 December,
dinner 24 and 31 December
and August bank holiday –
booking essential

Opened back in 2003, The Wolseley did not take long to earn iconic status, thanks to its stylish décor, celebrity following and smooth service. Its owners, Chris Corbin and Jeremy King, created a restaurant in the style of a grand European café, all pillars, arches and marble. Open from breakfast until late, the flexible menu offers everything from Austrian and French classics to British staples, so the daily special could be coq au vin or Lancashire hotpot. Pastries come from the Viennoiserie and lunch merges into afternoon tea. So, one table could be tucking into Beluga caviar or a dozen oysters while their neighbours enjoy a salt beef sandwich or eggs Benedict. The large clock reminds you that there are probably others waiting for your table.

Wright Brothers Soho

fish and seafood

13 Kingly St.
W1B 5PW
(020) 7434 3611
www.thewrightbrothers.co.uk

Menu £17/19 – Carte £23/54

⊖ Oxford Circus
Closed 25-27 December
and bank holidays

Bigger than the original Wright Brothers in Borough Market, this branch is spread over three levels but the best seats are on the lower floor and certainly at the counter if you want to watch the expert oyster shucking. Oysters are the first choice of many as they grow their own in Cornwall; the plates of fruits de mer are also popular and designed for sharing. The menu is divided between cold and hot starters and 'house staples' which include everything from prawn cocktail to fish pie. The specials board also has plenty on offer, from sardines on toast to a perfectly judged whole sea bream. Desserts are something of an afterthought – it's all about fishy things here. There's an all-day menu and the restaurant opens out into Kingly Court.

Yauatcha ✿

15 Broadwick St
✉ W1F 0DL
✆ (020) 7494 8888
www.yauatcha.com

⊖ Tottenham Court Road
Closed 24-25 December
and lunch 26 December
and 1 January

Menu £29, £40/55 – Carte £23/48

A/C
🍽
🍸
🕐
☀
VISA
M©
AE

No cuisine or style of eating is immune from revolution, due largely to the changing ways we all live our lives. Go to Hong Kong and you'll see that even dim sum is evolving and has come to mean so much more than merely snacks to accompany the daytime drinking of tea. In London Yauatcha has always been at the heart of this change and its success is not hard to understand. The food is so good and the surroundings so slick and stylish that customers found it hard to be in and out in their allotted time – so now you can keep hold of your table for a couple of hours. They have also put in a bar on the ground floor which means you can wait for your table in a little more comfort. Three dim sum per person followed by some noodles or a stir-fry should be enough. Stand-out dishes are the scallop shui mai, prawn cheung fun, the wonderfully light baked venison puff and the Kung Po chicken. Those who prefer something sweet to accompany their Silver Needle white tea from Fujian can also come for cakes, tarts and pastries during the day.

First Course	*Main Course*	*Dessert*
• Scallop shui mai with tobiko caviar.	• Dover sole with shiitake and soya.	• Raspberry delice.
• Pork and chive box dumpling.	• Salt and pepper quail.	• Pear and almond tart with Guanaja ice cream.

Strand · Covent Garden

It's fitting that Manet's world famous painting 'Bar at the Folies Bergère' should hang in the **Strand** within a champagne cork's throw of theatreland and Covent Garden. This is the area perhaps more than any other which draws in the ticket-buying tourist, eager to grab a good deal on one of the many shows on offer, or eat and drink at fabled shrines like J.Sheekey or Rules. It's here the names already up in lights shine down on their potential usurpers: celeb wannabes heading for The Ivy, West Street's perennially fashionable restaurant. It's here, too, that Nell Gwyn set up home under the patronage of Charles II, while Oscar Wilde revelled in his success by taking rooms at the Savoy.

The hub of the whole area is the piazza at **Covent Garden,** created by Inigo Jones four hundred years ago. It was given a brash new lease of life in the 1980s after its famed fruit and veg market was pulled up by the roots and re-sown in Battersea. Council bigwigs realised then that 'what we have we hold', and any further redevelopment of the area is banned. Where everyone heads is the impressive covered market, within which a colourful jumble of arts and crafts shops gels with al fresco cafés and classical performers proffering Paganini with your cappuccino. Outside, under the portico of St Paul's church, every type of street performer does a turn for the tourist trade. The best shops in Covent Garden, though, are a few streets north of the market melee, emanating out like bicycle spokes from Seven Dials.

For those after a more highbrow experience, one of London's best attractions is a hop, skip and *grand jeté* from the market. Around the corner in **Bow Street** is the city's famed home for opera and ballet, where fire – as well as show-stopping performances – has been known to bring the house down. The **Royal Opera House** is now in its third incarnation, and it gets more impressive with each rebuild. The handsome, glass-roofed Floral Hall is a must-see, while an interval drink at the Amphitheatre Café Bar, overlooking the piazza, is de rigeur for show goers. At the other end of the Strand the **London Coliseum** offers more opera, this time all performed in English. Down by Waterloo Bridge, art lovers are strongly advised to stop at **Somerset House** and take in one of London's most sublime collections of art at the Courtauld Gallery. This is where you can get up close and personal to Manet's barmaid, as well as an astonishing array of Impressionist masters and twentieth century greats. The icing on the cake is the compact and accessible eighteenth century building that houses the collection: real icing on a real cake can be found in a super little hidden-away café downstairs.

Of a different order altogether is the huge **National Gallery** at

AGE / PHOTONONSTOP

Trafalgar Square which houses more than two thousand Western European pieces (it started off with 38). A visit to the modern Sainsbury Wing is rewarded with some unmissable works from the Renaissance. It can get just as crowded in the capital's largest Gallery as in the square outside, so a good idea is to wander down **Villiers Street** next to Charing Cross station and breathe the Thames air along the Victoria Embankment. Behind you is the grand Savoy Hotel, which reopened in 2010 after major refurbishment;

for a better view of it, you can head even further away from the crowds on a boat trip from the **Embankment,** complete with on-board entertainment. And if the glory of travel in the capital, albeit on the water, has whetted your appetite for more, then pop into the impressively renovated Transport Museum in Covent Garden piazza, where gloriously preserved tubes, buses and trains from the past put you in a positive frame of mind for the real live working version you'll very probably be tackling later in the day.

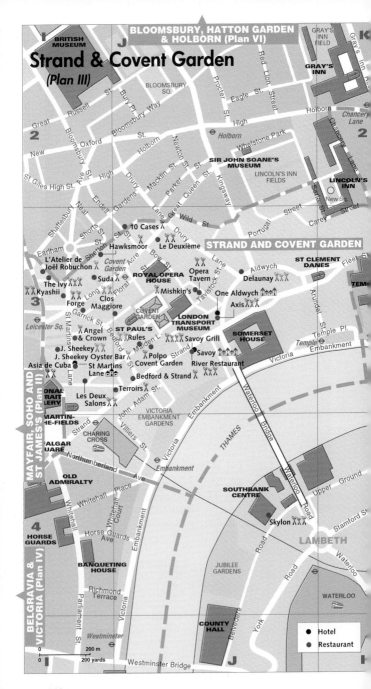

Strand & Covent Garden
(Plan III)

BLOOMSBURY, HATTON GARDEN & HOLBORN (Plan VI)

STRAND AND COVENT GARDEN

BRITISH MUSEUM
BLOOMSBURY SQ.
GRAY'S INN FIELD
GRAY'S INN
Russell St.
Bury Pl.
Great Russell St.
Bloomsbury Way
New Oxford St.
Proctor St.
Eagle St.
High
Red Lion St.
Holborn
Holborn
Chancery Lane
Whetstone Park
St Giles High St.
Shaftesbury Ave
Bloomsbury St.
High Holborn
Endell St.
Newton St.
Drury
Macklin St.
Parker St.
SIR JOHN SOANE'S MUSEUM
Kingsway
LINCOLN'S INN FIELDS
Chancery Lane
LINCOLN'S INN
New Sq.
Gardens
Great Queen St.
Wild St.
Portugal St.
Carey St.
Serle St.
Earlham St.
Shorts Gardens
Shelton St.
10 Cases
Hawksmoor
Le Deuxième
Bow St.
Drury Lane
Aldwych
ST CLEMENT DANES
Fleet St.
Neal St.
L'Atelier de Joël Robuchon
Covent Garden
ROYAL OPERA HOUSE
Opera Tavern
Delaunay
TEMP
Long Acre
Suda
Floral St.
Mishkin's
Tavistock St.
One Aldwych
The Ivy
Kyashii
Clos Maggiore
Forge
J. Sheekey
Garrick St.
Bedford St.
COVENT GARDEN
ST PAUL'S
LONDON TRANSPORT MUSEUM
Axis
Leicester Sq.
St Martin's Lane
Maiden Ln.
SOMERSET HOUSE
Arundel St.
Temple Pl.
Angel & Crown
Rules
Strand
Savoy Grill
Temple
Embankment
J. Sheekey Oyster Bar
Polpo Covent Garden
Savoy
River Restaurant
Asia de Cuba
St Martins Lane
Bedford & Strand
Victoria Embankment
Les Deux Salons
Terroirs
John Adam St.
VICTORIA EMBANKMENT GARDENS
NATIONAL PORTRAIT GALLERY
MAYFAIR, SOHO AND ST JAMES'S (Plan II)
ST MARTIN-IN-THE-FIELDS
Strand
Villiers St.
THAMES
Waterloo Bridge
Upper Ground
TRAFALGAR SQUARE
CHARING CROSS
Victoria Embankment
OLD ADMIRALTY
Northumberland Ave
Whitehall Place
Whitehall Court
SOUTHBANK CENTRE
Waterloo Road
Stamford St.
HORSE GUARDS
Whitehall
Horse Guards Ave
Embankment
Skylon
LAMBETH
BANQUETING HOUSE
Richmond Terrace
Parliament St.
Victoria
JUBILEE GARDENS
Road
Waterloo
BELGRAVIA & VICTORIA (Plan IV)
Westminster
WATERLOO
COUNTY HALL
York Road
Belvedere Road
Westminster Bridge

● Hotel
● Restaurant

0   200 m
0   200 yards

L'Atelier de Joël Robuchon ✿✿

French ✕

13-15 West St.
✉ WC2H 9NE
☎ (020) 7010 8600
www.joelrobuchon.co.uk

⊖ Leicester Square
Closed 25-26 December,
1 January, Sunday and August bank
holiday Monday

Menu £28/125 – Carte £35/69

A/C

VISA

MC

AE

L'Atelier de Joël Robuchon

STRAND & COVENT GARDEN ▶ PLAN III

London's L'Atelier de Joël Robuchon differs from his other 'branches' dotted around the world's culinary hotspots by being two restaurants under one roof: on the ground floor is L'Atelier itself, with an open kitchen and large counter; upstairs is the monochrome La Cuisine, a slightly more structured, sleek and more brightly-lit affair with table seating. Apart from a few wood-fired dishes upstairs, the menus are largely similar. The cooking is artistic, creative and occasionally playful; it is technically very accomplished and highly labour intensive – there are over thirty chefs in the building – but it is never overworked and each dish is perfectly balanced, its flavours true and its taste exquisite. French is the predominant influence, supported by other Mediterranean flavours, and ordering a number of smaller dishes is the best way to fully appreciate Robuchon's craft and vision, although your final bill can be pretty lofty. Service is expertly timed and confident and sitting at the counter will give you some insight into this most polished of operations.

First Course

- Green asparagus cappuccino with golden croutons.
- Veal pâté with foie gras and pistachio.

Main Course

- Quail stuffed with foie gras and truffle mashed potatoes.
- Cod in yuzu broth with lily bulbs.

Dessert

- Creamy Manjari chocolate, bitter chocolate sorbet and 'Oreo' cookie.
- Crispy meringue, lemon sorbet, avocado and banana cream.

Angel & Crown

British traditional

I3

58 St Martin's Ln
✉ WC2N 4EA
✆ (020) 7748 5244
www.theangelandcrown.com

⊖ Leicester Square.
Closed 25 December

Carte £23/34

A/C
☀
VISA
MC
AE
①

Tourist spots and good food are rarely enjoyed together and London is no exception, but fortunately the gastropub revolution is now creeping into the West End. The Angel & Crown is part of the Martin Brothers' portfolio which includes The Well and The Gun and here they've converted a handsome Victorian pub in the heart of theatre-land. The ground floor, with its pewter tankards hanging above the bar, is the sort of place you want to stand up in; most of the eating is done upstairs in the dining room. The menu wisely sticks to British dishes, with nothing to scare away the out-of-towners, and uses decent ingredients, so the pie may be venison and bone marrow and the sausages that go with the mash and onion gravy are made using wild boar.

Asia de Cuba

Asian

I3

St Martins Lane Hotel,
45 St Martin's Ln ✉ WC2N 3HX
✆ (020) 7300 5500
www.morganshotelgroup.com

⊖ Charing Cross

Menu £19/25 – Carte £41/66

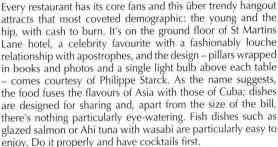

Every restaurant has its core fans and this über trendy hangout attracts that most coveted demographic: the young and the hip, with cash to burn. It's on the ground floor of St Martins Lane hotel, a celebrity favourite with a fashionably louche relationship with apostrophes, and the design – pillars wrapped in books and photos and a single light bulb above each table – comes courtesy of Philippe Starck. As the name suggests, the food fuses the flavours of Asia with those of Cuba; dishes are designed for sharing and, apart from the size of the bill, there's nothing particularly eye-watering. Fish dishes such as glazed salmon or Ahi tuna with wasabi are particularly easy to enjoy. Do it properly and have cocktails first.

Axis

modern XXX

One Aldwych Hotel,
1 Aldwych ✉ WC2B 4RH
℘ (020) 7300 1300
www.onealdwych.com

⊖ Temple
Closed Sunday and Monday

Menu £20 (lunch and early dinner) – Carte £34/39

A/C

Expectation is everything and the spiral marble staircase leading down to this restaurant always adds a little excitement. The room, which must have one of the highest ceilings in London, is neatly laid out and service is well-organised, if perhaps a little too formal for its own good. One wise decision was the moving of the bar to downstairs; this means there is always a little noise, even when the restaurant has a lull just after the theatre-goers have left. They have made the menu a little lighter by adding salads and a seafood section. More European influences now also sit alongside the British dishes, so you can have smoked salmon, salt beef and a treacle sponge or scallops with chorizo, beef bourguignon and a crème brûlée.

VISA
MC
AE
①

STRAND & COVENT GARDEN ▶ PLAN III

Bedford & Strand

British traditional X

1a Bedford St
✉ WC2E 9HH
℘ (020) 7836 3033
www.bedford-strand.com

⊖ Charing Cross
Closed 24 December-2 January,
Sunday and bank holidays –
booking essential

Menu £18 – Carte £19/38

VISA
MC
AE
①

Maybe it's the basement location or the discreet entrance, but Bedford & Strand has an almost secretive, clubby feel. The bar dominates proceedings but in a good way – you'll hear the laughter as you come down the stairs – and the character of the place makes you quickly forget about its subterranean location. Wine is given equal billing with the food; the list is sensibly laid out and there's plenty by the glass and carafe. The food menu complements it well and is appealingly to the point; highlights are the British classics like shepherd's pie, potted crab and treacle tart. The young staff make up in eagerness what they lack in direction and the atmosphere is pleasantly unhurried, despite its proximity to scores of theatres.

Clos Maggiore

French XX

J3

33 King St
✉ WC2E 8JD
✆ (020) 7379 9696
www.closmaggiore.com

⊖ Leicester Square
Closed 24-25 December

Menu £16/23 – Carte £32/44

Any West End restaurateurs still half-hearted about pre and post theatre dining should come to Clos Maggiore to see how it can be done: the menu represents excellent value, the kitchen is well organised and the staff get on with the serving, which means the theatregoer doesn't have to keep checking the time. Clos Maggiore is also one of the most romantic restaurants around – just be sure to ask for the table in the enchanting conservatory at the back, with its retractable roof. The chef is from Provence and you can almost smell the lavender when reading his menu. The French dishes are sophisticated in their make while the ingredients come mostly from the British Isles. The wine list has great depth and reflects the owner's passion.

ⓝ Delaunay

modern XXX

J3

55 Aldwych
✉ WC2B 4BB
✆ (020) 7499 8558
www.thedelaunay.com

⊖ Temple
Closed dinner 24 December, 25 December
and August bank holiday –
booking essential

Carte £18/50

Just like The Wolseley, its hugely successful older sibling, The Delaunay was inspired by the grand cafés of Europe and boasts a similar celebrity clientele, yet this is more than a mere replica. It may have opened in 2011, but the 150-seater dining room manages to evoke the 1920s with all its wood panelling, brass and leather. The menu is also more mittel-European, with great schnitzels and wieners featuring prominently. Daily specials could include daube of beef or fish stew, or you could just come for some eggs or a salad – it's that sort of place. There's a nostalgic element too; you'll find Black Forest gateau, banana split, and even a cover charge. The staff are engaging and swift but never make you feel rushed.

Le Deuxième

J3

modern ✕✕

65a Long Acre
✉ WC2E 9JH
☎ (020) 7379 0033
www.ledeuxieme.com

⊖ Covent Garden
Closed 24-25 December

Menu £17 (lunch) – Carte £31/38

Don't think that because it's busy in the early evening before curtain-up in all the local theatres that's it's going to quieten down when all the early-diners have gone – it seemingly stays busy most of the evening, most nights. This certainly gives the room plenty of energy but it also means that this is the sort of place where, if you get the attention of the waiter or waitress, you'll want to be ready with your order so as not to waste the opportunity. The menu offers an extensive range of dishes, whose influences come largely from within Europe. In amongst the pastas and the salads are some fairly classic French dishes and this is where the kitchen's experience lies. Side dishes, though, can quickly bump up the bill.

Les Deux Salons

I3

French ✕✕

40-42 William IV St
✉ WC2N 4DD
☎ (020) 7420 2050
www.lesdeuxsalons.co.uk

⊖ Charing Cross
Closed 25-26 December and 1 January

Menu £18 (weekday lunch) – Carte £25/51

After the success of Arbutus and Wild Honey, Will Smith and Anthony Demetre turned their attention towards France and came up with Les Deux Salons – a Parisian brasserie so authentic in its look you half expect to see Sartre sitting in the corner. Of the two salons, the ground floor is the more atmospheric and visually impressive, with its smoked mirrors, globe lights, zinc-topped bar and striking mosaic floor. The menu makes for an appealing read; you'll find French classics like bouillabaisse, assorted meats grilled on the Josper and even the occasional interloper from this side of the Channel, like cottage pie; desserts are full-on Gallic and all the better for it. It's been busy since opening its doors; service is swift, but not pushy.

Forge

modern ✗✗

13

14 Garrick St
✉ WC2E 9BJ
☎ (020) 7379 1432
www.theforgerestaurant.co.uk

⊖ Leicester Square
Closed 2 days Easter and 24-26 December

Menu £15/30 – Carte £24/48

A/C
😊
☀
VISA
Ⓜ©
AE

For those who can't decide what they want to eat or at what time, there is The Forge. Open all day, every day, with last orders at midnight, it offers an exhaustive choice of dishes to satisfy both the late-riser and the early-reveller. Omelettes and oysters vie with snails and salads; there's a pasta section and main courses range from whole Dover sole to liver and bacon; so whether it's tournedos Rossini or a hamburger you're after, you'll probably find what you want. Waiters weave between tables and make up in confidence what they sometimes lack in direction. The décor mixes the old with the new and, while the front of the restaurant is more intimate, the back is more fun. There is a good value pre and post theatre menu.

Hawksmoor

meats and grills ✗

13

11 Langley St
✉ WC2H 9JG
☎ (020) 7420 9390
www.thehawksmoor.com

⊖ Covent Garden
Closed 24-26 and 31 December,
1-2 January and Sunday dinner

Menu £22/25 – Carte £39/62

A/C
💠
⅋
🍸
😊
VISA
Ⓜ©
AE

Impressive renovation work from those clever Hawksmoor people turned this former brewery cellar into a very atmospheric restaurant whose primary function is the serving and eating of red meat – a suitably apt activity as one 18C owner of the brewery used to host a steak club. You'll get a friendly greeting at the bottom of the stairs and can either eat in the bar or in the large and bustling dining room with its ersatz industrial look. Steaks from Longhorn cattle lovingly reared in North Yorkshire and dry-aged for at least 35 days are the stars of the show. A blackboard shows availability and meat is priced per 100g. But beware as side orders and competitive over-ordering on the size of the cut can push up the final bill.

The Ivy

13

B r i t i s h   t r a d i t i o n a l XXX

1-5 West St
✉ WC2H 9NQ
✆ (020) 7836 4751
www.the-ivy.co.uk

⊖ **Leicester Square**
Closed 25-26 December

Menu £22 – Carte £38/50

The members-only Ivy Club may have siphoned off the top tier of regulars but The Ivy restaurant continues to attract new blood. It's still the sort of place where everyone looks up from their food to see who's just arrived but nowadays that's just as likely to be a reality TV contestant as a theatrical knight. Getting a table is still a challenge; try calling on the day – if they offer the bar, accept, because you may get bumped up into the main room. But the great thing about The Ivy is that it's impossible not to find the menu appealing: perfectly gratinated shepherd's pie, plump fishcakes, eggs Benedict, nursery puddings – they're all here and all done well. Staff earn their crust by frequently but discreetly re-laying the tables.

J. Sheekey

13

f i s h   a n d   s e a f o o d XX

28-34 St Martin's Ct.
✉ WC2 4AL
✆ (020) 7240 2565
www.j-sheekey.co.uk

⊖ **Leicester Square**
Closed 25-26 December –
booking essential

Carte £31/75

Named after the restaurant's first chef who cooked for its then owner Lord Salisbury, J. Sheekey proves that longevity and tradition need not mean old and crusty. It is as fashionable now as it was in 1896 and remains one of the first choices for the theatrical world and those whose business is show. The wood panelling and silver on the tables add to the timeless British feel and service is as charming and efficient as ever. Fish and seafood are handled deftly: the Arbroath smokie and potted shrimps are permanent fixtures and the fish pie and lemon sole are rightly renowned. Avoiding pre and post-theatre times will shorten the odds of your getting a table and ask for 'dining room 4' which is the largest of the five rooms.

J. Sheekey Oyster Bar

13

fish and seafood ✗

33-34 St Martin's Ct.
✉ WC2 4AL
✆ (020) 7240 2565
www.j-sheekey.co.uk

⊖ Leicester Square
Closed 25-26 December and 1 January

Carte £32/72

And you can't even see the join. When the opportunity arose for J. Sheekey to expand next door, the obvious decision would have been to extend the restaurant which has, after all, been working well since 1896. Instead, they decided to create this terrific oyster bar – and for that we should all be grateful. There are four or five tables but you're much better off sitting at the bar as you can chat with the chaps behind it and, if you're on the far side, watch the chefs in action. The tablemat doubles as a menu, which offers the same high quality seafood as next door but at slightly lower prices. Along with favourites like oysters and the individual fish pie, come dishes designed for sharing such as the fruits de mer.

Kyashii

13

Japanese ✗✗

4a Upper St Martin's Ln
✉ WC2H 9NY
✆ (020) 7836 5211
www.kyashii.co.uk

⊖ Leicester Square
Closed 25 December and 1 January

Carte £22/46

Another restaurant satisfying the demand for contemporary Japanese food and glossy surroundings is Kyashii, housed in premises formerly occupied by The Kingly Club. The ground floor is an eye-catching mix of cream leather, mirrors and fish tanks, contrasting nicely with a long dark marble sushi bar; and if you think the music's too loud then you're too old to be here. Cooking is well-executed and the kitchen adds just enough originality to give the food personality. Kushiyaki skewers and single bowl Teishoku lunches are specialities. Shaker, whose name presumably refers to their impressive selection of cocktails rather than the religious sect known for their furniture, is the name of the achingly trendy bar upstairs.

N Mishkin's

25 Catherine St
✉ WC2B 5JS
☎ (020) 7240 2078
www.mishkins.co.uk

⊖ Covent Garden
Closed 24-26 and 31 December-2 January

Carte £16/25

The Jewish-American deli, of the sort found on Manhattan's Lower East Side, was the inspiration behind this fun creation from the Polpo people. The menu is an appealing (non-kosher) blend of classics such as lox beigel, chopped liver and salt beef, along with nibbles like cod cheek popcorn. The Reuben sandwich may not bulge like its transatlantic cousin but it will satisfy most appetites; the crispy lamb belly also hits the spot. Delis aren't often associated with cocktails but it works here and the gin based drinks are great. The place has that ubiquitous distressed urban look; try to book one of the red booths if you're with a group or just grab a seat at the bar. In a further break with tradition, staff are young and accommodating.

Opera Tavern

23 Catherine St.
✉ WC2B 5JS
☎ (020) 7836 3680
www.operatavern.co.uk

⊖ Covent Garden
Closed 24-26 and 31 December,
1-2 January and Sunday dinner

Menu £35/40 – Carte £11/36

That many of its more touristy areas now boast some decent restaurants is testament to London's maturing dining scene. Opera Tavern comes from the people who brought you Salt Yard and Dehesa, so they know what they're doing, but this time they're doing it in a converted old boozer dating from 1879, albeit one that's had a complete makeover. If you haven't booked a table in the upstairs dining room then try your luck on the lively ground floor; order 2 or 3 dishes per person and be prepared to share – stand-outs are the Ibérico ham, chorizo with piquillo pepper and crispy squid. The wine list also swings between Spain and Italy and includes some rare and ancient grape varieties. The staff are all reassuringly confident and clued up.

STRAND & COVENT GARDEN ▶ PLAN II

121

Polpo Covent Garden

Italian 🗶

6 Maiden Ln.
✉ WC2E 7NA
☎ (202) 7836 8448
www.polpo.co.uk

⊖ Leicester Square
Closed 24-26 December –
(bookings not taken at dinner)

Carte £12/30

After sewing up Soho with their first three restaurants, this clever little group then turned its attention to neighbouring Covent Garden to open this Venetian bacaro. Behind the delicately embroidered linen screens is another shrewdly designed spot, with a tin ceiling imported from New York and church pews contrasting with the ersatz industrial look. It covers two floors – the ground floor is best. Over-ordering is easy, as the small plates are surprisingly filling, with delights such as the wonderfully fresh flavours of pizzette of white anchovy vying with fennel and almond salad, fritto misto competing with spaghettini and meatballs. A no-bookings policy after 5.30pm means that there will be queues but turnover is naturally quick.

River Restaurant

modern 🗶🗶🗶

Savoy Hotel,
Strand ✉ WC2R 0EU
☎ (020) 7836 4343
www.fairmont.com/savoy

⊖ Charing Cross

Menu £28 – Carte £40/71

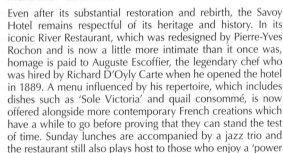

Even after its substantial restoration and rebirth, the Savoy Hotel remains respectful of its heritage and history. In its iconic River Restaurant, which was redesigned by Pierre-Yves Rochon and is now a little more intimate than it once was, homage is paid to Auguste Escoffier, the legendary chef who was hired by Richard D'Oyly Carte when he opened the hotel in 1889. A menu influenced by his repertoire, which includes dishes such as 'Sole Victoria' and quail consommé, is now offered alongside more contemporary French creations which have a while to go before proving that they can stand the test of time. Sunday lunches are accompanied by a jazz trio and the restaurant still also plays host to those who enjoy a 'power breakfast'.

Rules

British traditional 🍴🍴

35 Maiden Ln
✉ WC2E 7LB
☎ (020) 7836 5314
www.rules.co.uk

⊖ Leicester Square
Closed 25-26 December –
booking essential

Carte £35/56

Some restaurants don't even last 1798 days; Rules opened in 1798, at a time when the French were still revolting, and has been a bastion of Britishness ever since. Virtually every inch of wall is covered with a cartoon or painting and everyone from Charles Dickens to Buster Keaton has passed through its doors. The first floor is now a bar; time it right and you'll spot some modern-day theatrical luminaries who use it as a Green Room. The hardest decision is whether to choose the game, which comes from their own estate in the Pennines, or one of their celebrated homemade pies. Be sure to leave room for their proper puddings, which come with lashings of custard - no wonder John Bull was such a stout fellow. It makes you proud.

Savoy Grill

British traditional 🍴🍴🍴

Savoy Hotel,
Strand ✉ WC2R 0EU
☎ (020) 7592 1600
www.gordonramsay.com/thesavoygrill

⊖ Charing Cross

Menu £26 (weekday lunch) – Carte £30/102

The Savoy Grill prepared for the future by going back to its roots. Archives were explored, designers briefed and much money spent, with the result that The Savoy Grill has returned to the traditions that made it famous. As befits the name, it is the charcoal grilling of meats that takes centre stage. Beef from the Lake District and Essex is dry-aged for a minimum of 35 days and offered in an impressive selection of cuts. There's also a daily trolley – it could be beef Wellington one day, leg of lamb the next – and an enticing section entitled 'Roasts, Braises and Pies'. The shiny art deco inspired interior evokes the 1930s, photos of past guests adorn the walls and even the table layout and numbering remains true to the original.

Suda

I3

Thai ✕

23 Slingsby Pl, St Martin's Courtyard
✉ WC2E 9AB
✆ (020) 7240 8010
www.suda-thai.com

⊖ Covent Garden

Carte £15/22

This shiny Thai restaurant in the new St Martin's Courtyard development looks remarkably like a branded chain that's about to be rolled out and, as Oscar Wilde said, "It is only shallow people who do not judge by appearances". However, the quality of its food and the care taken in its preparation far exceeds one's expectations. OK, so the 'street' food may have had a wash and brush up and heat warnings on certain dishes are overplayed but the kitchen still delivers enough familiar flavours on a cold January night to transport you back to Sukhumvit Road. Som tam spicy salads are a speciality, as are creamy curries and there's plenty for veggies. Come in a group, sit upstairs and order cocktails and plenty of dishes to share.

 # 10 Cases

J3

French ✕

16 Endell St
✉ WC2H 9BD
✆ (020) 7836 6801
www.the10cases.co.uk

⊖ Covent Garden
Closed Easter, Christmas-
New Year and bank holidays –
booking essential

Carte £24/33

It's a simple but effective idea: serve an unpretentious daily changing menu with a choice of 3 starters, 3 main courses and 3 desserts accompanied by a wine list of 10 reds and 10 whites, all available by the glass, carafe or bottle; 10 cases of each wine are bought – hence the name – and when they're finished the wine is changed. The cooking is straightforward and honest and the menu is supplemented by nibbles such as potted crab or roasted garlic. The food suits the cosy bistrot feel of the place and though the portions may be rather small, so too are the prices. The wines are well chosen and the mark-ups limited, so most bottles are priced between £19 and £35; the 50cl carafes are particularly good value.

Terroirs

J3

5 William IV St
✉ WC2N 4DW
✆ (020) 7036 0660
www.terroirswinebar.com

⊖ **Charing Cross**
Closed 25-26 December, 1 January,
Sunday and bank holidays

Carte £25/37

The ground floor is as busy and as fun as ever but you can also eat 'Downstairs at Terroirs', where the menu is slightly different and there's a greater variety of cooking methods used; there are also dishes for two such as the roast Landaise chicken. Tables down here are a little bigger which makes sharing easier and, despite being two floors down, it is more atmospheric. If you recognise the banquette seating it's because it comes from Mirabelle. Meanwhile, both levels share the same respect for flavoursome and satisfying French cooking, with added Italian and Spanish influences. The wine list is interesting, varied and well-priced. Service remains a mixed bag and can be of the headless chicken variety.

Remember, stars
(✿✿✿...✿) are awarded
for cuisine only! Elements
such as service and décor
are not a factor.

Belgravia · Victoria

The well-worn cliché 'an area of contrasts' certainly applies to these ill-matched neighbours. To the west, Belgravia equates to fashionable status and elegant, residential calm; to the east, Victoria is a chaotic jumble of back-packers, milling commuters and cheap-and-not-always-so-cheerful hotels. At first sight, you might think there's little to no common ground, but the umbilical cord that unites them is, strange to say, diplomacy and politics. Belgravia's embassies are dotted all around the environs of **Belgrave Square,** while at the furthest end of bustling Victoria Street stands **Parliament Square.**

Belgravia – named after 'beautiful grove' in French - was developed during the nineteenth century by Richard Grosvenor, the second Marquess of Westminster, who employed top architect Thomas Cubitt to come up with something rather fetching for the upper echelons of society. The grandeur of the classical designs has survived for the best part of two centuries, evident in the broad streets and elegant squares, where the rich rub shoulders with the uber-rich beneath the stylish balconies of a consulate or outside a high-end antiques emporium. You can still sample an atmosphere of the village it once was, as long as your idea of a village includes exclusive designer boutiques and even more exclusive mews cottages.

By any stretch of the imagination you'd have trouble thinking of **Victoria** as a village. Its local railway station is one of London's major hubs and its bus station brings in visitors from not only all corners of Britain, but Europe too. Its main 'church', concealed behind office blocks, could hardly be described as humble, either: **Westminster Cathedral** is a grand concoction based on Istanbul's Hagia Sophia, with a view from the top of the bell tower which is breathtaking. From there you can pick out other hidden charms of the area: the dramatic headquarters of Channel 4 TV, the revolving sign famously leading into New Scotland Yard, and the neat little Christchurch Gardens, burial site of Colonel Blood, last man to try and steal the Crown Jewels. Slightly easier for the eye to locate are the grand designs of **Westminster Abbey,** crowning glory and resting place of most of England's kings and queens, and the neo-gothic pile of the **Houses of Parliament.** Victoria may be an eclectic mix of people and architectural styles, but its handy position as a kind of epicentre of the Westminster Village makes it a great place for political chit-chat. And the place to go for that is The Speaker, a pub in Great Peter Street, named after the Commons' centuries-old peacekeeper and 'referee'. It's a backstreet gem, where it's not unknown for a big cheese from the House to be filmed over a pint.

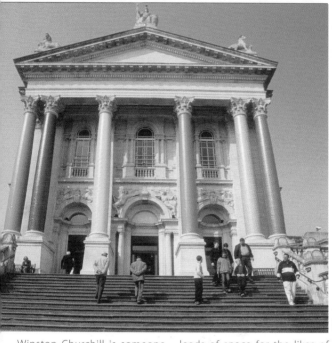

visitlondon.com

Winston Churchill is someone who would have been quite at home holding forth at The Speaker, and half a mile away in King Charles Street, based within the **Cabinet War Rooms** – the secret underground HQ of the war effort - is the Churchill Museum, stuffed full of all things Churchillian. However, if your passion is more the easel and the brush, then head down to the river where another great institution of the area, **Tate Britain,** gazes out over the Thames. Standing where the grizzly Millbank Penitentiary once festered, it offers, after the National Gallery, the best collection of historical art in London. There's loads of space for the likes of Turner and Constable, while Hogarth, Gainsborough and Blake are well represented, too. Artists from the modern era are also here, with Freud and Hockney on show, and there are regular installations showcasing upwardly mobile British talent. All of which may give you the taste for a trip east along the river to Tate Modern. This can be done every twenty minutes courtesy of the Tate-to-Tate boat service, which handily stops enroute at the London Eye, and, even more handily, sports eye-catching Damien Hirst décor and a cool, shiny bar.

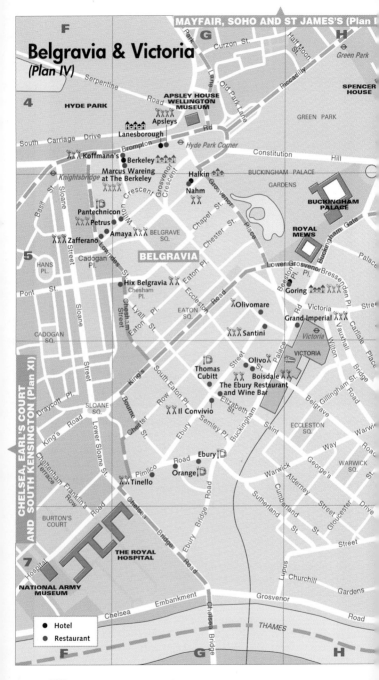

Belgravia & Victoria
(Plan IV)

Hotel ●

Restaurant ●

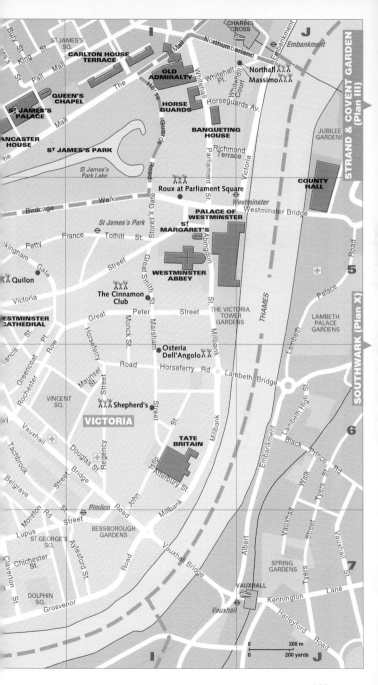

Amaya ✿

Indian XXX

Halkin Arcade, 19 Motcomb St
✉ SW1X 8JT
✆ (020) 7823 1166
www.realindianfood.com

⊖ Knightsbridge
Closed dinner 25 December

Menu £20/70 – Carte £35/69

A/C
🍸
🕐
☀
VISA
MC
AE
DC

Amaya

You know you're doing something right when imitators start appearing everywhere. The quality and consistency of the food at Amaya keeps it busy, but if you haven't booked it's still worth turning up as they try to accommodate everyone and their stylish bar is a great place in which to wait. To best experience the variety and range of the menu, order a number of small plates to share and then finish with a curry or biryani – or else plump for the Gourmet or Tasting menus where the selection has already been made for you. The tandoor, the tawa griddle and the Sigri charcoal grill are used to great effect here and the spicing enhances the natural flavours of the ingredients. Seafood is handled well, with rock oysters, grouper and prawns competing with the ever popular tandoori monkfish. The delicate and flavoursome lamb chops are another dish that almost everyone seems to order – and one shouldn't ignore the imaginative vegetable dishes either. The best tables are by the open kitchen where the immaculate chefs work almost silently beside the grill and tandoor.

First Course

- King scallops with light herb sauce.
- Tandoori black pepper chicken tikka.

Main Course

- Crispy baby chicken, green chilli, thyme and lemon.
- Tandoori monkfish tikka.

Dessert

- Saffron and rose panna cotta.
- Unripe mango brûlée.

Apsleys ✿

G4

Lanesborough Hotel,
Hyde Park Corner
✉ SW1X 7TA
☎ (020) 7333 7254
www.apsleysrestaurant.com

⊖ Hyde Park Corner

Menu £35 (lunch) – Carte £59/81

BELGRAVIA & VICTORIA ▶ PLAN IV

The Lanesborough

Heinz Beck is a German-born chef responsible for some pretty exceptional Italian cooking in his restaurant La Pergola in Rome. Apsleys is very much his creation and he is actively involved in the operation, although he does have a head chef who is extremely committed and passionate about his craft. The sourcing of the finest ingredients is the starting point; vegetables are imported from Italy but meat and fish are from much nearer to home. Proving that not all Italian food has to be of the rustic, thrown-together variety, the cooking displays a deft, light touch and there are subtle hints of innovation, such as in one of the signature dishes, carbonara fagottelli. Designed by the ubiquitous Adam Tihany, the room is elegant and undeniably opulent, but its grandeur never intimidates, thanks largely to the assured serving team who are adept at putting their guests at ease. They are also well-versed in the menu and offer fuller explanations, which is just as well as the menu descriptions are understated to say the least.

First Course

- Fish crudo.
- Veal terrine with cannellini beans and carrots.

Main Course

- Carbonara fagottelli.
- Suckling pig.

Dessert

- Chocolate soufflé with vanilla and raspberry.
- Coffee mousse and rum.

Boisdale

regional 𝕏𝕏

15 Eccleston St
✉ SW1W 9LX
📞 (020) 7730 6922
www.boisdale.co.uk

⊖ **Victoria**
Closed Christmas,
Saturday lunch and Sunday

Menu £20 – Carte £28/80

Acres of tartan, whiskies galore, haggis, mash and neeps - Boisdale couldn't be more Scottish if it sang 'Scots Wha Hae' and did the Highland Fling. Owner Ranald Macdonald bought various parts of the building at different times, hence the charmingly higgledy-piggledy layout. The original Auld Restaurant is the more characterful; the Macdonald Bar has more buzz and nightly live jazz and a large cigar selection add to the masculine feel. The menu features plenty of Scottish produce, from Orkney herring to Shetland scallops, but the stand-outs are the four varieties of smoked salmon, followed by the 28-day aged Aberdeenshire cuts of beef. Ignore the lacklustre tomato and watercress garnish and just savour the quality of the meat.

The Cinnamon Club

Indian 𝕏𝕏𝕏

30-32 Great Smith St
✉ SW1P 3BU
📞 (020) 7222 2555
www.cinnamonclub.com

⊖ **St James's Park**
Closed 26 December,
1 January and Sunday

Menu £22/24 – Carte £28/74

It may still look like a library, albeit a smart one with lovely parquet flooring, original wood panelling and a gallery of bookcases, but this Grade II listed building is actually home to some pretty ambitious modern Indian cooking. You can come for breakfast – eschew the fry-up and try the spiced scrambled eggs or rice cakes instead; lunch sees a good value set menu, while at dinner the main menu is supplemented by a monthly changing themed menu resolving around perhaps game of Indo-Malaysian fish but this plethora of menus can put the kitchen under some pressure. Presentation is quite arty and tandoori dishes stand out. The atmosphere is buzzy and the basement bar is funky; service is well organised but perhaps a little over-formal.

Il Convivio

G6

Italian  XX

143 Ebury St
✉ SW1W 9QN
✆ (020) 7730 4099
www.ilconvivio.co.uk

⊖ Sloane Square
Closed Christmas-New Year, Easter,
bank holidays and Sunday

Menu £20/24 – Carte £29/51

A/C
⟨⟩
VISA
MC
AE

If passing by, you'll find yourself being drawn in by the appealing façade of this handsome Georgian townhouse – and there's usually an eager welcome to boot, whether you're a regular or first-timer. Inside is equally pleasant, with Dante's poetry embossed on the wall to remind you you're in an Italian restaurant and a retractable roof at the back, under which sit the best tables. All pasta is made on the top floor of the house; the squid ink spaghetti with lobster is a menu staple. Dishes are artfully presented but not so showy as to compromise the flavours. Artisanal cheeses are carefully selected and looked after, while service is confident and able. Using the private dining room allows you to imagine being the owner of the house.

Ebury

G6

modern

11 Pimlico Rd
✉ SW1W 8NA
✆ (020) 7730 6784
www.theebury.co.uk

⊖ Sloane Square.
Closed 23-28 December
and bank holidays

Carte £22/40

A/C
☼
VISA
MC
AE

Grab a passing waiter to get yourself seated otherwise they'll assume you've just come for a drink at the bar and will ignore you. Once you've got your feet under one of the low-slung tables, however, you'll find everything moves up a gear. This is a rather smart affair and provides an object lesson in how to draw in punters. That means a varied menu, from burger to black bream, assorted salads that show some thought, three vegetarian dishes and main courses that display a degree of originality. Add to that a conscientious kitchen, a wine list that offers plenty by the glass and carafe, and weekend brunch that goes on until 4pm and it's little wonder the place is always so busy. The waiters come with French accents and self-confidence.

The Ebury Restaurant and Wine Bar

modern XX

G6

139 Ebury St.
✉ SW1W 9QU
✆ (020) 7730 5447
www.eburyrestaurant.co.uk

⊖ Victoria
Closed Christmas-New Year

Menu £19 (lunch and early dinner) – Carte £26/46

A/C
☼
VISA
M©
AE

There are probably many reasons why Ebury Wine Bar has been going strong for over 50 years but likeability and adaptability must surely be two. It has an endearing honesty that is largely down to the eagerness of the longstanding staff, and changing habits have meant that the focus is now more on the food than the wine; even the bar offers a decent snack menu. Go through to the dining room, with its trompe l'oeil, and you'll find a kitchen that brings imaginative international influences to some dishes but is equally happy doing the classics such as lamb cutlets or liver and bacon. The set menu includes a glass of champagne; there are separate dairy and gluten free menus and the wine list is thoughtfully compiled and keenly priced.

Goring

British traditional XXX

H5

Goring Hotel,
15 Beeston Pl, Grosvenor Gdns
✉ SW1W 0JW
✆ (020) 7396 9000 – **www**.thegoring.com

⊖ Victoria
Closed Saturday lunch

Menu £38/50

A/C
⅏
☼
VISA
M©
AE
①

Like the hotel in which it is found, The Goring dining room is a paean to all things British and is perfect for those who still like things done 'properly'. Designed by Viscount Linley, the room is as urbane as it is serene; its staff are supremely proficient and service is not without a little theatre. The chef tours the country looking for the best ingredients for his unambiguously British menu; his beef comes from the Castle of Mey estate, his lobsters are Scottish and his butter from Gloucestershire. On the menu you'll find potted game and jugged hare, beef Wellington, poached salmon, and eggs Drumkibo, which was a favourite dish of the late Queen Mother. Lunch – here still called luncheon— features a daily special from the trolley.

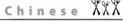

Grand Imperial

Chinese 🗙🗙🗙

Grosvenor Hotel,
101 Buckingham Palace Rd ✉ SW1W 0SJ
☎ (020) 7821 8898
www.grandimperiallondon.com

⊖ Victoria

Menu £17 – Carte £22/41

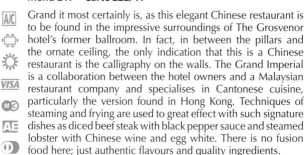

Grand it most certainly is, as this elegant Chinese restaurant is to be found in the impressive surroundings of The Grosvenor hotel's former ballroom. In fact, in between the pillars and the ornate ceiling, the only indication that this is a Chinese restaurant is the calligraphy on the walls. The Grand Imperial is a collaboration between the hotel owners and a Malaysian restaurant company and specialises in Cantonese cuisine, particularly the version found in Hong Kong. Techniques of steaming and frying are used to great effect with such signature dishes as diced beef steak with black pepper sauce and steamed lobster with Chinese wine and egg white. There is no fusion food here; just authentic flavours and quality ingredients.

Hix Belgravia

modern 🗙🗙

Belgraves Hotel,
Pont St ✉ SW1X 9EJ
☎ (020) 3189 4850
www.hixbelgravia.co.uk

⊖ Knightsbridge

Carte £31/50

Mark Hix has grown his mini empire on the back of his pro-local, pro-British and pro-seasonal reputation but this is his first venture which reflects his thoughts on other cuisines. Accordingly, the menu provides a hotchpotch of dishes from around the globe, offering everything from Vietnamese chicken broth to veal Holstein and steak tartare to risotto nero, although those who look to Blighty for their nourishment will be reassured by the list of steaks and chops. It works for the same reason all his other restaurants work: the cooking is simple and the produce is excellent. The restaurant is on the ground floor of Belgraves, a newcomer to the London hotel scene, and is enlivened with contemporary artwork and brightened by large windows.

Koffmann's

French 🗙🗙🗙

G4

Berkeley Hotel,
Wilton Pl. ✉ SW1X 7RL
☎ (020) 7235 1010
www.the-berkeley.co.uk

⊖ Knightsbridge

Menu £22/26 – Carte £39/90

Retirement isn't for everyone and, it appears, it wasn't for Pierre Koffmann. After years of rumour and following the success of his 'pop-up' restaurant in Selfridges, one of London's most fêted chefs came back to the stove and returned to his previous address, albeit on the other side of the building. Those with fond memories of his classic dishes will enjoy getting reacquainted with the scallops with squid ink or the braised pig's trotter. This time around his food stays truer to his Gascon roots, although the gutsy flavours can sometimes be compromised in the dish's final execution. The dining room's off-white colour and textured walls add to the light, fresh feel; the further in you go, the better the table.

Massimo

Italian 🗙🗙🗙

J4

Corinthia Hotel,
10 Northumberland Ave. ✉ WC2N 5AE
☎ (020) 7998 0555
www.massimo-restaurant.co.uk

⊖ Embankment
Closed Sunday

Menu £25 – Carte £30/69

David Collins has been responsible for designing some of London's most striking restaurants but few can match the grandeur of Massimo. This huge room is dominated by vast, striped Corinthian columns; beautiful mosaics and plenty of marble augment the feeling of unrelenting luxury, while leather-covered booths add some warmth and comfort to proceedings. Taking up the challenge provided by these surroundings is a kitchen specialising in seafood and while the menu may be written in Italian, the cooking could be considered largely Mediterranean. Dishes are kept fairly classical in influence and relatively simple in make-up, and although the food may not always live up to the splendour of the room, the prices do.

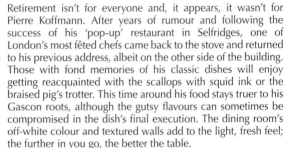

Marcus Wareing
at The Berkeley ✿ ✿

Berkeley Hotel,
Wilton Pl. ✉ SW1X 7RL
☎ (020) 7235 1200
www.marcus-wareing.com

⊖ **Knightsbridge**
Closed 1 January and Sunday

Menu £38 (weekday lunch), £80

Marcus Wareing at The Berkeley

Thanks to Koffmann's on its north side, The Berkeley is book-ended by two good restaurants. On his side of the hotel, Marcus Wareing delivers a formal dining experience involving confident and expertly constructed dishes, in surroundings that are quite sombre yet undoubtedly comfortable. He remains a chef who appreciates the importance of using the best quality produce and, as such, will treat a carrot with as much respect as he does a lobster. His 'Prestige' and 'Gourmand' menus allow the diner to sample the full diversity of his cooking, which is mostly French in its influences and techniques but is not afraid of a little originality here and there. Indeed, there is quite a bold approach brought to some of the dishes. Desserts are a strength of the kitchen and, if you are one of those who likes to see how it's all done, then consider the Chef's Table, which is one of the best in town. Service is structured and deliberate but now comes with a little more personality than seen in previous years.

First Course
- Mackerel, scallop, pine nut and yuzu.
- Foie gras, pineapple, cinnamon and brioche.

Main Course
- Suckling lamb with beans, oregano and Flower Marie.
- Halibut, cockles, razor clams and fennel.

Dessert
- Horlicks, honey and whisky.
- Coffee, Marsala and mascarpone.

Nahm

G5

Halkin Hotel,
5 Halkin St ✉ SW1X 7DJ
☎ (020) 7333 1234
www.halkin.como.bz

⊖ Hyde Park Corner
Closed lunch Saturday
and Sunday – booking advisable

Menu £25/30 – Carte £40/47

A/C
◌
VISA
M C
A E
○

An appealing mix of copper tones, wood and candlelight, along with an understated hint of Asian design, allows the restaurant to blend effortlessly into the slick and stylish surroundings of the boutique Halkin hotel in which it is located. The cuisine served here is based on Royal Thai traditions and the flavours and combinations of ingredients are authentic. However, the cooking has lost some of its essential vitality, which is one of the fundamental elements of Thai cuisine, and dishes can sometimes be let down by careless execution. Perhaps it was the opening of another Nahm, this time in Bangkok itself, that lead to the slight drop in the standard here at the original outpost.

Northall

J4

Corinthia Hotel,
Whitehall Pl. ✉ SW1A 2BD
☎ (020) 7321 3100
www.thenorthall.co.uk

⊖ Embankment

Menu £25/35 – Carte £27/70

A/C
☼
VISA
M C
A E
○

The Corinthia Hotel's British restaurant not only celebrates our indigenous food but also champions its producers by acknowledging them all on the menu. It is certainly an appealing document with the likes of potted shrimps, Dover sole meunière and roast venison with swede alongside a grilled section using Cumbrian shorthorn cattle aged for 28 days. The kitchen is also not averse to looking across the Channel for the occasional influence. The restaurant occupies two rooms; the most appealing is the more modern room with its bar counter and booths while the other section is more formally arranged and better suited for a business lunch. An attractive 'market place' set up with cheese and meat displays links the two rooms.

Olivo

G6

21 Eccleston St
✉ SW1W 9LX
☎ (020) 7730 2505
www.olivorestaurants.com

⊖ Victoria
Closed lunch Saturday-Sunday
and bank holidays –
booking essential

Menu £24 (lunch) – Carte £28/44

The cooking at Olivo has always been highly capable and reassuringly reliable, which does tend to make up for the service which is never quite as engaging as you hope it will be. Nevertheless this is a popular, pleasant and relaxed little neighbourhood Italian, with vivid blues and yellows, rough wooden floorboards and intimate lighting. The menu showcases the robust flavours of Sardinia and changes fortnightly, although some dishes, such as spaghetti bottarga and linguine with crab, remain permanent features. There are normally a few daily specials – particularly for the regulars – dishes are clearly prepared with care and desserts continue the regional theme; try sebada, a traditional Sardinian cheese fritter.

Olivomare

G5

10 Lower Belgrave St
✉ SW1W 0LJ
☎ (020) 7730 9022
www.olivorestaurants.com

⊖ Victoria
Closed bank holidays

Carte £31/42

Italian seafood, particularly Sardinian seafood, is celebrated here at Olivomare, a bright and lively restaurant whose design owes as much to Barbarella as it does M.C. Escher. Bottarga naturally features and not just with spaghetti – it also comes with Sardinian artichokes and even burrata. The stews are terrific as are the couscous soups; the octopus, whether in a salad, a stew or just roasted is always worth ordering. For pud the 'gelato allo yoghurt' is good and is just one of the items that can also be bought from their well-stocked deli next door. The wine list is a little limited by the glass but otherwise this is a very warmly run and understandably popular local, where freshness and simplicity combine to great effect.

Orange

G6

modern

37 Pimlico Rd
✉ SW1W 8NE
℘ (020) 7881 9844
www.theorange.co.uk

⊖ Sloane Square.

Carte £23/47

The Belgravia-Victoria-Pimlico quarter is clearly working for the team behind The Thomas Cubitt and Pantechnicon because their latest pub, The Orange, is within shouting distance of their other two and appears to be equally busy. There are a couple of differences: this pub has bedrooms; nicely decorated and named after the local streets, and the food is a little more down-to-earth and family-friendly. Pizza in the bar from their wood-fired oven is always a popular choice, or enjoy rustic European cooking in the upstairs restaurant, which, unusually, is noisier than the bar. The building's stucco-fronted façade may be quite grand but the colonial feel inside and the particularly friendly service create a pleasantly laid-back atmosphere.

Osteria Dell' Angolo

I6

Italian

47 Marsham St.
✉ SW1P 3DR
℘ (020) 3268 1077
www.osteriadellangolo.co.uk

⊖ St James's Park
Closed Easter, 18 August-1 September, 23-26 December-1-7 January, Saturday lunch, Sunday and bank holidays

Menu £17 (lunch) – Carte £31/42

Depending on whether you come for lunch or dinner you will either find this restaurant opposite the Home Office a bustling spot occupied by lots of men in suits talking shop, or a relaxed neighbourhood Italian populated by immaculately coiffured locals. Either way, the food will be good and the service switched on. The menu is a little more approachable these days, with homemade pasta dishes a highlight along with the seafood dishes – the chef is from Naples, and the all-Italian team are a personable bunch who know their regulars. The wine list has been thoughtfully compiled, although closer scrutiny of expense claims these days mean that some of the gems in the wine cave don't fly off the shelves quite as quickly as they once did.

Pantechnicon

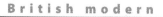 **British modern**

10 Motcomb St
✉ SW1X 8LA
✆ (020) 7730 6074
www.thepantechnicon.com

⊖ Knightsbridge.
Closed 25 December-1 January –
booking advisable

Carte £27/55

BELGRAVIA & VICTORIA ▶ PLAN IV

It may be the very antithesis of the spit 'n' sawdust pub, but The Pantechnicon is still a very welcoming and busy local. The brightly run ground floor is crammed with tables and works on a first-come-first-served basis; upstairs you'll find a far more formal, Georgian style dining room and there's even a top floor cocktail bar – this is Belgravia after all. Wisely, the same menu is served throughout – an appealing mix of the refined and the comforting. Castle of Mey 28-day aged steaks and salt and chilli squid are the two most popular choices; home-smoked salmon, burgers and fish pie are also done well. The name comes from the horse-drawn wagons that once transported the belongings of locals to and from a repository on Motcomb Street.

Roux at Parliament Square

French

RICS, Parliament Sq.
✉ SW1P 3AD
✆ (020) 7334 3737
www.rouxatparliamentsquare.co.uk

⊖ Westminster
Closed 23 December-4 January, Saturday,
Sunday and bank holidays

Menu £25 (lunch) – Carte £36/56

In this part of Westminster, chartered surveyors and Members of Parliament have never been faced with a plethora of restaurants from which to choose, but the opening of Roux at Parliament Square has helped fill the void. Knowing that the Roux is Michel, of Le Gavroche fame, means that the cooking was never going to be anything other than intricate and visually impressive – but while the base is French, the kitchen does have a lighter than expected touch and flavours are contemporary. The decoration is cool and comfortable, with plenty of natural light flooding through the Georgian windows. Service comes from a well-trained team but is not without personality and there is a particularly attractive private dining room in the library.

Pétrus ❀

1 Kinnerton St
✉ SW1X 8EA
✆ (020) 7592 1609
www.gordonramsay.com/petrus

⊖ **Knightsbridge**
Closed 25 December and Sunday

Menu £30/75

  ♿
  A/C
  🖼
  🍽Ⓥ
  🎱
  VISA
  M⒞
  AE

Gordon Ramsay Holdings

Following his divorce from Marcus Wareing, Gordon Ramsay came away with custody of the name Pétrus and he used the estate's name for this smart Belgravia restaurant, in challengingly close proximity to the premises of his former protégé. It's attractively decorated in understated tones of silver, oyster and – to add warmth and as a nod to the name – claret. Tables are immaculately dressed and service is under the watchful eye of an experienced team who never let things get too reverential. Downstairs is the 'show' kitchen with its horseshoe shaped chef's table, for those whose enjoyment of a meal is sharpened by watching a large brigade of chefs – in this case around 14 – beavering away in front of them. Sceptical diners should initially try lunch, when they'll find a set menu that won't break the bank. There are also vegetarian and chef's menus alongside the appealing à la carte of French-based dishes. In a break with tradition and in a nod to Thomas Keller, the cheese trolley is replaced by a single cheese offered as a 'savoury pudding'.

First Course

- Fricassée of langoustines, snails and chicken wing.
- Loin of rabbit and cannelloni of confit leg.

Main Course

- Roasted veal fillet with tongue, anchovies, and artichokes.
- Lobster tail with asparagus and trompettes.

Dessert

- Chocolate sphere with milk ice cream and honeycomb.
- Star anise crème brûlée, caramelised pear and liquorice.

Quilon ✿

Indian 🍴🍴🍴

Crowne Plaza London - St James Hotel,
41 Buckingham Gate
✉ SW1E 6AF
☏ (020) 7821 1899
www.quilon.co.uk

⊖ St James's Park
Closed 25 December

Menu £24/43 – Carte £28/53

Quilon

An extensive 2012 makeover left this longstanding Indian restaurant looking slick and contemporary. A stylish bar was added, along with a striking private dining room which comes with its own kitchen. These elegant surroundings provide the ideal backdrop to chef Sriram Aylur's accomplished cooking, which focuses on India's southwest coast. 'Progression' is one of his watchwords and he has overseen a transformation in the food which is now considerably lighter than much Indian cuisine. There's a high degree of originality in some of the dishes, such as his own version of black cod and his imaginative dishes involving game, but traditionalists will still find much to savour, whether that's masala dosa or a fish curry with coconut. The crab cakes are a delight and the colourful and crisp okra is very moreish. The serving team are charming and helpful; the wine list has been thoughtfully compiled to complement the food and there's an interesting selection of beers too. The re-launch of Quilon is something to be celebrated by all lovers of Indian food.

First Course	Main Course	Dessert
• Char-grilled scallops with mango and chilli relish.	• Venison coconut fry.	• Hot vermicelli kheer with rose ice cream.
• Chicken sukke.	• Goan-spiced seared sea bass.	• Caramelised banana pudding.

Santini

G5

29 Ebury St
✉ SW1W 0NZ
☎ (020) 7730 4094
www.santinirestaurant.com

⊖ Victoria
Closed Easter, 24-26 December,
1 January and lunch Saturday-Sunday

Carte £30/66

Like many of its bronzed customers, Santini really comes into its own in the summer: the white walls and marble flooring are crisp and cooling and the terrace must be one of the largest around. Family-owned since 1984, it has never been the cheapest Italian around but then this was never the sort of place that pretended to be accessible to all and the service is decidedly old-school; the type that intimidated you when you were young. But the food, with its mild Venetian accent, is very good. Homemade pastas are excellent and the zabaglione is a gloriously rich concoction. Further evidence of the restaurant's self-belief is in the number of times its name appears in dishes, so you can follow insalata Santini with branzino Santini.

Shepherd's

I6

Marsham Ct., Marsham St.
✉ SW1P 4LA
☎ (020) 7834 9552
www.langansrestaurants.co.uk

⊖ Pimlico
Closed Saturday,
Sunday and bank holidays –
booking essential

Carte £26/37

Looking at the number of shiny pates and pin-striped suits that pile into Shepherd's for lunch you'd be forgiven for thinking that 'Blair's Babes' never left much of a legacy. This is a classic, old-school blokey institution that could show some of those new restaurants a thing or two. For starters, it runs on wheels and gives the punters what they want. The atmosphere is animated throughout, but it's worth asking for one of the booths. The menu is a combination of classic dishes and brasserie favourites but your best bet is to head for those bits of the menu that read like a UKIP manifesto – the fiercely British specialities, like the daily roast or the Dover Sole, followed by an indulgent dessert like a sponge pudding.

Thomas Cubitt

G6

m o d e r n

44 Elizabeth St
✉ SW1W 9PA
☎ (020) 7730 6060
www.thethomascubitt.co.uk

⊖ Sloane Square.
Closed Christmas and New Year –
booking essential

Menu £18 (weekday lunch) – Carte £32/45

The Thomas Cubitt is a pub of two halves: on the ground floor it's perennially busy and you can't book which means that if you haven't arrived by 7pm then you're too late to get a table. However, you can reserve a table upstairs, in a dining room that's a model of civility and tranquillity. Here, service comes courtesy of a young team where the girls are chatty and the men unafraid of corduroy. Downstairs you get fish and chips; here you get pan-fried fillet of brill with oyster beignet and truffled chips. The cooking is certainly skilled, quite elaborate in its construction and prettily presented. So, take your pick: upstairs can get a little pricey but is ideal for entertaining the in-laws; if out with friends then crowd in downstairs.

Tinello

G6

I t a l i a n ✗✗

87 Pimlico Rd
✉ SW1W 8PH
☎ (020) 7730 3663
www.tinello.co.uk

⊖ Sloane Square
Closed Sunday –
booking essential at dinner

Carte £29/44

Italian restaurants have always thrived in this neighbourhood but it's no bad thing for a newcomer to shake things up and that's exactly what Tinello is doing. It is run by two Italian brothers, Max and Federico, who previously worked as sommelier and head chef respectively at Locanda Locatelli. The majority of the menu leans on their native Tuscany for inspiration and this is especially evident in the tempting antipasti or 'small eats' section. Pasta is exemplary and main courses ooze confidence. Service is undertaken with a refreshing earnestness and the sleek restaurant is spread over two floors; the ground floor is more fun, but if you are downstairs you do get to see the kitchen in action through the glass windows.

Zafferano

F5

15 Lowndes St
✉ SW1X 9EY
✆ (020) 7235 5800
www.zafferanorestaurant.co.uk

⊖ **Knightsbridge**
Booking essential

Menu £26 (weekday lunch) – Carte £29/56

Zafferano may be a senior member of London's Italian restaurant fraternity but for the gilded few who live in Belgravia's grand terraces and white stucco houses, it is more like their local canteen –and the restaurant is sensible enough to realise that looking after these guests is their primary concern. The menu is written for those who like their Italian food to be reassuringly familiar and, as everyone has their favourite dishes, the kitchen has settled into something of a routine. Unfortunately this has led to a little complacency, with some of the sparkle going out of the cooking. But the place does still deliver on the bustle and bonhomie, especially if you are sitting in the main room rather than in the extension.

A/C
VISA
MC
AE

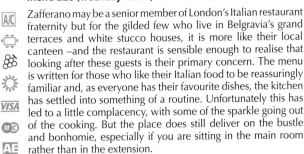

Good food without
spending a fortune?
Look for the Bib
Gourmand 😋.

Regent's Park · Marylebone

The neighbourhood north of chaotic Oxford Street is actually a rather refined place where shoppers like to venture for the smart boutiques, and where idlers like to saunter for the graceful parkland acres full of rose gardens and quiet corners. In fact, Marylebone and Regent's Park go rather well together, a moneyed village with a wonderful park for its back garden.

Marylebone may now exude a fashionable status, but its history tells a very different tale. Thousands used to come here to watch executions at Tyburn gallows, a six hundred year spectacle that stopped in the late eighteenth century. Tyburn stream was covered over, and the area's modern name came into being as a contraction of St Mary by the Bourne, the parish church. Nowadays the people who flock here come to gaze at less ghoulish sights, though some of the inhabitants of the eternally popular Madame Tussauds deserved no better fate than the gallows. South across the busy Marylebone Road, the preponderance of swish restaurants and snazzy specialist shops announces your arrival at **Marylebone High Street.** There are patisseries, chocolatiers, cheese shops and butchers at every turn, nestling alongside smart places to eat and drink. At St Marylebone Church, each Saturday heralds a posh market called Cabbages & Frocks, where artisan food meets designer clothing in a charming garden. Further down, the century old Daunt Books has been described as London's most beautiful bookshop: it has long oak galleries beneath graceful conservatory skylights. Close by, the quaintly winding Marylebone Lane boasts some truly unique shops like tiny emporium The Button Queen, which sells original Art Deco, Victorian and Edwardian buttons. In complete contrast, just down the road from here is the mighty **Wigmore Hall,** an art nouveau gem with great acoustics and an unerringly top-notch classical agenda that can be appreciated at rock-bottom prices. Meanwhile, art lovers can indulge an eclectic fix at the **Wallace Collection** in **Manchester Square,** where paintings by the likes of Titian and Velazquez rub shoulders with Sevres porcelain and grand Louis XIV furniture.

Regent's Park – an idyllic Georgian oasis stretching off into London's northern suburbs - celebrated its two hundredth birthday in 2011. Before architect John Nash and his sponsor The Prince Regent gave it its much-loved geometric makeover, it had been farming land, and prior to that, one of Henry VIII's hunting grounds. His spirit lives on, in the sense that various activities are catered for, from tennis courts to a running track. And there are animals too, albeit not roaming free, at **London Zoo,** in the park's northerly section. Most people,

C. Eymenier / MICHELIN

though, come here to while away an hour or two around the boating lake or amble the Inner Circle which contains **Queen Mary's Gardens** and their enchanting bowers of fragrant roses. Others come for a summer sojourn to the Open Air Theatre where taking in a performance of 'A Midsummer Night's Dream' is very much *de rigueur*. The Regent's Canal provides another fascinating element to the park. You can follow its peaceful waters along a splendid walk from the **Little Venice** houseboats in the west, past the golden dome of the **London Central Mosque,** and on into the north-west confines of Regent's Park as it snakes through London Zoo, before it heads off towards Camden Lock. On the other side of Prince Albert Road, across from the zoo, the scenic glory takes on another dimension with a climb up Primrose Hill. Named after the grassy promontory that sets it apart from its surrounds, to visitors this is a hill with one of the best panoramas in the whole of London; to locals (ie, actors, pop stars, media darlings and the city set) it's an ultra fashionable place to live with pretty Victorian terraces and accordingly sky-high prices. Either way you look at it (or from it), it's a great place to be on a sunny day with the breeze in your hair.

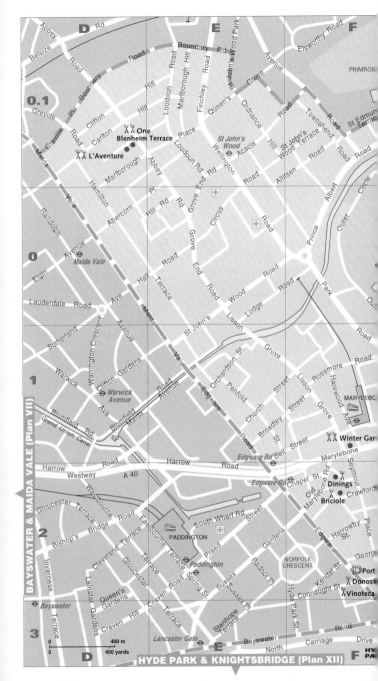

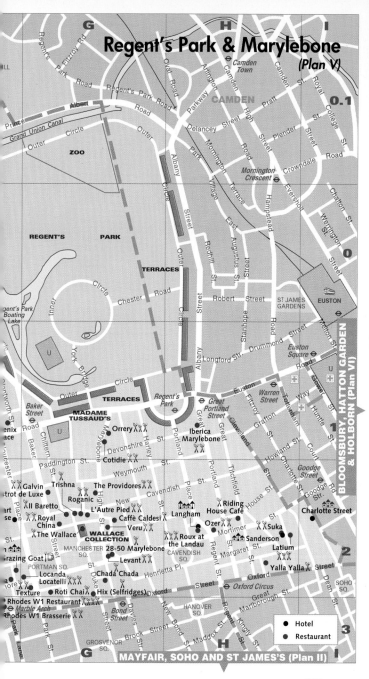

Regent's Park & Marylebone
(Plan V)

Camden Town

CAMDEN

0.1

ZOO

Grand Union Canal

REGENT'S   PARK

Mornington Crescent

O

ST JAMES
GARDENS

EUSTON

TERRACES

Regent's Park
Boating
Lake

BLOOMSBURY, HATTON GARDEN
& HOLBORN (Plan VI)

TERRACES

York Bridge

Great
Portland
Street

Euston
Square

Warren
Street

1

Baker
Street

MADAME
TUSSAUD'S

Orrery ✗✗✗

Iberica
Marylebone ✗✗

Goodge
Street

Cotidie ✗✗

Goodge
St.

✗✗ Galvin
strot de Luxe

Trishna ✗✗ The Providores ✗✗

Charlotte Street

✗ Riding
House Café

Roganic ●

All Baretto ✗

L'Autre Pied ✗✗

Caffè Caldesi ✗✗

Langham

Ozer ✗✗

✗ Suka

Royal
China ●

Veru ✗

✗✗✗ Roux at
the Landau

Sanderson

✗The Wallace

WALLACE
COLLECTION

28-50 Marylebone ✗

Latium
✗✗

razing Goat

MANCHESTER
SQ.

Levant ✗✗

Yalla Yalla ✗ Street

PORTMAN SQ.

Locanda
Locatelli ✗✗✗

Chada Chada ✗

Oxford

Oxford Circus

SOHO
SQ.

Texture ● Roti Chai ✗

Hix (Selfridges) ✗

Rhodes W1 Restaurant ✗✗✗

Bond
Street

HANOVER
SQ.

Rhodes W1 Brasserie ✗✗

Marble Arch

GROSVENOR
SQ.

● Hotel
● Restaurant

MAYFAIR, SOHO AND ST JAMES'S (Plan II)

151

L'Autre Pied ✿

G2

5-7 Blandford St.
✉ W1U 3DB
✆ (020) 7486 9696
www.lautrepied.co.uk

⊖ Bond Street
Closed 4 days Christmas,
1 January and Sunday dinner

Menu £19, £68/68 – Carte £34/58

L'Autre Pied

Head Chef Andy McFadden's food is marked out by a refreshing lack of showiness on the plate. He and his team present their dishes in a fairly natural way so that, despite some of the constructions being quite elaborate, the final result never looks too fiddly or overworked. The kitchen gets in whole animals – venison is a particular strength here – and creates robust yet easy to eat dishes which also provide very pleasing contrasts in textures. The chef's greater confidence and the restaurant's growing reputation have resulted in the presence of more luxury ingredients on the à la carte but prices are not stratospheric when one considers the levels of skill involved; the albeit simpler set lunch menu represents very good value indeed. The restaurant remains very different in style from its older sibling, Pied à Terre; it's very much part of the local 'village' and has a more casual, buoyant atmosphere. Ask for a table by the window as the middle section can be something of a thoroughfare.

First Course	Main Course	Dessert
• Ceviche of scallops, black quinoa and dill oil.	• Suckling pig, purple carrot and sea buckthorn purée.	• Bitter sweet chocolate crème, whisky and espresso granité.
• Roast foie gras with tea-marinated prunes and nutmeg.	• Poached megrim sole, champagne and oyster velouté.	• Baked vanilla cheesecake with mandarin sorbet.

L'Aventure

French

DO/1

3 Blenheim Terr
✉ NW8 0EH
✆ (020) 7624 6232
www.laventure.co.uk

⊖ St John's Wood
Closed 19-31 August,
first week January, Saturday lunch,
Sunday and bank holidays

Menu £19/31

Tailor-made for anyone with a sound grasp of French wishing to impress a date - the menu is written entirely in French so politely decline the waiter's offer of a quick translation and wait for the admiring looks. What's more, if it's a warm day, you'll be sitting in the enchanting front terrace where the shrubs are covered in twinkly lights. This is a charming neighbourhood restaurant with a cosy and warm interior, owned and run by the delightful Catherine who'll make you feel you're being unfaithful if you don't return. The set menu is good value at lunch but pricier at dinner when the well-heeled locals come out. Expect the French bourgeois classics, from artichoke salad to rack of lamb and an ile flottante to finish.

Il Baretto

G2

Italian

43 Blandford St.
✉ W1U 7HF
✆ (020) 7486 7340
www.ilbaretto.co.uk

⊖ Baker Street
Closed 25-26 December,
lunch 31 December and 1 January

Carte £20/58

Arjun Waney, the man behind Roka, Zuma and La Petite Maison, gives Italy a go here. The site had been Italian for a while and came complete with the wood-fired oven which is undoubtedly the star of the show. The ground floor wine bar doubles as a reception/holding area for the main basement room which comes with reclaimed-brick walls and terracotta tiled flooring; the open kitchens somehow compensate for the lack of windows. Look for dishes marked in red on the extensive menu, such as the succulent lamb cutlets or the whole sea bass as they are cooked in the wood-fired oven or on the robata grill. Unless you're sticking to pizza, the final bill can be more than expected. Staff are in black and display varying degrees of commitment.

Briciole

F2

20 Homer St
✉ W1H 4NA
☏ (020) 7723 0040
www.briciole.co.uk

⊖ Edgware Road
Closed 25-26 December

Carte £11/25

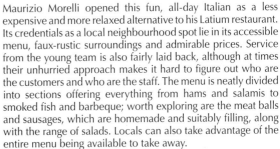

Maurizio Morelli opened this fun, all-day Italian as a less expensive and more relaxed alternative to his Latium restaurant. Its credentials as a local neighbourhood spot lie in its accessible menu, faux-rustic surroundings and admirable prices. Service from the young team is also fairly laid back, although at times their unhurried approach makes it hard to figure out who are the customers and who are the staff. The menu is neatly divided into sections offering everything from hams and salamis to smoked fish and barbeque; worth exploring are the meat balls and sausages, which are homemade and suitably filling, along with the range of salads. Locals can also take advantage of the entire menu being available to take away.

Caffé Caldesi

G2

118 Marylebone Ln. (1st floor)
✉ W1U 2QF
☏ (020) 7487 0753 /4
www.caldesi.com

⊖ Bond Street

Menu £14/20 – Carte £20/44

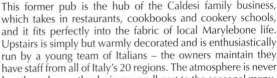

This former pub is the hub of the Caldesi family business, which takes in restaurants, cookbooks and cookery schools, and it fits perfectly into the fabric of local Marylebone life. Upstairs is simply but warmly decorated and is enthusiastically run by a young team of Italians – the owners maintain they have staff from all of Italy's 20 regions. The atmosphere is never less than cheery, thanks in no small part to the seasonal menu, which offers up classics from across Italy that have one thing in common – they are generously proportioned and really deliver on flavour; the pasta dishes are particularly satisfying. On the ground floor you'll find a less structured operation with a slightly abridged but more accessibly priced menu.

Chada Chada

Thai ✗

16-17 Picton Pl.
✉ W1U 1BP
☎ (020) 7935 8212
www.chadathai.com

⊖ Bond Street
Closed 25 December and
lunch Sunday-Monday

Carte £17/36

A/C

VISA

MC

AE

Chada Chada exudes a sense of authenticity that eludes the plethora of chain restaurants surrounding James Street. The menu offers a comprehensive tour around all parts of Thailand – for the main course you choose your primary ingredient, such as prawn or duck, and then decide on the best accompaniments. The kitchen does the familiar well, which makes sense as it has a regular following who know what they like. It also doesn't hang around in sending forth the dishes, which not only come in generous proportions but are also well-priced for W1; the only problem is accommodating all of the dishes on the small tables. There's another branch in Battersea which, surprisingly, is somewhat smarter than its West End cousin.

ℕ Cotidie

Italian ✗✗

50 Marylebone High St
✉ W1U 5HN
☎ (020) 7258 9878
www.cotidierestaurant.com

⊖ Baker Street
Closed Christmas

Menu £25 (lunch) – Carte £35/55

A/C

🍷

☼

VISA

MC

AE

Having made his name in San Pietro in Cariano, acclaimed chef Bruno Barbieri left to embark on new opportunities and so far these have included judging 'Masterchef Italia' and opening this restaurant in Marylebone Village. It occupies the former Café Luc site which didn't need much work as it's an elegant and comfortable space. 'Cotidie' means 'everyday' which, in this instance, refers to the oft changing menu rather than the style of food which is sophisticated and imaginative and seeks inspiration from all of Italy's regions. Pasta dishes stand out, like the Sardinian malloreddus with bottarga; desserts such as the Machiavelli cup-cream are also very satisfying, although prices, especially at dinner, can be a little alarming.

Dinings

J a p a n e s e ✕

22 Harcourt St.   ⊖ Edgware Road
✉ W1H 4HH   Closed Christmas, Saturday lunch
✆ (020) 7723 0666   and Sunday – booking essential
www.dinings.co.uk

Menu £13 (weekday lunch) – Carte £18/57

VISA
Ⓜ©
ÆE
①

In Tokyo the hanging sign outside would be considered positively flamboyant but in London it's the very definition of discretion, making this sweet little place easy to miss. There are half a dozen seats at the counter on the ground floor and a few tables downstairs in the somewhat claustrophobic basement; but wherever you sit, it's hard not to be charmed by it all. The menu is an extensive document, supplemented by blackboard specials, and takes many of its influences from the style of Japanese food found at Nobu, the owner's alma mater: accordingly, highlights are the more creative dishes like the 'sashimi four ways'. The temptation is to order plenty to share but beware because the prices can make this an expensive activity.

ⓝ Donostia

B a s q u e ✕

10 Seymour Pl   ⊖ Marble Arch
✉ W1H 7ND   Closed Christmas, Sunday
✆ (020) 3620 1845   dinner and Monday
www.donostia.co.uk

Carte £13/30

Ⓜ©
ÆE
①

As London's love affair with tapas continues, many diners are now keen on learning more about Spain's regional specialties. The bright and lively Donostia, which is the Basque name for San Sebastiàn, was opened by two young owners inspired by this coastal municipality. Anyone who has visited the area, known for the quality of its restaurants and its terrific pintxos, will recognise classic Basque dishes like cod with pil-pil sauce, chorizo from the native pig Kintoa and tender, slow-cooked pig's cheeks. Add in a thoughtful wine list along with the traditional drinks of cider and Txakoli and you have a winning recipe. You can book a table but it's worth trying for one of the 10 seats at the marble counter in front of the kitchen.

Galvin Bistrot de Luxe

G2

French

66 Baker St.
✉ W1U 7DJ
☎ (020) 7935 4007
www.galvinrestaurants.com

⊖ Baker Street
Closed 25-26 December,
1 January and dinner 24 December

Menu £20/22 – Carte £31/50

Despite the enormous success of Galvin La Chapelle in The City, brothers Chris and Jeff Galvin have never taken their eyes off the ball here at their eponymous 'bistrot de luxe' in Baker Street. Regulars still flock here for the clubby, relaxed atmosphere and the traditional French food, which may look simple on the plate but is carefully constructed behind the scenes. The emphasis is very much on flavour; the kitchen's understanding and appreciation of ingredients, and the classic combinations in which they are used, really come through. The menu has enough variety to satisfy those happy to indulge but those with one eye on the cost should come for lunch or before 7pm if they want to take advantage of a good value fixed menu.

Grazing Goat

F2

British traditional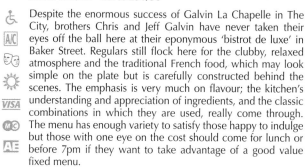

6 New Quebec St
✉ W1H 7RQ
☎ (020) 7724 7243
www.thegrazinggoat.co.uk

⊖ Marble Arch.
Booking essential at dinner

Carte £27/46

The Portman Estate, owners of some serious real estate in these parts and keen to raise the profile of its investment, encouraged an experienced pub operator more at home in Chelsea and Belgravia to venture a little further north and take over the old Bricklayers Arms. Renamed in homage to a past Lady Portman (who grazed goats in a field where the pub now stands as she was allergic to cows' milk), it is now a smart city facsimile of a country pub. It's first-come-first-served in the bar but you can book in the upstairs dining room. Pub classics are the order of the day, such as pies or Castle of Mey steaks, and Suffolk chicken is cooked on the rotisserie. The eight bedrooms are nicely furnished, with their bathrooms resembling Nordic saunas.

Hix (Selfridges)

modern 🍴

G2

Mezzanine Fl, Selfridges, 400 Oxford St
✉ W1A 1AB
📞 (020) 7499 5400
www.hixatselfridges.co.uk

⊖ Bond Street
Closed 25 December
and Sunday dinner

Menu £18 (lunch) – Carte £19/94

It comes as no surprise to learn that this outpost of Mark Hix's expanding group, found on the mezzanine floor of Selfridges overlooking the designer handbags, is an altogether daintier affair than his muscular Chop House in Clerkenwell. It mirrors the opening hours of the store so breakfast kicks things off at 9.30am and the champagne bar offers refuelling opportunities throughout the day. Lunch comes with the buzz generated by the promise of some post-prandial shopping, although the affordable wine list could make this a risky proposition. The cooking is a little lighter and more European than his other restaurants and there are also more salads; but it does share their philosophy of serving unadorned food using home-grown ingredients.

Iberica Marylebone

Spanish 🍴🍴

H1

195 Great Portland St
✉ W1W 5PS
📞 (020) 7636 8650
www.ibericalondon.co.uk

⊖ Great Portland Street
Closed 1 January,
Sunday dinner and bank holidays

Carte £30/75

In 2012, after successfully launching a second branch in Canary Wharf, the original Iberica here at the top end of Great Portland Street was given a fresh new look. It's a sizeable space spread over two floors and comes divided into assorted areas so instead of taking the table you're offered, politely ask if you can wander around first – some prefer the intimacy of upstairs, others the bustle of the ground floor with its bar and deli. Along with an impressive array of Iberico hams, cured meats and cheeses are plenty of tapas style dishes to share. Highlights include the more filling dishes such as glossy black rice with cuttlefish and prawns, and a slowly braised beef cheek. Charming young staff are on hand to offer advice.

Latium

Italian XXX

21 Berners St.
⊠ W1T 3LP
☎ (020) 7323 9123
www.latiumrestaurant.com

⊖ Oxford Circus
Closed 25-26 December,
1 January, Saturday lunch,
Sunday and bank holidays

Menu £23, £34/34

A/C
VISA
MC
AE

The last revamp made it brighter and more contemporary but such is the loyalty of its followers that a simple lick of paint would have been enough. There's now a window into the kitchen for those who like to know where their food comes from, and a chef's table for those who want to watch them at it. Tables by the entrance are given away first but it's worth asking to be seated further in; you'll almost certainly be accommodated as staff are a friendly and considerate bunch. The chef-owner is from Lazio, hence the name, so expect cooking that is free from over-elaboration. Recipes from across Italy also feature and many use British ingredients. The good value lunch menu changes weekly and homemade ravioli is the speciality.

Levant

Lebanese XX

Jason Ct., 76 Wigmore St.
⊠ W1U 2SJ
☎ (020) 7224 1111
www.levant.co.uk

⊖ Bond Street
Closed 25-26 December

Carte £25/35

A/C
☼
VISA
MC
AE

The enticing scent of joss sticks and hookah pipes, pumping Arabic beats and belly dancing mean that Levant is guaranteed to provide a more exotic dining experience than most restaurants. Its basement location, lanterns and low-slung bar add further to the mystique and, as with anywhere offering a hint of spice, diners adopt the principle of safety in numbers and come in larger groups. With all these elements, it is almost a surprise to discover that equal care and enthusiasm has gone into the food. The kitchen uses good ingredients to create satisfying Lebanese dishes ideal for sharing. Avoid the more expensive set menus and head for the à la carte, with its appealing selection of falafel, pastries, char-grills and slow-roasted specialities.

REGENT'S PARK & MARYLEBONE ▶ PLAN V

Locanda Locatelli

G2

Italian 🍴🍴🍴

8 Seymour St.
✉ W1H 7JZ
✆ (020) 7935 9088
www.locandalocatelli.com

⊖ Marble Arch
Closed 25-26 December and 1 January

Carte £29/62

🦽 A/C 🍇 ☀ VISA MC AE

Locanda Locatelli

When your clientele is made up of lots of buffed and shiny people then it is important that you're looking pretty good yourself. So every year the cherry wood is given a fresh coat of varnish and the tan leather seating gets a good clean and this keeps the room looking dapper and slick. Despite the vicissitudes of fashion, Locanda Locatelli has remained an ever popular choice for the cognoscenti, thanks largely to the excellence of the cooking. The large serving team in their black shirts and white ties may look like they've just come from a Sicilian wedding, but they get the job done with alacrity and efficiency. The menu offers around ten dishes per section so there is enough choice for everyone, even those with food allergies. Pasta is a perennial highlight, especially the risotto and gnocchi, and desserts, which always include the toothsome tiramisu and tart of the day, are expertly rendered with flair and care. Thinly sliced calf's head makes an interesting start, while unfussy presentation allows the quality of fish to really shine.

First Course

- Pan-fried scallops with celeriac purée and saffron vinaigrette.
- Pappardelle with broad beans and rocket.

Main Course

- Roast rabbit leg, polenta and Parma ham.
- Black sea bream with bagna cauda sauce.

Dessert

- Tasting of Amedei chocolate.
- Cheesecake with vanilla, violet jelly and strawberry sorbet.

One Blenheim Terrace

innovative ✗✗

1 Blenheim Terrace
✉ NW8 0EH
☎ (020) 7372 1722
www.oneblenheimterrace.co.uk

⊖ St John's Wood
Closed Monday

Carte £26/41

For his first solo venture the young chef has taken on premises that proved unsuccessful for the two previous incumbents, so support from St John's Wood locals is going to be vital. He hopes to draw them in by doing something a little different: some of his dishes are re-interpretations of '60s and '70s classics like crepe Suzette and beef Wellington. However, this is less about nostalgia and more about modern cooking techniques as the updated dishes bear little relation to the original – which may actually be no bad thing in some cases. It is not as gimmicky as it sounds and clearly there is talent in the kitchen. The restaurant itself comes into its own in the summer, thanks to the large terrace and glazed front section.

Orrery

modern ✗✗✗

55 Marylebone High St
✉ W1U 5RB
☎ (020) 7616 8000
www.orrery-restaurant.co.uk

⊖ Regent's Park
Booking essential

Menu £25/48

Enthusiastic post-prandial shopping can be a perilously expensive pastime – the danger is doubled here as Orrery is perched temptingly above a Conran shop. These are actually converted stables from the 19C but, such is the elegance and style of the building, you'd never know. What is sure is the long, narrow restaurant looks its best when the daylight floods in; on warm days make time to have a drink on the terrific rooftop terrace. To complement these charming surroundings you'll be offered a bewildering array of menus, all of which feature quite elaborate, modern European cooking. Dishes are strong on presentation and there is the occasional twist but it's usually done with some meaning rather than merely straining for effect.

Ozer

H2

5 Langham Pl., Regent St.
✉ W1B 3DG
✆ (020) 7323 0505
www.ozer.co.uk

⊖ Oxford Circus

Carte £18/44

There are plenty of London restaurants ideal for a romantic dinner; Ozer is not one of them. Come here with a group of friends, though, and you'll have a fun time because its large bar, excitable noise levels, flat-out service, frantic atmosphere and, above all, the sharing of food make this a great party restaurant. Huseyin Ozer's bewildering array of menus may take time to plough through but that is because there are plenty of highlights. Ignore incongruous interlopers like black cod and go for the Turkish and Ottoman specialities, such as borek, kofte and the extensive selection of chargrilled meats. The food is not only enjoyable but also comes with a health dividend which justifies any enthusiastic over-ordering.

Phoenix Palace

F1

5 Glentworth St.
✉ NW1 5PG
✆ (020) 7486 3515
www.phoenixpalace.co.uk

⊖ Baker Street
Closed 25 December –
bookings advisable at dinner

Carte £26/50

Phoenix Palace may be around the corner from Baker Street but is the sort of vast restaurant that could just as easily be found off Stanley Street in Hong Kong. Come in a large group and there'll be a table big enough to accommodate you; order plenty of dishes to share and they'll be delivered swiftly by the well-drilled staff. The menu may be disconcertingly long but the dishes to go for are the Cantonese specialities like the soups, the roast meats and the king prawn dishes, along with the 'chef's specials' like fish maw with conpoy and winter melon. Dim sum is served until 5pm and is very popular with business types and locals. Ask for a table on the raised section which gives you a good view of this well-oiled machine.

Portman

F2

51 Upper Berkeley St   ⊖ Marble Arch.
✉ W1H 7QW
✆ (020) 7723 8996
www.theportmanmarylebone.com

Menu £15 (weekday lunch) – Carte £23/32

When it went by the name of The Masons Arms this pub was widely known for its gruesome history. It was here that the condemned, on their way to Tyburn Tree gallows, would take their last drink, which purportedly led to the phrase "one for the road". Reincarnated as The Portman, the pub these days boasts a less disreputable clientele who are more attracted by the quality of the cooking. Food is served all day and you can choose to eat in the busy ground floor bar or in the unexpectedly formal upstairs dining room, all thick-pile carpet and starched tablecloths. Fortunately, the style of food remains thoroughly down-to-earth and satisfying and is accompanied by a well-organised wine list and an interesting selection of cocktails.

The Providores

G2

109 Marylebone High St.   ⊖ Bond Street
✉ W1U 4RX   Closed 24 December-4 January
✆ (020) 7935 6175
www.theprovidores.co.uk

Carte £47/67

'Marylebone Village' offers so many restaurants and cafés that it's becoming a destination in itself. Included in the roll call is this fusion restaurant within a former Edwardian pub. The warmth of the staff and the general buzz hit you immediately in the ground floor Tapa Room, where tables and tapas are shared. Upstairs is a slightly more sedate room but the staff are equally charming. Here all dishes come in starter size to "minimise food envy" and allow for sharing; three courses plus a dessert should suffice. There is no doubting the quality of the ingredients, although sometimes there's a flavour or two too many on the plate. The wine list champions New Zealand. Bookings are needed upstairs; downstairs, it's first-come-first-served.

Rhodes W1 (Brasserie)

F3

modern XX

Cumberland Hotel, Great Cumberland Pl.   ⊖ Marble Arch
✉ W1H
✆ (020) 7616 5930
www.rhodesw1.com

Menu £20 (lunch) – Carte £22/40

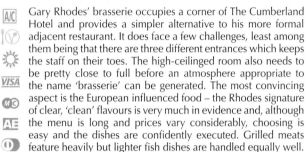

Gary Rhodes' brasserie occupies a corner of The Cumberland Hotel and provides a simpler alternative to his more formal adjacent restaurant. It does face a few challenges, least among them being that there are three different entrances which keeps the staff on their toes. The high-ceilinged room also needs to be pretty close to full before an atmosphere appropriate to the name 'brasserie' can be generated. The most convincing aspect is the European influenced food – the Rhodes signature of clear, 'clean' flavours is very much in evidence and, although the menu is long and prices vary considerably, choosing is easy and the dishes are confidently executed. Grilled meats feature heavily but lighter fish dishes are handled equally well.

Riding House Café

H2

modern X

43-51 Great Titchfield St   ⊖ Oxford Circus
✉ W1W 7PQ   Closed 25-26 December
✆ (020) 7927 0840
www.ridinghousecafe.co.uk

Carte £19/35

For their third project, the owners of The Garrison and Village East ventured uptown, albeit to an area hitherto untroubled by the presence of decent restaurants. It's less a café, more an all-day Manhattan-style brasserie and cocktail bar, with some charming touches of quirky design. You turn left for the restaurant but it's more fun in the main section where you can't book – either at a counter facing the kitchen or on a large refectory table where you rub shoulders with strangers. It's the same menu throughout, starting with breakfast and followed by a choice of 'small plates' along with more straightforward main courses like steak or burgers. It's easy to over-order so stick with the small plates which have a bit more zing to them.

Rhodes W1 (Restaurant) ✿

F3

Cumberland Hotel, Great Cumberland Pl.
✉ W1H 7DL
☎ (020) 7616 5930
www.rhodesw1.com

Menu £26, £50/50

⊖ **Marble Arch**
Closed 2 weeks January,
2 weeks August, Saturday lunch,
Sunday, Monday and bank holidays
– booking advisable

REGENT'S PARK & MARYLEBONE ▶ PLAN V

Rhodes W1

Gary Rhodes may be one of the proudest promoters of British recipes and ingredients but here at his eponymous restaurant the kitchen looks more towards France for inspiration. Where his influence is most obvious is in the uncluttered presentation on the plate; this often belies the work which has gone into each dish, and the ease with which the dishes can be eaten. The cooking is certainly refined but that's never at the expense of flavour and, while the constructions are imaginative in their make-up, they are achieved without recourse to using strange combinations of ingredients. Kelly Hoppen's room design almost compensates for the lack of windows and, unlike most restaurants – where economic imperatives necessitate the re-laying of dining tables over the course of an evening— here, whichever one of the 12 tables you find yourself sitting at, it's yours for however long you want it, so there's no need to look anxiously at your watch around dessert time. Staff do their bit to ensure that proceedings never get too starchy.

First Course

- Roquefort mousse with pickled apple purée and Waldorf salad.
- Fillet of mackerel with honey and sesame caramel.

Main Course

- Slow-cooked sea trout with mussels and curried emulsion.
- Spiced lamb with crisp shoulder and lemon and cumin jus.

Dessert

- Peanut butter parfait, with banana and lime sorbet.
- Mandarin 'arctic roll' with blood orange and mandarin sorbet.

Roganic

G2

innovative 🍴🍴

19 Blandford St
✉ W1U 3DH
✆ (020) 7486 0380
www.roganic.co.uk

⊖ **Baker Street**
Closed 25-26 December, Sunday and
Monday – booking advisable

Menu £29/80

[A/C] [🍸Ⓥ] [VISA] [MC] [AE] [①]

Whether occupying premises for two years still counts as being a 'pop-up' restaurant is a moot point but what is sure is that Roganic, the London outpost of Simon Rogan's L'Enclume restaurant in the Lake District, has garnered plenty of fans in a relatively short time. The choice for customers is between 3, 6 or 10 course tasting menus – and the original, inventive and delicate dishes use plenty of ingredients from their own small farm. The departure of the head chef in 2012 led to the promotion of his sous chef; he's a L'Enclume old boy so regular visitors to Cartmel will recognise more of the dishes served here. The lease runs out in the summer of 2013 but work is already afoot to find a more permanent London base.

 # Roti Chai

G2

Indian 🍴

3 Portman Mews South
✉ W1H 6HS
✆ (020) 7408 0101
www.rotichai.com

⊖ **Marble Arch**

Menu £25/35 – Carte £18/31

[A/C] [🍹] [☼] [VISA] [MC] [AE] [①]

The very colourful Roti Chai represents the new wave of modern yet informal Indian restaurants and also shows what can be done to a huge concrete shell with a little imagination. It's divided in two: the ground floor is about quick and easy pan-Indian street food, from Dhokla chickpea cake to 'Railway' lamb curry, and no bookings are taken; the downstairs 'dining room', with its faux-industrial aesthetic, is somewhat swankier and more expensive but bookable. Here the separate kitchen offers a contemporary update of Indian home cooking, in such dishes as crisp Chennai-style chicken and plump and tasty Bengali crab cakes. It's fun, enthusiastically run and a little different, from the spirited T-shirted waiting team to the Indian cocktails.

Roux at the Landau

French

H2

Langham Hotel,
1c Portland Pl., Regent St. ✉ W1B 1JA
✆ (020) 7965 0165
www.rouxatthelandau.com

⊖ Oxford Circus
Closed Saturday lunch
and Sunday

Menu £40 (lunch and early dinner) – Carte £40/78

It does have its own street entrance but it's best to enter this grand, oval-shaped restaurant from the hotel, as you don't often get the chance to walk through a 'wine corridor'. The hotel brought in the considerable experience of the Roux organisation – which means Albert and Michel Jr – to add vigour and ambition to the operation. Classical, French-influenced cooking is the order of the day but one can detect the emergence of a lighter style of cuisine with the odd twist. The restaurant is also sensible enough to keep its more traditionally minded regulars happy by ensuring that their favourites, like grilled Dover Sole, remain constants. The daily special from the trolley goes down well with the busy lunchtime corporates.

Royal China

Chinese

G2

24-26 Baker St
✉ W1U 7AB
✆ (020) 7487 4688
www.royalchinagroup.co.uk

⊖ Baker Street

Menu £30/40

It could be just as at home in Hong Kong's Wanchai or Central districts but, as it is, Royal China sits very comfortably in Baker Street. The large kitchen is staffed exclusively by Chinese chefs, including the early rising dim sum chef, who is responsible for the specialities served between midday and 5pm each day. The Cantonese dishes are strong on aroma and colour and, while the restaurant does not sell a great deal of seafood due to a lack of tank space, the lobster dishes remain one of the more popular choices. However, it is the barbecued meats, assorted soups, stir-fries and the choice of over 40 different types of dim sum that draw the large groups and ensure that this branch of the Royal China group remains as bustling as ever.

Suka

✗✗

Sanderson Hotel,
50 Berners St ⊠ W1T 3NG
📞 (020) 7300 5588
www.morganshotelgroup.com

⊖ Oxford Circus

Menu £23/50

🅰🅲
🍸
☀
VISA
Ⓜ🅒
🅰🅴
Ⓓ

The Long Bar is one of the busiest parts of the Sanderson hotel so be prepared to fight your way through to get to Suka, the hotel's Malaysian restaurant. The place has an easy-going charm and a menu designed to be shared between friends; just choose between the high stools on one side and the more traditional seating parallel to the open kitchen. The menu offers an appealing précis of the multicultural nature of Malaysian cuisine and features street food alongside more sophisticated dishes. Nasi Lemak, the closest thing to a national dish, is a good place to start and comes with a choice of assorted curries and braised meats. Laksa is suitably creamy and filling, and fruits with which to finish are in abundance.

 28°-50° Marylebone

✗

15-17 Marylebone Ln.
⊠ W1U 2NE
📞 (020) 7486 7922
www.2850.co.uk

⊖ Bond Street
Closed 25 December

Menu £19 (lunch and early dinner) – Carte £21/30

🅰🅲

🐟
☀
VISA
Ⓜ🅒
🅰🅴

If only wine bars had looked like this in the '80s. The second 28°-50° from the people behind Texture restaurant follows the successful formula adopted in their first branch in The City. That means a well-priced wine list where everything is offered in sizes ranging from a mouthful or a glass to a carafe or a bottle, and a supplementary Collectors' List with an impressive roll-call of largely Old World classics. On the food-front, grilled meats from their coal burning oven are the highlight of the menu, while salads, soups and starters all come in a choice of size. You can also simply pop in for a plate of charcuterie, salmon or cheese to share with your wine. Service is as bright as the room which is dominated by the central counter bar.

Texture ✿

innovative 🗙🗙

G2

34 Portman St.
✉ W1H 7BY
☎ (020) 7224 0028
www.texture-restaurant.co.uk

⊖ Marble Arch
Closed Christmas-New Year,
2 weeks August, Sunday
and Monday

Menu £20 (lunch)/79 – Carte £51/71

Chef-owner Agnar Sverrisson and his business partner Xavier Rousset, who trained as a sommelier, have steadily gone about creating an exceedingly good restaurant. The Champagne bar at the front has become a destination in itself and is separated from the restaurant by a large cabinet so you never feel too detached from it. The high ceilings add a little grandeur and the service is very pleasant, with staff all ready with a smile. Agnar's cooking is a little less showy than when Texture opened in 2007 and is all the better for that; you feel he's now cooking the food he wants to cook rather than the food he thought he should be cooking. Iceland is his country of birth so it is no surprise to find lamb, cod (whose crisp skin is served with drinks), langoustine and skyr, the dairy product that nourished the Vikings. There's considerable technical skill and depth to the cooking but dishes still appear light and refreshing and, since the use of cream and butter is largely restricted to the desserts, you even feel they're doing you good.

First Course

- Graflax and smoked salmon with horseradish.
- Asparagus with parmesan, hazelnut and olives.

Main Course

- Lightly salted cod, barley risotto and prawns.
- Rib-eye of beef, ox cheek, horseradish and olive oil béarnaise.

Dessert

- Skyr with rhubarb, muesli and ginger.
- Passion fruit soup with basil ice cream.

Trishna 🕸

G2

15-17 Blandford St.
✉ W1U 3DG
📞 (020) 7935 5624
www.trishnalondon.com

⊖ **Baker Street**
Closed 25-28 December
and 1-3 January

Menu £19 (lunch) – Carte £20/37

Michelin

The coast of southwest India provides many of the influences at this crisply decorated, double fronted modern Indian restaurant. The menu is full of appealing dishes, ranging from the playful – try their own mini version of 'fish and chips' as a starter – to the original; the succulent guinea fowl comes with lentils, fennel seed and star anise. However, the undoubted star of the show is a version of the dish made famous by the original Trishna in Mumbai: brown crab, in this case from Dorset, comes with lots of butter and a little kick of wild garlic; it is so wondrously rich no man alone can finish a bowl, and you'll be licking your lips for days afterwards. All the dishes are as fresh tasting as they are colourful and there is even a recommended wine to go with each one. Doing things a little differently also extends to the cocktail list, although the mango chutney martini is perhaps one brave step too far. Ignore the slightly dodgy acoustics or the occasional need to prompt the staff and just enjoy some wonderfully satisfying Indian food.

First Course
- Char-grilled tiger prawns with mustard and garlic.
- Potato chat.

Main Course
- Fish tikka with dill raita.
- Dorset brown crab.

Dessert
- Mango kheer and pistachio.
- Lemongrass malai.

Verru

69 Marylebone Ln
✉ W1U 2PH
☎ (020) 7935 0858
www.verru.co.uk

⊖ Bond Street

Menu £13/15 – Carte £28/35

The great thing about this part of town is that you can still come across tiny, tucked away restaurants doing something a little different. This is a warm, genially run and smartly dressed little place but it's not just the look that's appealing on a winter's night: Verru's chef-owner is Estonian and accordingly his cooking not only displays a Baltic boldness of flavour but also uses influences from the more northerly parts of Europe. Despite the occasional tendency to gild the lily, the kitchen produces dishes that have an appealing frankness to them but they are also underpinned by some sound classical techniques – and you certainly won't leave hungry. Sit at the front for more atmosphere; at the back for greater intimacy.

Vinoteca

15 Seymour Pl.
✉ W1H 5BD
☎ (020) 7724 7288
www.vinoteca.co.uk

⊖ Marble Arch
Closed 24-26, 31 December,
1 January, bank holiday Mondays and
Sunday dinner –
booking advisable

Carte £22/33

They've transferred the winning formula from their Clerkenwell original, so expect a great selection of wines, gutsy and wholesome cooking, young and enthusiastic staff and almost certainly a wait for a table. One side of the room is given over to shelves of wine; not only is the selection immeasurably appealing but the staff display both a knowledge and, more importantly, enormous enthusiasm when giving advice. The daily changing menu takes its cue from the sunnier parts of Europe and includes thoughtfully compiled salads and good charcuterie. There are also some firmly British dishes too, like mutton and oyster pie, and each one comes with its own wine pairing recommendation. It's great fun, basic in comfort and always very busy.

The Wallace

French ✗

G2

Hertford House, Manchester Sq
✉ W1U 3BN
✆ (020) 7563 9505
www.thewallacerestaurant.com

⊖ Bond Street
Closed 24-26 December –
(lunch only and
dinner Friday-Saturday)

Menu £26 – Carte £28/40

☀
VISA
MC

The Wallace Collection of 18 and 19C decorative art is one of London's finest, if lesser known museums and is found within Sir Richard and Lady Wallace's former home, Hertford House. Go through the French windows in what was once the dining room of this imposing mansion and you'll find yourself in a vast, glass-roofed courtyard. The restaurant occupies one half, a café the other, and, while there are often large groups in for lunch, there is room for everyone. The menu is heavily influenced by France but the kitchen keeps things relatively light. The à la carte is wide-ranging and includes plenty of terrines along with fruits de mer, but the menu du jour represents much better value and usually offers a nicely balanced selection of dishes.

Winter Garden

Mediterranean ✗✗

F1

The Landmark London Hotel,
222 Marylebone Rd ✉ NW1 6JQ
✆ (020) 7631 8000
www.landmarklondon.co.uk

⊖ Edgware Road

Menu £27 (lunch) – Carte £34/55

A/C
☀
🚗
VISA
MC
AE

Dining options tend to get more limited once you find yourself north of Marylebone Road, so the Winter Garden at the Landmark Hotel is a useful place to have up your sleeve, particularly if that sleeve is covered with a business suit. The kitchen displays a pleasing lightness of touch and the best dishes are those of a Mediterranean persuasion. At lunchtime the set menu is nicely balanced and served promptly, which is one of the reasons it's a good spot for meetings – Marylebone Station around the corner being the other reason. Dinner is more leisurely paced and more popular with hotel guests, with assorted grilled dishes adding to the choice. A pianist gallantly tries to help fill the enormous atrium in which the restaurant sits.

Yalla Yalla

Lebanese ✗

H2

12 Winsley St.
✉ W1W 8HQ
✆ (020) 7637 4748
www.yalla-yalla.co.uk

⊖ Oxford Circus
Closed 25-26 December,
1 January and Sunday

Carte £19/26

Close to the clamour of Oxford Street is this fun, good value restaurant whose Beirut street food is much tastier than anything you'll find along the Edgware Road. The name means "Hurry up!" which is a message no doubt endorsed by those waiting for a table as bookings are only taken for larger parties. The crowds come for the broad selection of mezze, which ranges from fattoush and sawda djej (chicken livers) to soujoc (spicy sausages). For the main course, succulent charcoal-grilled lamb dishes stand out, while desserts come from the enticing pastry corner. They also do a brisk takeaway trade in flatbreads, pastries and wraps. Wines from the Bekaa Valley are available alongside the juices and teas. The tiny, original branch is in Soho.

Zayna

Indian ✗✗

F2

25 New Quebec St.
✉ W1H 7SF
✆ (020) 7723 2229
www.zaynarestaurant.co.uk

⊖ Marble Arch

Menu £10/25 – Carte £18/34

When a restaurant is named after the owner's daughter you know there's going to be a lot of love around. Zayna reflects the personality of Riz Dar who spent his formative years around Kashmir and Punjab and whose first job was in his father's restaurant in Pakistan. It's no surprise then to find a menu of North Indian and Pakistani delicacies. It comes divided according to cooking method, from the pan, grill, tawa or oven; but look out for the refined street food using offal. He is passionate about produce: spices are roasted and ground in house and only halal meat and free-range chicken are used. Dishes come packed with flavour, although the final bill can quickly mount up. The ground floor is the more elegant of the two rooms.

Bloomsbury · Hatton Garden · Holborn

A real sense of history pervades this central chunk of London. From the great collection of antiquities in the British Museum to the barristers who swarm around the Royal Courts of Justice and Lincoln's Inn; from the haunts of Charles Dickens to the oldest Catholic church in Britain, the streets here are dotted with rich reminders of the past. Hatton Garden's fame as the city's diamond and jewellery centre goes back to Elizabethan times while, of a more recent vintage, Bloomsbury was home to the notorious Group (or Set) who, championed by Virginia Woolf, took on the world of art and literature in the 1920s.

A full-on encounter with **Holborn** is, initially, a shock to the system. Coming up from the tube, you'll find this is where main traffic arteries collide and a rugby scrum regularly ensues. Fear not, though; the relative calm of London's largest square, part-flanked by two quirky and intriguing museums, is just round the corner. The square is **Lincoln's Inn Fields,** which boasts a canopy of characterful oak trees and a set of tennis courts. On its north side is **Sir John Soane's Museum,** a gloriously eccentric place with twenty thousand exhibits where the walls open out like cabinets to reveal paintings by Turner and Canaletto. On its south side, the Hunterian Museum, refitted a few years ago, is a fascinating repository of medical bits and pieces. Visitors with a

Damien Hirst take on life will revel in the likes of animal digestive systems in formaldehyde, or perhaps the sight of half of mathematician Charles Babbage's brain. Others not so fascinated by the gory might flee to the haunting silence of **St Etheldreda's church** in Ely Place, the only surviving example of thirteenth-century Gothic architecture in London. It survived the Great Fire of 1666, and Latin is still the language of choice.

Contemplation of a different kind takes centre stage in the adjacent **Hatton Garden.** This involves eager-eyed couples gazing at the glittering displays of rings and jewellery that have been lighting up the shop fronts here for many generations, ever since the leafy lane and its smart garden environs took the fancy of Sir Christopher Hatton, a favourite of Elizabeth I. After gawping at the baubles, there's liquid refreshment on hand at one of London's most atmospheric old pubs, the tiny Ye Old Mitre hidden down a narrow passageway. The preserved trunk of a cherry tree stands in the front bar, and, by all accounts, Elizabeth I danced the maypole round it (a legend that always seems more believable after the second pint).

Bloomsbury has intellectual connotations, and not just because of the writers and artists who frequented its townhouses in the twenties. This is where the University of London has its headquarters, and it's also home

C. Eymenier / MICHELIN

to the **British Museum,** the vast treasure trove of international artefacts that attracts visitors in even vaster numbers. As if the exhibits themselves weren't lure enough, there's also the fantastic glass-roofed Great Court, opened to much fanfare at the start of the Millennium, which lays claim to being the largest covered public square in Europe. To the north of here by the Euston Road is the **British Library,** a rather stark red brick building that holds over 150 million items and is one of the greatest centres of knowledge in the world. Meanwhile,

Dickens fans should make for the north east corner of Bloomsbury for the great man's museum in **Doughty Street:** this is one of many London houses in which he lived, but it's the only one still standing. He lived here for three years, and it proved a fruitful base, resulting in Nicholas Nickleby and Oliver Twist. The museum holds manuscripts, letters and Dickens' writing desk. If your appetite for the written word has been truly whetted, then a good tip is to head back west half a mile to immerse yourself in the bookshops of Great Russell Street.

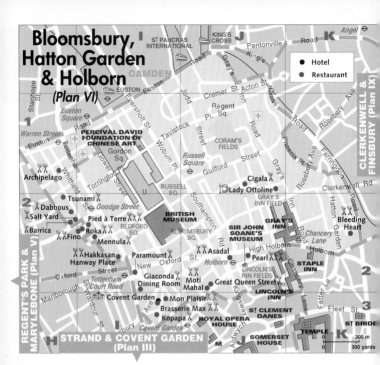

Bloomsbury, Hatton Garden & Holborn

(Plan VI)

| | Hotel |
| | Restaurant |

Archipelago

H1

110 Whitfield St.
⊠ W1T 5ED
✆ (020) 7383 3346
www.archipelago-restaurant.co.uk

⊖ **Goodge Street**
Closed 24-27 December,
Saturday lunch, Sunday and
bank holidays

Menu £26/33 – Carte £27/38

AC

VISA

MC

AE

Bored with beef? Tired of chicken? How about some zebra? Or a little crocodile? Not only is the gloriously oddball Archipelago unlike any other restaurant in London but tales of your meal can also be used to frighten small children. 'Exploring the exotic' is their slogan although 'eating the exotic' would be more exact: the menu reads like an inventory at an omnivore's safari park and the place itself resembles an eccentric Oriental bazaar that's rapidly running out of space. Several dishes are given an Asian twist and side dishes include the 'love-bug salad' made with locusts and crickets. Apart from a somewhat laborious reservation system, it's all great fun and the experience will certainly be memorable.

Asadal

K o r e a n XX

J2

227 High Holborn
⊠ WC1V 7DA
✆ (020) 7430 9006
www.asadal.co.uk

⊖ **Holborn**
Closed 25-26 December, 1 January
and Sunday lunch

Carte £20/30

AC

MC

AE

If it was any nearer Holborn Tube station you'd need an Oyster card to get in. But head down the stairs and you'll soon be oblivious to what's going on at street level, thanks to a comfortable room which is divided up and kitted out with lots of wood. Those unfamiliar with Korean food will find that, by and large, the menu explains itself, since many of the dishes have had their photo taken. One thing to note is that the more there are in your party the better, as sharing is the key. Kimchi provides the perfect starter; there's plenty of seafood but the stars of the show are the hotpots, the delicate dumplings and the barbecues where meats are cooked on the hot-plate on the table. The young staff cope well with the early evening rush.

Barrica 😊

H2

62 Goodge St
✉ W1T 4NE
☎ (020) 7436 9448
www.barrica.co.uk

⊖ **Goodge Street**
Closed 25-26 December, 1 January,
Sunday and bank holidays –
booking essential

Carte £18/20

If the zeitgeist is epitomised by informality and sharing then it's little wonder that tapas bars are sprouting up all over the place. Barrica opened in close proximity to a couple of well-established competitors but manages to hold its own. You'll have to fight through the after-work group at the front to get to the tables and noise levels can overawe at times, but the food is good and the atmosphere fun. The menu is sensibly laid out and supplemented by daily specials. Highlights include braised veal cheeks, duck rillettes and marinated sardines. Cured meats hang above the bar and the cosy room is warm and intimate. If you haven't got a booking, you may get a counter seat or else you can try the Spanish way of eating standing up.

Bleeding Heart

K2

Bleeding Heart Yard (off Greville St.)
✉ EC1N 8SJ
☎ (020) 7242 8238
www.bleedingheart.co.uk

⊖ **Farringdon**
Closed 24 December-1 January,
Saturday, Sunday and bank holidays
– booking essential

Menu £25 (weekday lunch) s – Carte £27/50 s

Dickensian tales of murder and intrigue still haunt the wonderfully evocative Bleeding Heart Yard, while contented bankers and modern day industrialists sit in its candlelit and atmospheric restaurant, feasting on classic French cuisine. Weekly changing set menus sit alongside the fairly pricey à la carte, which comes written in French and English, and well-drilled French staff exhibit a fair degree of personality. The kitchen can sometimes overcomplicate dishes so you're better off going for the more traditional choices with their relative simplicity. The wine list is a splendid affair and the owners have their own estate in New Zealand. If you want something altogether less formal then cross the yard for the Bistro.

Brasserie Max

I3 — modern XX

Covent Garden Hotel,
10 Monmouth St. ✉ WC2H 9HB
✆ (020) 7806 1007
www.firmdalehotels.com

⊖ Covent Garden
Booking essential

Menu £25 – Carte £28/60

Okay, so it does a brisk trade in afternoon tea but this is much more than your usual hotel restaurant. For a start, the surroundings are refreshingly free from chintz and on offer is an equally interesting cocktail list – one end of the room is dominated by a large zinc bar. Meanwhile, the menu is appealingly accessible and will always have something on it that seems just right, whether you're grabbing a bite before the theatre or making an evening of it. There are Asian and Mediterranean influences, carefully compiled salads and plenty of grilled meats. Just beware that side orders can push the final bill up and that staff are sometimes a little reluctant to admit to running a better value TDH menu alongside the à la carte.

A/C VISA AE

Cigala

J1 — Spanish X

54 Lamb's Conduit St.
✉ WC1N 3LW
✆ (020) 7405 1717
www.cigala.co.uk

⊖ Russell Square
Closed bank holidays – booking essential

Menu £18 (lunch) – Carte £23/39

Tapas and small plates may be all the rage these days but Cigala has been going about its business in the part-pedestrianised Lamb's Conduit Street for a few years now. It's not just local medics, lawyers and advertising execs who flock here in their droves – the combination of hassle-free surroundings, sensible prices and an accessible menu means it appeals to a wide audience, with the result that staff can sometimes be a little overwhelmed. Highlights include grilled black pudding, hams from the open kitchen counter, homemade chorizo and squid with mojo sauce. Those in no great hurry should order one of the filling paellas. The entirely Spanish wine list includes some interesting sherries and cocktails.

A/C VISA AE

N Dabbous 🕸

modern 𝕏

12

39 Whitfield St
✉ W1T 2SF
✆ (020) 7323 1544
www.dabbous.co.uk

⊖ **Goodge Street**
Closed 23 December-15 January,
29 March-2 April, two weeks August,
Sunday and Monday –
booking essential

Menu £24/49 – Carte £22/30

Dabbous

There are many London restaurants that are hard to get into but, more often than not, that's because they appeal to those whose business is show. A table at Dabbous is currently one of the hottest tickets in town but that owes more to the fact that Ollie Dabbous is an extremely talented chef and his cooking is something special. An advocate of the 'less is more' approach, his food comes with elegantly restrained finesse and a bewitching purity. His cooking is also influenced by his two primary alma maters – Le Manoir aux Quat' Saisons and Texture – with the result that some dishes owe more to classical theories while others are guided by more modern techniques and ideas. Most tables go for the 7-course Tasting menu which showcases his stimulating and sublime combinations of ingredients and things kick off straight away with the arrival of a wonderful warm seeded loaf (in a paper bag) with homemade butter. The room is ersatz industrial, with ubiquitous exposed ducting and pendant lighting, although there is a simple elegance to the place, with its 14 wooden tables.

First Course

- Mixed alliums in a chilled pine infusion.
- Salad of fennel, lemon balm and pickled rose petals.

Main Course

- Barbecued Iberico pork, savoury acorn praline and homemade vinegar.
- Braised halibut with lemon verbena.

Dessert

- Chocolate ganache, basil moss and sheep's milk ice cream.
- Custard cream pie.

Fino

Spanish XX

33 Charlotte St (entrance on Rathbone St.)
✉ W1T 1RR
✆ (020) 7813 8010
www.finorestaurant.com

⊖ **Goodge Street**
Closed Saturday lunch,
Sunday and bank holidays

Carte £16/44

Fino's basement location and discreet entrance engender in its clientele that warm, satisfyingly smug feeling of being 'in the know'. While it is more formally structured than most restaurants that serve tapas, the atmosphere is always lively and the crowd, particularly at night, is pleasingly mixed. Start with a sherry and some coquetas while you scour the sensibly laid out menu. The young staff all know what's on offer and the more effort you put in with them the more they'll be inclined to offer guidance. Then order a bottle of Albariño and dig in; seafood is a delight, especially the squid from the plancha. Dishes are easy to share and, as in life, the more people in your party the greater will be your enjoyment.

Giaconda Dining Room ☺

modern X

9 Denmark St.
✉ WC2H 8LS
✆ (020) 7240 3334
www.giacondadining.com

⊖ **Tottenham Court Road**
Closed 3 weeks August, 2 weeks Easter,
2 weeks Christmas-New Year, Saturday
lunch, Sunday, Monday and bank holidays
– booking essential

Carte £24/35

In the shadow of Centre Point lies a frayed little area that's 'not quite Soho'. Here you'll find Denmark Street - London's own historic Tin Pan Alley – which is home to the Giaconda Dining Room. Aussies Paul and Tracey Merrony have a small but perfectly formed little place; spartanly decorated, busy from day one and great fun. Paul describes his cooking as "Frenchy, with day trips to Italy", which translates on the plate as confident, gutsy, no-nonsense and immeasurably satisfying. Tripe; steak tartare; pork sausage stew; risotto; a deconstructed pig's trotter and a daily changing fish or grilled special - there's something for everyone and, with most wine bottles in the £20s, it's all done at a credit-crunch busting price.

Great Queen Street 🏵

British modern ✗

J2

32 Great Queen St
✉ WC2B 5AA
📞 (020) 7242 0622

⊖ Holborn
Closed Christmas-New Year, Sunday dinner
and bank holidays – booking essential

Carte £18/33

VISA
_MC_

This is one of those restaurants that is perfect on a cold winter's night, with its candlelight, burgundy coloured walls, busy atmosphere and, most importantly, its heartwarming food. Its popularity does mean that service can sometimes need a prompt but there is no doubting the staff's enthusiasm for the food they serve. The menu descriptions are unapologetically concise but then dishes come equally unembellished. There's little difference between what constitutes a starter or main course and there's always a daily special or two. Highlights are the shared dishes such as the roast chicken crown or the shoulder of lamb, but offal is also done very well. Wine is served in tumblers and the list is thoughtfully put together.

Kopapa

Asian influences ✗

I3

32-34 Monmouth St
✉ WC2H 9HA
📞 (020) 7240 6076
www.kopapa.co.uk

⊖ Covent Garden
Closed 25 December – booking advisable

Menu £25/37 – Carte £24/39

[AC]
🍵
🍷
🍸
😷
☀
VISA
_MC_
[AE]

Too often 'fusion' cooking demands the addition of the prefix 'con', but, like many of his fellow Kiwis, Peter Gordon is a chef with a greater understanding of this sort of culinary promiscuity. Kopapa, a Maori word for a gathering, is his just-drop-in-anytime place; it's ideal for Covent Garden and is staffed by many of his enthusiastic countrymen. Ok, it may be cramped and austerely kitted out, but this isn't about long, lingering lunches, more about grabbing a table and getting stuck in. There's a wide choice, from breakfast items to quick bites and platters, but the highlights are found in the tapas section. You may not recognise all the ingredients listed, but you'll know that your taste buds have been given a workout.

Hakkasan Hanway Place ❀

Chinese ✕✕

12

8 Hanway Pl.
✉ W1T 1HD
✆ (020) 7927 7000
www.hakkasan.com

Carte £50/82

⊖ **Tottenham Court Road**
Closed 24-25 December

Hakkasan

The original, subterranean Hakkasan remains as cool and seductive as ever and, despite the opening of another branch in Mayfair, its popularity shows no sign of slowing. Despite the size and general bustle, it is actually possible to have quite an intimate experience here, thanks to the clever lighting and good acoustics. However, service can be a little hit and miss and depends largely on who your waiter is and their level of enthusiasm. Lunchtime dim sum is a real highlight, although they sometimes appear curiously reluctant to offer you that particular menu. There are 20 chefs in the kitchen, many of whom are, like the head chef, from Singapore. The extensive menu is laid out clearly and logically, although there can be a marked difference in price between similar sounding dishes. Cantonese remains the starting point but the kitchen adds its own signature of inventiveness to give the dishes zip and the flavours depth. One thing the waiting staff do get right is telling you when you've unwittingly but understandably succumbed to over-ordering.

First Course	*Main Course*	*Dessert*
• Peking duck with Royal Beluga caviar.	• Roasted silver cod.	• Jivara hazelnut bomb.
• Dim sum platter.	• Jasmine tea-smoked chicken.	• Chilled melon soup.

BLOOMSBURY, HATTON GARDEN & HOLBORN ▶ PLAN VI

183

N # Lady Ottoline

J1

11a Northington St
✉ WC1N 2JF
📞 (020) 7831 0008
www.theladyottoline.com

⊖ Chancery Lane.
Closed 24-26 December
and bank holidays

Menu £14 (weekdays) – Carte £21/33

Apart from some repair work on the cornicing and the tiled floor, this substantial red-brick Victorian pub is largely unchanged from when it was called The Kings Arms. The menus in the packed and slightly chaotic ground floor bar and the Queen Anne style upstairs dining room are not hugely different: cold winter nights see dishes like braised pig cheeks with lentils or venison haunch with squash purée. The kitchen takes more care with its cooking than one expects and dishes deliver on flavour. There's also a large selection of wine by the glass. This is the second pub for this husband and wife team and a sister to Princess of Shoreditch. It is named after the society hostess who was a friend to the Bloomsbury set.

Mennula

I2

10 Charlotte St
✉ W1T 2LT
📞 (020) 7636 2833
www.mennula.com

⊖ Goodge Street
Closed 25-26 December, 1 January, lunch
Saturday-Sunday and bank holidays
– bookings advisable at dinner

Menu £18 – Carte £28/42

Sicilian specialities provide the highlights at this sweet little spot which has firmly established itself on Charlotte Street. The ebullient chef-owner, who now has his son in the kitchen with him, cooks with a passion and his generosity and ambition is evident on the plate. Start with homemade Sicilian stuzzichini, which includes such delicacies as arancini and roasted almonds (hence the name mennula); do also order a typical Sicilian pasta dish such as spaghetti with sardines, pine nuts, sultanas and fennel. At first one feels the service may be a little too formal for this small room but it comes with genuine warmth and is nicely paced. The more intimate area is at the back but it's also worth asking for one of the booths.

Mon Plaisir

French ✗✗

19-21 Monmouth St.
✉ WC2H 9DD
☎ (020) 7836 7243
www.monplaisir.co.uk

⊖ **Covent Garden**
Closed Christmas-New Year,
Sunday and bank holidays

Menu £13/24 – Carte £29/48

Mon Plaisir couldn't be more French if it wore a beret and whistled La Marseillaise; but because this institution has been around since the 1940s, and under the current ownership since the '70s, it can also give one an unexpected but palpable sense of old London. It's divided into four rooms, all of which have slightly different personalities but share the Gallic theme; even the bar was reportedly salvaged from a Lyonnais brothel. Service may lack some of the exuberance of the past but that's just down to the relative lack of experience of the current serving team. All the authentically tasting classics are on offer, from snails to terrines, duck to coq; the set menu represents good value while the à la carte can be a little pricey.

Moti Mahal

Indian ✗✗

45 Great Queen St.
✉ WC2B 5AA
☎ (020) 7240 9329
www.motimahal-uk.com

⊖ **Holborn**
Closed Christmas, Sunday and lunch
Saturday and bank holidays

Menu £15/49 – Carte £24/46

To get the most out of your visit to Moti Mahal, order dishes from the menu which follows the path of the Grand Trunk Road, built in the 16C and stretching the 2500km from Bengal to the North West of India and the Pakistan border. This journey also takes little detours along the way to include specialities cooked on a clamp grill and there is no distinction between starters and main courses – just order a selection to share with your table. There is also a 'classics' menu for those who insist on only ordering dishes with recognisable names. The flavoursome cooking is done with care and service is conscientious and endearing. The restaurant is split between a bright and busy ground floor and a more intimate basement level.

Paramount

I2

modern ✗

Centre Point (31st floor)
101-103 New Oxford St.
✉ WC1A 1DD
☎ (020) 7420 2900 – **www**.paramount.uk.net

⊖ Tottenham Court Road
Closed 25-26 December
and Sunday dinner

Menu £24 (lunch and early dinner) – Carte £32/51

Restaurants with great views usually hope you'll spend so much time gawping out of the window that you won't notice the quality of the cooking. But Paramount, on the 32nd floor of the iconic Grade II listed Centre Point building, is owned by experienced restaurateur Pierre Condou and he has invested in a decent kitchen team. Getting to the restaurant can be a little laborious as you first get buzzed in on the ground floor, go to reception, get in a lift and then repeat the name-giving at another reception. But this is a fun place with keen staff and sweeping views across London; there's also a champagne bar one floor up. The ambition of the kitchen is shown by the presence of a tasting menu; cooking is surprisingly elaborate and the ingredients are good.

Pearl

J2

French ✗✗✗

Chancery Court Hotel,
252 High Holborn ✉ WC1V 7EN
☎ (020) 7829 7000
www.pearl-restaurant.com

⊖ Holborn
Closed 2 weeks August,
Sunday, lunch Saturday
and bank holidays

Menu £22/25 – Carte £48/63

A room as grand as this has to be busy otherwise the tables feel a little cast adrift. This former banking hall is within what was once Pearl Assurance's HQ; its high ceiling, chandeliers and columns certainly add some grandeur to proceedings but they clearly didn't make life easy when it came to adding the lighting. Waiting staff come dressed in black and are an enthusiastic, well-drilled bunch who do a good job ensuring that the surroundings don't become the main event. Chef Jun Tanaka, who pulls in plenty of the customers himself thanks to his television appearances, offers a menu high in originality but grounded in a classical French base. The wine list is a particularly impressive tome in both its depth and variety.

Pied à Terre ✿

innovative 𝖃𝖃𝖃

34 Charlotte St
✉ W1T 2NH
✆ (020) 7636 1178
www.pied-a-terre.co.uk

Menu £28/75

⊖ Goodge Street
Closed last week December-3 January,
Saturday lunch, Sunday and bank
holidays – booking essential

Pied a Terre

Having celebrated its 21st birthday in 2012, Pied à Terre appears to be in rude health. Marcus Eaves is the fourth chef to have led the kitchen since its birth and has settled in nicely now with a new team behind him. He has not changed the style of food here too much although his dishes do display more of his own personality by being bolder in flavour. More imaginative than ground-breaking, his food is refined without being over-complicated and his menu makes appealing reading. Wine remains a very strong element here; the two weighty tomes list over 700 bins, with considerable depth and quality across all major regions. Apart from a striking new feature on the wall – made from monkfish skin, by the way – the restaurant remains largely unchanged which means it's intimate for some, a little claustrophobic for others. Service can be a touch chaotic in the early evening so let it settle by having an aperitif in the under-used first floor room. If you're a party of 6 or more then ask for the semi-private table in the window.

First Course

- Lobster with suckling pig belly and peanut dressing.
- Spiced pig head and crab raviolo, shiso and kaffir lime broth.

Main Course

- Veal with tarragon brioche, morels and parmesan.
- Fillet of monkfish with Tokyo turnips, watercress purée, mustard and clam vinaigrette.

Dessert

- Tart of Earl Grey tea, milk and vanilla gel with bergamot ice cream.
- Rhubarb, white chocolate and cardamom millefeuille.

Roka

Japanese ✕✕

I2

37 Charlotte St
✉ W1T 1RR
☎ (020) 7580 6464
www.rokarestaurant.com

⊖ Goodge Street
Plan V
Closed 25 December

Menu £50 – Carte £18/89

&
A/C
☼
VISA
MC
AE
⊙

Roka has one of those appealingly perceptible pulses that only really busy, well-run restaurants enjoy. It attracts a handsome crowd although they don't just come to glory in their mutual attractiveness but to share food that's original, easy to eat and just as pretty as they are. The kitchen takes the flavours, delicacy and strong presentation standards of Japanese food and adds its own contemporary touches. The menu can appear bewildering but just skip the set menus and order an assortment from the various headings; ensure you have one of the specialities from the on-view Robata grill. Sometimes too many dishes can arrive at once but the serving team are a friendly and capable bunch and they'll ease up on the delivery if you ask.

Salt Yard ☺

Mediterranean ✕

H2

54 Goodge St.
✉ W1T 4NA
☎ (020) 7637 0657
www.saltyard.co.uk

⊖ Goodge Street
Closed 24 December-4 January, Saturday
lunch and Sunday

Carte £14/24

A/C
🍴
🎋
VISA
MC
AE
⊙

The ground floor is the more boisterous and you'll feel like you're in the middle of a fun party; downstairs is better if you don't know your dining companion that well, although it too is full of life. This is all about tapas, although not just about Spanish tapas. One side of the menu has bar snacks, charcuterie and cheese but after ordering some olives or boquerones, turn over and you'll find three headings: Fish, Meat and Vegetable – one plate of each per person should do it. Unusual dishes, like braised gurnard with smoked Jersey Royals, sit alongside more traditional pairings like duck breast with parsnip purée. Prices are excellent; sharing is encouraged and service, young and sincere. Spain and Italy dominate the wine list.

Tsunami

Japanese ✗

93 Charlotte St.
✉ W1T 4PY
☎ (020) 7637 0050
www.tsunamirestaurant.co.uk

⊖ Goodge Street
Closed Saturday lunch and Sunday

Menu £15 (weekday lunch) – Carte £14/47 s

A/C
VISA
MC
AE

You'll never find anyone from Clapham in Nobu or Roka because they always insist they have their own cheaper version in Tsunami. Now we all have the opportunity of seeing what they mean, thanks to their second branch here in the West End. Appropriately enough, it is at the less showy end of Charlotte Street but is prettily decorated with lacquered walls and a floral motif, with colour changing lights and lounge music. Staff have good intentions but do tend to go missing at crucial moments. The contemporary Japanese food is carefully prepared and the menu covers all points and includes plenty of originality. Seafood, whether grilled, as tempura or as sashimi salad, is a highlight and much can be shared without breaking the bank.

BLOOMSBURY, HATTON GARDEN & HOLBORN ▶ PLAN V

Bib Gourmand ☺
indicates our inspectors'
favourites for good value.

Bayswater · Maida Vale

There may not appear to be an obvious link between Maida Vale and Italy, but the name of this smart area to the west of central London is derived from a battle fought over two hundred years ago in Southern Italy, and the most appealing visitor attraction in the neighbourhood is the charming canalside **Little Venice.** To stroll around here on a summer's day brings to mind promenading in a more distant European clime; it's hard to believe that the ear-shattering roar of the Westway is just a short walk away. South of this iconic elevated roadway – a snaking route out from Maryle-bone to the western suburbs – is Bayswater, a busy area of impo-sing nineteenth century buildings that's the epicentre of London's Middle Eastern community.

During its Victorian heyday, **Bayswater** was a grand and gla-morous address for affluent and elegant types who wanted a giant green space (Hyde Park) on their doorstep. The whole area had been laid out in the mid 1800s, when grand squares and cream stuccoed terraces started to fill the acres between Brunel's curvy Paddington station and the park. But during the twentieth century Bayswater's cachet nose-dived, stigmatised as 'the wrong side of the park' by the arrivistes of Knightsbridge and Kensington. Today it's still a backpacker's pa-radise: home to a bewildering number of shabby tourist hotels,

bedsits and B&Bs, converted from the grand houses. But this tells only a fraction of the modern story, because the area is under-going a massive facelift that will transform it forever. The hub of this makeover is the **Paddington Basin,** a gigantic reclamation of the old Grand Union Canal basin in the shadow of the rail terminus. From a ramshackle wasteground, it's now a shimmering zone of metal, steel and glass, a phantas-magoria of blue chip HQs, homes, shops and leisure facilities. Even the barges have been turned into permanently moored 'retail op-portunities'. Tree-lined towpaths along the perimeter complete the picture of a totally modern waterscape.

Lovers of the old Bayswater can still relish what made it famous in the first place: radiating out from **Lancaster Gate,** away from Hyde Park, is a web of streets with hand-some squares and tucked-away mews, and it still retains pockets of close-knit communities, such as Porchester Square, west of Pad-dington station. Meanwhile, the 'cathedral' of the area, Whiteleys shopping centre in **Queensway**, remains a pivotal landmark, as it has been for more than a century. Just beyond Whiteleys heading away from central London, **West-bourne Grove** is still reassuringly expensive, or at least the bit that heads determinedly towards Not-ting Hill. But the wind of change has rustled other parts of the

neighbourhood: Connaught Street has evolved into a villagey quarter of boutiques, galleries and restaurants, while, further west, Craven Hill Gardens is the height of chic, courtesy of The Hempel, a boutique hotel.

Little Venice pretty much acts as a dividing line between Bayswater and Maida Vale. Technically, it's the point where the Paddington arm of the Grand Union Canal meets the **Regent's Canal,** but the name, coined by poet Robert Browning who lived close by, has come to encompass the whole area just to the north of the soaring Westway. Narrow boat moorings vie for attention alongside the cafés and pubs that mercifully lack the frantic high street buzz so typical of their kind away from the water's edge. The permanently moored boats were here a long time before those upstarts at Paddington Basin. This is where you can find old-time favourites including a floating art gallery and a puppet theatre barge, and all overseen by the Warwick Castle pub, a stalwart of the area that's a minute's walk from the canal. Suitably refreshed, a wander round the residential streets of Maida Vale is very pleasant, dominated by the impressive Edwardian blocks of flats that conjure up a distinctive well-to-do scene.

191

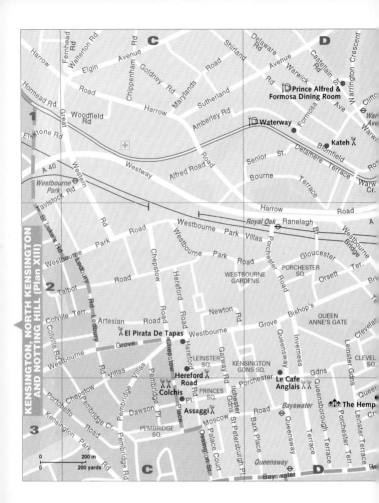

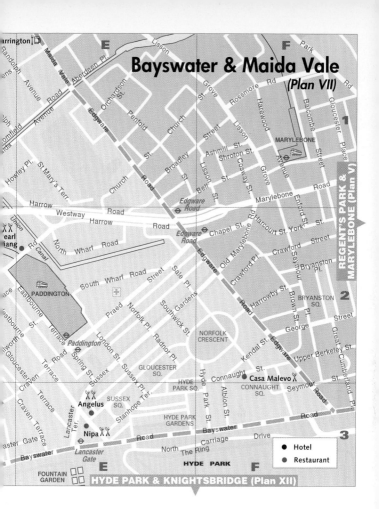

Bayswater & Maida Vale
(Plan VII)

REGENT'S PARK & MARYLEBONE (Plan V)

MARYLEBONE

PADDINGTON

NORFOLK CRESCENT

Casa Malevo

GLOUCESTER SQ.

NORFOLK SQ.

HYDE PARK SQ.

Angelus

SUSSEX SQ.

CONNAUGHT SQ.

BRYANSTON SQ.

Nipa

HYDE PARK GARDENS

- ● Hotel
- ● Restaurant

FOUNTAIN GARDEN

HYDE PARK & KNIGHTSBRIDGE (Plan XII)

HYDE PARK

Angelus

E3

French ✗✗

4 Bathurst St.
✉ W2 2SD
☎ (020) 7402 0083
www.angelusrestaurant.co.uk

⊖ Lancaster Gate
Closed 24 December-2 January

Menu £20 (lunch) – Carte £40/56

[A/C]

This 19C former pub, with its Murano chandeliers and art nouveau mirrors, has a warm and inclusive feel, and much of the credit for that goes to its very hospitable owner, Thierry Tomasin, who knows all his regulars and has put together an equally committed team. Along with the front restaurant, there is a surprisingly large sitting area at the back. Thierry has resisted the temptation to put in more tables, although with the downstairs area and a chef's table in the kitchen he probably has enough. The cooking style is French with British ingredients and he has a 'proper' kitchen which does the right things at the right time of year: who could resist braised ox cheek on a cold winter's night? Equal thought has gone into the wine list.

[VISA]
[M©]
[AE]

Assaggi

C3

Italian ✗

39 Chepstow Pl, (1st Floor)
✉ W2 4TS
☎ (020) 7792 5501

⊖ Bayswater
Closed 2 weeks Christmas,
Sunday and bank holidays –
booking essential

Carte £41/54

Assaggi has always been about simplicity, from the pared-down surroundings of this room above a pub to the handwritten bill at the end. The cooking has also always been about honest flavours and quality produce but a little inconsistency in delivery means that sometimes dishes don't always shine as they can. This is a pity because Assaggi has always been a spirited and inclusive restaurant and showed everyone that good food need not be accompanied by great ceremony. What hasn't changed is the warm and effusive service and the great atmosphere; its many regulars, who are kissed on the way in and the way out, treat the place like their local trattoria. However, for most of us, the prices represent a special night out.

Le Café Anglais

modern ✗✗

D2

8 Porchester Gdns
✉ W2 4BD
✆ (020) 7221 1415
www.lecafeanglais.co.uk

⊖ Bayswater
Closed 25-26 December and 1 January

Menu £23/27 – Carte £31/48

A/C
☀
VISA
MC
AE

The terminal blandness of Queensway received a boost when Rowley Leigh, formerly of Kensington Place, opened this vast brasserie within Whiteley's, the Grade II listed shopping centre. His place shares the same conviviality and culinary accessibility as 'KP' but on a bigger scale and with better acoustics. The art deco styling, leather banquettes and big windows may reflect Whiteley's 1911 roots but it's still best to take the lift up from the side entrance. The menu offers a huge range of brasserie classics, from rabbit rillettes and the wonderful parmesan custard to the daily specials and meats turning slowly on the rotisserie. The wine list is resolutely Old World. You can always just pop in and sit at the oyster bar.

Casa Malevo

Argentinian ✗

F2

23 Connaught St
✉ W2 2AY
✆ (020) 7402 1988
www.casamalevo.com

⊖ Marble Arch

Menu £15 (weekday lunch) – Carte £19/41

A/C
⊡
☀
VISA
MC
AE

Carnivores are in clover these days due to the high number of places specialising in the cooking of red meat. Adding to the choice is this local Argentinian restaurant, with its bare brick walls and intimate lighting. Kick off by sharing the 'picada de campo': a board of grilled peppers, focaccia, pork cheek terrine and chicken matambre; then select from the grill, a piece of beef imported from Argentina – rib-eye, sirloin or fillet. The accompaniments may not quite come up to the mark but when you've got a steak and a bottle of Malbec from their exclusively Argentinian wine list, what else do you need? Those who have brought their own defibrillator can share the 'parrillada' containing rib-eye, fillet, chicken, lamb, chorizo and morcilla.

195

 **Colchis**

o t h e r   w o r l d   k i t c h e n s   ✗✗

39 Chepstow Pl.
✉ W2 4TS
✆ (020) 7221 7620
www.colchisrestaurant.co.uk

⊖ Bayswater
Closed Christmas-New Year and Monday

Carte £21/35

Students of classical mythology will recognise the name Colchis as the destination of the Argonauts; students of London's diverse restaurant scene will see it as an opportunity to experience another cuisine. Hearty cooking from the former Soviet State of Georgia, with its Mediterranean and Middle Eastern influences, is celebrated at this former pub which now has a contemporary look. Starters include khachapuri (leavened bread stuffed with cheese) and lobio mchadit (a hearty red kidney bean stew with corn cakes) and for a main course it has to be shashlyk (lamb, pork or veal kebabs from the grill) which come with great roast potatoes. If you're still not full, then finish with medoki, a traditional sponge cake.

Hereford Road

B r i t i s h   m o d e r n   ✗

3 Hereford Rd.
✉ W2 4AB
✆ (020) 7727 1144
www.herefordroad.org

⊖ Bayswater
Closed 24 December-3 January and
27-29 August – booking essential

Menu £16 (weekday lunch) – Carte £20/29

Hereford Road is, first and foremost, a local restaurant. Lunch is a relaxed affair, with the room brightened by the large domed skylight, while dinner is the livelier feast, where everyone gives the impression that they walked here. Owner-chef Tom Pemberton is often the first person you see as the open kitchen is by the entrance – this was once a butcher's shop. He is an acolyte of St John and his cooking shares the same principles but not the same prices. So expect seasonal, British ingredients in very tasty dishes devoid of frippery. Offal is handled with aplomb and dishes designed for two, such as the shoulder of lamb or the whole oxtail, are so good you won't actually want to share them. Staff are enthusiastic and articulate.

Kateh

D1

5 Warwick Pl
✉ W9 2PX
✆ (020) 7289 3393
www.kateh.net

⊖ **Warwick Avenue**
Booking essential – (dinner only and lunch
Friday-Sunday)

Carte £20/27

Booking is imperative if you want to join those locals who have already discovered what a little jewel they have here in the form of this buzzy, busy Persian restaurant. Kateh is a type of rice from the Gilan Province in Iran; the fishermen there cook it to a sticky consistency and mix it with their daily catch. It features as a traditional accompaniment here, along with herbs and fruits. The baby calamari is delicious, the stews are very satisfying and the grilling is expertly done over charcoal. Warm sesame-coated flatbreads are moreish and be sure to finish with an authentic dessert like 'kolouche' (date and walnut pastries) along with tea made with cardamom. There's a delightful decked terrace at the back.

Nipa

E3

Lancaster London Hotel,
Lancaster Terr ✉ W2 2TY
✆ (020) 7551 6039
www.niparestaurant.co.uk

Thai ✗✗

⊖ Lancaster Gate
Closed Christmas-NewYear,
Saturday lunch and Sunday

Menu £13/29 – Carte £23/32

You'll find Nipa to be a little oasis of calm and hospitality, once you've made it up to the first floor of the Royal Lancaster and sidestepped the businessmen on their laptops in the adjacent lounge. Its teak panelling and ornaments are all imported from Thailand and they've done a convincing job of replicating the original Nipa in Bangkok's Landmark Hotel – if anything, it's even a little smarter. The menu is comprehensive, with a mix of the recognisable blended with more regional specialities. Dishes are marked 1-3 in chillies for their respective heat, come in decent sizes and the harmonious blend of flavours and textures successfully delivers what the aromas promise. Set menus are at the back and provide a convenient all-round experience.

Pearl Liang

Chinese

E2

8 Sheldon Sq., Paddington Central
✉ W2 6EZ
☎ (020) 7289 7000
www.pearlliang.co.uk

⊖ Paddington
Closed 24 and 25 December

Menu £25/38 – Carte £12/53

Chain restaurants tend to dominate corporate developments like 'Paddington Central' therefore thanks should be extended to Pearl Liang for flying the flag of independence. The weighty menu dedicates each page to a different main ingredient, be it poultry, fish, prawns or duck. There is the occasional interloper from other Asian cuisines but it's best to stick to the Chinese specialities. Prices allow for enthusiastic ordering and the prawn and pork dishes score highly, especially the king prawn with chilli. It's a big place whose large tables are more likely to be occupied by business types than families but the fast and furious service gives it an authentic edge. The surrounding offices make use of the takeaway lunch menu.

El Pirata De Tapas

Spanish

C2

115 Westbourne Grove
✉ W2 4UP
☎ (020) 7727 5000
www.elpiratadetapas.co.uk

⊖ Bayswater
Closed 24-26 December, 26-27 August and
1 January

Menu £10/25 – Carte £19/25

Spanish restaurants and tapas-style eating satisfy our appetite for a shared, less structured dining experience and El Pirata is no exception. It's spread over two floors, although you wouldn't want to be the first table downstairs, and is decorated in a contemporary yet warm style. The staff give helpful advice on a menu that is quite lengthy but helpfully divided up into sections, from charcuterie to fish, croquettes to vegetarian, meat to paellas; there are also a couple of appealing and balanced set menus and the pricing structure is far from piratical. The kitchen shows respect for traditional flavours but is not afraid of trying new things or adding a note of playfulness to some dishes. A good place to come with friends.

Prince Alfred &
Formosa Dining Room

D1

m o d e r n 🍺

5A Formosa St
✉ W9 1EE
✆ (020) 7286 3287
www.theprincealfred.com

Menu £12/16 – Carte £24/47

Original plate glass, panels and snugs make The Prince Alfred a wonderful example of a classic Victorian pub. Unfortunately, the eating is done in the Formosa Dining Room extension on the side but at least it's a lively room with capable cooking. There's a rustic theme running through the menu, with a strong British accent, so traditionalists will enjoy the fish pie, potted trout, steak and ale pie and calves liver but there are also risottos, parfaits and terrines for those whose tastes are more continental. The open kitchen is not averse to sprucing up some classics, for example your burger arrives adorned with foie gras and truffles. Prices are realistic, even with a charge made for bread, and the friendly team cope well under pressure.

Waterway

D1

m o d e r n 🍺

54 Formosa St
✉ W9 2JU
✆ (020) 7266 3557
www.thewaterway.co.uk

Carte £23/34

A canalside setting offering refreshment to passing narrowboaters; a large terrace besieged by drinkers; and live music on a Thursday night – it sounds like a pub and even has the necessary warmth and bustle, but inside it's all surprisingly smart. There's a bar occupying one side and a restaurant the other, with no sign anywhere of any spit or sawdust. The menu and cooking are both comparable to the most urbane of urban gastropub: the muscular flavours of black pudding with chorizo and hen's egg are in contrast to its delicate presentation, while fillet of bream with prawn mash reveals the kitchen's lighter touch. Things tail off somewhat with desserts but prices are realistic. Service is youthful, bubbly and capable.

City of London · Clerkenwell Finsbury · Southwark

Say what you like about London, **The City** is the place where it all started. The Romans developed this small area – this square mile – nearly two thousand years ago, and today it stands as the economic heartbeat of not only the capital, but the country as a whole. Each morning it's besieged with an army of bankers, lawyers and traders, and each evening it's abandoned to an eerie ghost-like fate. Of course, this mass exodus is offset by the two perennial crowd-pullers, **St Paul's** and the **Tower of London**, but these are both on the periphery of the area, away from the frenetic commercial zone within. The casual visitor tends to steer clear of the City, but for those willing to mix it with the daytime swarm of office workers, there are many historical nuggets hidden away, waiting to be mined. You can find here, amongst the skyscrapers, a tempting array of Roman ruins, medieval landmarks and brooding churches designed by Wren and Hawksmoor. One of the best ways of encapsulating everything that's happened here down the centuries is to visit the Museum of London, on London Wall, which tells the story of the city from the very start, and the very start means 300,000 BC.

For those seeking the hip corners of this part of London, the best advice is to head slightly northwest, using the brutalist space of the **Barbican Arts Centre** as your marker. You're now entering **Clerkenwell**. Sliding north/south through here is the bustling and buzzy **St John Street,** home to some of the funkiest eating establishments in London, their proximity to **Smithfield** meat market giving a clue as to much of their menus' provenance. Clerkenwell's revivalist vibe has seen the steady reclamation of old factory space: during the Industrial Revolution, the area boomed with the introduction of breweries, print works and the manufacture of clocks and watches. After World War II, decline set in, but these days city professionals and loft-dwellers are drawn to the area's zeitgeist-leading galleries and clubs, not to mention the wonderful floor-to-ceiling delicatessens. Clerkenwell is home to The Eagle, one of the city's pioneering gastropubs and still a local favourite, which even has its own art gallery upstairs. Meanwhile, the nearby **Exmouth Market** teems with trendy bars and restaurants, popular with those on their way to the perennially excellent dance concerts at Sadler's Wells Theatre.

The area was once a religious centre, frequented by monks and nuns; its name derives from the parish clerks who performed Biblical mystery plays around the Clerk's Well set in a nunnery wall. This can be found in **Farringdon Lane** complete with an exhibition explaining all. Close by in St John's Lane is the 16C gatehouse which is home to the Museum of the

C. Eymenier / MICHELIN

Order of St John (famous today for its ambulance services), and chock full of fascinating objects related to the Order's medieval history.

Not too long ago, a trip over London Bridge to **Southwark** was for locals only, its trademark grimness ensuring it was well off the tourist map. These days, visitors treat it as a place of pilgrimage as three of London's modern success stories reside here. **Tate Modern** has become the city's most visited attraction, a huge former power station that generates a blistering show of modern art from 1900 to the present day, its massive turbine hall a must-see feature in itself. Practically next door but a million miles away architecturally is Shakespeare's **Globe,** a wonderful evocation of medieval showtime. Half a mile east is the best food market in London: **Borough Market.** Foodies can't resist the organic, feel-good nature of the place, with, its mind-boggling number of stalls selling produce ranging from every kind of fruit and veg to rare-breed meats, oils, preserves, chocolates and breads. And that's just for hors-d'œuvres…

201

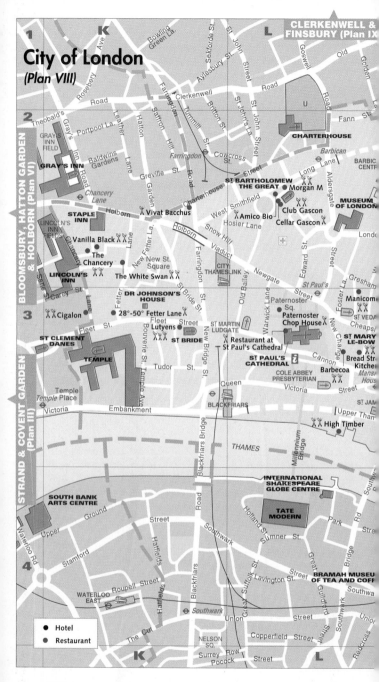

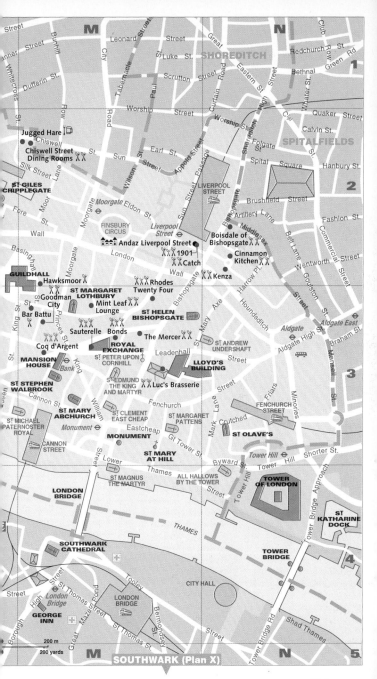

Street

Leonard   Street

Tanner Street
Whitecross
Bunhill
City
St Luke St.
Scrutton   Street
Great   Eastern   St.
SHOREDITCH
Redchurch
Club Row
Green Rd
1

Dufferin St.
Tabernacle
Paul
Curtain   Road
High   Street
Bethnal
Whaler St.
Clara
Quaker   Street
Calvin St.
SPITALFIELDS

Row
Worship   Street
Worship   Street
Shoreditch
Folgate   St.
Hanbury St.

Jugged Hare
Chiswell
Chiswell Street
Dining Rooms ✗✗
Silk Street   Lane
St.
Earl   St.
Sun   Street
Appold Street
Sun Street Passage
Spital
Spital   Square   St.
2

ST GILES
CRIPPLEGATE
Fore   St.
Moor   Lane
Wall
Moorgate
Eldon St.
Liverpool
Street
LIVERPOOL
STREET
Brushfield   Street
Artillery Lane
Middlesex
Fashion St.

Basinghall
Moorgate
FINSBURY
CIRCUS
London
Liverpool
Street
Andaz Liverpool Street
1901
✗✗✗ Catch
Boisdale of
Bishopsgate ✗✗
Cinnamon
Kitchen ✗✗
Bishopsgate
Brushfield
Bell Lane
Wentworth   Street
Goulston   St.
Commercial   Street

Wall
Kenza ✗✗
Harrow Pl.
Aldgate East
Braham St.

GUILDHALL
Hawksmoor ✗
Goodman
City ✗✗✗
Bar Battu
King St.
Princes
St.
ST MARGARET
LOTHBURY
Mint Leaf ✗✗
Lounge
Rhodes
Twenty Four
ST HELEN
BISHOPSGATE
St Mary Axe
Houndsditch
Aldgate
Aldgate High St.
3

Sauterelle   Bonds
Coq d'Argent ✗✗✗
MANSION
HOUSE
Bank
King   William
ROYAL
EXCHANGE
ST PETER UPON
CORNHILL
The Mercer ✗✗
Leadenhall   Street
ST ANDREW
UNDERSHAFT
LLOYD'S
BUILDING
Friars
Minories
Mansell   St.

ST STEPHEN
WALBROOK
Cannon   Street
ST EDMUND
THE KING
AND MARTYR ✗✗ Luc's Brasserie
Fenchurch   Street
FENCHURCH
STREET

ST MICHAEL
PATERNOSTER
ROYAL
ST MARY
ABCHURCH
Monument
CANNON
STREET
ST CLEMENT
EAST CHEAP
Eastcheap
MONUMENT
Monument
ST MARGARET
PATTENS
Mark   Lane
Crutched
Fenchurch
Gt Tower St.
ST OLAVE'S

Lower   Thames   Street
ST MARY
AT HILL
Byward   St.
Tower Hill
Shorter St.
4

LONDON
BRIDGE
ST MAGNUS
THE MARTYR
London
Street
ALL HALLOWS
BY THE TOWER
Tower Hill
Tower
TOWER
OF LONDON
Tower Bridge Approach
ST
KATHARINE
DOCK

THAMES

SOUTHWARK
CATHEDRAL
TOWER
BRIDGE

Tooley   Street
CITY HALL
Tower Bridge Rd
Shad Thames

St Thomas
London
Bridge
Great Maze Pond
LONDON
BRIDGE
Bermondsey

George St.
Borough High
GEORGE
INN
St Thomas St.

200 m
200 yards

SOUTHWARK (Plan X)

203

Clerkenwell & Finsbury
(Plan IX)

SHOREDITCH

KING SQ.

BARTHOLOMEW SQ.

Old Street ⊖

CHARTERHOUSE SQ.

Barbican ⊖

BARBICAN CENTRE

ST BARTHOLOMEW THE GREAT

MUSEUM OF LONDON

ST GILES CRIPPLEGATE

FINSBURY SQ.

Moorgate ⊖

FINSBURY CIRCUS

0   200 m
0   200 yards

CITY OF LONDON (Plan VIII)

205

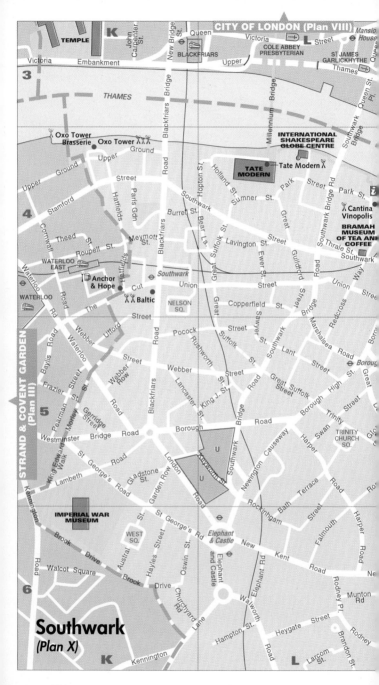

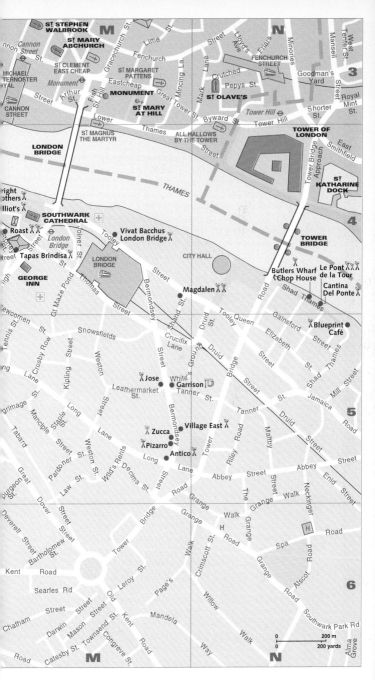

ST STEPHEN WALBROOK
ST MARY ABCHURCH
Cannon Street
MICHAEL PATERNOSTER ROYAL
ST CLEMENT EAST CHEAP
Monument
Arthur St.
CANNON STREET
Lime St.
Fenchurch St.
Street
Gracechurch St.
ST MARGARET PATTENS
Eastcheap
MONUMENT
Fish St. Hill
ST MARY AT HILL
Mincing La.
Great Tower St.
Mark La.
Crutched
Pepys St.
ST OLAVE'S
Byward St.
Tower Hill
Lloyd's Ave
Friars
Minories
FENCHURCH STREET
Goodman's Yard
Shorter St.
Royal Mint St.
Mansell
West Tenter St.

London Bridge
Lower Thames Street
ST MAGNUS THE MARTYR
ALL HALLOWS BY THE TOWER
Tower Hill
TOWER OF LONDON
East Smithfield
Tower Bridge Approach
ST KATHARINE DOCK

THAMES

right others
Elliot's
SOUTHWARK CATHEDRAL
Roast
London Bridge
Tapas Brindisa
GEORGE INN
Newcomen St.
Vivat Bacchus London Bridge
Joiner St.
Tooley St.
St. Thomas St.
LONDON BRIDGE
Bermondsey St.
CITY HALL
Magdalen
TOWER BRIDGE
Butlers Wharf Chop House
Le Pont de la Tour
Cantina Del Ponte
Shad Thames
Gainsford St.
Blueprint Café
Mill Street

Tennis St.
Crosby Row
Snowsfields
Weston St.
Kipling St.
Crucifix Lane
Druid St.
Queen Elizabeth Street
Shad Thames St.
Jamaica Road

Pilgrimage St.
Manciple St.
Long Lane
Staple St.
Jose
Leathermarket St.
White Tanner St.
Garrison
Druid Street
Tanner St.
Druid Street
Maltby St.
St.

Great Dover St.
Tabard St.
Pardoner St.
Law St.
Weston St.
Wild's Rents
Zucca
Pizarro
Antico
Village East
Long Lane
Tower Bridge Road
Riley Road
Abbey Street
Grange
The Grange
Grange Walk
Neckinger
Enid Street

Deverell Street
Bartholomew St.
Dover Street
Decima St.
Bridge Walk
Grange
H Road
Crimscott St.
Walk
Spa Road
H
Road
Alscot Road
Grange Road

Kent Road
Searles Rd
Chatham Street
Darwin Street
Mason Street
Townsend St.
Catesby St.
Congreve St.
Old Kent Road
Page's Walk
Leroy St.
Mandela Way
Willow Walk
Way
Southwark Park Rd
Alma Grove

0   200 m
0   200 yards

M   N

207

Amico Bio

Vegetarian

L2

44 Cloth Fair
✉ EC1A 7JQ
✆ (0207) 6007 778
www.amicobio.co.uk

⊖ Barbican
▶ **Plan VIII**
Closed 25 December, Saturday lunch,
Sunday and bank holidays

Menu £18 – Carte approx. £22

Opening a vegetarian restaurant just yards from Smithfield Market may seem like a grand ironic gag but a dish of the baked red peppers with capers and olives could turn the most committed of carnivores. This simple little Italian place is owned by an experienced chef and his cousin and all their organic produce comes from their family farm in Capua. The menu changes as the produce comes and goes so don't be surprised if a dish suddenly runs out. The cooking is light and fresh with combinations of flavours that remain true to the chef's upbringing in Campania. He's happy to engage with his customers so it's worth asking for his recommendations. Photos of the farm adorn the walls and prices are unimpeachably generous.

Anchor & Hope

British modern

K4

36 The Cut
✉ SE1 8LP
✆ (020) 7928 9898

Carte £19/34

⊖ Southwark.
▶ **Plan X**
Closed Christmas-New Year, Sunday
dinner, Monday lunch and bank holidays
– bookings not accepted

The Anchor & Hope is still running at full steam and its popularity shows no sign of abating. It's not hard to see why: combine a menu that changes with each service and is a paragon of seasonality, with cooking that is gutsy, bold and wholesome, and you end up with immeasurably rewarding dishes like suckling kid chops with wild garlic, succulent roast pigeon with lentils or buttermilk pudding with poached rhubarb. The place has a contagiously congenial feel and the staff all pull in the same direction; you may spot a waiter trimming veg or a chef delivering dishes. The no-reservation policy remains, so either get here early or be prepared to wait – although you can now book for Sunday lunch, when everyone sits down at 2pm for a veritable feast.

Antico

Italian ✗

214 Bermondsey St
✉ SE1 3TQ
✆ (020) 7407 4682
www.antico-london.co.uk

⊖ London Bridge
▶ **Plan X**
Closed Sunday dinner and Monday

Menu £15/18 – Carte £20/41

Art galleries, markets, pubs, bars, restaurants, independent shops, even a local festival…if only all our streets resembled Bermondsey Street. In 2012 Antico was added to the list of dining options along the strip following the conversion of an antique warehouse – hence the name. This is a bright and breezy corner spot, with exposed brick walls acknowledging its past and a downstairs lounge bar a nod to the present. The Italian food is honest and straightforward; the homemade pasta dishes like slow-roasted pork shoulder tortelloni are especially good and there is always a seasonal ragu, risotto and sorbet on the blackboard. The atmosphere is fun, the cocktails are good and the clientele is pleasingly mixed in age and affluence.

Baltic

other world kitchens ✗✗

74 Blackfriars Rd
✉ SE1 8HA
✆ (020) 7928 1111
www.balticrestaurant.co.uk

⊖ Southwark
▶ **Plan X**
Closed 24-27 December and 1 January
– bookings advisable at dinner

Menu £15/39 – Carte £23/34

Baltic has been going for over a decade and is as busy as ever, serving over 100 diners every night. The façade may have faded over time but the atmosphere inside is as contagious as ever, as the noise from the bar competes with the clatter from the large dining area at the back. Just kick back, order a vodka and get down to choosing from the menu. If you don't know your pierogi from your pelmeni, don't panic – most of the staff are Polish so help is at hand. Starters include soups such as botwinka and zurek; blinis come with all the toppings and meat dishes outnumber fish choices 2 to 1. Just be sure you're wearing your eating-boots because portions are big and dishes are packed with flavour. There's jazz on Sunday nights.

Bar Battu

48 Gresham St
✉ EC2V 7AY
✆ (020) 7036 6100
www.barbattu.com

⊖ Bank
▶ **Plan VIII**
Closed 24 December-2 January, Saturday,
Sunday and bank holidays

Menu £18 – Carte £24/38

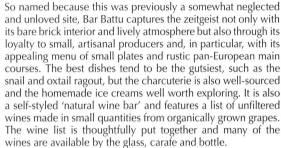

So named because this was previously a somewhat neglected and unloved site, Bar Battu captures the zeitgeist not only with its bare brick interior and lively atmosphere but also through its loyalty to small, artisanal producers and, in particular, with its appealing menu of small plates and rustic pan-European main courses. The best dishes tend to be the gutsiest, such as the snail and oxtail ragout, but the charcuterie is also well-sourced and the homemade ice creams well worth exploring. It is also a self-styled 'natural wine bar' and features a list of unfiltered wines made in small quantities from organically grown grapes. The wine list is thoughtfully put together and many of the wines are available by the glass, carafe and bottle.

Barbecoa

20 New Change Passage
✉ EC4M 9AG
✆ (020) 3005 8555
www.barbecoa.com

⊖ St Paul's
▶ **Plan VIII**
Closed 25-26 December – booking
essential

Carte £30/95

There are many things that us Brits lead the world in, but barbecuing ain't one of them. So we owe thanks to American chef Adam Perry Lane who, in collaboration with our own Jamie Oliver, set up this restaurant to show us how it should be done. For a start, the kitchen has all the right kit to ensure the prime meats are cooked to perfection, whether that's rib-eye or half a chicken. But to really see the standard to aim for when next entertaining in your garden, order the pulled pork shoulder with BBQ sauce and cornbread. If you haven't quite got the appetite for crispy pig cheeks, then try one of the interesting salads; by dessert you may be willing to share so go for Chocolate Nemesis, Jamie's homage to his alma mater.

Bistrot Bruno Loubet

K1

Zetter Hotel,
St John's Sq., 86-88 Clerkenwell Rd. ✉ EC1M 5RJ
☎ (020) 7324 4444
www.thezetter.com

⊖ Farringdon
▶ **Plan IX**
Booking advisable

Carte £29/36

The original Bistrot Bruno's heyday in Soho was around 1994, at a time when London house prices were struggling to recover, England were no-shows at the World Cup and Silvio Berlusconi was Italy's prime minister. So 2010 seemed as good a time as any for Bruno Loubet to return to the capital after his sojourn in Australia. He did surprise a few people by pitching up in Clerkenwell, at the trendy Zetter hotel, but it's a good fit for his satisfying and rustic cooking. There is actually more depth and sophistication to the food than the menu suggests and it's not exclusively French: a little Asian spicing or Moroccan flavour can find their way in too. The room is bright; the staff unhurried and the clientele self-assured.

Blueprint Café

modern

N5

Design Museum, Shad Thames,
Butlers Wharf ✉ SE1 2YD
☎ (020) 7378 7031
www.blueprintcafe.co.uk

⊖ London Bridge
▶ **Plan X**
Closed Sunday dinner
except mid-June-August

Menu £13/23 – Carte £23/40

2012 may have seen its first change of head chef for nearly 16 years but it's business as usual at this bright white restaurant above the Design Museum. The cooking remains light, uncomplicated and easy to eat as they make the most of seasonal ingredients and use them in complementary ways. The set menus come with very appealing price tags and this is a great choice of restaurant on a sunny day thanks to the retractable windows and views of the river and Tower Bridge. The local area has far more bustle to it than when the restaurant opened at the end of the '80s and the opera glasses allow those with window tables to zoom in on the passers-by below, with the knowledge that, as you're one floor up, they won't notice you doing so.

Boisdale of Bishopsgate

N2

Swedeland Crt., 202 Bishopsgate
✉ EC2M 4NR
☏ (020) 7283 1763
www.boisdale.com

⊖ Liverpool Street
▶ **Plan VIII**
Closed Christmas, bank holidays,
Saturday and Sunday

Menu £20 – Carte £25/74

A narrow alley littered with drinkers and smokers is perhaps an unlikely place in which to find old-fashioned Scottish hospitality. The ground floor is given over to the guiltless consumption of champagne and oysters but the main event happens in the vaulted cellar below, with its long bar and green leather seating – ask for one of the three booths or table 13 which comes with its own alcove. The menu is varied but it's best to stick to the Scottish staples: smoked salmon, roast haggis with mash and neeps and, in particular, the 28 day dry-aged cuts of beef. The wine list is strong on top end producers from the Auld Alliance partner; cigars and whiskies are also in abundance, while live jazz accompanies all this revelry.

Bonds

M3

Threadneedles Hotel,
5 Threadneedle St. ✉ EC2R 8AY
☏ (020) 7657 8088
www.bonds-restaurant.com

⊖ Bank
▶ **Plan VIII**
Closed Saturday,
Sunday and bank holidays

Menu £24 (lunch) – Carte £29/55

Bonds repays the investment of its customers by providing plenty of interest, in both the menu choice and the surroundings. This former banking hall dates from the 1850s and its marble, pillars and panelling make it a grand old room in which to house a restaurant. The cooking is equally bold and the experienced kitchen produced well-versed dishes that are unfussy and keep their roots largely within Europe. Slow-cooking is a popular technique and is used with veal shin, rump of lamb and pork belly, while fish from Newhaven is handled deftly. Service is up to speed at lunch; dinner is less frenzied, when the lower lighting helps create a more intimate atmosphere. The cocktail list makes the adjacent bar worth visiting.

N Bread Street Kitchen

modern ✕✕

10 Bread St   ⊖ St Paul's
✉ EC4M 9AJ   ▶ **Plan VIII**
✆ (020) 3030 4050   Closed 25 December – booking advisable
www.breadstreetkitchen.com

Carte £27/59

Influenced perhaps by the time he has spent in the US in recent years, Bread Street Kitchen is Gordon Ramsay's take on New York loft-style dining. With floor-to-ceiling windows, a large bar, thumping music, an open kitchen running down one side and enough zinc ducting on the ceiling to kit out a small industrial estate, the space is big, butch and full of buzz. In a further departure from his usual style of operation, the food is quite simple and rustic – think modern bistro dishes with the odd touch of refinement – and there is enough choice to provide something for everyone. The short rib burger is a best seller; the wood oven is used to good effect with dishes like braised pork collar and the desserts are particularly well done.

Butlers Wharf Chop House

British traditional ✕

36e Shad Thames, Butlers Wharf   ⊖ London Bridge
✉ SE1 2YE   ▶ **Plan X**
✆ (020) 7403 3403
www.chophouse-restaurant.co.uk

Carte £24.50/55

A chophouse means meat and, where there is meat, there are usually men. You'll see plenty of them here, their suit jackets slung over their seats as they get stuck into a charcoal-grilled rib-eye or prepare to wrestle with a game bird. The menu is a paean to all things British so other choices such as steak and kidney pudding or lamb with haggis are equally sturdy; finish off with sticky toffee puddings and you'll wonder if you'll ever be hungry again. The large room comes with light wood panelling that'll prompt cricketers to think of linseed oil and the bar at the entrance end offers a simpler and cheaper menu. Come in the summer for a table on the fantastic terrace – few restaurants can match the stunning views.

CITY OF LONDON, CLERKENWELL, FINSBURY & SOUTHWARK ▶ PLAN VIII

Cantina Del Ponte

N4

36c Shad Thames, Butlers Wharf
✉ SE1 2YE
✆ (020) 7403 5403
www.cantina.co.uk

⊖ London Bridge
▶ **Plan X**
Closed 25-27 December

Menu £15/19 – Carte £19/35

A refurbishment a few years back revitalised this Italian stalwart. They kept the large mural on one wall and created a pleasantly relaxing, faux-rustic environment. The menu was also tweaked: it was out with the pizzas and in with a greater degree of authenticity. The focus is on appealing and flavoursome dishes and the set menu represents decent value. There's an appealing selection on offer, with the focus very much on recognisable standards and old favourites. However, flavours are well-defined and portions are bigger than expected. The wine list covers all of Italy and there's ample choice by the glass. The first tables to go on a summer's day are naturally those on the riverside terrace under the awning.

Cantina Vinopolis

L4

No.1 Bank End
✉ SE1 9BU
✆ (020) 7940 8333
www.cantinavinopolis.com

⊖ London Bridge
▶ **Plan X**
Closed bank holidays

Menu £26 (weekdays) – Carte £27/62

One of the advantages of a restaurant being beneath huge Victorian arches is that larger parties are in no danger of dominating the room: the rumble of passing trains and a vast vaulted brick ceiling ensure that any extra noise is easily absorbed. Cantina is the restaurant attached to the wine museum, Vinopolis, and its wine list is appropriately impressive in its range and reach. But this isn't just a restaurant for oenologists: due care is also given to the food, which comes with a healthy Mediterranean glow. The à la carte can be a little pricey but the set menu, which is not too dissimilar and offers an adequate selection, represents better value. Salads are satisfying and the open kitchen also handles fish particularly well.

Caravan

K1

11-13 Exmouth Market
✉ EC1R 4QD
✆ (020) 7833 8115
www.caravanonexmouth.co.uk

⊖ Farringdon
▶ **Plan IX**
Closed Christmas-New Year
and Sunday dinner –
booking advisable

Carte £22/31

A discernible Antipodean vibe pervades this casual eatery, from the laid-back, easy-going charm of the serving team to the kitchen's confident combining of unusual flavours; even in the excellent flat-whites served by the barista. There's an ersatz industrial feel to the room and a randomness to the decorative touches that belies the seriousness of the ambition. The 100% Arabica beans are roasted daily in the basement, the wine list features an unusual selection of producers and plenty of organic wines, and the owners' travels (hence the name) inform the innovative and inventive cooking. There's something for everyone, from breakfast to small plates to share, or even main courses for two – this really is a caravan of love.

Catch

M2

Andaz Liverpool Street Hotel,
40 Liverpool St. ✉ EC2M 7QN
✆ (020) 7618 7200
www.andazdining.com

⊖ Liverpool Street
▶ **Plan VIII**
Closed Christmas, Easter,
Saturday and Sunday

Menu £25 – Carte £36/49

Catch has been fashioned out of a cordoned off corner of the Andaz hotel's ground floor, in what was the original hotel entrance but still manages to look quite glamorous thanks to the marble and the ornate ceiling. The first thing you notice is the vast chilled area which is bursting with a wonderful selection of assorted shellfish. The kitchen does have a slight tendency to over-complicate some of the dishes so it's best to stick to the classics, like the home-cured salmon, fish and chips or Dover sole. However, the real stars of the show are the six varieties of oysters, all in tip-top form; indeed, plenty of regulars just pop in for a glass of champagne and the 'oyster experience' where they are served four different ways.

Cellar Gascon

L2

59 West Smithfield
✉ EC1A 9DS
✆ (020) 7600 7561
www.cellargascon.com

Menu £13 (lunch) – Carte £18/26

⊖ Barbican
▶ **Plan VIII**
Closed Christmas-New Year, Saturday,
Sunday and bank holidays – booking
essential at lunch

Tucked into the side of Club Gascon is their narrow cellar, which began life as a wine bar with a few nibbles thrown in but now, with the whole 'small plates' thing being all the rage, the food enjoys more of a starring role. It's not unlike a smart tapas bar and the monthly changing menu has plenty of treats: pâtés, rillettes, farmhouse hams, cheeses and even some salads for the virtuous, but the Toulouse sausages and the Gascony pie of duck and mushrooms really stand out. The terrific value 'express' lunch, which includes a dish of the day, is hard to beat and understandably popular. The wine list is a shorter version of next door's and focuses on France's south west; they also hold monthly wine tasting evenings.

The Chancery

K2

9 Cursitor St
✉ EC4A 1LL
✆ (020) 7831 4000
www.thechancery.co.uk

Menu £35

⊖ Chancery Lane
▶ **Plan VIII**
Closed 24 December-4 January,
Saturday lunch and Sunday

The Chancery is an elegant, discreet restaurant that's so close to the law courts you'll assume your fellow diners are barristers, jurors, or the recently acquitted. The ground floor, with its contemporary artwork and smartly laid tables, is more comfortable than the basement, although there are plans afoot to expand into next door. The menu is appealing concise and understated and most of the dishes have a reassuringly classical backbone, whether that's the mackerel escabeche or the saddle of rabbit. The kitchen clearly knows what it is doing – flavours are bold and sauces are a particular highlight. The service team can seem a little withdrawn at first – maybe it's dealing with all those formal legal types – but they do get the job done.

Chiswell Street Dining Rooms

British modern ✗✗

Montcalm London City at The Brewery Hotel,
56 Chiswell St ⊠ EC1Y 4SA
℘ (020) 7614 0177
www.chiswellstreetdining.com

⊖ Barbican
▶ Plan VIII

Carte £30/52

The Martin brothers used their successful Botanist restaurant as the model for their corner spot at the former Whitbread brewery. As it also acts as a hotel dining room for the Montcalm Hotel, it's open for breakfast, but the place really comes alive in the evening, thanks to its lively cocktail bar. There's a pleasing Britishness to the menu and the kitchen makes good use of nearby Billingsgate, with classics like whole Cornish lemon sole, and poached langoustines. Those who prefer more muscular cooking can head for the Hereford snail and smoked bacon pie or Aberdeen Angus rib-eye; and who cannot fail to smile when they see 'Knickerbocker Glory' on a menu? The smartly kitted-out staff cope very well with the constant buzzy atmosphere.

Cicada

Asian ✗

132-134 St John St
⊠ EC1V 4JT
℘ (020) 7608 1550
www.rickerrestaurants.com

⊖ Farringdon
▶ Plan IX
Closed 25 December, 1 January,
Saturday lunch and Sunday

Carte £20/36

You'll need to book ahead to guarantee a table at this busy, noisy and infectiously entertaining Pan-Asian restaurant, which was the first in Will Ricker's London-wide chain. The semi-booth seating and open style kitchen add to the general drama and the bar is more than just an addendum to the restaurant. A pot of knives, forks and chopsticks on each table allow you to decide just how authentic you want the experience to be. The varied and lengthy menu changes often but perennial favourites like chilli salt squid are constants. The Chinese element is quite strong and dim sum forms a large part but there's also more Japanese influence than in the other branches, which comes in the form of sashimi, maki rolls and tempura.

CITY OF LONDON, CLERKENWELL, FINSBURY & SOUTHWARK ▶ PLAN VIII

Cigalon

K3

115 Chancery Ln
✉ WC2A 1PP
✆ (020) 7242 8373
www.cigalon.co.uk

⊖ Chancery Lane
▶ **Plan VIII**
Closed 24 December-2 January,
Saturday, Sunday and bank holidays

Menu £20/25 – Carte £21/43

A/C
📶
VISA
MC
AE

A huge skylight bathes the room in light while the kitchen pays homage to the food of Provence – this is a restaurant that really comes into its own in the summer. A former auction house for law books, the space is stylishly laid out, with the booths in the centre being the prized seats – ask for No.9 if you want to watch the chefs in action. Along with the traditional dishes such as soupe au pistou, bouillabaisse, salade niçoise and pieds et paquets are popular grilled dishes such as venison, and there's even the occasional detour to Corsica. Equal thought went into the name: it refers to both a 1935 Marcel Pagnol film about a haughty chef and the local name for the summer cicada. There's also a busy bar downstairs in the cellar.

Cinnamon Kitchen

N2

9 Devonshire Sq
✉ EC2M 4YL
✆ (020) 7222 2555
www.cinnamonclub.com

⊖ Liverpool Street
▶ **Plan VIII**
Closed Sunday and bank holidays

Menu £15/75 – Carte £20/44

🛖
A/C
📶
VISA
MC
AE
①

Having successfully established Westminster's Cinnamon Club and made it a popular choice with those who run the country, the team behind it opened a second branch here in The City, to appeal to those who own, or thought they owned, the country. This is all about contemporary Indian dining: the cooking is creative and original, the surroundings light and unobtrusive and the service keen and sprightly. The menu bears little resemblance to the usual Indian fare and includes ingredients like quinoa, red deer and scallops. The arresting presentation doesn't come at the expense of the punchy flavours. The grill section is worth exploring and enthusiastic amateur cooks should position themselves at the Tandoor Bar to watch all the action.

Clerkenwell Kitchen

modern ✕

27-31 Clerkenwell Cl
✉ EC1R 0AT
✆ (020) 7101 9959
www.theclerkenwellkitchen.co.uk

Carte £17/23

⊖ Farringdon
▶ **Plan IX**
Closed Christmas-New Year,
Saturday, Sunday and bank holidays
– booking advisable – (lunch only)

Time spent working in Dorset with Hugh Fearnley-Whittingstall has clearly influenced Emma, the owner of this busy, tucked away eatery: she sources her ingredients from small producers who use traditional methods and is committed to sustainability, recycling and the reduction of food miles. But this is more than just a worthy enterprise – the food is rather good too. Local office workers flock in for breakfast and takeaway sandwiches but it is well worth booking for the appealing daily changing lunch menu. Two of the six main courses will be vegetarian and offer, along with dishes like venison and pancetta pie, plenty of freshness and flavour. Even the juices are seasonal and the tarts, pies and cakes are all made daily.

Comptoir Gascon 😊

French ✕

61-63 Charterhouse St.
✉ EC1M 6HJ
✆ (020) 7608 0851
www.comptoirgascon.com

Menu £15 (lunch) – Carte £17/29

⊖ Farringdon
▶ **Plan IX**
Closed Christmas-New Year,
Sunday, Monday and bank holidays
– booking essential

This buzzy restaurant should be subsidised by the French Tourist Board as it does more to illustrate one component of Gascony's famed 'douceur de vivre' – sweetness of life – than any glossy brochure. The wines, breads, foie gras, duck and cheeses all celebrate SW France's reputation for earthy, proper man-food. The menu is divided into 'mer', 'vegetal' and 'terre'; be sure to order duck, whether as rillettes, confit or in a salade Landaise. After these big flavours, it'll come as a relief to see that the desserts, displayed in a cabinet, are delicate little things. The prices are also commendable; even the region's wine comes direct from the producers to avoid the extra mark-up. There's further booty on the surrounding shelves.

Club Gascon ✿

French ✗✗

L2

57 West Smithfield
✉ EC1A 9DS
✆ (020) 7796 0600
www.clubgascon.com

Menu £25/65 – Carte £40/50

⊖ Barbican
▶ **Plan VIII**
Closed Christmas - New Year,
Saturday lunch, Sunday and bank
holidays – booking essential

A/C

VISA

MC

AE

Club Gascon

Those living in Gascony enjoy a diet with the highest fat content in France yet they tend to live longer than their compatriots. Leaving aside the magical powers of Armagnac, this 'Gascony paradox' is surely reason enough to explore further this most indulgent of cuisines. Chef-owner Pascal Aussignac is passionate about all things south-western: get him started on the quality of the produce and he'll talk the hind legs off an âne. Whilst familiar ingredients appear on the menu, the cooking is surprisingly contemporary and often quite original; the ambition may not always be matched by the execution but the dishes will certainly grab your attention. Lunch is a slightly pared down version of the evening menu but the tasting menu remains the benchmark and comes with some intelligent and well considered wine matches. Service is appropriately and unapologetically Gallic, while marble pillars, panelling and huge floral displays add grandeur to the high-ceilinged room, which was once a Lyons Corner House.

First Course

- Braised snails with tulip and wild fennel infusion.
- Grilled duck foie gras with grapes.

Main Course

- Langoustine and squid with saffron pearls and pig's trotter.
- Venison loin on violet tea embers, roasted quince.

Dessert

- Turrón and foie gras macaroon.
- Carpaccio of figs, honeycomb and clove ice cream.

Coq d'Argent

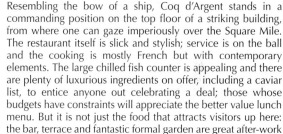

French XXX

M3

1 Poultry
✉ EC2R 8EJ
☎ (020) 7395 5000
www.coqdargent.co.uk

⊖ Bank
▶ **Plan VIII**
Closed 25-27 December, 1 January,
Saturday lunch, Sunday dinner and bank
holidays – booking essential

Menu £28 – Carte £34/58

Resembling the bow of a ship, Coq d'Argent stands in a
commanding position on the top floor of a striking building,
from where one can gaze imperiously over the Square Mile.
The restaurant itself is slick and stylish; service is on the ball
and the cooking is mostly French but with contemporary
elements. The large chilled fish counter is appealing and there
are plenty of luxurious ingredients on offer, including a caviar
list, to entice anyone out celebrating a deal; those whose
budgets have constraints will appreciate the better value lunch
menu. But it is not just the food that attracts visitors up here:
the bar, terrace and fantastic formal garden are great after-work
spots or venues for private parties.

ⓝ Crooked Well

modern

O2

16 Grove Ln
✉ SE5 8SY
☎ (020) 7252 7798
www.thecrookedwell.com

⊖ Denmark Hill (Rail)
▶ **Plan XVII**
Closed Monday lunch

Carte £19/30

Three friends scoured the south of England before finding this
old boozer in Camberwell. They've done it up very cleverly
because it manages to look both new and lived-in at the
same time and also feels like a proper 'local'. There's a strong
emphasis on beers, great cocktails and an interesting wine list
with plenty available by the glass and pichet, but the pub's
growing reputation is mostly down to its food. The kitchen
mixes things up by offering stout, traditional classics like
rabbit and bacon pie alongside more playful dishes such as a
deconstructed Peach Melba. There are lots of things 'on toast'
at lunchtime, while dishes like Scotch egg with Heinz tomato
soup are designed to evoke memories of childhood.

Elliot's

modern ✗

12 Stoney St., Borough Market
✉ SE1 9AD
☏ (020) 7407 7436
www.elliotscafe.com

⊖ London Bridge
▶ **Plan X**
Closed 25-26 December –
booking advisable

Carte £19/46

If you want to satisfy the powerful Pavlovian pangs induced by the bounty on display in Borough Market then head for Elliot's Café. This unpretentious spot sources its ingredients directly from the market and has a kitchen that's wise enough not to muck about with them too much. It's open from breakfast time onwards and the menu is concise, regularly changing and instantly appealing. Earthy and uncomplicated dishes like squid with aioli and dukkah, and beef cheek with market-fresh winter vegetables, will leave anyone feeling sated and satisfied; many just pop in for their burger which has quickly established its own fan-base. The appeal of Elliot's Café lies in the fact that it does the simple things well.

Garrison

Mediterranean 🍺

99-101 Bermondsey St
✉ SE1 3XB
☏ (020) 7089 9355
www.thegarrison.co.uk

⊖ London Bridge.
▶ **Plan X**
Closed 25-27 December –
booking essential at dinner

Carte £20/34

You'd be hard pressed to find a more charming pub than The Garrison. With its appealing vintage look, warm atmosphere and delightful staff, it's the perfect antidote to those hard-edged boozers that we've all accidentally found ourselves in at some point. Open from 8am for smoothies and breakfast, it gets busier as the day goes on – and don't bother coming for dinner if you haven't booked. Booth numbers 4 and 5, opposite the open kitchen, are the most popular while number 2 at the back is the cosiest. Daily specials on the blackboard supplement the nicely balanced menu and the cooking is perky and bright, with a subtle Mediterranean slant. Salads are done well and there's a daily steak, while puds are of a more traditional bent.

Goodman City

11 Old Jewry
✉ EC2R 8DU
☎ (020) 7600 8220
www.goodmanrestaurants.com

⊖ Bank
▶ **Plan VIII**
Closed Saturday, Sunday and
bank holidays

Menu £22 (lunch) – Carte £28/77

The Mayfair branch proved such a success that the opening of a second steakhouse was inevitable. For it, they chose the more appropriate setting of a semi-industrial looking space in The City, perfect for this incontestably macho style of food. Steaks are obviously the stars of the show: the corn-fed USDA beef is imported a tonne at a time and wet-matured for 60 days; the Scottish and Irish beef is grass-fed. Competitive eating from suited City types mean that steaks weighing an impressive 700g are the most popular; the meats are cut to order in the kitchen using a band saw. Commendably – and perhaps unusually for a steakhouse – equal care goes into the other dishes, whether that's calamari to start, or a sorbet at the end.

Green

K1

British traditional 🍺

29 Clerkenwell Gn
✉ EC1R 0DU
☎ (020) 7490 8010
www.thegreenec1.co.uk

⊖ Farringdon.
▶ **Plan IX**
Closed 25-30 December

Carte £19/30

29 Clerkenwell Green dates from 1580 and had become a tavern by 1720. It's therefore fitting that, after decades being used firstly as offices and then as a restaurant, The Green is now back to being known as a pub. Appetising and imaginative bar snacks like hog shank on toast are to be had in the ground floor bar, but the intimate upstairs is where the real eating goes on. Here you'll find an appealing menu of fresh, seasonal ingredients which might include Devon crab, Cornish mackerel, Wiltshire trout or Suffolk pork. The traditional fish pie is a favourite of many and the puds on the blackboard continue the British theme. Lunches get pretty busy with those wearing suits but dinner is more relaxed and the clientele in less of a hurry.

Hawksmoor

meats and grills X

M2

10-12 Basinghall St
⊠ EC2V 5BQ
✆ (020) 7397 8120
www.thehawksmoor.com

⊖ Bank
▶ **Plan VIII**
Closed 22 December-2 January,
Saturday, Sunday and bank holidays
– booking essential

Carte £39/62

A/C ⊟ ⊡ ⊗ ⊽ VISA MC AE

Fast and furious, busy and boisterous, the third Hawksmoor provides another testosterone filled celebration of the serious business of beef eating– this is about red meat, red wine and red faced City types in duels to see who can order the biggest steak. It's a handsome room, with its low ceiling, leather seating and wood panelling, which was once used in specimen cupboards at the Natural History Museum. It comes with a great cocktail list and an impressive wine list offering plenty of Mouton Rothschild for when bonuses are handed out. The Longhorn steaks are nicely aged, particularly the D-Rump, and well-rested before coming to the table. With notice you can order 'meat feasts' which take you on a 7-course 'tour of a cow'.

High Timber

modern XX

L3

8 High Timber St.
⊠ EC4V 3PA
✆ (020) 7248 1777
www.hightimber.com

⊖ Mansion House
▶ **Plan VIII**
Closed 25-30 December,
1-4 January, Saturday dinner,
Sunday and bank holidays

Menu £17 (lunch) – Carte £26/55

⋜ ⋔ A/C ⊡ VISA MC AE ⓪

Surprisingly few restaurants in London overlook the river, especially on the north side, so High Timber is already off to a good start. Add an impressive wine cellar with over 900 bins, including much from the owners' homeland of South Africa, and you've virtually guaranteed a good night out. Heavy wood tables and slate floors lend a slightly rustic look to what is the ground floor of a purpose-built office block; but the room has a fluid feel, as diners are encouraged to visit the cellar or indeed the cheese room to make their choice. The highlight of the concise, seasonal menu is the beef from the grill; they use 28-day matured Cumbrian beef, cut to order from the bone. Dishes have a muscular vigour and come served on slate or chopping boards.

Hix Oyster and Chop House

British traditional ✕

L2

36-37 Greenhill Rents
✉ EC1M 6BN
✆ (020) 7017 1930
www.hixoysterandchophouse.co.uk

⊖ Farringdon
▶ **Plan IX**
Closed 25-29 December, bank holidays,
Saturday lunch and Sunday dinner

Menu £18 (lunch and early dinner) – Carte £27/59

Utilitarian surroundings, seasonal British ingredients, plenty of offal and prissy-free cooking: this may sound like a description of St John but was in fact Mark Hix's first solo venture and the start of his rapidly expanding restaurant empire. Smithfield Market seems an appropriate location for a restaurant that not only celebrates Britain's culinary heritage with old classics like rabbit brawn, nettle soup and beef and oyster pie but also reminds us of our own natural bounty, from sand eels and asparagus, whiting to laver bread. It's also called an Oyster and Chop House for a reason, with four types of oyster on offer as well as plenty of meat, including Aberdeen beef aged for 28 days and served on the bone.

José 😀

Spanish ✕

M5

104 Bermondsey St
✉ SE1 3UB
✆ (020) 7403 4902
www.josepizarro.com

⊖ London Bridge
▶ **Plan X**
Closed Christmas and Sunday dinner
– bookings not accepted

Carte approx. £25

Included on any list of 'things to be enjoyed while standing up' must surely be the eating of tapas. Here at this snug Bermondsey tapas bar they don't take bookings, but fear not – just turn up and you'll get in because they pack 'em in like boquerones and that adds to the charm. The eponymous José was formerly with Brindisa in Borough Market, so he knows what he's doing and is usually found at the counter carving the wonderful acorn-fed Iberico ham. Five plates per person should be more than enough but it's hard to stop ordering when you see what the person next to you has got. The food is dictated by the markets; you'll find the daily fishy dishes on the blackboard. There's a great list of sherries and all wines are available by the glass.

 Ⓝ Jugged Hare

British traditional 🍽️🍺

42 Chiswell St   ⊖ Barbican.
✉ EC1Y 4SA   ▶ **Plan VIII**
☎ (020) 7614 0134   Booking advisable
www.thejuggedhare.com

Carte £23/51

A/C

The famous 18C recipe created by Hannah Glasse, the UK's first domestic goddess, provided the inspiration for the renaming of this Grade II listed pub, previously known as The King's Head. It's an apt name because committed vegetarians may feel ill at ease – and not just because of the collection of glass cabinets in the bar which showcase the art of taxidermy. The atmospheric and appealingly noisy dining room, which has a large open kitchen running down one side, specialises in stout British dishes, with Denham Estate venison, Yorkshire guinea fowl and Cumbrian Longhorn steaks from the rotisserie and the grill being the highlights. If the main course doesn't fill you, puddings like treacle tart or bread and butter pudding will.

VISA
MC
AE
①

Kenza

Lebanese 🍴🍴

10 Devonshire Sq.   ⊖ Liverpool Street
✉ EC2M 4YP   ▶ **Plan VIII**
☎ (020) 7929 5533   Closed Saturday lunch,
www.kenza-restaurant.com   Sunday and bank holidays

Menu £21 (lunch) – Carte £15/30

A/C

Proving that a party atmosphere and good food are not mutually exclusive, Kenza's Middle Eastern exotica instantly transports you away from the city institutions above. It's not easy to find which adds a frisson of expectation, as does descending the staircase into a room full of Moroccan tiles, beaded lamps, lanterns, silk cushions, mosharabi screens and thumping lounge music. Most of the menu is Lebanese but with Moroccan influences; meze is varied and satisfying and the best main courses are slow-cooked lamb shoulder, chargrilled chicken and marinated swordfish; all meat is Halal. Larger parties need not waste time choosing and can order the 'feasting' menus thus allowing more time to appreciate the skills of the belly dancers.

VISA
MC
AE
①

Luc's Brasserie

French 🍴🍴

17-22 Leadenhall Mkt
✉ EC3V 1LR
✆ (020) 7621 0666
www.lucsbrasserie.com

Menu £18 – Carte £25/64

⊖ Bank
▶ **Plan VIII**
Closed 24 December-2 January, Saturday,
Sunday and bank holidays – booking essential
at lunch – (lunch only and dinner Tuesday-
Thursday)

Go into Leadenhall Market and look up – that's Luc's Brasserie, a restaurant which first appeared in the late 1890s and was reinvigorated and re-launched in 2006. The top floor is fairly sedate but the main room - from where you can admire the Victorian splendour of the market – is where the action is. The menu is an unapologetic paean to all things French, from snails to steak tartare, confit of duck to crème brûlée. The kitchen wisely sticks to conventional and classic recipes and it's easy to see why ties are quickly loosened. Staff do their bit by getting on with things but do so with a smile. As one would expect, the mood relaxes somewhat on the three nights they open for dinner, when a fixed price menu is also available.

Lutyens

modern 🍴🍴🍴

85 Fleet St.
✉ EC4Y 1AE
✆ (020) 7583 8385
www.lutyens-restaurant.com

Menu £26/22 – Carte £28/61

⊖ St Paul's
▶ **Plan VIII**
Closed 1 week Christmas-New Year,
Saturday, Sunday and bank holidays

Having built one restaurant empire, Sir Terence Conran appears to have embarked on creating another. Lutyens opened in 2009 following the success of Boundary, and boasts that unmistakeable Conran look: timeless and effortless good looks mixed with functionality. He also found another building of note: the restaurant is within what was the HQ of Reuters and is named after its architect, Sir Edwin. The menu is an appealing Anglo-French affair, with an assortment of classics ranging from parfaits and fruits de mer to Dover sole and roast grouse, along with dishes from the rotisserie; sushi even makes an incongruous appearance. Service is clued-up but perhaps a little more formal than it needs to be. There's a busy bar on the Fleet Street side.

Magdalen

152 Tooley St.
✉ SE1 2TU
☎ (020) 7403 1342
www.magdalenrestaurant.co.uk

⊖ London Bridge
▶ **Plan X**
Closed bank holidays,
Sunday and lunch Saturday

Menu £16 (weekday lunch) – Carte £27/40

A/C
VISA
MC
AE

The Magdalen's kitchen is a clever one: super sourcing and direct contact with farmers take care of the ingredients; the cooking demonstrates a solid, unshowy technique and the influences are kept largely from within the British Isles. Shoulder of Middle White pork with fennel and lemon is a highlight and the rabbit leg with broad beans leaves you wondering why this meat isn't sold in every supermarket. French toast with apricots and vanilla ice cream provides a suitably comforting finale. The lunch menu is a steal, the wine list has been thoughtfully put together by someone who knows the menu well and staff are an eager, genial bunch. The restaurant is divided between two floors; it's unusually more fun on the ground floor.

Manicomio

6 Gutter Ln.
✉ EC2V 8AS
☎ (020) 7726 5010
www.manicomio.co.uk

⊖ St Paul's
▶ **Plan VIII**
Closed 1 week Christmas, Saturday,
Sunday and bank holidays

Carte £27/51

A/C
VISA
MC
AE

You'll find this sibling to the King's Road branch on the first floor of a Norman Foster designed building. On the ground floor is the deli/café while the bar is kept separately on the top floor and is away from the restaurant, which makes a nice change in this part of town. The owners' other business is importing Italian produce so they know their cipollas. There's also plenty of British meat, game and fish but prepared in an Italian way, with top notch Italian accompaniments. The cooking covers many regions, with daily specials; one or two side dishes are needed for the main course and these, together with the bread, may bump the final bill up somewhat. The room has a bright, fresh feel and all the furniture is imported from Italy.

Medcalf

K1

British traditional ✗

40 Exmouth Mkt.
✉ EC1R 4QE
✆ (020) 7833 3533
www.medcalfbar.co.uk

⊖ Farringdon
▶ **Plan IX**
Closed 31 December-3 January,
Sunday dinner and bank holidays –
booking essential

Carte £25/30

There is something very 'proper' about Medcalf: maybe it's the no-frills décor celebrating the original butcher's shop that was here from 1912 (the lights are held up by meat hooks); maybe it's the loud and buzzy pub-like atmosphere, with the good range of draught beers, wines by the glass and assorted snacks; or maybe it's the fresh, appealing and very seasonal British cooking, with dishes like Barnsley chop or calves liver, which has a satisfyingly robust, masculine feel to it. Whatever it is, it works as the restaurant gets very busy, very quickly. Those who think jellies and foams should only be found at children's playtime rather than on a dinner plate will find much to celebrate here at Medcalf.

The Mercer

M3

modern ✗✗

34 Threadneedle St
✉ EC2R 8AY
✆ (020) 7628 0001
www.themercer.co.uk

⊖ Bank
▶ **Plan VIII**
Closed 25 December, Saturday,
Sunday and bank holidays

Menu £39/49 – Carte £26/40

The credit crunch means it's even less likely that a restaurant will ever be converted into a bank so, at the moment, the trend remains from bank to restaurant; here at The Mercer you can even see where the tellers used to sit. The high ceilings and windows let in plenty of light and the place has a pleasingly animated brasserie feel, with service that is slick and well paced. Open from breakfast, the kitchen concentrates on familiar flavours and comforting classics. While the cooking may not always live up to the promise of the menu, it is nonetheless satisfying. Scottish beef features in the Grill section and there are daily specials which could be corned beef hash or a fish pie. There's a huge choice of wines by the glass or carafe.

Mint Leaf Lounge

Indian 🍴🍴

12 Angel Ct., Lothbury
✉ EC2R 7HB
📞 (020) 7600 0992
www.mintleaflounge.com

⊖ Bank
▶ **Plan VIII**
Closed 22 December-3 January,
Saturday lunch and Sunday

Menu £18 (lunch) – Carte £29/51

This was formerly NatWest's HQ and has been turned into a stylish and slick Indian restaurant. The bar is bigger and the dining area smaller than the original branch in St James's, but with the stock market the way it's been, you can't blame them for that. The menu cleverly allows for flexibility in that many of the dishes are available in both starter and main course size and the presentation on the plate is quite contemporary. The majority of influences come from the more southerly parts of India and dishes demonstrate genuine care in preparation. Fish, meat or vegetarian platters are available and there's a good value set lunch menu. Knowledgeable staff in ubiquitous black provide nicely paced service.

The Modern Pantry

other world kitchens 🍴

47-48 St John's Sq.
✉ EC1V 4JJ
📞 (020) 7553 9210
www.themodernpantry.co.uk

⊖ Farringdon
▶ **Plan IX**
Closed 25-26 December and
1 January – booking advisable

Menu £20 (lunch) – Carte £28/41

This Georgian building has been everything from a foundry to a carpentry workshop but these days plays host to New Zealander Anna Hansen's fusion restaurant. The smart glass doors lead into a simple, crisp space; there's an upstairs too, split between two rooms, which offers a little more intimacy but lacks the buzz of downstairs. The kitchen's peregrinations are reflected in a menu that has few boundaries. You'll probably need to ask for an explanation of at least one ingredient but the staff are clued up, which is no mean feat since menus change daily as ingredients come in. Despite all that's happening on the plate, flavours are well-judged and complementary. Most dishes also come with thoughtfully suggested wine matches.

Ⓝ Morgan M

50 Long Ln
✉ EC1A 9EJ
✆ (020) 7609 3560
www.morganm.com

⊖ Barbican
▶ **Plan VIII**
Closed 24-30 December,
Saturday lunch and Sunday

Menu £26 (lunch and early dinner) – Carte £41/51

Morgan Meunier, a proud Frenchman from Champagne, moved his Islington restaurant lock, stock and barrel to this spot opposite Smithfield Market in late 2011, hoping to gain a few new customers whilst also keeping hold of the ones he's nurtured over the years. Things are kept in a classical vein, from the formally dressed dining room to the menu rooted in French tradition; the choice is between seasonal or vegetarian set menus or the à la carte, with the lunch menu doubling as the pre-theatre. The cooking exhibits plenty of bold flavours, although occasionally the hand can be a little heavy. Small plates are served downstairs, where bookings aren't taken. The serving team give you their full attention.

Morito

32 Exmouth Mkt
✉ EC1R 4QE
✆ (020) 7278 7007
www.morito.co.uk

⊖ Farringdon
▶ **Plan IX**
Closed 24 December-3 January and
bank holidays – bookings not accepted

Carte approx. £25

Morito may not seduce you with its looks but once you start eating you'll find it hard to tear yourself away. This authentic tapas bar comes courtesy of the owners of next door Moro and shares their passion for Moorish cuisine. It's modestly kitted out but endearingly so, with a two-tone formica counter and half a dozen small tables; just turn up and if they haven't got space they'll take your number and you can have a drink in Exmouth Market while you wait. Seven or eight dishes between two should be enough but at these prices you can never overspend. Highlights of the immensely appealing menu include jamon and chicken croquetas and succulent lamb chops with cumin and paprika, all served in authentic earthenware dishes.

Moro

34-36 Exmouth Mkt
✉ EC1R 4QE
✆ (020) 7833 8336
www.moro.co.uk

⊖ Farringdon
▶ **Plan IX**
Closed 24 December-3 January,
bank holidays and Sunday dinner –
booking essential

Carte £28/37

Not only has Moro been a feature of Exmouth Market for over 15 years, but it's still one of the busiest restaurants around. Anyone left frustrated by not getting a table should consider just pitching up and sitting at the zinc-topped bar: it's a great spot for tapas and some wonderful sherries, you'll get the full benefit of the wondrous aromas from the open kitchen and be able to watch the chefs in action. Moorish cooking is the draw which means Spain and the Muslim Mediterranean. The wood-burning oven and charcoal grill provide the smokiness and charring to improve and enhance the poultry, meat and sourdough bread. The cooking is colourful and invigorating and the menu changes fully every two weeks.

1901

Andaz Liverpool Street Hotel,
Liverpool St. ✉ EC2M 7QN
✆ (020) 7618 7000
www.andaz.com

⊖ Liverpool Street
▶ **Plan VIII**
Closed Christmas,
Saturday lunch and Sunday

Menu £25 (lunch) – Carte £34/51

1901 is the redecorated, rebranded and relaunched version of what was previously called Aurora. It's one of several restaurants within the Andaz hotel and is very much their flagship. This is a hugely impressive room, which they've painted white to make the eye-catching cupola even more striking. A cocktail bar has been added, along with a cheese and wine room; the cheeses being of predominantly British provenance. The cooking is mostly French in preparation and technique but stoutly British in terms of the ingredients it uses. A refined and delicate touch is evident in dishes such as poached halibut with saffron potatoes and the smoked haddock boudin. There is an army of staff on hand who are well-practised but also friendly.

North Road ✿

69-73 St John St
✉ EC1M 4AN
✆ (020) 3217 0033
www.northroadrestaurant.com

⊖ Farringdon
▶ **Plan IX**
Closed 23 December- 2 January,
Saturday lunch and Sunday

Menu £25 (weekday lunch)/67 – Carte £36/45

VISA

North Road

Tired of cooking alone at his restaurant 'Fig' in Barnsbury, chef-owner Christoffer Hruskova made the move to a more conspicuous neighbourhood when he took over the premises previously occupied by The Clerkenwell Dining Rooms. Consequently, he is enjoying far greater exposure in these coolly designed and elegantly understated surroundings. His Danish roots and culinary training are most evident on the plate: dishes are prepared using little or no butter or cream, he makes expert use of sous-vide techniques but often keeps the actual cooking of ingredients to a minimum by serving many items either raw or smoked, sometimes in hay. He is also fully respectful of the seasons and his produce is largely sourced from small suppliers around the British Isles, including fish from Cornwall and Dorset, shellfish from Scotland, herbs from Kent and meat from Norfolk. The spacious dining room is equally devoid of unnecessary frills and frippery and its clean, fresh feel suits the style of cooking perfectly.

First Course

- Scallops, carrot, sea buckthorn and sea urchin.
- Pickled mackerel and buttermilk, cucumber and dill.

Main Course

- Breast, tail and loin of English rose veal with morel broth.
- Monkfish and 'bakskud', sea vegetables and seaweed butter.

Dessert

- Birch parfait, malt and Douglas fir pine.
- 'Strawberry field'.

Oxo Tower

modern

K4

Oxo Tower Wharf (8th floor), Barge House St
✉ SE1 9PH
✆ (020) 7803 3888
www.harveynichols.com

⊖ Southwark
▶ **Plan X**
Closed 25 December,
dinner 24 December and lunch 26
December

Carte £44/67

There can be few brighter restaurants than this one on the 8th floor of the Oxo Tower, thanks to its huge windows and enthusiastic application of white paint. The menu provides a fairly promising read, with dishes made up of ingredients from the luxury end of the spectrum, although the kitchen doesn't always quite deliver the goods. Meanwhile, service is a little more ceremonial than the brasserie next door and all this is reflected in the prices – the final bill can dazzle as much as the surroundings, so at least try to get a table by the window to make it memorable. Lunchtimes are largely invaded by city types from across the river, while at night the restaurant becomes a popular setting for those celebrating special occasions.

Oxo Tower Brasserie

modern X

K4

Oxo Tower Wharf (8th floor), Barge House St
✉ SE1 9PH
✆ (020) 7803 3888
www.harveynichols.com

⊖ Southwark
▶ **Plan X**
Closed 24 December dinner and
25 December

Carte £34/57

The light-filled, glass-encased brasserie on the eighth floor of the iconic Oxo Tower makes much of its riverside location but that's not to say that this is just a spot for a summer's day as the bold, zingy Mediterranean flavours ensure that the cooking is bright and sunny even when it's dull outside. They've moved the bar to the front so that everyone gets a better view these days. Even so, if you've never asked for a window table before, then now is the time to start. Better still, ask for the terrace and face east towards St Paul's for the best views. Staff do their bit by being a responsive bunch and the place really rocks in the evenings. It's much more fun than their restaurant and the prices are friendlier too.

Paternoster Chop House

British traditional ✗

L3

Warwick Ct., Paternoster Sq.
✉ EC4M 7DX
☎ (020) 7029 9400
www.paternosterchophouse.co.uk

Menu £23 – Carte £30/49

⊖ St Paul's
▶ **Plan VIII**
Closed 22 December-2 January,
Saturday,
Sunday dinner and bank holidays

If you could make just one restaurant legally obliged to serve British food then it would probably be the one that lies in the shadow of St Paul's Cathedral, one of Britain's most symbolic landmarks. Fortunately, Paternoster Chop House negates the need for a bye-law by offering classics from all parts of these isles. The first thing you see on the neatly laid-out menu is the comfortingly patriotic sight of a 'Beer of the Day'. Their livestock comes from small farms, their fish from day boats in the southwest and all the old favourites are present and correct: native oysters, cottage pie, potted hough, liver and bacon, and apple crumble. The dining room is large and open; you might have to fight your way through the busy bar.

Peasant

British modern

L1

240 St John St
✉ EC1V 4PH
☎ (020) 7336 7726
www.thepeasant.co.uk

Menu £28/35 – Carte £25/36

⊖ Farringdon.
▶ **Plan IX**
Closed 25 December-1 January and bank
holidays except Good Friday –
booking essential

From the outside it may be starting to look its age, but this senior member of the gastropub movement still pulls in plenty of punters. Come evening, you have two choices: stay in the bar and compete for a spare table with the city boys having a post-work pint, or book a table in the sanctuary of the sedate upstairs dining room with its circus-themed prints and posters. Downstairs comes with an easy, eat-on-the-hoof type of menu: squid tempura and sharing boards such a cheese or meze stand out and are ideal accompaniments to a pint. In the restaurant, dishes such as sea bream with capers and brown shrimps, and honey-roast duck with celeriac purée, come with a greater degree of sophistication but still deliver on flavour.

Le Pont de la Tour

N4

36d Shad Thames, Butlers Wharf
✉ SE1 2YE
✆ (020) 7403 8403
www.lepontdelatour.co.uk

⊖ London Bridge
▶ **Plan X**

Menu £18, £30/45

For over 20 years, Le Pont de la Tour has been the flagship restaurant of the Butlers Wharf development. Decoratively, it may not look quite as striking as it did in 1991 but there is no doubting the glory of its location, especially in summer when you can sit on the terrace and look out over the river and Tower Bridge. During the week the place is largely populated by noisier corporate types but at weekends the room takes on a more romantic air. The set price menu, which includes a few dishes which carry supplements, is not dissimilar to that found in a bistro moderne, but if you want even more rustic choices such as pork rillettes or coq au vin then sit in the livelier cocktail bar and grill, with its evening pianist.

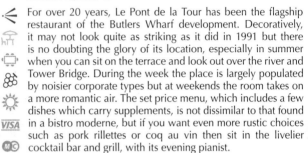 Pizarro

M5

171-173 Bermondsey St
✉ SE1 3UW
✆ (020) 7378 9455
www.josepizarro.com

⊖ Borough
▶ **Plan X**
Closed 24-28 December –
(bookings not taken at dinner
and weekend lunch)

Carte £23/30

José Pizarro has a refreshingly simple way of naming his establishments: first came José, a bustling tapas bar, and now there's Pizarro, a larger, more structured restaurant a few doors down. Neither place take reservations so be prepared to wait, even though there's not a great deal of bar space here to do so. It is, though, worth persevering for a seat at one of the counters facing the street or the kitchen, at the large communal table or even at the prized semi-circular booths, because the food's good and the atmosphere fun. Go for the small plates; dishes such as prawns with piquillo peppers and jamón are as tasty as they are easy on the eye. Larger plates could include hake with artichoke and pork fillet with mash and almonds.

Redhook

89 Turnmill St
✉ EC1M 5QU
☎ (020) 7065 6800
www.redhooklondon.com

⊖ Farringdon
▶ **Plan IX**
Closed Easter, 25 December,
Saturday lunch and Sunday –
bookings advisable at dinner

Brooklyn comes to Clerkenwell in the shape of Redhook, an appealingly designed American-style restaurant whose refreshingly unambiguous menu specialises in seafood and steaks. There's assorted fish and some pasta on the menu but most diners will be busy chowing down on the Canadian lobster or the assorted cuts of beef which come from Scotland, Ireland and the US; even that '70s symbol of culinary excess, 'surf & turf', makes a comeback here. The kitchen handles the ingredients with care and desserts are not as sweet as those served in the US. Staff contribute to the pleasant atmosphere; California dominates the wine list and the bare brick walls, booths and a faux industrial aesthetic add to the New York feel.

Restaurant at St Paul's Cathedral

L3

British modern X

St Paul's Churchyard
✉ EC4M 8AD
☎ (020) 7248 2469
www.restaurantatstpauls.co.uk

⊖ St Paul's
▶ **Plan VIII**
Closed Easter and 25 December –
booking advisable – (lunch only)

Menu £26 – Carte approx. £29

Tucked away in a corner of the crypt of Sir Christopher Wren's 17C masterpiece is this earnest little restaurant, offering respite to tired tourists and weary worshippers. The kitchen prepares everything from scratch and rightly promotes and celebrates all things British in both the food and the accompanying list of drinks – even the back of the menu is graced with a collection of interesting local food facts. Start by sharing some nibbles such as wild boar salami or potted shrimp; move on to corned beef hash or a shepherd's pie and finish with a comforting Bakewell tart or some Neal's Yard cheeses. Service is done on the run but the staff are a friendly bunch and if you stay put for long enough, they'll start serving afternoon tea.

Rhodes Twenty Four ✿

British modern XXX

Tower 42, (24th floor) 25 Old Broad St
✉ EC2N 1HQ
℡ (020) 7877 7703
www.rhodes24.co.uk

⊖ Liverpool Street
▶ **Plan VIII**
Closed Christmas-New Year, Saturday,
Sunday and bank holidays

Carte £38/64

Enduring the airport-like security in the lobby of Tower 42 and having your ears pop as the lift speeds you up to the 24th floor are both worth it because the views from this restaurant on the 24th floor are great and the food is even better. The main restaurant overlooks the 'Gherkin' while the private dining rooms look across at the 'Shard'— but do ask for a window table otherwise you won't see much. This being The City means that your fellow diner is more likely to be the male of the species in a suit, but come a little later in the evening and the room begins to fill with people paying their own bill and not talking business. A Gary Rhodes menu is instantly recognisable as he's never needed a passing bandwagon to champion British produce or use words like 'pie', 'crumble' and 'pudding'. His team of protégés in the kitchen ensure that the dishes come without unnecessary adornment and that they deliver on flavour. The serving team are slick and efficient but shouldn't be afraid of exhibiting a little more personality.

First Course	Main Course	Dessert
• Glazed lobster omelette thermidor.	• Steamed mutton and onion suet pudding with buttered carrots.	• Rhodes Twenty Four signature pudding plate.
• Game pie with celeriac and game gravy.	• Stone bass with creamed celeriac and wild mushrooms.	• Bread and butter pudding.

Roast

M4

The Floral Hall, Borough Mkt
✉ SE1 1TL
✆ (0845) 3473 00
www.roast-restaurant.com

⊖ London Bridge
▶ **Plan X**
Closed 25-26 December and 1 January
– booking essential

Carte £34/60

It's in the one place where you don't look when you find yourself in the deliciously enticing surroundings of Borough Market – up. Jump into the lift and upstairs you'll be greeted and led into a vast room; the best seats are in the raised section beyond the bar. It's always busy here and the young team are a friendly bunch, although they can sometimes appear to be a man down. The food is all about being British and proud of it, reflecting the values of the market below and the importance of provenance. Start with the cocktail of the week, move on to Cornish herring or Arbroath smokie, followed by roast lamb or steak and onion pudding and finish with a Bakewell tart or rhubarb crumble. You'll leave whistling 'Land of Hope and Glory'.

Sauterelle

M3

The Royal Exchange
✉ EC3V 3LR
✆ (020) 7618 2483
www.sauterelle-restaurant.co.uk

⊖ Bank
▶ **Plan VIII**
Closed Saturday,
Sunday and bank holidays,

Menu £20/35 – Carte £33/55

Sauterelle enjoys a hugely impressive setting on the mezzanine floor of The Royal Exchange and looks down over the Grand Café below which was the original trading floor. This City landmark was rebuilt in 1844, but its layout remains largely true to Sir Thomas Gresham's 1565 original. The striking ceiling and ornate arches add to the already comfortable feel of the restaurant. The menu is largely French, but more contemporary than classic which means the addition of the occasional Italian note. The kitchen certainly doesn't skimp on luxury ingredients: foie gras, turbot, Anjou pigeon and Pyrenean lamb make regular appearances and are appreciated by big spending customers for whom the credit crunch is but a distant memory.

St John ⊛

L2

26 St John St
✉ EC1M 4AY
☎ (020) 3301 8069
www.stjohnrestaurant.com

Carte £25/43

⊖ Farringdon
▶ **Plan IX**
Closed Christmas-New Year, Saturday
lunch, Sunday dinner and bank
holidays, – booking essential

St John

Despite opening a Soho outpost, there's been no drop in standards here. The walls, painted in a shade of detention centre white, add to the utilitarian feel of the room which was a smokehouse in the 19C. There's no standing on ceremony; indeed no ceremony at all, and that makes dining at St John such a joyful experience as the focus is entirely directed at the food. You can play it safe and go for some crab and then roast beef but this is the place to try new flavours, whether that's the cuttlefish or the ox tongue. Game is a real favourite and the only gravy will be the blood of the bird – this is natural, 'proper' food. Seasonality is at its core – the menu is rewritten for each service – and nothing sums up the philosophy more than the potatoes and greens: they are always on the menu but the varieties and types change regularly. The waiters wear chef's jackets and spend time in the kitchen so they know what they're talking about. There are dishes for two as well as magnums of wine for real trenchermen – and be sure to order a dozen warm madeleines to take home.

First Course
- Roast bone marrow and parsley salad.
- Asparagus and hot butter.

Main Course
- Roast Middle White loin and braised fennel.
- Ox tongue and chips.

Dessert
- Eccles cake and Lancashire cheese.
- Gooseberry trifle.

Skylon

modern XXX

1 Southbank Centre, Belvedere Rd
✉ SE1 8XX
✆ (020) 7654 7800
www.skylon-restaurant.co.uk

⊖ Waterloo
▶ **Plan III**
Closed 25 December
and Sunday dinner

Menu £29, £45/45

The original Skylon was a steel structure built for the Festival of Britain in 1951 to promote better quality design. Its name now lives on as the restaurant within the Royal Festival Hall, which was built just yards from where this 'vertical feature' once stood. The South Bank is now a much appreciated area of London and the restaurant offers wonderful river views. It's a large space, with a busy central cocktail bar, a formally laid out restaurant on one side and a simpler grill-style operation on the other. The latter serves fishcakes, burgers, steaks and the like; the restaurant uses more expensive ingredients and puts a modern spin on classic combinations. Be sure to ask for a window table.

Tapas Brindisa

Spanish X

18-20 Southwark St, Borough Market
✉ SE1 1TJ
✆ (020) 7357 8880
www.tapasbrindisa.com

⊖ London Bridge
▶ **Plan X**
Bookings not accepted

Carte £16/31

The owners spent years importing Spanish produce so it was no surprise that their restaurant on the edge of Borough Market took off immediately. It not only provided the blueprint for many of the tapas bars that subsequently sprung up over London but was also one of the first restaurants not to take bookings— a less welcome but still understandable policy that has also become more widespread. The place has an infectious energy and vitality and the young staff are as efficient as they are unflappable. Start with a glass of Fino and crisp parcels of morcilla, then share a selection of hand-carved Ibérico hams and robust, generously sized dishes such as Galician style hake, black rice with squid and braised ox cheeks.

CITY OF LONDON, CLERKENWELL, FINSBURY & SOUTHWARK ▶ PLAN III

241

Tate Modern (Restaurant)

British modern ✗

L4

Tate Modern (7th floor), Bankside ⊖ Southwark
✉ SE1 9TG ▶ **Plan X**
✆ (020) 7887 8888 Closed 24-26 December –
www.tate.org.uk (lunch only and dinner Friday-Saturday)

Carte £24/37

Floor to ceiling windows on two sides and a large mural on a third allow light and colour to fill this large restaurant on the 7th floor of the Tate Modern and balance all that black. Even if you don't get a window table you'll still get a great view of St Paul's. There's seating for 145 but they stop taking reservations when they get to 100 to allow for the impulse diner. Lunch starts at 11.30 and ends at 3pm so there's every possibility of getting in but waiting at the bar is no hardship. The menu is an appealing mix of light, seasonal, fresh and zesty dishes, with a daily fish from Newlyn. The influences are mostly British, with the occasional Italian note. There's a good choice of wines by the glass and carafe as well as interesting soft drinks.

28°-50° Fetter Lane

French ✗

K3

140 Fetter Ln ⊖ Temple
✉ EC4A 1BT ▶ **Plan VIII**
✆ (020) 7242 8877 Closed Saturday,
www.2850.co.uk Sunday and bank holidays

Menu £16 (lunch) – Carte £27/35

All things vinous are celebrated at this cellar restaurant and wine bar, which is named after the latitudes between which most wine-making grapes are grown. Owned by the people behind Texture restaurant, it offers a good choice of grilled meats, charcuterie, cheese and assorted European dishes – and all the dishes come with a pleasing, underlying simplicity which allows the wine star billing. Oenophiles will appreciate the carefully compiled wine list which consists of 17 reds and 17 whites, all available by the glass, carafe and bottle; sherries and dessert wines are not forgotten either. The Collector's List offers some real gems; the cross section of regions is spot on and the wines are served at their perfect temperatures.

Vanilla Black

Vegetarian ✗✗

17-18 Tooks Ct.
✉ EC4A 1LB
☎ (020) 7242 2622
www.vanillablack.co.uk

⊖ Chancery Lane
▶ **Plan VIII**
Closed 2 weeks Christmas-New Year,
Saturday lunch and Sunday

Menu £19, £24/35

[A/C]
[𝒱]
VISA
MC
AE

Those who think vegetarian food is all nut cutlets and knitted muesli should get along to Vanilla Black. Run by a Teesside couple who had a restaurant of the same name in York, they prove that vegetarian food can be varied, flavoursome and filling. The room is neat but quite stark and crisp in its decoration; sufficient warmth comes from the owner and her team of waiting staff. The set-priced menu represents fair value and the cooking displays sufficient originality and imagination. Certainly no one leaves hungry as the flavoursome dishes use liberal amounts of cheese and potato. This is a proper restaurant that could heal the wounds of any carnivore scarred in their youth by an unpleasant vegetarian experience.

Village East

modern ✗

171-173 Bermondsey St
✉ SE1 3UW
☎ (0207) 3576 082
www.villageeast.co.uk

⊖ London Bridge
▶ **Plan X**
Closed 25-26 December

Carte £23/50

[A/C]
[⊡]
[☼]
VISA
MC
AE

Clever name - sounds a bit downtown Manhattan; but while Bermondsey may not be London's East Village, what Village East does is give this part of town a bit more 'neighbour' and a little less 'hood'. It's tricky to find so look for the glass façade and you'll find yourself in one of the bars, still wondering if you've come to the right place. Once, though, you've seen the open kitchen you know the dining area's not far away. Wood, brick, vents and large circular lamps give it that warehouse aesthetic. The menu is laid out a little confusingly but what you get is ample portions of familiar bistro-style food, as well as some interesting combinations. The separately priced side dishes are not really needed and can push the bill up.

Vinoteca

modern ✗

L2

7 St John St.
✉ EC1M 4AA
✆ (020) 7253 8786
www.vinoteca.co.uk

⊖ Farringdon
▶ **Plan IX**
Closed 25-26 December, 1 January,
bank holidays and Sunday

Carte £18/31

Vinoteca, a self-styled 'bar and wine shop', comes divided into two tiny rooms and is always so busy that you'll almost certainly have to wait for a table. But what makes this frenetic place so special is the young and very passionate team who run it so well. The wine list is thrilling: it is constantly evolving and covers all regions, including less familiar territories along with the organic and the biodynamic. In circumstances such as these, the food can often be an afterthought but here it isn't. Alongside the cheeses and the cured meats that are available all day are classic dishes like pear, chicory and Roquefort salad; potted shrimps; bavette steak and panna cotta; all fresh tasting, well-timed and enjoyable.

Vivat Bacchus

other world kitchens ✗

K2

47 Farringdon St
✉ EC4A 4LL
✆ (020) 7353 2648
www.vivatbacchus.co.uk

⊖ Farringdon
▶ **Plan VIII**
Closed Christmas and New Year, Saturday,
Sunday and bank holidays

Menu £15/19 – Carte £22/50

Both the name and the Paul Cluver barriques outside offer clues about the make-up of this bustling City spot: it revolves around wine and the owner is South African. From four cellars come a hugely impressive 500 labels and 15,000 bottles, not only paying homage to major players like Château Latour, d'Yquem, Lafite and Romanée Conti, but also featuring South African jewels like Meerlust Rubicon – if you can button-hole owner Gerrie, he'll give you a tour. The restaurant attracts an ebullient City crowd and the menu complements the wine: steaks and charcuterie dominate and the sharing platters are perfect with a glass or three. Ostrich and kangaroo also feature and you can choose your perfectly ripened cheese from the cheese room.

Vivat Bacchus London Bridge

M4 o t h e r w o r l d k i t c h e n s ✕✕

4 Hays Ln
✉ SE1 2HB
☎ (0207) 2340 891
www.vivatbacchus.co.uk

⊖ London Bridge
▶ **Plan X**
Closed Christmas and New Year,
Saturday lunch, Sunday
and bank holidays

Menu £15/19 – Carte £22/50

The owners have sensibly avoided the temptation to tamper with a winning formula and so their second branch closely follows the style of the original in The City. That means a packed wine bar on the ground floor where city types quaff wines with relish and feast on 'world platters' from assorted countries. This then leads down to a slightly industrial looking basement restaurant, with a fantastic cellar and cheese room. Buying 'en primeur', they have created an impressive list with a large South African section and such is their enthusiasm that staff almost drool over oenophiles. The food is appropriately robust and also contains South African specialities, including the excellent roast springbok. Be sure to sample the cheese.

Well

L1 B r i t i s h m o d e r n 🍴🍺

180 St John St
✉ EC1V 4JY
☎ (020) 7251 9363
www.downthewell.com

⊖ Farringdon.
▶ **Plan IX**
Closed 25-26 December

Carte £24/36

The Well is perhaps more of a locals pub than many others found around these parts. It's all quite small inside but, thanks to some huge sliding glass windows, has a surprisingly light and airy feel, and the wooden floorboards and exposed brick walls add to the atmosphere of a committed metropolitan pub. Monthly changing menus offer modern dishes ranging from potted shrimps to foie gras and chicken liver parfait or sea trout and samphire, as well as classic English puddings like Eton Mess and some particularly good cheeses. The downstairs bar with its seductive lighting and fish tank is only available for private hire; check out the picture of a parched desert and a well which follows the curve of the wall on your way down.

CITY OF LONDON, CLERKENWELL, FINSBURY & SOUTHWARK ▶ PLAN X

The White Swan

modern ✗✗

K2

108 Fetter Ln
✉ EC4A 1ES
✆ (020) 7242 9696
www.thewhiteswanlondon.com

⊖ Chancery Lane
▶ **Plan VIII**
Closed 25-26 December, Saturday,
Sunday and bank holidays

Menu £16/36 – Carte £26/39

A/C
VISA
M©
AE

You'll find something akin to an assault course at the White Swan because to get to the first floor restaurant you have to fight your way through the drinkers in the ground floor bar and, at lunch time, this is more challenging than you think. Once upstairs, you'll find a small, neat room and service that is polite and friendly but also well-paced and professional. The mirrored ceiling and large windows add plenty of light, although the closeness of the tables can make private conversation tricky. However, the cooking is good enough to induce the odd contented silence. It is classical in its base but with the occasional contemporary tweak and dishes display a certain refinement. Pricing is also fair when one considers the location.

Wright Brothers

fish and seafood ✗

M4

11 Stoney St., Borough Market
✉ SE1 9AD
✆ (020) 7403 9554
www.thewrightbrothers.co.uk

⊖ London Bridge
▶ **Plan X**
Closed bank holiday Mondays –
booking advisable

Carte £26/41

VISA
M©
AE

If you want to take a breather from the hordes at Borough Market then nip into Wright Brothers, but do it early as it quickly fills. Their motto is 'not just oysters' but then they do excel in them – hardly surprising when you consider that this small place started as an oyster wholesaler. Grab a table and enjoy them raw or cooked, by candlelight, along with the perfect accompaniment – a glass of porter – or else share a bench or the counter and opt for a platter of fruits de mer and a bottle of chilled Muscadet. If the bivalve is not your thing, then there are daily specials such as skate knobs, as well as pies and, for dessert, either chocolate truffles or crème brûlée. An air of contentment reigns.

Zucca

M5

184 Bermondsey St
✉ SE1 3TQ
☎ (020) 7378 6809
www.zuccalondon.com

⊖ Borough
▶ **Plan X**
Closed 24 December-10 January,
Easter, Sunday dinner and Monday –
booking essential at dinner

Carte £18/27

[A/C]
⟨⟩
[V]
⅍
VISA
⊕
AE

The suitably fresh faced young chef-owner seems to have got it all pretty spot-on: the simple but informed Italian cooking is driven by the ingredients, the prices are more than generous, the room is bright and crisp and the service, sweet and responsive. The antipasti forms the largest part of the weekly changing menu and the hard part – especially if you're sharing – is knowing when to stop ordering; but do always include the zucca fritti – the pumpkin speciality. The kitchen team are an unflustered group, largely because they don't fiddle with the food and know that less equals more. The freshly baked breads come with Planeta olive oil; there are usually two pasta dishes and the aromas that fill the room make it hard to leave.

The sun is out – let's eat alfresco! Look for 🛱.

Chelsea · Earl's Court · Hyde Park · Knightsbridge · South Kensington

Though its days of unbridled hedonism are long gone - and its 'alternative' tag is more closely aligned to property prices than counter-culture - there's still a hip feel to **Chelsea.** The place that put the Swinging into London has grown grey, distinguished and rather placid over the years, but tourists still throng to the **King's Road,** albeit to shop at the chain stores which have steadily muscled out SW3's chi-chi boutiques. It's not so easy now to imagine the heady mix of clans that used to sashay along here, from Sixties mods and models to Seventies punks, but for practically a quarter of a century, from the moment in 1955 when Mary Quant opened her trend-setting Bazaar, this was the pavement to parade down.

Chelsea's most cutting-edge destination these days is probably the gallery of modern art that bears the name of Margaret Thatcher's former favourite, Charles Saatchi. Which isn't the only irony, as Saatchi's outlandishly modish exhibits are housed in a one-time military barracks, the Duke of York's headquarters. Nearby, the traffic careers round **Sloane Square,** but it's almost possible to distance yourself from the fumes by sitting amongst the shady bowers in the centre of the square, or watching the world go by from a prime position in one of many cafés. Having said that, *the* place to get away from it all, and

yet still be within striking distance of the King's Road, is the delightful **Physic Garden,** down by the river. Famous for its healing herbs for over 300 years, it's England's second oldest botanic garden.

Mind you, if the size of a green space is more important to you than its medicinal qualities, then you need to head up to **Hyde Park,** the city's biggest. Expansive enough to accommodate trotting horses on Rotten Row, swimmers and rowers in the Serpentine, up-to-the-minute art exhibitions at the Serpentine Gallery, and ranting individualists at Speakers' Corner, the park has also held within its borders thousands of rock fans for concerts by the likes of the Rolling Stones, Simon and Garfunkel and Pink Floyd.

Just across from its southern border stands one of London's most imperious sights, The **Royal Albert Hall,** gateway to the cultural hotspot that is South Kensington. Given its wings after the 1851 Great Exhibition, the area round **Cromwell Road** invested heavily in culture and learning, in the shape of three world famous museums and three heavyweight colleges. But one of its most intriguing museums is little known to visitors, even though it's only a few metres east of the Albert Hall: the Sikorski is, by turns, a moving and spectacular showpiece for all things Polish.

248

No one would claim to be moved by the exhibits on show in nearby **Knightsbridge,** but there are certainly spectacular credit card transactions made here. The twin retail shrines of Harvey Nichols and Harrods are the proverbial honey-pots to the tourist bee, where a 'credit crunch' means you've accidentally trodden on your visa. Between them, in **Sloane Street,** the world's most famous retail names line up like an A-lister's who's who. At the western end of Knightsbridge is the rich person's Catholic church of choice, the Brompton Oratory, an unerringly lavish concoction in a baroque Italianate style. Behind it is the enchanting Ennismore Gardens Mews, a lovely thoroughfare that dovetails rather well with the Oratory.

Further west along Old Brompton Road is **Earl's Court,** an area of grand old houses turned into bedsits and spartan hotels. An oddly bewitching contrast sits side by side here, the old resting alongside the new. The old in this case is Brompton Cemetery, an enchanting wilderness of monuments wherein lie the likes of Samuel Cunard and Emmeline Pankhurst. At its southwest corner, incongruously, sits the new, insomuch as it's the home of a regular influx of newcomers from abroad, who are young, gifted and possessed of vast incomes: the players of Chelsea FC.

C. Eymenier/MICHELIN

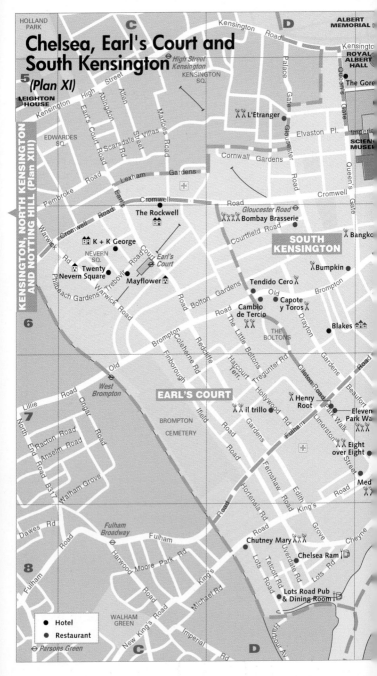

Chelsea, Earl's Court and South Kensington

(Plan XI)

HOLLAND PARK

LEIGHTON HOUSE

ALBERT MEMORIAL

ROYAL ALBERT HALL

The Gore

L'Etranger

Kensington Road

Palace Gate

Queen's Gate

Elvaston Pl.

Imperial

SCIENCE MUSEUM

High Street Kensington

KENSINGTON SQ.

High Street

Allen Street

Abingdon Road

Marloes Road

Scarsdale Villas

Earl's Court Road

Kensington

EDWARDES SQ.

Pembroke Road

Lexham Gardens

Cornwall Gardens

Cornwall Road

Queen's Gate

KENSINGTON, NORTH KENSINGTON AND NOTTING HILL (Plan XIII)

Cromwell Road

The Rockwell

Gloucester Road

Bombay Brasserie

Cromwell Road

SOUTH KENSINGTON

Courtfield Road

Bangko

Warwick Rd

Cromwell Road

K + K George

NEVERN SQ.

Twenty Nevern Square

Philbeach Gardens

Warwick Road

Trebovir Road

Earl's Court Road

Mayflower

Earl's Court

Bolton Gardens

Bumpkin

Tendido Cero

Old Brompton Road

Cambio de Tercio

Capote y Toros

Drayton Gardens

Blakes

THE BOLTONS

The Little Boltons

Redcliffe

Brompton Road

Coleherne Rd

Finborough Road

Old Brompton Road

West Brompton

EARL'S COURT

Harcourt Terr.

Treguntar Rd

Hollywood Rd

Gilston Road

Beaufort

Lillie Road

Ongar Road

Tracton Road

North End Road B317

Anselm Road

Waltham Grove

BROMPTON CEMETERY

il trillo

Ifield Road

Gardens

Fulham Road

Fernshaw Road

Henry Root

Park Walk

Limerston St

Eleven Park Wa

Eight over Eight

Edith Grove

Med

Dawes Rd

Fulham Road

Fulham Broadway

Harwood Road

Moore Park Rd

Fulham Road

Hortensia Rd

King's Road

King's Road

Telcott Rd

Uverdale Rd

Cheyne

Chutney Mary

Chelsea Ram

WALHAM GREEN

New King's Road

Michael Rd

King's Road

Lots Road

Lots Rd.

Lots Road Pub & Dining Room

Imperial Rd

Harbour Av

• Hotel
• Restaurant

Parsons Green

250

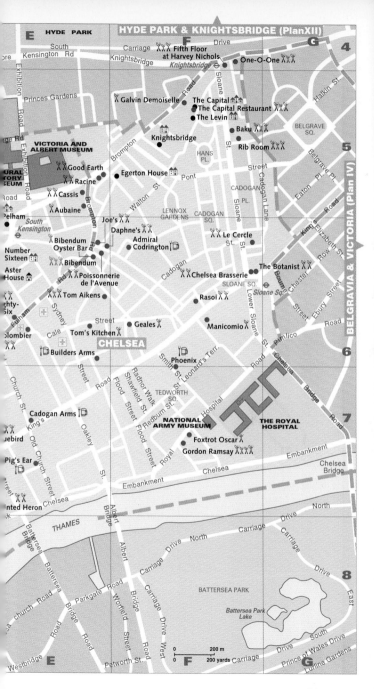

E   HYDE PARK

F   G   4

South Kensington Rd

Knightsbridge

Carriage   Drive

Fifth Floor at Harvey Nichols

Knightsbridge

One-O-One

Princes Gardens

Exhibition Road

Galvin Demoiselle

The Capital
The Capital Restaurant
The Levin

Baku

BELGRAVE SQ.

VICTORIA AND ALBERT MUSEUM

Brompton

Knightsbridge

HANS PL.

St.

Rib Room

5

NATURAL HISTORY MUSEUM

Good Earth

Racine

Cassis

Aubaine

Egerton House

Brompton

Walton St.

Pont   Street

CADOGAN LANE

CADOGAN PL.

Sloane

St.

Belgrave Pl.

Eaton Pl.

King's

Elizabeth St.

BELGRAVIA & VICTORIA (Plan IV)

Road

Pelham

South Kensington

Joe's

Daphne's

LENNOX GARDENS

CADOGAN SQ.

Le Cercle

St.   St.

Number Sixteen

Aster House

Bibendum Oyster Bar

Bibendum

Poissonnerie de l'Avenue

Admiral Codrington

Cadogan

Chelsea Brasserie

The Botanist

Cadogan

SLOANE SQ.

Sloane Sq.

Lower

Chester

Ebury

Row

Street

6

Eighty-Six

Fulham

Sydney

Tom Aikens

Rasoi

Bourn

Sloane

St.

Pimlico

Road

Colombier

Cale

Street

Tom's Kitchen

Geales

Manicomio

CHELSEA

Builders Arms

Smith St.

Radnor Walk

Shawfield St.

St. Leonard's Terr.

Phoenix

Chelsea

Bridge

Road

7

Church St.

Cadogan Arms

Bluebird

Pig's Ear

King's

Old Church Street

Oakley

Flood Street

Redburn St.

Royal

TEDWORTH SQ.

NATIONAL ARMY MUSEUM

Hospital

THE ROYAL HOSPITAL

Chelsea   Bridge

Foxtrot Oscar

Gordon Ramsay

Embankment

Embankment   Chelsea

Chelsea Bridge

Painted Heron   Chelsea

Albert   Bridge

THAMES

Battersea   Bridge

Church Road

Albert   Bridge

Parkgate   Road

Worfield   Street

Carriage   Drive   North

Carriage   Drive

Carriage

Drive

East

8

BATTERSEA PARK

Battersea Park Lake

Westbridge

E

Road

Petworth St.

F

0   200 m
0   200 yards

Prince of Wales Drive

Carriage

Lurline Gardens

G

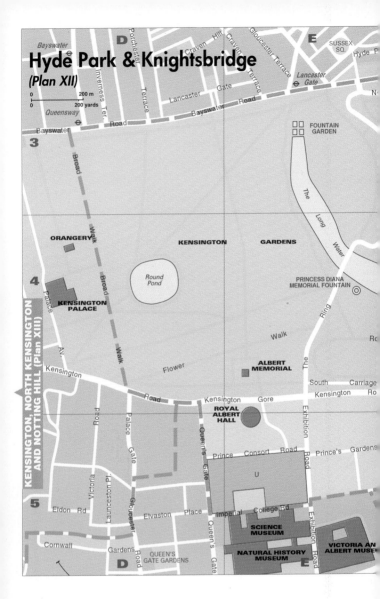

Hyde Park & Knightsbridge
(Plan XII)

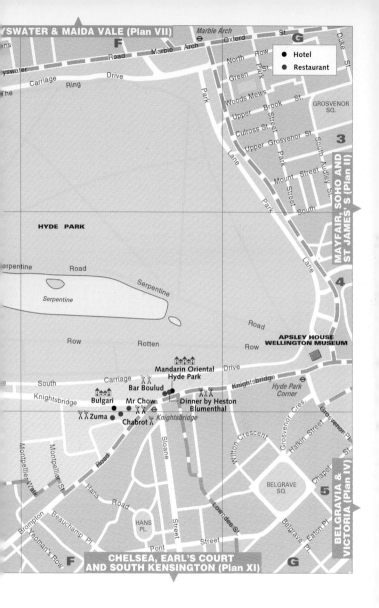

Admiral Codrington

modern

F6

17 Mossop St
✉ SW3 2LY
✆ (020) 7581 0005
www.theadmiralcodrington.com

⊖ South Kensington.
▶ **Plan XI**
Closed 24-26 December

Carte £22/43

If you're going to make one of your pubs the flagship of your bourgeoning organisation then it makes sense to choose the one that has 'Admiral' in its title. Cirrus Inns now run 'The Cod' and managed to touch it all up without tampering with it too much. Lunch means some fresh fish or a club sandwich in either the front bar or the rather smart restaurant with its retractable roof; in the evening the bar sticks to just serving drinks. Start with the terrific snacks, like pork crackling with apple sauce, then head for the more familiar, tried-and-tested dishes from the monthly-changing menu. Beef is big here and is aged in-house; the burgers have become popular, with new combinations communicated by Twitter.

Aubaine

French 🍴

E5

260-262 Brompton Rd.
✉ SW3 2AS
✆ (020) 7052 0100
www.aubaine.co.uk

⊖ South Kensington
▶ **Plan XI**

Carte £22/52

This was the first of the bourgeoning Aubaine brand and it is easy to understand the appeal. A country style aesthetic is coupled with functionality and flexibility, so that a brisk morning coffee trade is followed by brunch, then a more structured lunch and dinner. Influences are European but the kitchen has its feet firmly set in France. Highlights include well-timed scallops and a decent rib-eye. Desserts are presented on a tray, to remind you this is also a place where one can pick up bread and pastries for home. The midday lunching ladies give way to a more mixed crowd in the evenings and service is young and eager. If you've got an appetite, then you may find it pricier than you expected but it's an easy place to like.

Baku

other world kitchens XXX

164 Sloane St (1st Floor) ⊖ Knightsbridge
✉ SW1X 9QB ▶ **Plan XI**
✆ (020) 7235 5399
www.bakulondon.com

Carte £29/56

If evidence is needed that London is the culinary centre of the universe then simply look at the different cuisines on offer. In 2012 Azerbaijan was added to the list thanks to Baku, named after the capital and offering diners a fairly opulent, firmly run restaurant along with a far more characterful bar. Start with a fresh fruit sherbet and then traditional arishta soup. Sturgeon from the Caspian Sea features, both from the tandir and as one of the popular kebabs; and its caviar is there for the big spenders. Try a saj, a choice of meat cooked with peppers and onions on a dome shaped pan, along with plov – saffron rice. Spicing is quite subtle and, as some dishes have been lightened a little, it's worth ordering quite a few dishes.

Bangkok

Thai X

9 Bute St ⊖ South Kensington
✉ SW7 3EY ▶ **Plan XI**
✆ (020) 7584 8529 Closed 24 December-2 January and Sunday
www.bangkokrestaurant.co.uk

Carte £23/33

You don't survive for over 40 years in London's capricious restaurant scene without doing something right. Bangkok opened at a time when few knew what a wok was and was the first restaurant to introduce us to fresh and zesty soups, delicate fishcakes, rich curries and moreish noodles. Over the years, Thai restaurants have sprung up throughout the UK, many of them smart and sophisticated, but Bangkok remains resolutely traditional in both its cooking and its uncomplicated surroundings and for that we should be grateful. The laminated menu lists about 20 dishes and the cooking is so fresh and satisfying and, with such down-to-earth prices, that you feel the restaurant should be sponsored by Thailand's Tourist Board.

Bar Boulud

F4

French 🍴🍴

Mandarin Oriental Hyde Park Hotel,
66 Knightsbridge ✉ SW1X 7LA
☎ (020) 7201 3899
www.barboulud.com

⊖ Knightsbridge
▶ **Plan XII**

Menu £23 – Carte £26/54

[A/C]

Lyon-born Daniel Boulud built his considerable reputation in New York and these two cities now inform the menu here at his London outpost. Order a plate of excellent charcuterie while you look at the menu; sausages are a highlight and there are plenty of classic French dishes, from fruits de mer to coq au vin, but it's the burgers that steal the show. Designed by Adam Tihany, the restaurant makes the best of its basement location which was previously used by the Mandarin Oriental Hotel as a storeroom. Don't think you'll be in exile if they lead you to a table around the corner: it's a good spot and you'll be facing the open kitchen. Service is fast and furious; prices are sensible and the place is noisy, fashionable and fun.

VISA

M/C

AE

Bibendum

E6

French 🍴🍴🍴

Michelin House, 81 Fulham Rd.
✉ SW3 6RD
☎ (020) 7581 5817
www.bibendum.co.uk

⊖ South Kensington
▶ **Plan XI**
Closed 24-26 December and 1 January

Menu £27/30 – Carte £36/66

[A/C]

Bibendum is now well into its twenties but very little has changed over those years, which is why it remains a favourite restaurant for so many. Matthew Harris' cooking continues to produce the sort of food that Elizabeth David would adore – it's mostly French but with a subtle British point of view. The set lunch menu has now been joined by a small à la carte selection; evening menus are handwritten and the roast chicken with tarragon for two remains a perennial presence. Side dishes can bump the final bill up further than expected but the food is easy to eat and satisfying. The striking character of Michelin's former HQ, dating from 1911, is perhaps best appreciated at lunch when the sun lights up the glass Bibendum - the Michelin Man.

VISA

M/C

AE

Bibendum Oyster Bar

fish and seafood ✗

Michelin House, 81 Fulham Rd.
✉ SW3 6RD
☎ (020) 7589 1480
www.bibendum.co.uk

⊖ South Kensington
Closed 24-26 December and
1 January – bookings not accepted

Carte £21/64

The plateau de fruits de mer, for two, is the house speciality here. It includes crab, langoustines, prawns, oysters, winkles and whelks and will leave anyone satisfied and, when the sun is shining, pleased with the world in general. You'll find other appealing classics, from potted shrimps to egg mayonnaise, assorted salads and, predictably enough, a selection of oysters. The accessible wine list includes 460ml pots. It is all served in a relaxed continental-style café, with a mosaic floor and colourful ceramic tiles depicting the early days of French motoring – as befits any establishment located in the former foyer of Michelin House. The crustacea stall and florist at the front of the building attract plenty of passers-by.

Bluebird

British modern ✗✗

350 King's Rd.
✉ SW3 5UU
☎ (020) 7559 1000
www.bluebird-restaurant.co.uk

⊖ South Kensington
▶ **Plan XI**

Menu £25 – Carte £26/47

The last refurbishment may have softened the huge space a little but Bluebird still delivers the atmosphere and excitement one expects from such a large industrial space. A former garage built in 1923, it houses everything from a wine store and café to a food shop and private members club, with the restaurant as the centrepiece. The kitchen champions British produce and highlights its provenance, be it Herdwick mutton, Cumbrian beef or Goosnargh chicken. It also features British cheeses along with seasonal fruit and veg. That being said, not all the dishes are so Anglo-centric: there are assorted pasta choices and the occasional French classic. Sunday roasts and a children's menu ensure that all bases are covered.

Bombay Brasserie

Indian ✗✗✗✗

D6

Courtfield Rd.
✉ SW7 4QH
☎ (020) 7370 4040
www.bombaybrasserielondon.com

⊖ Gloucester Road
▶ **Plan XI**
Closed 25-26 December – bookings
advisable at dinner

Menu £43/48 – Carte £29/47

Going strong since 1982, The Bombay Brasserie has always been one of the smartest Indian restaurants around, but a few years ago it emerged with a brand new look which revitalised the whole place. Plushness abounds, from the deep carpet and huge chandeliers of the large main room to the show kitchen of the conservatory and the very smart bar. The staff also got a new look with their burgundy waistcoats, but they continue to offer charming and professional service. The menu wasn't forgotten either and was overhauled by Hemant Oberoi. They replaced the predictable with the more creative, while at the same time respecting traditional philosophies; influences are a combination of Bori, Parsi, Maharashtrian and Goan cuisine.

The Botanist

modern ✗✗

F6

7 Sloane Sq
✉ SW1W 8EE
☎ (020) 7730 0077
www.thebotanistonsloanesquare.com

⊖ Sloane Square
▶ **Plan XI**
Closed 25-26 December

Carte £29/53

Unlike say New Yorkers, Londoners seemingly prefer their bars separate from their restaurants, which is a shame as The Botanist demonstrates how well the two can coexist. You enter first into the bar and, by osmosis, its general bustle adds to the convivial atmosphere of the adjoining bright and warm restaurant. The place always appears full of people who 'get' what a restaurant should feel and sound like. The menu mixes cheffy descriptions like 'escabeche' with more prosaic words like 'pie' so expect a choice that includes terrines, fish from Billingsgate or more ambitious numbers like pigeon with Puy lentils. Dishes are unfussy in appearance – always a sign of a confident kitchen – and deliver on flavour.

Builders Arms

E6

British traditional 🍺

13 Britten St
✉ SW3 3TY
☎ (020) 7349 9040
www.geronimo-inns.co.uk

⊖ South Kensington.
▶ **Plan XI**
Closed 25-26 December – bookings not
accepted

Carte £21/41

A/C
☀
VISA
MC
AE

The Builders Arms is very much like a packed village local –
the only difference being that, in this instance, the village is
Chelsea and the villagers are all young and prosperous. The
inside delivers on the promise of the smart exterior but don't
expect it to be quiet as drinkers are welcomed just as much
as diners. In fact, bookings are only taken for larger parties
but just tell the staff that you're here to eat and they'll sort
you out. The cooking reveals the effort that has gone into the
sourcing of some decent ingredients; the rib of beef for two
is a perennial favourite. Dishes are robust and satisfying and
are not without some flair in presentation. Wine is also taken
seriously and their list has been thoughtfully put together.

Bumpkin

D6

British traditional ✗

102 Old Brompton Rd
✉ SW7 3RD
☎ (020) 7341 0802
www.bumpkinuk.com

⊖ Gloucester Road
▶ **Plan XI**

Carte £30/37

A/C

☀
VISA
MC
AE

Their slogan is "for city folk who like a little country living",
which is exactly the reason why many of the moneyed in this
prosperous neighbourhood bought weekend retreats. This
Bumpkin follows the success of the Notting Hill branch and
they've largely repeated the formula by creating a restaurant
with a pub-like informality that champions British produce. The
rear room, with its large open-plan kitchen, is the more fun of
the two and service is spirited and friendly. Quarterly printed
menus double as placemats, with additional daily specials on
the board. Expect lots of pies, burgers using Welsh Black beef
and hotpots, with the simpler dishes often being the best ones.
Weekend brunches and Sunday roasts are very popular.

Cadogan Arms

British traditional

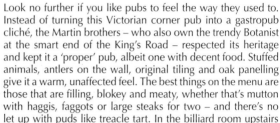

298 King's Rd
✉ SW3 5UG
✆ (020) 7352 6500
www.thecadoganarmschelsea.com

⊖ South Kensington.
▶ **Plan XI**
Closed 25-26 December – bookings
advisable at dinner

Carte £25/36

A/C
☼
VISA
M©
AE

Look no further if you like pubs to feel the way they used to. Instead of turning this Victorian corner pub into a gastropub cliché, the Martin brothers – who also own the trendy Botanist at the smart end of the King's Road – respected its heritage and kept it a 'proper' pub, albeit one with decent food. Stuffed animals, antlers on the wall, original tiling and oak panelling give it a warm, unaffected feel. The best things on the menu are those that are filling, blokey and meaty, whether that's mutton with haggis, faggots or large steaks for two – and there's no let up with puds like treacle tart. In the billiard room upstairs you'll find three American 8-ball pool tables available to hire by the hour; snacks can be had up there too.

Cambio de Tercio

Spanish ✗✗

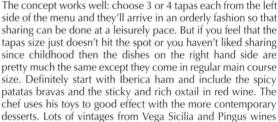

163 Old Brompton Rd.
✉ SW5 0LJ
✆ (020) 7244 8970
www.cambiodetercio.co.uk

⊖ Gloucester Road
▶ **Plan XI**
Closed 25 December

Menu £40 – Carte £18/54 s

A/C
☐
▤
⑰
⅍
☼
VISA
M©
AE
①

The concept works well: choose 3 or 4 tapas each from the left side of the menu and they'll arrive in an orderly fashion so that sharing can be done at a leisurely pace. But if you feel that the tapas size just doesn't hit the spot or you haven't liked sharing since childhood then the dishes on the right hand side are pretty much the same except they come in regular main course size. Definitely start with Iberica ham and include the spicy patatas bravas and the sticky and rich oxtail in red wine. The chef uses his toys to good effect with the more contemporary desserts. Lots of vintages from Vega Sicilia and Pingus wines feature, along with Alion and Roda. Service gets better the more you visit. They also own the tapas bar across the road.

The Capital Restaurant

The Capital Hotel,
22-24 Basil St. ⊠ SW3 1AT
𝒸 (020) 7591 1202
www.capitalhotel.co.uk

⊖ Knightsbridge
▶ **Plan XI**
Booking essential

Menu £25 (lunch)/75 – Carte £44/58

The Capital Hotel has always felt a little like a smart country house transplanted to London, so it is perhaps fitting that its restaurant is elegant, restrained and thoroughly well dressed. The staff are as charming as they are efficient and service is as polished as the silver; there is even a little theatre, with the rack of lamb, for instance, carved at the table. The French kitchen is classically trained but the presentation of the dishes leans more towards the modern and ingredients are suitably luxurious, with ravioli filled with foie gras and omelettes made with lobster. The wine list comes with an impressive international reach and includes wines from the owner's own estate in the Loire Valley.

Capote y Toros

157 Old Brompton Road
⊠ SW5 0LJ
𝒸 (020) 7373 0567
www.cambiodetercio.co.uk

⊖ Gloucester Road
▶ **Plan XI**
Closed Sunday and Monday – (dinner only)

Carte £14/51

From the owners of not-quite-next-door Cambio de Tercio comes the compact and vividly coloured Capote y Toros which celebrates sherry, tapas and ham. Named after the matador's cape and his foe, there are enough bullfighting references to satisfy enthusiasts of Hemingway proportions, including a large wall of photos. However, it is sherry that takes centre stage and there's a huge variety and choice on offer. Those as yet unmoved by this most underappreciated of wines should start by trying 5 varieties in a 'flight'. Meanwhile, the menu revolves around about 25 dishes; try 3 per person. The Iberico ham is excellent and the octopus will make the queuing worthwhile – bookings aren't taken. Sherry is also used extensively in the cooking.

Cassis

French 🍴🍴

E5

232-236 Brompton Rd.   ⊖ South Kensington
✉ SW3 2BB   ▶ **Plan XI**
☎ (020) 7581 1101   Closed 25 December
www.cassisbistro.co.uk

Menu £21/55 – Carte £30/68

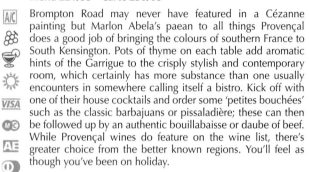

Brompton Road may never have featured in a Cézanne painting but Marlon Abela's paean to all things Provençal does a good job of bringing the colours of southern France to South Kensington. Pots of thyme on each table add aromatic hints of the Garrigue to the crisply stylish and contemporary room, which certainly has more substance than one usually encounters in somewhere calling itself a bistro. Kick off with one of their house cocktails and order some 'petites bouchées' such as the classic barbajuans or pissaladière; these can then be followed up by an authentic bouillabaisse or daube of beef. While Provençal wines do feature on the wine list, there's greater choice from the better known regions. You'll feel as though you've been on holiday.

Le Cercle

French 🍴🍴

F6

1 Wilbraham Pl.   ⊖ Sloane Square
✉ SW1X 9AE   ▶ **Plan XI**
☎ (020) 7901 9999   Closed Christmas and New Year, Sunday,
www.lecercle.co.uk   Monday and bank holidays

Menu £19/35 – Carte £24/38

Knowing this is owned by the same team as Club Gascon may lead to the raising of false hopes, as this is an altogether different operation. Le Cercle positions itself as a fashionable stop on the celebrity circuit and has the unsmiling receptionist and the managers with Secret Service ear pieces to prove it. Lunch sees a bewildering mix of business types and senior local ladies but what is certain is that it all comes alive at dinner; and its drapes and high ceiling do give it a fairly striking look. Where it does follow the same theme as its City sister is in the menu format, whereby you order three or four small dishes per person from the various sections. Dishes are nicely balanced and the French flavours pronounced.

Chabrot

F5

French ✗

9 Knightsbridge Grn
✉ SW1X 7QL
☎ (020) 7225 2238
www.chabrot.co.uk

⊖ Knightsbridge
▶ **Plan XII**
Closed 25 December and 1 January

Menu £23 (dinner) – Carte £27/57

A/C
🎱
☼
VISA
MC
AE
①

In 2011 Thierry Laborde, formerly of Le Gavroche, got together with three friends – a sommelier, a restaurant manager and a florist – to open Chabrot, a bistro that couldn't be more French if it wore a beret and sang 'La Mer'. The kitchen looks to the SW of France and the Basque country for most of its inspiration. Sharing a board of Basque charcuterie is a good way to start and there are plenty of hearty offerings like roast foie gras as a main course, along with snails, octopus skewers and veal-stuffed cabbage. Add a few daily specials and a plat du jour and there should be something for everyone. If you really can't decide on what to order, the tables are so close you can simply take a peek at what your neighbour has chosen.

Chelsea Brasserie

F6

French ✗✗

The Sloane Square Hotel,
7-12 Sloane Sq. ✉ SW1W 8EG
☎ (020) 7896 9988
www.sloanesquarehotel.co.uk

⊖ Sloane Square
▶ **Plan XI**
Closed Sunday dinner

Menu £24/28 – Carte £31/54

A/C
🎭
VISA
MC

If you're not going on to either the Royal Court or Cadogan Hall theatres then it may be best to alert your waiter; they are clearly so used to getting their customers fed and watered before curtain up that they sometimes find it hard to shift down a gear later on. It's no surprise that it is so busy early evening because their theatre menus represent excellent value. The menus, like the waiters, are mostly French born with some intercontinental experience. Vegetarians get plenty of choice and carnivores should be satisfied with the selection from the grill. The cooking has a breezy confidence and hits the spot. The front section of the restaurant attached to the bar is more fun, while tables at the back are quieter.

Chelsea Ram

British modern ❭◻

D8

32 Burnaby St
✉ SW10 0PL
✆ (020) 7351 4008
www.geronimo-inns.co.uk/thechelsearam

⊖ Fulham Broadway.
▶ **Plan XI**
Closed 25 December

Menu £25/30 – Carte £19/33

A/C

VISA

M©

AE

It's easy to see why the Chelsea Ram is such a successful neighbourhood pub: its somewhat secreted position means there are few casual passers-by to upset the peace, the locals appreciate the relaxed and warm feel of the place and the pub provides them with just the sort of food they want. That means proper pub grub, with highlights being things on toast, like chicken livers or mushrooms, and the constant presence of favourites like The Ram burger or haddock and leek fishcake; prices are fair and portions large. They do take bookings but somewhat reluctantly, as they always want to keep a table or two for that spontaneous visit. The Chelsea Ram's winning formula is that it's comfortable just being what it is – a friendly, reliable local.

Chutney Mary

Indian XXX

D8

535 King's Rd.
✉ SW10 0SZ
✆ (020) 7351 3113
www.realindianfood.com

⊖ Fulham Broadway
▶ **Plan XI**
Closed dinner 25 December – (dinner only and lunch Saturday-Sunday)

Menu £20/45 – Carte £33/53

A/C

VISA

M©

AE

When Chutney Mary opened in 1990 it signalled the arrival of a new-wave of cosmopolitan Indian restaurants. Instead of the basic beer and curry house aesthetic we got smart surroundings, regional specialities, cocktails and even suggested wine pairings for the meal – and it's a combination that is still working successfully today. The place is deceptively large and comes with framed silks, mirrors, candles and prints; if you're a couple then ask for a table in the slightly less hectic conservatory. Dishes come from all across India and range in style from luxurious fish dishes from the south to redefined street food. The kitchen uses plenty of British produce and employs chefs from the different Indian regions to ensure authenticity.

Le Colombier

French 🍴🍴

145 Dovehouse St.   ⊖ South Kensington
✉ SW3 6LB   ▶ **Plan XI**
☎ (020) 7351 1155
www.le-colombier-restaurant.co.uk

Menu £20 (lunch) – Carte £32/60

Le Colombier is as warm and welcoming as it is honest and reliable and thereby offers proof that being a good neighbourhood restaurant takes more than just being in a good neighbourhood. French influences abound, from the accents of the staff and the menu content to the inordinate amount of double cheek kissing that occurs – most of the customers appear to know one another or feel they should like to know one another. In summer, when the full-length windows fold back, the terrace is the place to sit although the under-floor heating ensures the place is equally welcoming in winter. Oysters, game in season, veal in various forms and regional cheeses are the highlights, as are the classic desserts from crêpe Suzette to crème brûlée.

Daphne's

Italian 🍴🍴

112 Draycott Ave.   ⊖ South Kensington
✉ SW3 3AE   ▶ **Plan XI**
☎ (020) 7589 4257   Closed 25-26 December – booking
www.daphnes-restaurant.co.uk   essential

Carte £29/49

One wonders if theatrical agent Daphne Rye opened her eponymous restaurant as a means of keeping her resting actors busy. Forty years on and Daphne's is a chic Chelsea institution; there's even a branch in Barbados for those who can't live without their vongole on holiday. The narrow room is Tuscan in its look and the best seats are those at the front by the large windows. The many regulars clearly like the reassurance of familiarity so the kitchen sticks largely to a tried and tested assortment of Italian classics but prepared with greater care than one usually expects in an Italian restaurant with a 'celebrity' following. The lunch menu is good value and the occasional new dish, like salt-baked sea bass, gets in under the radar.

Dinner by Heston Blumenthal ✿

F4

Mandarin Oriental Hyde Park Hotel, ⊖ Knightsbridge
66 Knightsbridge ⊠ SW1X 7LA ▶ Plan XII
✆ (020) 7201 3833
www.dinnerbyheston.com

Menu £32 (weekday lunch) – Carte £50/65

Mandarin Oriental Hyde Park

For a country with a less than stellar reputation for the quality of its food, we need reminding sometimes about the glories of our own culinary heritage. So hats off then to Heston Blumenthal because his mischievously named restaurant at the Mandarin Oriental Hyde Park should stir feelings of pride in all of us regarding our native cuisine. Don't come expecting 'molecular' alchemy; the menu reads like a record of historic kitchen triumphs, with the date of origin attached to each dish and a fashionably terse list of its parts; on the reverse you can read more. A kitchen brigade of 45 works with calm efficiency, meticulous attention to detail and intelligence to produce food that looks deceptively 'simple' but tastes sublime. The large, light room has quirky touches, like wall sconces shaped as jelly moulds, but the main focus is on the open kitchen, with its oversized watch mechanics powering the spit to roast the pineapple that goes with the Tipsy Cake (c.1810).

First Course	*Main Course*	*Dessert*
• Mandarin meat fruit.	• Spiced pigeon with ale and artichokes.	• Tipsy cake with spit-roast pineapple.
• Nettle porridge.	• Cod in cider.	• Chocolate bar.

Eight over Eight

Asian 🍴🍴

392 King's Rd
✉ SW3 5UZ
☏ (020) 7349 9934
www.rickerrestaurants.com

⊖ South Kensington
▶ **Plan XI**
Closed 24-27 December

Carte £19/54

A major fire a few years ago meant that Eight over Eight stayed shut for quite a few months, but anyone who missed it too much during this period needed only to nip up to Notting Hill to find another one of Will Ricker's trendy Asian restaurants. From the day it reopened it has been full, so maybe its customers are more loyal than anyone thought; they are certainly a handsome bunch and many of them seem to know one another. The restaurant was largely unchanged in its look; it just feels a little plusher and is better lit. Wisely, they didn't change the menu either; its influences stretch across a number of countries in South East Asia and dishes are designed for sharing. Highlights are the creamy curries and anything that's crispy.

Eighty-Six

modern 🍴🍴

86 Fulham Rd, (1st Floor)
✉ SW3 6HR
☏ (020) 7052 9620
www.86restaurant.co.uk

⊖ South Kensington
▶ **Plan XI**
Closed 24-29 December and Sunday
– (dinner only)

Menu £21 – Carte £33/55

If you want proof that the economic meltdown barely troubled the inner reaches of Chelsea then come along to this converted Georgian townhouse, as it's not just its name that evokes the carefree days of the '80s. Catering to those who know their Verbier from their Verdelho, it mixes three decorative styles – baroque, rococo and bling – to create a glamorous, gilded jewel for SW3's young movers and shakers. Upstairs from the cocktail bar is the dining room, where you'll find an over-eager service team and a dinner menu that roams around Europe. Here, the kitchen's strengths lie in the simpler, more rustic dishes, especially those that make use of British ingredients and rare breeds such as Tamworth pork or Galloway beef.

Eleven Park Walk

D7

Italian 🍴🍴🍴

11 Park Walk
✉ SW10 0AJ
℘ (020) 7352 3449
www.11parkwalk.co.uk

⊖ South Kensington
▶ **Plan XI**
Closed 25 December

Carte £29/64

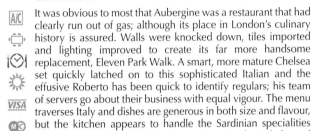

It was obvious to most that Aubergine was a restaurant that had clearly run out of gas; although its place in London's culinary history is assured. Walls were knocked down, tiles imported and lighting improved to create its far more handsome replacement, Eleven Park Walk. A smart, more mature Chelsea set quickly latched on to this sophisticated Italian and the effusive Roberto has been quick to identify regulars; his team of servers go about their business with equal vigour. The menu traverses Italy and dishes are generous in both size and flavour, but the kitchen appears to handle the Sardinian specialities with added care. The menu can get quite pricey but is balanced by a wine list that offers plenty of choice for under £25.

L'Etranger

D5

innovative 🍴🍴

36 Gloucester Rd.
✉ SW7 4QT
℘ (020) 7584 1118
www.etranger.co.uk

⊖ Gloucester Road
▶ **Plan XI**
Booking essential

Menu £25 (lunch) – Carte £31/57

Messing around with classic French cooking is considered sacrilegious in certain parts of France but L'Etranger has escaped the tyranny of tradition by locating itself in South Kensington, London's own little Gallic ward. It offers an eclectic mix off French dishes that are heavily influenced by Japan, so a veal chop will come with wasabi sauce and salmon is poached in sake. Not every dish has a Nipponese constituent but it certainly makes for an original experience. The room is dark and moody and better suited to evenings, while service is a little more formal than it need be. The clientele is a mix of well-heeled locals and homesick French and Japanese émigrés, who also appreciate the depth and breadth of the impressive wine list.

Fifth Floor at Harvey Nichols

modern XXX

F4

109-125 Knightsbridge
✉ SW1X 7RJ
☏ (020) 7235 5250
www.harveynichols.com

⊖ Knightsbridge
▶ **Plan XI**
Closed Christmas and Sunday dinner

Menu £25 – Carte £35/48

Pressure is now on the restaurant to hold its own against the alluring look of the revamped and well stocked food hall, here on the fifth floor of Harvey 'Nics'. It certainly seems to have got its appearance right by not being too stuffy and it handles the contrasting nature of lunch and dinner with aplomb: for the former it's mostly shoppers and at night is far more intimate. Dishes are bright, light and unfussy and some of the starters and mains are now available as tasting plates, which either catches the zeitgeist by providing greater flexibility or is a tacit acknowledgment that its clientele could never be accused of overeating. What the staff may lack in wit they more than make up for in the looks department.

Foxtrot Oscar

British traditional X

F7

79 Royal Hospital Rd.
✉ SW3 4HN
☏ (020) 7352 4448
www.gordonramsay.com/foxtrotoscar

⊖ Sloane Square
▶ **Plan XI**
Closed 25 December – booking essential

Menu £18/25 – Carte £23/53

There are always plenty of locals in Foxtrot Oscar, which is not something you can say about many of Gordon Ramsay's restaurants. The fact that this is probably his least known is perhaps a factor. The burgundy walls and black and white photos give it an almost '80s bistro feel and there's also a downstairs, which is actually quite a nice spot and not merely an overflow. The lunch menu is appealing priced; the dinner à la carte is more mixed. Your best bet is to skip the starters and head for something braised or slow-cooked which should satisfy anyone's hunger. Another good choice is the Foxtrot burger, which arrives on a board, accompanied by tomato relish and some enormous chips. Regulars are well looked after.

CHELSEA, SOUTH KENSINGTON, EARL'S COURT, HYDE PARK & KNIGHTSBRIDGE ▶ PLAN XI

 Galvin Demoiselle

French ✗

Ground Floor Food Hall, Harrods,
87-135 Brompton Rd ✉ SW1X 7XL
☎ (020) 7730 1234
www.galvinrestaurants.com

⊖ Knightsbridge
▶**Plan XI**
Closed 25 December and Sunday dinner
– bookings not accepted

Carte £31/36

A/C
VISA
MC
AE
①

The Galvin brothers' bourgeoning company now includes this smart and distinctively dressed café, which you'll find on the mezzanine floor of Harrods food hall. Their French-accented menu sensibly acknowledges the unavoidable truth that most people are in the building primarily to shop and so you won't find anything too heavy, elaborate or time consuming. A different soup is served each day, along with a choice of five salads; there's assorted charcuterie and carefully prepared, easy-to-eat dishes like cocottes or their popular baked lobster fishcake. You can also pop in for morning coffee and a pastry or afternoon tea and a French Fancy and, although it's not inexpensive, they have got the tone and style of the service just right.

Geales

fish and seafood ✗

1 Cale St.
✉ SW3 3QT
☎ (020) 7965 0555
www.geales.com

⊖ South Kensington
▶ **Plan XI**
Closed 25-26 December,
1-2 January and Monday

Menu £10 – Carte £21/39

A/C
◌
☼
VISA
MC
AE

Good fish and chips shouldn't just be the preserve of visiting tourists who are hoping to catch up on new episodes of the Benny Hill Show while they're here. We all need reminding of their appeal sometimes and, for this, there is Geales. Don't be fooled by the "Established 1939" sign outside, as this branch opened in 2010. It occupies the site of Tom Aikens' short-lived chippy but the extraction system has clearly improved as there has been no uprising by locals worried about frying fumes permeating their Colefax and Fowler. The place is charmingly decorated, cosy and warmly run and the menu successfully mixes the classics with the more modern, so there's fried haddock along with soft shell crab tempura. Puds are wholesome and homemade.

Good Earth

Chinese

233 Brompton Rd.
✉ SW3 2EP
☏ (020) 7584 3658
www.goodearthgroup.co.uk

⊖ Knightsbridge
▶ **Plan XI**
Closed 23-31 December

Carte £21/48

The Brompton Road branch of this small chain has been a reliable constant for many a year and is suitably authentic on all levels: the service is brisk, the menu lengthy, cooking is dependable and desserts are not worth bothering with. There is no particular bias, save for a few Sichuan dishes, but they do use plenty of higher-end ingredients like scallops and Dover sole. Included among the set menus is the Lobster Dinner, a reminder of the restaurant's location and target market. More unusual dishes are often introduced but it's the old favourites and classic combinations that sell. Unlike most restaurants spread over two floors, here the basement level is actually the busier and more popular choice than the ground floor.

Henry Root

French 𝕏

9 Park Walk
✉ SW10 0AJ
☏ (020) 7352 7040
www.thehenryroot.com

⊖ South Kensington
▶ **Plan XI**
Closed 25-27 December – booking advisable

Carte £21/42

It was from his flat in Park Walk that satirist William Donaldson skewered many of the good and the great of his day through the letters of his eccentric alter ego, Henry Root. Now this little restaurant in the same street has adopted his name, which is surely a far better tribute than any blue plaque. The decoration is an appropriately curious mix of styles so expect everything from Jimi Hendrix photos to a stuffed salmon. The menu is appealingly divided into nibbles, salads, small plates, main courses and charcuterie. Terrines and ballotines are done well, as are traditional offerings like coq au vin or sea bass with cucumber and beetroot. Puddings often include a couple delivered from the nursery end of dessert-making.

CHELSEA, SOUTH KENSINGTON, EARL'S COURT, HYDE PARK & KNIGHTSBRIDGE ▶ PLAN XI

Gordon Ramsay ✿ ✿ ✿

French XXXX

F7

68-69 Royal Hospital Rd.
✉ SW3 4HP
✆ (020) 7352 4441
www.gordonramsay.com

⊖ Sloane Square
▶ **Plan XI**
Closed Christmas, Saturday and
Sunday – booking essential

Menu £45/95

A/C
🍴🟢
🍇
VISA
MC
AE

Gordon Ramsay Holdings

The steadfast Jean-Claude is one of London's most experienced maitre d's and has been a reassuring presence here at Gordon Ramsay's flagship restaurant since the day it opened. He has instilled in his team the same care and passion for the art of service as he has demonstrated over the years; they are not only effortlessly composed but also undertake their work without the slightest arrogance or aloofness. The result is that an air of calm pervades this bright and fresh looking room, which was designed by the ubiquitous David Collins. Meanwhile, in the kitchen, head chef Clare Smyth is now revealing more of her own personality through her cooking; the menu being a little more daring and the combinations more original. The Menu Prestige offers the complete experience, with G. Ramsay classics alongside Clare's newer creations, but her passion is most evident in the exquisite dishes from the Seasonal Inspiration dinner menu. Just like Claude, Clare looks at every detail: a dainty little silver trowel stops you getting cocoa from the chocolate petit fours on your fingers.

First Course

- Poached Scottish lobster tail with lardo di colonnata and vegetables à la grecque.
- Sautéed foie gras with roasted veal sweetbreads.

Main Course

- Suckling pig, crispy belly, roasted loin, sausage, chou farci and braised leg.
- Fillet of sea bass, monk's beard, oyster and caviar sauce.

Dessert

- Lemonade parfait with honey, bergamot and sheep's milk yoghurt sorbet.
- Blackcurrant, fennel and yoghurt génoise with violet sorbet.

il trillo

Italian ✗✗

D7

4 Hollywood Rd
✉ SW10 9HY
✆ (020) 3602 1759
www.iltrillo.net

⊖ Earl's Court
▶ **Plan XI**
Closed 2 weeks August, 2 weeks Christmas
and Monday – (dinner only and lunch
Saturday-Sunday)

Carte £29/57

The Bertuccelli family have been making wine and running a restaurant in the Tuscan Hills for over 30 years. Two of the brothers are now in London, running this smart neighbourhood restaurant which showcases the produce and wine from their region. A third brother, who's an architect, designed the room and nearly everything was brought over from Italy, from the marble to the tables and chairs. Most of the ingredients are shipped over weekly too, either from their own farm or suppliers they've known for years. The cooking is gutsy and the breads and homemade pasta stand out, as does the signature dish of stuffed onions cooked in Vermentino. The courtyard has been transformed into a pleasant decked garden, complete with lemon trees.

Joe's

modern ✗✗

E6

126 Draycott Ave
✉ SW3 3AH
✆ (020) 7225 2217
www.joseph.co.uk

⊖ South Kensington
▶ **Plan XI**
Closed 24-26 December, Easter Sunday and
dinner Sunday-Monday

Menu £20 (lunch) – Carte £23/34

Back in the '80s when the only thing bigger than the hair were the shoulder pads, Joe's was the place to be seen. Three decades later, it is once again a fashionable hang-out but this time a less excitable one with better food. The concise fortnightly changing menu is understated but at the same time appealingly intriguing. The cooking is fresh and vibrant and comes with Mediterranean overtones. Daily changing pulses and diminutive desserts give some clues as to the target audience, while midweek breakfasts and weekend brunches will power-up shoppers for the day ahead. Tables just past the bar are best for people-watching; those beyond are suited to anyone wanting to escape those prying eyes. Service is engaging but relaxed.

CHELSEA, SOUTH KENSINGTON, EARL'S COURT, HYDE PARK & KNIGHTSBRIDGE ▶ PLAN XI

Lots Road Pub & Dining Room

British traditional

D8

114 Lots Rd
✉ SW10 0RJ
✆ (020) 7352 6645
www.lotsroadpub.com

⊖ Fulham Broadway.
▶ **Plan XI**

Carte £21/31

Lots Road Pub and its customers are clearly happy with one another as it has introduced a customer loyalty scheme, whereby anyone making their fifth visit is rewarded with a discount. Lunch is geared more towards those just grabbing a quick bite but dinner sees a choice that could include oysters, mussels or a savoury tart; the Perthshire côte de boeuf is the house speciality. There are also pies and casseroles, in appropriate pub-like sizes, and even salads for those after something light. Service remains bright and cheery, even on those frantic Thursday nights when the pub offers 'Thursday Treats' with wine tasting and nibbles. The only disappointment is the somewhat ordinary bread for which they make a not insubstantial charge.

Manicomio

Italian

F6

85 Duke of York Sq., King's Rd.
✉ SW3 4LY
✆ (020) 7730 3366
www.manicomio.co.uk

⊖ Sloane Square
▶ **Plan XI**
Closed 1 January, 24-26 and 31 December

Carte £30/44

If anywhere encapsulates King's Road's journey from counterculture hub to retail playground it is Duke of York Square and its outlets. Among these is Manicomio, a glossy Italian restaurant which doesn't need to rely solely on weary shoppers as it also draws visitors from the Saatchi Gallery next door, a fact that shows just what an inspired location this was. Its success is also helped by an accessible menu, offering a greatest hits of easy-to-eat Italian food. Cooking is undertaken with care and the simplest dishes are the best ones, although prices do reflect the Chelsea postcode. Service remains sufficiently perky for one to forgive occasional moments of forgetfulness. The terrific front terrace fills quickly in nearly all seasons.

Marco

French ✕✕

Stamford Bridge, Fulham Rd.
✉ SW6 1HS
✆ (020) 7915 2929
www.marcorestaurant.org

⊖ Fulham Broadway
▶ **Plan XVIII**
Closed Christmas, Easter,
Sunday and Monday – booking advisable
– (dinner only)

Carte £32/52

A section of Manchester United fans was once derided as being prawn sandwich eaters; London expectations being what they are, at Chelsea's ground you get a brasserie from Marco Pierre White. Some will inevitably cry foul and shed a tear for football's working class roots; others will cheer for this evidence of our growing culinary maturity. Both sides, though, should applaud the menu, which offers classics galore such as grilled Dover sole, assorted roasts and Scottish steaks. This being a polyglot club means other nationalities are also represented, in this case a bit of Italy and France, and more sophisticated fare such as foie gras terrine or duck confit is available. Puddings are a particular highlight.

Mr Chow

F4

Chinese ✕✕

151 Knightsbridge
✉ SW1X 7PA
✆ (020) 7589 7347
www.mrchow.com

⊖ Knightsbridge
▶ **Plan XII**
Closed 1 January, 24-26 December, Easter
Monday dinner and Monday lunch

Menu £25 (lunch) – Carte £38/63

Chinese food, Italian waiters, swish surroundings, steep prices and immaculately coiffured regulars: it's an unusual mix that clearly works because Mr Chow has already celebrated its fortieth birthday. Even if you're not recognisable, you'll get a friendly welcome and the champagne chariot will be wheeled towards you. The laminated menu is long but clearly divided between sections entitled 'from the sea', 'from the land' and 'from the sky'; chickens will be pleased to find themselves in this last category. The cooking is far better than you expect, with genuine care shown. The desserts are thoroughly European and come on a trolley, with tarts the speciality. Your final bill won't be clearly itemised but this doesn't seem to bother anyone.

Medlar ✿

E7

438 King's Rd
✉ SW10 0LJ
✆ (020) 7349 1900
www.medlarrestaurant.co.uk

⊖ South Kensington
▶ **Plan XI**

Menu £26/40

Medlar

Being a customer should be the easiest thing in the world so it can sometimes be a little dispiriting to have to sit through yet another explanation of a restaurant's 'concept'. Medlar proved to be a success from day one precisely because it wasn't trying to be different or original – the two young owners just wanted to have a really great neighbourhood restaurant and that is exactly what they have created here. Both are alumnae of Chez Bruce which proved to be a pretty good blueprint for what they had in mind. David and his front of house team get the tone of the service just right – it's warm, knowledgeable and reassuring but never intrusive, while Joe, in the kitchen, concentrates on producing carefully executed dishes using a mix of French techniques and British ingredients, where the component flavours marry perfectly. A year spent in Sydney added a lighter tone to his cooking so having all three courses is the natural choice – especially when paired with a bottle from their impressive list of burgundies and clarets.

First Course

- Crab raviolo with samphire and brown shrimps.
- Foie gras ballotine salad with smoked duck breast.

Main Course

- Under blade fillet, bone marrow, triple-cooked chips and béarnaise.
- Halibut with scallops, cauliflower purée and trompettes.

Dessert

- Vanilla cheesecake with poached rhubarb and hazelnut crumble.
- Chocolate delice with milk ice cream.

One-O-One

Sheraton Park Tower Hotel,   ⊖ Knightsbridge
101 Knightsbridge ✉ SW1X 7RN   ▶ **Plan XI**
℘ (020) 7290 7101
www.oneoonerestaurant.com

Menu £22 (lunch) – Carte £48/77

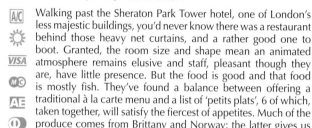

AC
☼
VISA
MC
AE
①

Walking past the Sheraton Park Tower hotel, one of London's less majestic buildings, you'd never know there was a restaurant behind those heavy net curtains, and a rather good one to boot. Granted, the room size and shape mean an animated atmosphere remains elusive and staff, pleasant though they are, have little presence. But the food is good and that food is mostly fish. They've found a balance between offering a traditional à la carte menu and a list of 'petits plats', 6 of which, taken together, will satisfy the fiercest of appetites. Much of the produce comes from Brittany and Norway; the latter gives us the King crab legs which are the stars of the show. The kitchen is not afraid of adding a little playfulness to its classical base.

Painted Heron

112 Cheyne Walk   ⊖ Gloucester Road
✉ SW10 0DJ   ▶ **Plan XI**
℘ (020) 7351 5232   Closed 24-25 December
www.thepaintedheron.com

Menu £20/45 – Carte £25/38

🏠
AC
☼
VISA
MC
AE

They call their style "modern Indian" which, in essence, means the kitchen's influences come from across the land; from Kashmir and Rajasthan to Kerala and Goa. Fish, largely from Hastings, is handled dextrously and seasonal game often features on the menu, whether that's the tandoor pigeon breasts, the partridge with red chilli paste or grouse in a southern stew. Flavours tend to be well-defined and balanced. The room is bigger than you think and has quite a formal feel, thanks largely to the style of service from the young team, but it's broken up into nooks and crannies and hence quite intimate. The open courtyard is an attractive feature and, despite its tiny entrance and tucked away location, the restaurant always appears to be busy.

Phoenix

F6

23 Smith St   ⊖ Sloane Square.
✉ SW3 4EE   ▶ **Plan XI**
☎ (020) 7730 9182   Closed 25 December
www.geronimo-inns.co.uk/thepheonix

Menu £18/28 – Carte £23/36

The same menu is served throughout and, while the bar has plenty of seating and a civilised feel, head to the warm and comfortable dining room at the back if you want a more structured meal or you're impressing a date. Blackboard specials supplement the menu which keeps things traditional: fish on a Friday, a pasta of the day and the likes of fishcakes or sausage and mash with red onion jam. For lunch, you'll find some favourites for late-risers, like eggs Benedict and, in winter, expect the heartening sight of crumbles or plum pudding. Wines are organised by their character, with nearly 30 varieties offered by the glass. The side dishes can bump up the final bill but The Phoenix remains a friendly and conscientiously run Chelsea local.

Pig's Ear

E7

35 Old Church St   ⊖ South Kensington.
✉ SW3 5BS   ▶ **Plan XI**
☎ (020) 7352 2908
www.thepigsear.info

Carte £29/45

This Chelsea pub may not look much like a foodie spot from the outside, or indeed from the inside, but it does have a refreshing honesty to it. Lunch is in the rough-and-ready ground floor bar, decorated with everything from 'Tintin' pictures to covers of 'Sounds' newspaper. There's a decent choice of 5-6 main courses and a wine list on a blackboard. With its wood panelling and dressed tables, the upstairs dining room provides quite a contrast, but the atmosphere is still far from starchy. Here the menu displays a little more ambition but cooking remains similarly earthy and the wine list has plenty of bottles under £30. The kitchen knows its way around an animal: slow-cooked dishes such as pork cheeks are done particularly well.

Poissonnerie de l'Avenue

f i s h   a n d   s e a f o o d   ✕✕

E6

82 Sloane Ave.
✉ SW3 3DZ
☎ (020) 7589 2457
www.poissonneriedelavenue.com

⊖ South Kensington
▶ **Plan XI**
Closed Easter and 25-26 December

Menu £30 (lunch) – Carte £31/66

There is something heartening about dining in a restaurant that is older than its waiters. Poissonnerie de l'Avenue began life in 1946 but the owner is still to be found greeting his customers – many of whom look as though they've been coming since the doors first opened – as old friends, as indeed many are. This is a restaurant all about traditional hospitality and it's easy to understand its longevity. The wood-panelled room has an air of luxury; service is well-organised and the cooking is done 'properly'. The menu is a large affair: expect about 18 starters with everything from oysters to smoked salmon and the same number of seafood and fish main courses. The well-groomed clientele hardly blink when handed the inevitably large bill.

Racine

F r e n c h   ✕✕

E5

239 Brompton Rd
✉ SW3 2EP
☎ (020) 7584 4477
www.racine-restaurant.com

⊖ South Kensington
▶ **Plan XI**
Closed Christmas

Menu £16 (lunch and early dinner) – Carte £30/51

Racine is as authentic a French brasserie as you can get at this end of the tunnel. The accents are thick; the baguettes are fresh and the room's wood and leather have that reassuring lived-in look. Some of the clientele, who are a mature and confident bunch, give the impression that they come here on a weekly basis and it's easy to understand why: along with the authentically prepared classics, such as steak tartare, tête de veau or fruits de mer, are plenty of other dishes that hit the spot, along with well priced lunch and early evening menus. Try to avoid the tables in the middle of the room because, on windier days, you'll find yourself assailed by the occasional gust of wind, whenever somebody opens the front door.

Rasoi 🏵

Indian ✗✗

F6

10 Lincoln St
✉ SW3 2TS
📞 (020) 7225 1881
www.rasoirestaurant.co.uk

⊖ Sloane Square
▶ **Plan XI**
Closed 25-26 December
and Saturday lunch

Menu £27/59

Rasoi

With his outposts in Geneva, Mauritius and Dubai, Vineet Bhatia proves that Indian food is as open to innovation and interpretation as any other cuisine. Fortunately for fans of his original branch here in Chelsea, he has a team of loyal lieutenants who are more than capable of ensuring that things remain consistently good. What really comes across in his modern Indian food is the delicate balance of flavours and the superb quality of the ingredients. For a rounded experience of his unique style, go for the 7-course 'Prestige' menu. On the à la carte, the 'street food' chaats are almost a meal in themselves; the vegetarian dishes are as colourful as they are delicious and the desserts, such as 'Chocolate Cravings' come with more of a Western personality. Be sure to ask for a table in the larger room at the back of the house which has more personality than the one at the front, especially when filled with the sweet aroma of the smoke rising from the racks of lamb. Alternatively, come with friends and book one of the richly decorated private rooms on the first floor.

First Course

- Scallop and prawn brochette.
- Smoke-enclosed tandoori salmon.

Main Course

- Smoked herb-crusted rack of lamb.
- Sea bass two ways.

Dessert

- Rose petal mousse.
- Zaffran bar.

Rib Room

F5

meats and grills XXX

Jumeirah Carlton Tower Hotel,
Cadogan Place ✉ SW1X 9PY
✆ (020) 7858 7250
www.theribroom.co.uk

⊖ Knightsbridge
▶ **Plan XI**

Menu £30/55 – Carte £48/71

The Rib Room is something of a London institution and a restaurant designed for those who didn't get where they are today by wasting time looking at prices. The menu would delight the most traditional of British trenchermen: one can start with smoked salmon or half a dozen Angel oysters then move on to Dover sole, a steak or, more appropriately, rib of Aberdeen Angus. The kitchen does things properly and wisely avoids trying to be too clever. The last designer successfully managed to add a little elegance to the room while also maintaining the overriding sense of masculinity that's often associated with this style of dining. The bar is an integral part of the set up and lends the place a pleasant buzz.

Tendido Cero

D6

Spanish X

174 Old Brompton Rd.
✉ SW5 0BA
✆ (020) 7370 3685
www.cambiodetercio.co.uk

⊖ Gloucester Road
▶ **Plan XI**
Closed 25 December

Menu £30 – Carte £10/48

Abel Lusa has got things pretty sewn up at this end of Old Brompton Road: on one side of the road he owns Cambio de Tercio and Capote y Toros and opposite he has Tendido Cero, a warmly decorated tapas bar adorned with paintings of matadors. On offer is an appealing mix of familiar hot and cold tapas, from padron peppers and Pata Negra ham to boquerones and assorted croquetas, but there are also a few unusual choices, like a mini 'hamburger' made with sardines. Further highlights include Galician octopus, white bean stew with chorizo and pork cheeks with potato purée. Lunchtimes are relatively quiet affairs; it is at night when the place comes alive and the pace hots up. Service is more about efficiency than personality.

⒩ Tom Aikens ✿

E6

43 Elystan St.
✉ SW3 3NT
✆ (020) 7584 2003
www.tomaikens.co.uk

⊖ South Kensington
▶ **Plan XI**
Closed Christmas, Saturday lunch,
Sunday and bank holidays

Menu £29/50

♿ A/C ▦ 🍷 🎱 VISA Ⓜⓒ AE

Tom Aikens

Re-launched with new business partners, Tom Aikens'
eponymous restaurant now has an edgier look and a subtly
different style of cooking. The room resembles one of Lars
von Trier's more minimalistic film sets, with oak tables,
atmospheric lighting and assorted food–related aphorisms
stencilled on the walls. Service remains a little overformal
for the surroundings but the intentions are good. The menu
layout appears somewhat baffling at first but stick to the
6 or 8 course menus and you won't go wrong. The kitchen
follows the culinary zeitgeist by appearing to be influenced by
all things Scandinavian; each dish focused around one main
ingredient and presented on a variety of plates and bowls.
There are plenty of modern techniques on show, including
the occasional powdered ingredient, but there is no doubting
the innate skill and the pleasing contrasts in textures. All the
'extras' are pretty good too: the terrific breads come in warm
hessian bags, the canapés are excellent and the friandises are
presented in an old Oxo tin.

First Course	*Main Course*	*Dessert*
• Salt-fried duck egg with dandelion and sour onions.	• Braised short rib of beef, bone marrow and herb purée.	• Coffee crème and sponge with espresso syrup.
• Roast langoustine, herb mayonnaise, black olive crumb.	• Chorizo baked cod, 24 hour squid, cod soup.	• Pistachio brick, caramelised pistachio, pistachio milk.

Tom's Kitchen

E6

French ⚒

27 Cale St.
✉ SW3 3QP
📞 (020) 7349 0202
www.tomskitchen.co.uk

⊖ South Kensington
▶ **Plan XI**

Carte £29/62

The locals may not have taken to his fish and chip shop but they do seem to like his kitchen. This is a restaurant with a thoroughly sound plan: it's open from early in the morning until late at night and offers satisfying comfort food in relaxed surroundings. The tiled walls and open kitchen work well and there's an upstairs room for the overspill. With its shepherd's pie, sausage and mash, and belly of pork, the menu wouldn't look out of place in a pub; although, as the eponymous Tom is Tom Aikens, a few luxury ingredients like foie gras do sneak in. Bread, olives and side dishes can push up the final bill but it's a friendly place with a stress-free atmosphere. There's a less convincing second branch in Somerset House.

Zuma

F5

Japanese ⚒⚒

5 Raphael St
✉ SW7 1DL
📞 (020) 7584 1010
www.zumarestaurant.com

⊖ Knightsbridge
▶ **Plan XII**
Closed Christmas

Carte £20/96

Zuma may have become a global brand, with branches stretching from Istanbul to Hong Kong, but this is the original and it's still giving its fashionable band of fans – which includes a high quotient of celebrities and enough footballers to make up a whole team – exactly what they want. Glamorous surroundings with an open kitchen, a great cocktail bar, intelligent service and easy-to-share modern Japanese food mean that the large, stylish space is rarely less than bursting, especially at night. The menu covers all bases but instead of sushi, sashimi or tempura your best bet is to head straight for the delicately presented, modern constructions as well as those dishes cooked on the robata grill, which range from beef to sea bass.

Kensington · North Kensington · Notting Hill

It was the choking air of 17C London that helped put **Kensington** on the map: the little village lying to the west of the city became the favoured retreat of the asthmatic King William III who had Sir Christopher Wren build **Kensington Palace** for him. Where the king leads, the titled follow, and the area soon became a fashionable location for the rich. For over 300 years, it's had no problem holding onto its cachet, though a stroll down Kensington High Street is these days a more egalitarian odyssey than some more upmarket residents might approve of.

The shops here mix the everyday with the flamboyant, but for a real taste of the exotic you have to take the lift to the top of the Art Deco Barkers building and arrive at the Kensington Roof Gardens, which are open to all as long as they're not in use for a corporate bash. The gardens are now over seventy years old, yet still remain a 'charming secret'. Those who do make it up to the sixth floor discover a delightful woodland garden and gurgling stream, complete with pools, bridges and trees. There are flamingos, too, adding a dash of vibrant colour.

Back down on earth, Kensington boasts another hidden attraction in **Leighton House** on its western boundaries. The Victorian redbrick façade looks a bit forbidding as you make your approach, but step inside and things take a dramatic turn, courtesy of the extraordinary Arab Hall, with its oriental mosaics and tinkling fountain creating a scene like something from *The Arabian Knights.* Elsewhere in the building, the Pre-Raphaelite paintings of Lord Leighton, Burne-Jones and Alma-Tadema are much to the fore. Mind you, famous names have always had a hankering for W8, with a particular preponderance to dally in enchanting **Kensington Square,** where there are almost as many blue plaques as buildings upon which to secure them. William Thackeray, John Stuart Mill and Edward Burne-Jones were all residents.

One of the London's most enjoyable green retreats is **Holland Park,** just north of the High Street. It boasts the 400 year-old Holland House, which is a fashionable focal point for summer-time al fresco theatre and opera. Holland Walk runs along the eastern fringe of the park, and provides a lovely sojourn down to the shops; at the Kyoto Garden, koi carp reach hungrily for the surface of their pool, while elsewhere peacocks strut around as if they own the place.

Another world beckons just north of here – the seedy-cum-glitzy environs of **Notting Hill.** The main drag itself, Notting Hill Gate, is little more than a one-dimensional thoroughfare only enlivened by second hand record shops, but to its south are charming cottages with pastel shades in leafy streets, while to the north the appealing **Pembridge Road** evolves into

S. Ollivier / MICHELIN

the boutiques of Westbourne Grove. Most people heading in this direction are making for the legendary Portobello Road market – particularly on Saturdays, which are manic. The market stretches on for more than a mile, with a chameleon-like ability to change colour and character on the way: there are antiques at the Notting Hill end, followed further up by food stalls, and then designer and vintage clothes as you reach the Westway. Those who don't fancy the madding crowds of the market can nip into the Electric Cinema and watch a movie in supreme comfort: it boasts two-seater sofas and leather armchairs. Nearby there are another two film-houses putting the hip into the Hill – the Gate, and the Coronet, widely recognised as one of London's most charming 'locals'.

Hidden in a mews just north of **Westbourne Grove** is a fascinating destination: the Museum of Brands, Packaging and Advertising, which does pretty much what it says on the label. It's both nostalgic and evocative, featuring thousands of items like childhood toys, teenage magazines…and HP sauce bottles.

285

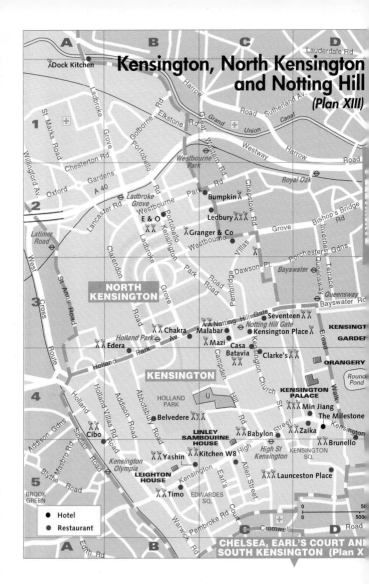

Kensington, North Kensington and Notting Hill
(Plan XIII)

Lauderdale Rd

Dock Kitchen

St Marks Road

Ladbroke Grove

Golborne Rd

Elkstone Rd

Harrow

Great Western Road

Grand Union Canal

Westway

Harrow Road

Willingford Av.

Chesterton Rd

Portobello

Gardens A 40

Oxford

Lancaster Rd

Ladbroke Grove

Westbourne

E & O

Portobello

Ladbroke Grove

Kensington

Westbourne Park

Park Rd

Bumpkin

Chepston Rd

Royal Oak

Ledbury

Granger & Co

Westbourne

Villas

Grove

Bishop's Bridge Rd

Inverness Terrace

Porchester Gdns

Queensway

Latimer Road

West

Cross

St Anns Road

Clarendon Road

Ladbroke Grove

NORTH KENSINGTON

Park

Road

Pembridge

Dawson Pl.

Bayswater

Queensway

Bayswater Rd

Route

Holland Park Av.

Chakra

Malabar

Notting Hill Gate

Notting Hill Gate

Seventeen

Kensington Place

KENSINGTON GARDEN

Edera

Holland

Park

Mazi

Casa Batavia

Campden

Clarke's

Kensington Church

Broad Walk

ORANGERY

Round Pond

KENSINGTON

HOLLAND PARK

U

Hill

St.

KENSINGTON PALACE

Belvedere

Min Jiang

The Milestone

Cibo

Addison Gdns

Sinclair Road

Holland Villas Rd

Addison Road

Abbotsbury Road

LINLEY SAMBOURNE HOUSE

Babylon

High St Kensington

Zaika

Kensington

KENSINGTON SQ.

Brunello

Blythe

Masbro Rd

Road

Kensington Olympia

Yashin

Kitchen W8

Earl's

Allen Street

Launceston Place

BROOK GREEN

LEIGHTON HOUSE

Timo

EDWARDES SQ.

Court

Cromwell

Road

Warwick Rd

Pembroke Rd

CHELSEA, EARL'S COURT AND SOUTH KENSINGTON (Plan X

Edith Rd

● Hotel
● Restaurant

0   50
0   500

Babylon

m o d e r n 🍴🍴

The Roof Gardens, 99 Kensington High St ((entrance on Derry St))
✉ W8 5SA
✆ (020) 7368 3993 – **www**.roofgardens.virgin.com

⊖ High Street Kensington
Closed 24-30 December,
1-2 January and Sunday dinner

Menu £20/47 – Carte £34/57

Once you've passed muster with Frosty the Doorman, take the lift up to the 7th floor and you'll find yourself staring at trees and shrubs - 1.5 acres of amazing rooftop garden. The restaurant's terrace must surely be one of the city's best spots for a cocktail and a view, with the easterly skyline visible through the oak and fruit trees. However, be aware that private parties often have exclusive access. The food can't always compete with this bucolic scene and presentation can sometimes be at the expense of flavour but the menu does offer plenty of choice. Dishes are not too heavy, which is a plus for later as dinner at weekends entitles you to access to The Club. You could also consider coming on a Tuesday as that's jazz night.

Belvedere

m o d e r n 🍴🍴🍴

Holland House, off Abbotsbury Rd.
✉ W8 6LU
✆ (020) 7602 1238
www.belvedererestaurant.co.uk

⊖ Holland Park
Closed 26 December,
1 January and Sunday dinner

Menu £20 (weekday lunch)/28 – Carte £32/48

Built in the 17C as the summer ballroom to the Jacobean Holland House, The Belvedere sits in a stunning position in Holland Park. It's hard to believe you're still in London but check the location first as signposts within the park are a little elusive. The ground floor is the more glittery, with mirrors, glass balls and a small bar area. Upstairs is more traditional in style and leads out onto the charming terrace, which is well worth booking in summer. Service remains decidedly formal. The menu covers all bases from eggs Benedict to even the occasional Thai offering, but it's worth sticking to the more classical, French influenced dishes as these are kitchen's strength. Produce is well-sourced and dishes nicely balanced. France dominates the wine list.

Brunello

D4

Baglioni Hotel,
60 Hyde Park Gate ✉ SW7 5BB
☎ (020) 7368 5900
www.baglionihotels.com

⊖ High Street Kensington

Menu £26/30 – Carte £42/74

AC
☀
VISA
MC
AE
DI

With all that gold and black, and velvet and glass, Brunello could never be accused of understatement. The restaurant, on the ground floor of the Baglioni hotel, unashamedly targets those who like a bit of bling with their branzino and pitches its à la carte prices at sufficiently lofty levels to ensure that passers-by will know to keep walking if they're underdressed. The Italian cooking is perfectly enjoyable and while the kitchen has a fairly promiscuous approach to culinary influences, it does use prime ingredients and is not averse to a little reinterpretation of the classics, such as tiramisu. The restaurant shares its space with a cocktail bar lounge – indeed, it's not always apparent where one ends and the other begins.

Bumpkin

C2

209 Westbourne Park Rd
✉ W11 1EA
☎ (020) 7243 9818
www.bumpkinuk.com

⊖ Westbourne Park

Carte £23/39

AC
⊡
☀
VISA
MC
AE

How refreshing to find a restaurant's name that sums up its spirit instead of merely repeating its street number or using the name of an obscure vegetable. Bumpkin, whose slogan is 'for city folk who like a little country living', champions British produce in quasi-rustic surroundings with a pub-like informality. Young, keen staff run around with 'Country Girl' or 'Country Boy' emblazoned on their T-shirts and the noisy open kitchen adds to the fun. The menu avoids being too earnest and focuses on using first-rate ingredients sensibly; the best dishes are the simplest ones, such as a 'Cow Pie' of which Desperate Dan would surely approve. Be sure to sit in the main room rather than in the corridor of uncertainty between it and the front bar.

Casa Batavia

C3

135 Kensington Church St
✉ W8 7LP
✆ (020) 7221 7348
www.casabatavia.com

⊖ **Notting Hill Gate**
Closed 25 December, Easter Sunday and
lunch Saturday – booking advisable

Menu £19 (weekday lunch) – Carte £24/36

A/C

VISA

M©

AE

In 2011 two friends from different backgrounds came together to open this intimate Italian restaurant on busy Kensington Church Street. The affable Paolo Boschi has been a recognisable figure on the London restaurant scene for many years, while Nicola Batavia established his reputation as a gifted chef in Turin in the late '90s. Here at Casa Batavia, Nicola oversees the menu and has installed one of his protégés as chef, while Paolo ensures that the service team are on their toes. The more refined cooking of Piedmont is the major influence on the menu, in such specialities as Castelmagno cheese with chestnut honey; potted rabbit with hazelnuts; pig's cheek with polenta and dried fruits; and, of course, panna cotta.

ⓝ Chakra

C3

157-159 Notting Hill Gate
✉ W11 3LF
✆ (020) 7229 2115
www.chakralondon.com

⊖ **Notting Hill Gate**
Closed 25-26 December, 1 January and
Easter Monday – booking advisable

Menu £30 (weekday dinner) – Carte £16/43

A/C

VISA

M©

AE

Ⓓ

Indian 'street food' may be all the rage these days but here at Chakra – which is named after the body's energy points – the influences come from the Royal kitchens of the Maharajahs, particularly those from the North Western province of Lucknow. A different chef is credited with running each section on the menu, whether that's the charcoal grill, griddle, clay oven or veg pan, and dishes are designed for sharing, although some of the prices tend to discourage too much ordering. The spicing is more subtle than usual, the aroma fresher and the presentation more striking, with the best dishes being the more traditional ones. Divided into two smart rooms, one white and one brown, the place is run by charming and elegant young ladies.

Cibo

Italian

A4-5

3 Russell Gdns
✉ W14 8EZ
☎ (020) 7371 6271
www.ciborestaurant.net

⊖ **Kensington Olympia**
Closed 1 week Christmas,
Easter and bank holidays

Menu £20/35 – Carte £26/44

Some of the sparkle may have dimmed since Cibo opened in 1989 but its band of local followers remain committed in their enthusiasm for this friendly Italian restaurant. The interior looks a tad weary these days but the quirky pictures celebrating the naked female form are still there and the imported hand-painted crockery is a nice touch. The ever-popular platter of grilled seafood dictates that the menu pretty much changes on a daily basis, although certain dishes can never be changed; some regulars can even guess who's in the kitchen that day by the degree of spicing. Service is friendly if a touch chaotic at times and while the opening front façade is a boon in summer, it can be draughty in winter, so ask for a table at the back.

Clarke's

modern XX

C4

124 Kensington Church St
✉ W8 4BH
☎ (020) 7221 9225
www.sallyclarke.com

⊖ **Notting Hill Gate**
Closed Christmas-New Year, Sunday dinner
and bank holidays – booking advisable

Carte £34/43

By constantly searching for the next big thing, many diners miss out on London's more dependable and worthy restaurants such as Clarke's, which has been a reassuring presence on Kensington Church Street since 1984. Regulars, of whom there are many, prefer the ground floor, although the tables downstairs benefit from the delicious aromas arising from the surprisingly serene open kitchen. The cooking remains true to Sally Clarke's founding principles of excellent ingredients and simple preparation and owes much to the influence of Alice Waters at Chez Panisse in San Francisco. There is a small, weekly changing à la carte plus 'Sally's Dinner Menu', a nicely balanced set price menu. The wine list has also been thoughtfully compiled.

Dock Kitchen

A0

Mediterranean ✗

Portobello Dock, 342-344 Ladbroke Grove ⊖ Ladbroke Grove
✉ W10 5BU   Closed 24 December-5 January
℘ (020) 8962 1610   and Sunday dinner
www.dockkitchen.co.uk

Menu £15 (lunch)/55 – Carte £26/41

VISA
MC
AE
①

What started as a pop-up restaurant became a permanent feature in this former Victorian goods yard and the space is shared with designer Tom Dixon, some of whose furniture and lighting is showcased here. The open kitchen dominates one end of the room where steel girders and exposed brick add to the industrial aesthetic. The similarities to Moro, River Café and Petersham Nurseries are palpable, not just in the refreshing lack of ceremony and the fashionable crowds that flock here, but also in the cooking, where quality ingredients are a given and natural flavours speak for themselves. The chef's peregrinations also inform his cooking; look out for his themed set menus which could be Sardinian one week, Moroccan the next.

E&O

B2

Asian ✗✗

14 Blenheim Cres.   ⊖ Ladbroke Grove
✉ W11 1NN   Closed 26-27 August,
℘ (020) 7229 5454   25-26 December and 1 January
www.rickerrestaurants.com

Menu £20/59 – Carte £18/57

A/C
⊡
☼
VISA
MC
AE
①

Once you've sidestepped the full-on bar of this Notting Hill favourite, a step from Portobello Road, you'll find yourself in a moodily sophisticated restaurant packed with the beautiful and the hopeful. The room is understatedly urbane, with slatted walls, large circular lamps and leather banquettes, while noise levels are at the party end of the auditory index. Waiting staff are obliging, pleasant and often among the prettiest people in the room. E&O stands for Eastern and Oriental and the menu journeys across numerous Asian countries, dividing itself into assorted headings which include dim sum, salads, tempura, curries and roasts. Individual dishes vary in size and price so sharing, as in life, is often the best option.

Edera

B4

148 Holland Park Ave.
✉ W11 4UE
✆ (020) 7221 6090
www.edera.co.uk

⊖ Holland Park

Carte £28/53

The last makeover made Edera warmer and more comfortable and, while it actually holds up to 75 people, it still manages to feel quite intimate. On a typical night it seems as though the vast majority of customers have been before, that they know one another and probably walked here. In comparison, the staff are a youthful bunch, but they are well-marshalled and quietly efficient. The menu is quite broad and portions are on the generous side so if you're having a pasta dish you may struggle with a fourth course. The list of daily specials is wisely printed so you don't have to try to memorise the waiter's recital; there is a Sardinian element to the cooking, with bottarga omnipresent, and the ingredients are first-rate.

ⓝ Granger & Co

C2

175 Westbourne Grove
✉ W11 2SB
✆ (020) 7229 9111
www.grangerandco.com

⊖ Bayswater
Closed 25-26 December
and 1 January – bookings not accepted

Carte £16/36

Having relocated from the sun of Sydney to the cool of Notting Hill, Bill Granger decided to open a local restaurant. He's brought with him that disarmingly charming 'matey' service that only Australians can do, his breakfast sweetcorn fritters and ricotta hotcakes and a zesty menu that features everything from pasta to pork chops. At dinner a BBQ section is added along with a daily fish dish, while various puds replace the cakes offered during the day. The room is bright and open, prices are reasonable and the Asian accents lend many of the dishes an easy-to-eat quality which makes you feel healthier than when you arrived and allows you to forget that you probably had to queue for a table.

Kensington Place

modern ✗

C3

201-209 Kensington Church St.
✉ W8 7LX
☎ (020) 7727 3184
www.kensingtonplace-restaurant.co.uk

⊖ Notting Hill Gate
Closed Sunday dinner and Monday lunch

Menu £17 (weekday dinner) – Carte £20/57

A/C
⟨⟩
VISA
MC
AE

It must have been quite difficult for the D&D group to re-establish Kensington Place, especially as Rowley Leigh, its well-known former chef, now operates in nearby Bayswater. One thing they have got right is the menu; they dispensed with an à la carte and in its place introduced a competitively priced set menu which offers plenty of choice. There are some supplements for the few dishes using pricier ingredients but these can be easily avoided. The cooking is modern and quite dainty at times and desserts are done well. Service is still speedy and copes easily with the numbers when it needs to. The addition of cushions has succeeded in softening the acoustics so it's also easier to have a conversation these days.

Malabar

Indian ✗✗

C3

27 Uxbridge St.
✉ W8 7TQ
☎ (020) 7727 8800
www.malabar-restaurant.co.uk

⊖ Notting Hill Gate
Closed 1 week Christmas –
(buffet lunch Sunday)

Menu £18/25 s – Carte £14/31 s

A/C
⟨⟩
☼
VISA
MC
AE

One of the reasons why Malabar has been going strong since 1983 is that it keeps on top of its appearance, as, it seems, do most of its Notting Hill customers. These days the front has a sleek, understated look; the interior is a fashionable grey and the staff do their bit by dressing in black. What doesn't change is the quality of the food, from the breads to the piping hot thalis. The favourites remain but the seafood section has been beefed up with the addition of a monkfish curry and a whole gilt-head bream; and just because the tandoori dishes sit beside the starters on the menu, don't assume they come in starter sizes. The excellent value Sunday buffet lunch, when children under 12 eat for free, still packs them in.

Kitchen W8 ✿

modern 🍴🍴

C5

11-13 Abingdon Rd
✉ W8 6AH
📞 (020) 7937 0120
www.kitchenw8.com

⊖ High Street Kensington
Closed 25-26 December
and bank holidays

Menu £18/30 – Carte £35/55

Over the years Abingdon Road has played host to a decent collection of restaurants but the general standard was raised considerably when Kitchen W8 arrived. This joint venture between Rebecca Mascarenhas, one of London's most experienced restaurateurs, and Philip Howard, luminary chef of The Square, has quickly established itself on the scene and it is easy to see why. For a start, their talented head chef has a crisp and confident style, which never lets presentation or construction compromise the clarity of the flavours. He also appreciates that diners don't come here to eat something they could knock up easily at home so his dishes have depth and a degree of originality. Furthermore, when one considers the quality of ingredients used and the manpower in the kitchen, prices are refreshingly restrained – and the weekly changing lunch menu is a steal. The place itself is quite big but comes divided into three smaller sections; the youthful looking staff ensure that the atmosphere remains light and relaxed, as befits a neighbourhood restaurant.

First Course

- Grilled white asparagus with thinly sliced veal, egg and truffle.
- Parfait of foie gras with apricot, camomile and sourdough toast.

Main Course

- Cod with brown shrimps and pickled cauliflower.
- Pigeon with hazelnut bulgur wheat, pickled beetroot, turnips and watercress.

Dessert

- Hazelnut ice cream with banana and lime caramel.
- Vanilla rice pudding parfait with English raspberries.

Launceston Place ✿

D5

1a Launceston Pl.
✉ W8 5RL
✆ (020) 7937 6912
www.launcestonplace-restaurant.co.uk

Menu £23/46

⊖ **Gloucester Road**
Closed 24-30 December,
Monday lunch and dinner
bank holiday Mondays –
bookings advisable at dinner

A/C

⛎

🌱🍷

☼

VISA

MC

AE

D

launceston place

Michelin

Keeping your regulars happy is half the battle for all neighbourhood restaurants and one way of ensuring they keep returning is to give them the sort of food they want to eat as well as the sort of food that complements the surroundings. Yorkshire-born Timothy Allen joined this longstanding Kensington landmark as head chef at the beginning of 2012 and his cooking appears to be a very good fit. He worked for chefs John Burton Race and Martin Burge for over ten years and their influences are evident in his own style of cooking which is refined without being dainty and, like most of the customers, sophisticated without being showy. Despite Launceston Place being part of the D&D group, the chef sources his own produce and works without interference. The restaurant comes divided into various areas and everyone has their favourite spot. The striking chocolate coloured walls and modern artwork add to the intimate and grown up feel. Service can sometimes feel a little overformal but its heart is in the right place.

First Course

- Scallop with glazed pork belly, apple and celeriac.
- Hot home-smoked mackerel, prawns, piquillo pepper and lemon confit.

Main Course

- Lamb with curried cauliflower, peas and broad beans.
- Brill with prawns, samphire and new season potatoes.

Dessert

- Baked English custard, poached rhubarb and apple ice cream.
- Caramel chocolate mousse and carpaccio of poached pear.

Ledbury ✿ ✿

modern XXX

127 Ledbury Rd.
✉ W11 2AQ
℘ (020) 7792 9090
www.theledbury.com

⊖ Notting Hill Gate
Closed 25-26 December, August bank
holiday and Monday lunch

Menu £30/80

The Ledbury

The Ledbury's Australian head chef, Brett Graham, is one of the more intelligent chefs around and his passion for quality ingredients really shines through. He is constantly on the lookout for new supplies and suppliers and knows what to do when he gets them. Hebridean lambs arrive whole and are then butchered, with every part of the beast used; game is also one of the kitchen's strengths – Brett is a keen shot. The kitchen is also firmly grounded in technique so that whenever a slightly unusual flavour or a little tease is introduced, it is done merely to enhance the dish. This is bravado cooking but without affectation. Even though the chef also has an involvement in The Harwood Arms, he does so without ever taking his eye off the ball here. Along with The Ashes, let's hope he's staying on this side of the world for a while. The room is elegant without being overdressed and the serving team are well organised and professional but they never forget that fundamentally this is a neighbourhood restaurant, albeit a rather good one.

First Course

- Buffalo milk curd with Saint-Nectaire and truffle toast.
- Scallop with fennel, liquorice and elderflower.

Main Course

- Breast and confit legs of grouse with foie gras and cherries.
- Dover sole with thyme milk skin, mussels and cauliflower.

Dessert

- Parfait of dried flowers, wild strawberries and vanilla tapioca.
- Passion fruit soufflé with Sauternes ice cream.

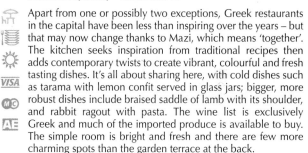

N Mazi

Greek ✗

12-14 Hillgate Rd
✉ W8 7SR
📞 (020) 7229 3794
www.mazi.co.uk

⊖ Notting Hill Gate
Closed 24-30 December

Menu £22 (lunch) – Carte £29/43

Apart from one or possibly two exceptions, Greek restaurants in the capital have been less than inspiring over the years – but that may now change thanks to Mazi, which means 'together'. The kitchen seeks inspiration from traditional recipes then adds contemporary twists to create vibrant, colourful and fresh tasting dishes. It's all about sharing here, with cold dishes such as tarama with lemon confit served in glass jars; bigger, more robust dishes include braised saddle of lamb with its shoulder, and rabbit ragout with pasta. The wine list is exclusively Greek and much of the imported produce is available to buy. The simple room is bright and fresh and there are few more charming spots than the garden terrace at the back.

Min Jiang

Chinese ✗✗✗

Royal Garden Hotel,
(10th Floor), 2-24 Kensington High St
✉ W8 4PT
📞 (020) 7361 1988 – **www**.minjiang.co.uk

⊖ High Street Kensington

Menu £40/45 – Carte £23/88

It's got great views of Kensington Palace and Gardens below (ask for tables 11 or 16) but because of its own good looks and its collection of vases influenced by the Ming Dynasty, this stylish Chinese restaurant on the 10th floor of the Royal Garden hotel can more than hold its own. The speciality is wood-fired Beijing duck in two servings; its glistening meat is carved at the table and one then has the difficult task of choosing one of the four options offered for the second serving. The cuisine covers all provinces, although Cantonese and Sichuan are the most dominant. The dim sum is good and the signature dishes include sea bass with shredded chicken, sautéed Gong Bao chicken and spicy pork belly with leeks.

Seventeen

C3

17 Notting Hill Gate ⊖ Notting Hill Gate
✉ W11 3JQ
☎ (020) 7985 0006
www.seventeen-london.co.uk

Menu £21/36 – Carte £17/41

Burdening itself with an instantly forgettable name may not have helped its cause but still, this stylish Chinese restaurant should be attracting more locals as it offers something a little different in this part of town. Things are all very moody and cool inside, with candlelight and Chinese artefacts adding to the charm. The ground floor is a dimly lit, intimate space and there's further seating downstairs, along with a bar and an attractively screened private room. Authentic Sichuan and Shanghainese dishes provide the highlights, such as pork lung slices in chilli sauce, Sichuan-style fish and Chongqing chicken. The chef is from Mainland China and also offers delicacies from other regions, such as Dung Po pork, a Hangzhou speciality.

Timo

B5

343 Kensington High St. ⊖ High Street Kensington
✉ W8 6NW Closed Christmas, bank holidays and
☎ (020) 7603 3888 Sunday – booking advisable
www.timorestaurant.net

Menu £12/19 – Carte £30/42

Step with purpose towards the entrance of Timo, otherwise you might find yourself being dazzled by the neon of the neighbouring Iranian shops or by the sales pitch of their enthusiastic owners. Once inside this comfortable and comforting Italian restaurant, head past the 'corridor' of tables and up to the more relaxing area at the back, with its deep banquette seating and effective lighting. The smart team deliver professional and conscientious service under the watchful eye of the owner, who knows his regulars and ensures they are looked after. The menu, supplemented by a few daily specials, offers a broad selection of recognisable specialities from across all regions and the cooking is neat, reliable and soundly executed.

Yashin

Japanese ✕✕

1A Argyll Rd.
✉ W8 7DB
✆ (020) 7938 1536
www.yashinsushi.com

⊖ High Street Kensington
Closed first Monday in month,
Christmas-New Year – booking essential

Carte £38/83

A/C
☼
VISA
MC
AE

Two experienced sushi chefs joined forces to create this contemporary restaurant with its crisp, appealing black and white theme. Their worthy ambition to wean diners off fermented soya bean is reflected in their grammatically challenging but charmingly equitable slogan: "without soy sauce…but if you want to". There are three omakase choices offering 8, 11 or 15 pieces of sushi selected by the chefs and served together. The quality of the fish is clear and originality comes in the form of minuscule garnishes adorning each piece and the odd bit of searing. Service is knowledgeable and endearing but be sure to ask for a counter seat as one of the joys of sushi comes from watching the dextrous knife skills and the deft handling of the fish.

Zaika

Indian ✕✕

1 Kensington High St.
✉ W8 5NP
✆ (020) 7795 6533
www.zaika-restaurant.co.uk

⊖ High Street Kensington
Closed 25-26 December,
1-2 January and Monday lunch

Menu £23/62 – Carte £31/49

A/C
☼
VISA
MC
AE

The smell of incense hits you immediately and is one clue that the days of this being a bank are long gone. To further disguise its previous function, the room is decorated in a theatrical way, with plenty of drapes, ornaments and lots of colour to counteract the high ceiling and all that rather imposing wood panelling. Lunch here is more about offering attractively priced set menus; at dinner everything goes up a notch and the majority of diners go for the 'Gourmand' menu, which comes with the option of wine pairings. There is certainly some originality to the sophisticated Indian cooking, and the kitchen uses plenty of quality British produce like Herdwick lamb and Scottish scallops, but sometimes the spicing can lack a degree of subtlety.

Greater London

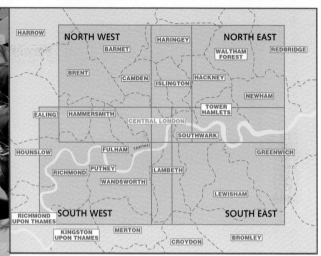

Ludovic Maisant/hemis.fr

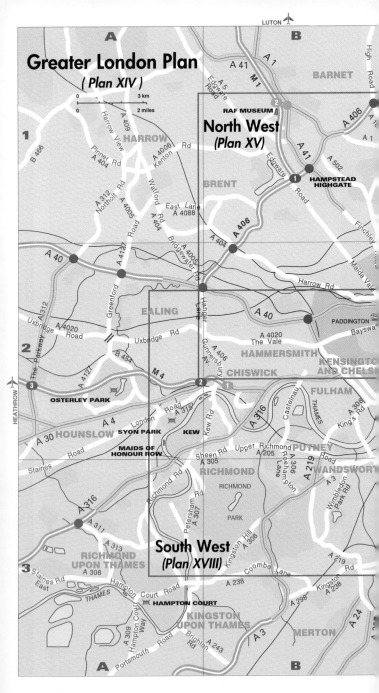

Greater London Plan
(Plan XIV)

LUTON

BARNET

RAF MUSEUM

North West
(Plan XV)

HARROW

HAMPSTEAD
HIGHGATE

BRENT

PADDINGTON
Bayswa

EALING

HAMMERSMITH

KENSINGTON
AND CHELSE

CHISWICK

FULHAM

HEATHROW

OSTERLEY PARK

PUTNEY

HOUNSLOW

SYON PARK

KEW

WANDSWORT

MAIDS OF
HONOUR ROW

RICHMOND

RICHMOND

PARK

South West
(Plan XVIII)

RICHMOND
UPON THAMES

THAMES

HAMPTON COURT

KINGSTON
UPON THAMES

MERTON

North-West London

Heading north from London Zoo and Regent's Park, the green baton is passed to two of the city's most popular and well-known locations: Hampstead Heath and Highgate Wood. In close proximity, they offer a favoured pair of lungs to travellers emerging from the murky depths of the Northern Line. Two centuries ago, they would have been just another part of the area's undeveloped high ground and pastureland, but since the building boom of the nineteenth century, both have become prized assets in this part of the metropolis.

People came to seek shelter in **Hampstead** in times of plague, and it's retained its bucolic air to this day. Famous names have always enjoyed its charms: Constable and Keats rested their brush and pen here, while the sculptors Henry Moore and Barbara Hepworth were residents in more recent times. Many are drawn to such delightful places as Church Row, which boasts a lovely Georgian Terrace. You know you're up high because the thoroughfares bear names like Holly Mount and Mount Vernon. The Heath is full of rolling woodlands and meadows; it's a great place for rambling, particularly to the crest of **Parliament Hill** and its superb city views. There are three bathing ponds here, one mixed, and one each for male and female swimmers, while up on the Heath's northern fringes, **Kenwood House,** along with its famous al fresco summer concerts, also boasts great art by the likes of Vermeer and Rembrandt. And besides all that, there's an ivy tunnel leading to a terrace with idyllic pond views.

Highgate Wood is an ancient woodland and conservation area, containing a leafy walk that meanders enchantingly along a former railway line to **Crouch End,** home to a band of thespians. Down the road at Highgate Cemetery, the likes of Karl Marx, George Eliot, Christina Rossetti and Michael Faraday rest in a great entanglement of breathtaking Victorian over-decoration. The cemetery is still in use – most recent notable to be buried here is Alexander Litvinenko, the Russian dissident.

Next door you'll find **Waterlow Park,** another fine green space, which, apart from its super views, also includes decorative ponds on three levels. Lauderdale House is here, too, a 16C pile which is now an arts centre; more famously, Charles II handed over its keys to Nell Gwynn for her to use as her North London residence. Head back south from here, and **Primrose Hill** continues the theme of glorious green space: its surrounding terraces are populated by media darlings, while its vertiginous mass is another to boast a famously enviable vista.

Of a different hue altogether is **Camden Town** with its buzzy edge, courtesy of a renowned

indie music scene, goths, punks, and six earthy markets selling everything from tat to exotica. Charles Dickens grew up here, and he was none too complimentary; the area still relishes its seamy underside. A scenic route out is the **Regent's Canal,** which cuts its way through the market and ambles to the east and west of the city. Up the road, the legendary Roundhouse reopened its arty front doors in 2006, expanding further the wide range of Camden's alt scene.

One of the music world's most legendary destinations, the **Abbey Road** studios, is also in this area and, yes, it's possible to join other tourists making their way over that zebra crossing. Not far away, in Maresfield Gardens, stands a very different kind of attraction. The Freud Museum is one of the very few buildings in London to have two blue plaques. It was home to Sigmund during the last year of his life and it's where he lived with his daughter Anna (her plaque commemorates her work in child psychiatry). Inside, there's a fabulous library and his working desk. But the pivotal part of the whole house is in another corner of the study – the psychiatrist's couch!

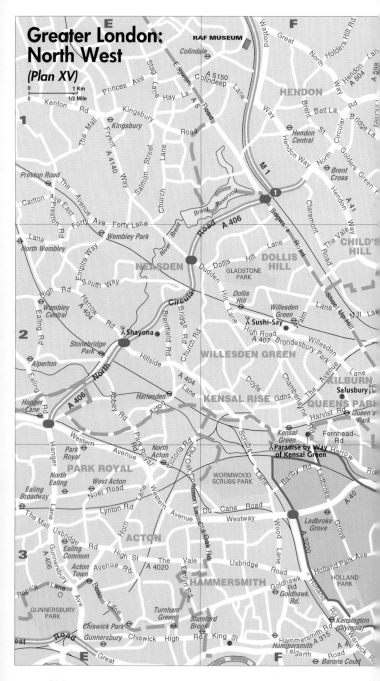

Greater London: North West
(Plan XV)

RAF MUSEUM

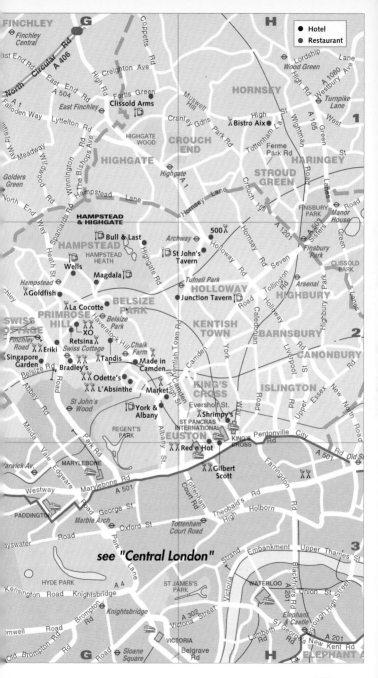

Legend
- ● Hotel
- ● Restaurant

G FINCHLEY
- ⊕ Finchley Central
- North Circular Rd A 406
- East End Rd
- A 1 Falloden Way
- Creighton Ave
- East End Rd A 504
- Fortis Green
- ⊕ Clissold Arms
- Lyttelton Rd
- Meadway
- Winnington Rd
- The Bishops Ave
- Wildwood Rd
- North End Way
- Golders Green
- Hampstead Lane
- **HAMPSTEAD & HIGHGATE**
- HIGHGATE WOOD
- ⊕ Highgate
- HIGHGATE A 1
- Spaniards Rd
- Heath St
- ⊕ Bull & Last
- HAMPSTEAD
- HAMPSTEAD HEATH
- ⊕ Wells
- Magdala ⊕
- Highgate Rd
- ✗ Goldfish
- BELSIZE PARK
- ✗ La Cocotte
- Haverstock Hill
- ⊕ Belsize Park
- PRIMROSE HILL
- SWISS COTTAGE
- ⊕ Finchley Road
- ✗✗ Eriki
- Singapore Garden
- ✗ Retsina
- ✗ XO
- ⊕ Swiss Cottage
- ✗✗ Tandis
- Belsize Rd
- ✗✗ Bradley's
- ✗✗ Odette's
- ✗✗ L'Absinthe
- Abbey Rd
- ⊕ St John's Wood
- Market ✗
- Made in Camden
- ⊕ York & Albany
- REGENT'S PARK
- Park Rd
- Albany St
- Maida Vale
- Edgware Rd
- ⊕ Warwick Av
- MARYLEBONE
- Westway
- Marylebone Rd A 501
- George St
- PADDINGTON
- Marble Arch
- Oxford St
- Bayswater Road
- *see "Central London"*
- HYDE PARK A 4
- Kensington Road
- Knightsbridge
- Cromwell Road
- Old Brompton Rd
- Brompton Rd
- ✗ Knightsbridge
- **G**
- Sloane Square

H HORNSEY
- Lordship Lane
- Wood Green
- High Rd
- Westbury Ave A 1080
- Turnpike Lane
- A 105 Green
- West Green
- St Wightman Rd
- ✗ Bistro Aix
- Muswell Hill
- Cranley Gdns
- CROUCH END
- Park Rd
- Ferme Park Rd
- Tottenham La
- HARINGEY
- STROUD GREEN
- Crouch Hill
- FINSBURY PARK
- Manor House
- A 1201
- A 503 Seven Sisters
- ⊕ Finsbury Park
- CLISSOLD PARK
- 500 ✗
- ✗ Archway
- St John's Tavern ⊕
- Holloway Rd
- Tufnell Park
- HOLLOWAY
- Seven Sisters Rd
- Tollington Rd
- Arsenal
- HIGHBURY
- Highbury Rd
- ● Junction Tavern ✗
- KENTISH TOWN
- Caledonian Rd
- BARNSBURY
- CANONBURY
- Kentish Town Rd
- Camden
- York Way
- Liverpool Rd
- Upper St
- Essex Rd
- New North Road
- ISLINGTON
- Camden High St
- KING'S CROSS
- Eversholt St.
- ✗ Shrimpy's
- ST PANCRAS INTERNATIONAL
- EUSTON
- KING'S CROSS
- Pentonville Rd
- City Rd
- Old St
- A 501
- Farringdon Rd
- ✗✗ Red n Hot
- ✗✗ Gilbert Scott
- Tottenham Court Rd
- Theobald's Rd
- Holborn
- High Holborn
- ✗✗
- Strand
- Embankment
- Upper Thames St
- Blackfriars Rd
- WATERLOO
- A 201
- Union St
- Elephant & Castle
- St George's Rd
- A 201
- Borough High Street
- New Kent Rd
- ST JAMES'S PARK
- Victoria Street
- A 302
- VICTORIA
- Belgrave Rd
- Lambeth Rd
- **H** ELEPHANT &

1
2
3

500

H2

Archway
782 Holloway Rd ✉ N19 3JH
℘ (020) 7272 3406
www.500restaurant.co.uk

⊖ Archway
Closed 2 weeks summer and 2 weeks
Christmas-New Year – booking essential
– (dinner only and lunch Friday-Sunday)

Carte £22/30

Named after the cute little Fiat and that couldn't be more appropriate because here is a restaurant that is small, fun, well-priced and ideal for London. The owner is an ebullient fellow who takes an active role in the service, as does the chef who likes to see the look of satisfaction on his customers' faces. Their shared passion is evident in the cooking: homemade breads and pastas are very good; the fluffy gnocchi with sausage ragu delivers a kick; the tender veal chop is a winner and the rabbit is the house special. The menu, which has occasional Sardinian leanings, changes regularly and the sheet of daily specials includes great little snacks to have with a drink. Black and white photos of old Holloway are the only incongruity.

St John's Tavern

H2

Archway
91 Junction Rd ✉ N19 5QU
℘ (020) 7272 1587
www.stjohnstavern.com

⊖ Archway.
Closed 25-26 December and 1 January
– bookings advisable at dinner – (dinner
only and lunch Friday-Sunday)

Carte £21/34

Having undergone an English Heritage restoration in recent years, St John's Tavern now stands as a beacon of hope on the stubbornly unchanging thoroughfare that is Junction Road. It doesn't disappoint inside either: the laid-back front bar does an appealing line in snacks like salt cod croquettes and mutton pasties, and there are few more warming spots in North London on a cold night than the large, boldly decorated rear dining room. The chefs list the provenance of their ingredients on a board next to the open kitchen, with Devon and Dorset seemingly the favoured counties. The daily menu is largely hardy and British but with nods to the Med; heartening terrines are a highlight, as is the delicious sourdough which is baked in-house.

Retsina

Belsize Park

48-50 Belsize Ln ✉ NW3 5AR

✆ (020) 7431 5855

www.retsina-london.com

⊖ **Belsize Park**

Closed 25-26 December,
1 January, Monday lunch
and bank holidays

Menu £19 (lunch) – Carte £21/45

Having outgrown their previous address on Regent's Park Road, the family owners moved to these larger premises in Belsize Park and the locals appear mighty grateful that they did. As in Greece, the place is all about two things: good food and pleasant service. The menu is unapologetically traditional and all the old favourites are there, from dolmades to soutzoukakia, kleftiko to stifado but the grill and the souvla are the stars of the show and the meats are gloriously juicy and tender. House specialties such as suckling pig or shoulder of lamb must be ordered 24 hours in advance. The dining room is split over two floors and is simply kitted out with tiles and Athenian artefacts. Service and atmosphere are both relaxed and friendly.

Tandis

Belsize Park

73 Haverstock Hill ✉ NW3 4SL

✆ (020) 7586 8079

www.tandisrestaurant.com

⊖ **Chalk Farm**

Closed 25 December

Carte £17/25

Haverstock Hill's maturing restaurant scene has now acquired a little exoticism thanks to Tandis and its enticing Iranian cooking. The appeal of this contemporary looking restaurant stretches way beyond the Iranian diaspora – plenty of locals also appear to have been seduced as soon as they tasted the traditional flat bread baked in a clay oven. A varied selection of invigorating 'koresht' stews and succulent 'kababs' form the mainstay of the menu but other specialities such as 'sabzi polo' and the rich and complex flavours of 'kashke bademjaan' are well worth exploring. Finish with some of their fine teas and a 'faloodeh', where rose water sorbet is matched with a sour cherry syrup. The best seats are to be found at the back.

XO

Asian ※※

Belsize Park
29 Belsize Ln. ⊠ NW3 5AS
✆ (020) 7433 0888
www.rickerrestaurants.com/xo

⊖ Belsize Park
Closed 25-26 December, 1 January and
bank holidays

Menu £15 (lunch) – Carte £21/33

Who knew Belsize Park was so trendy? Apart from estate agents, obviously. This branch of Will Ricker's small chain of glossy pan-Asian restaurants may not be quite as frenetic as the others but it still attracts plenty of shiny happy people, many of whom are holding hands. It follows the same theme as the others: a busy front bar that serves decent cocktails, behind which is the slick, uncluttered restaurant in shades of lime. The menu trawls through most of Asia; start with some warm edamame while reading through it. Highlights include the ever-popular crispy squid and the tender and tasty Indonesian lamb rendang curry but tempura is done with too heavy a hand. Sharing is the key, especially as those who come in large parties get the booths.

Made in Camden 😊

other world kitchens ✗

Camden Town
Roundhouse, Chalk Farm Rd
⊠ NW1 8EH
✆ (020) 7424 8495 – **www**.madeincamden.com

⊖ Chalk Farm
Closed 24-26 December,
1-2 January and Monday

Menu £10 (weekday lunch) – Carte £22/34

You'll find this large and relaxed bar and dining room attached to the side of the rejuvenated Roundhouse, which means it's at its most fun when it's jumping with people just before or after a show. The room's assorted posters will instil either a sense of curiosity or nostalgia, depending on your age, and the booths around the bar are a great spot for drinks. What really elevates the place, however, is the cooking; there is irony in the name because the kitchen has a global reach, from the Med to Asia. Serving small plates may be nothing new these days but here it's the combination of ingredients and flavours that sets it apart, whether that's fennel with feta and salted caramel or crispy chicken with black vinegar glaze.

Market

British modern ✗

Camden Town
43 Parkway ✉ NW1 7PN
📞 (020) 7267 9700
www.marketrestaurant.co.uk

⊖ **Camden Town**
Closed 25 December-3 January ,
Sunday dinner and bank holidays –
booking essential

Carte £25/33

A/C

VISA

M©

AE

①

The name is spot on because this is all about market fresh produce, seasonality and cooking that is refreshingly matter of fact, with big, bold flavour and John Bull Britishness. Dishes come as advertised, with no pointless ornamentation, and you can expect to find the likes of brawn, ox tongue fritters and devilled kidneys alongside stews and shepherd's pie in winter, followed by proper puddings, not desserts. But be sure to have lamb or beef dripping on toast as a pre-starter – it'll leave you licking your lips for the next few hours. The exposed brick walls, zinc-topped tables and old school chairs work very well and the atmosphere is fun without ever becoming too excitable. The terrific prices entice in plenty of passers-by.

York & Albany

 modern

Camden Town
127-129 Parkway ✉ NW1 7PS
📞 (020) 7388 3344
www.gordonramsay.com/yorkandalbany

⊖ **Camden Town.**
Booking essential

Menu £18 (weekday lunch)/21 – Carte £29/47

VISA

M©

AE

These days things are more egalitarian down at the York & Albany, a handsome 1820s John Nash coaching inn rescued by Gordon Ramsay after lying virtually derelict for years. Gone is the separation of bar and restaurant dining – you are now offered the same menu wherever you want to sit, whether that's in the bar, the back restaurant or downstairs next to the open kitchen. The menu has also been made a little more inclusive and now includes wood-fired pizzas and pasta dishes alongside more adventurous choices like lamb shoulder with braised celery and duck with hispi cabbage. It works well because the kitchen treats a burger with the same respect as they do a rib-eye steak, although service can still wobble at times. The bedrooms have character.

NORTH-WEST ▶ PLAN XV

311

Ⓝ Shayona

E2

Church End
54-62 Meadow Garth ✉ NW10 8HD
✆ (020) 8965 3365
www.shayonarestaurants.com

⊖ Stonebridge Park
Closed 12-14 November

Carte £11/17

Ⓐ/Ⓒ
Ⓥ
☼
VISA
Ⓜ/Ⓒ

Shayona sits in the shadow of Neasden's remarkable Shri Swaminarayan Mandir and is actually owned by the temple. In contrast to the splendour of this Hindu gem, the restaurant is housed within a building that looks, from the outside, a little like a supermarket and indeed somewhat resembles one from the inside too— but head past the sweet counter and you'll find yourself in a comfortable and vibrantly decorated room. The fresh, balanced cooking here is sattvic which means it is vegetarian and 'pure' and so avoids certain foods like onion or garlic. The large and varied menu covers all parts of India and includes curries from the north, dosas from the south and street snacks from Mumbai. There is no alcohol available so choose a refreshing lassi instead.

Bistro Aix

H1

Crouch End
54 Topsfield Par., Tottenham Ln.
✉ N8 8PT
✆ (020) 8340 6346 – **www**.bistroaix.co.uk

Closed 1 January –
(dinner only and
lunch Saturday-Sunday)

Menu £15 – Carte £24/43

Ⓐ/Ⓒ
▭
☼
VISA
Ⓜ/Ⓒ

Bistro Aix has enough local followers that it doesn't need to entice passers-by, which is just as well as there aren't too many boulevardiers wandering Tottenham Lane in search of duck confit. It's easy to see why Crouch Enders have taken the bistro to their hearts: the French food is unfussy and dependable, the surroundings are rustic and relaxed, the wine list is competitively priced and the atmosphere welcoming. The menu offers bags of choice, with around 20 starters and just as many main courses, and the kitchen does the classics, like snails, onion soup, rabbit with mustard, and tart Tatin, particularly well. There is the added attraction of a very appealingly priced set menu on Tuesday to Thursday and Sunday evenings.

Bull & Last

British traditional

G2

Dartmouth Park

168 Highgate Rd ✉ **NW5 1QS**
✆ (020) 7267 3641
www.thebullandlast.co.uk

⊖ **Tufnell Park.**
Closed 24- 25 December –
booking essential

Carte £23/45

Dartmouth Park locals know a good thing when they see it and The Bull and Last, always full of character and life, is most certainly a good thing. If you haven't booked, it's still worth trying your luck as they keep the odd table back – mind you, with enticing bar snacks like pig's trotter wontons and soft shell crab tempura, you may simply find happiness at the bar ordering some of these to go with your pint. The cooking is gloriously robust and generous and the menu mainly British with some pasta dishes thrown in. The kitchen knows its way around an animal too – the charcuterie boards are very popular. Puds are traditional; cheese is in good order and the homemade ice creams are good. And where else can you get marrowbone for your dog?

Red N Hot

Chinese 𝕏𝕏

H2/3

Euston

37 Chalton St ✉ **NW1 1JD**
✆ (020) 7388 0808
www.rednhotgroup.com

⊖ **Euston**
Closed 25 December

Menu £20/23 – Carte £16/25

The clue is in the name – this is all about the fiery pepper, so if you fancy Chinese food but also want something different then Red N Hot should fit the bill. Formerly called 'Snazz Sichuan', it was set up by an émigré from Sichuan and forms part of the New China Club which includes a members' club and an art gallery. If you don't already know that Sichuan cooking is hot then you soon will. Again, more clues lie in the name of dishes, like 'hot and numbing beef jerky' - so you can't say you weren't warned. And don't be fooled into thinking that a cold dish will be any less fiery. The ingredients are also a little different: stir-fried kidney, pig's blood mix, fried intestines and pig's ear in chilli oil; hotpots feature at lunch.

Clissold Arms

modern

Fortis Green   ⊖ East Finchley.
105 Fortis Green ⊠ N2 9HR
✆ (020) 8444 4224
www.clissoldarms.co.uk

Carte £23/41

Such is the growing reputation of The Clissold Arms that it may soon be better known for the quality of its cooking than its more long-standing claim to fame – that of having played host to The Kinks' first gig. Come at lunch and the menu and atmosphere make you feel you're in a proper pub, where you can expect classics like fishcakes or steak sandwiches. At dinner it all looks more like a restaurant, with loftier prices and slightly more ambitious, but still carefully prepared, dishes. The place is a lot bigger than you expect and, while staff could do with a little more guidance, it's often busy with locals grateful to have somewhere other than chain restaurants in their neighbourhood. The decked terrace has recently been extended.

La Cocotte

French

Hampstead   ⊖ Belsize Park
85b Fleet Rd ⊠ NW3 2QY   Closed Sunday dinner, Monday and lunch
✆ (020) 7433 3317   Tuesday-Thursday
www.la-cocotte.co.uk

Menu £14 (lunch) – Carte £22/35

First an Italian restaurant tried its luck here and now it is the turn of the French. With its tricolour above the door, onions and garlic hanging in the window and classic red checked tablecloths, one's initial impression is of cliché overload but this is countered by the presence of the affable, self-deprecating French owner. The menu provides a checklist of robust and capably prepared bourgeois classics, from terrines and rillettes to steak frites, but what sets it apart – and the clue is in the name – are the small, shallow iron pots of slow-cooked ingredients. These are a must, especially on a wintery night, and leave one feeling warmed and satisfied. The ground floor is the lively spot; upstairs is a little more intimate.

Goldfish

Asian ✗

G2

Hampstead ⊖ Hampstead
82 Hampstead High St ✉ NW3 1RE
✆ (020) 7794 6666
www.restaurantprivilege.com

Menu £10/20 – Carte £24/58

For some reason Hampstead has never been the easiest place in which to open a restaurant but it looks like Goldfish may be one to buck the trend. This sweet place calls its cooking 'modern Chinese' but really the kitchen looks to influences from across Asia. The à la carte menu is lengthy but highlights include anything involving crab, the fish dishes and some of the chef's own creations, such as the rich Mocha ribs. Prices at lunch are very reasonable, especially the dim sum which pulls in plenty of punters at weekends. The place is divided into three little rooms which all have their own style. Staff have their hearts in the right place and they remember their regulars, of whom there are growing numbers.

Magdala

modern

G2

Hampstead ⊖ Belsize Park.
2A South Hill Park ✉ NW3 2SB
✆ (020) 7435 2503
www.the-magdala.com

Carte £14/29

The Magdala is divided into three: on the right-hand side is the locals bar – you can eat here but not many do as it's a little dark and you'll feel like an impostor. Just go left, grab a seat anywhere and you'll be served. The third part of the operation is the upstairs, used as an extension at weekends or for hosting the monthly comedy club or fortnightly quiz. There's nothing on the menu to frighten the horses: there are burgers, sausages, paella and charcuterie plates or meze to share. However, the cooking is undertaken with greater care than you expect and you end up feeling as though you're in a country pub miles from the city. The owner certainly found a novel solution to the problem of keeping her chef – Reader, she married him.

Wells

B r i t i s h   m o d e r n

G2

Hampstead

30 Well Walk ✉ NW3 1BX
✆ (020) 7794 3785
www.thewellshampstead.co.uk

⊖ Hampstead.

Carte £24/39

The Wells is named after Chalybeate Well which, in 1698, was given to the poor of Hampstead – it's about 30 yards away, next to that BMW. Equidistant between Heath and High Street, this handsome pub is split in two: downstairs is the busier, more relaxed part of the operation, while upstairs you'll find a formally dressed dining room. Apart from a couple of extra grilled dishes downstairs, the two areas share a menu, which is cleverly balanced to satisfy all appetites from spirited dog walker to leisurely shopper. Salads or seared scallops can be followed by sea bass, assorted pasta or duck confit; puds are good and they do a decent crumble. Add a commendable range of ales and wines and you have a pub for all seasons.

Paradise by way of Kensal Green

B r i t i s h   m o d e r n

F2

Kensal Green

19 Kilburn Ln ✉ W10 4AE
✆ (020) 8969 0098
www.theparadise.co.uk

⊖ Kensal Green.
(dinner only and lunch Saturday
and Sunday)

Carte £23/39

Their slogan is 'they love to party at Paradise' and, frankly, who can blame them? This is so much more than just a pub, it's a veritable fun palace – upstairs plays host to everything from comedy nights to film clubs and you can even 'host your own roast' with friends in a private room. If you're coming in to eat then grab a squashy sofa in the Reading Room off the bar and share some of the terrific snacks; or sit in the dining room where the cooking is showy but satisfyingly robust. Whether it's potted meats, terrines, chateaubriand or poached turbot, it's clear that this is a very capable kitchen. The atmosphere throughout is great and helped along in no small way by a clued-up team who know their food.

L'Absinthe

G2

Primrose Hill
40 Chalcot Rd ✉ NW1 8LS
✆ (020) 7483 4848
www.labsinthe.co.uk

⊖ **Chalk Farm**
Closed August, Christmas and Monday

Menu £11 (weekday lunch) – Carte £19/31

A/C

L'Absinthe has succeeded on a site where so many tried and failed because it gives the locals exactly what they have clearly always wanted: a classic French bistro run with integrity and enthusiasm. It offers the sort of food that really hits the spot at the end of a working day: beef bourguignon, duck confit, steak frites or some fresh skate, with a crème brûlée to follow. The place has an authentic Gallic air too, with its Belle Époque posters and staff who are either French or can at least do a convincing accent. Don't be put off if they give you a table downstairs – even if you are the first down there, it'll soon fill up with regulars. The other great strength is the wine list: the owner merely charges corkage on the retail price.

VISA

MC

AE

Odette's

G2

Primrose Hill
130 Regent's Park Rd. ✉ NW1 8XL
✆ (020) 7586 8569
www.odettesprimrosehill.com

⊖ **Chalk Farm**
Closed 1 week Christmas

Menu £20/25 – Carte £32/49

It's amazing what a window can do: they installed a big one at the front of the restaurant and it opened the whole place up and made it feel far more welcoming. Locals used to regard Odette's as being a little bit standoffish but service is now a lot chattier and the atmosphere more relaxed, which in turn makes it feel more a part of the community. The cooking is also a little less complicated than it was and is all the better for it, although there is still depth to the dishes. Flavours are robust and braised dishes a highlight; the chef-owner also displays a passion for his Welsh roots. The lunch and early evening menus are a steal and change every fortnight; there are also tasting and vegetarian menus alongside the à la carte.

Salusbury

Italian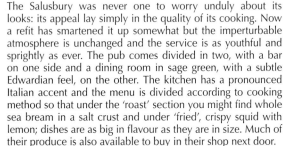

F2

Queens Park

50-52 Salusbury Rd ✉ NW6 6NN
✆ (020) 7328 3286
www.thesalusbury.co.uk

⊖ Queen's Park.
Closed 25-26 December
and Monday lunch

Carte £19/34

The Salusbury was never one to worry unduly about its looks: its appeal lay simply in the quality of its cooking. Now a refit has smartened it up somewhat but the imperturbable atmosphere is unchanged and the service is as youthful and sprightly as ever. The pub comes divided in two, with a bar on one side and a dining room in sage green, with a subtle Edwardian feel, on the other. The kitchen has a pronounced Italian accent and the menu is divided according to cooking method so that under the 'roast' section you might find whole sea bream in a salt crust and under 'fried', crispy squid with lemon; dishes are as big in flavour as they are in size. Much of their produce is also available to buy in their shop next door.

Gilbert Scott

British traditional ✖✖

H2/3

St Pancras

St Pancras Renaissance Hotel,
Euston Rd ✉ NW1 2AR
✆ (020) 7278 3888 – **www**.thegilbertscott.co.uk

⊖ King's Cross St Pancras

Menu £22 (weekdays) – Carte £29/42

Britain's less than stellar reputation for the quality of its food won't change until more people come and see what's cooking in our kitchens, so snaring those tourists as soon as they step off the Eurostar is no bad thing. Run under the aegis of Marcus Wareing and named after the architect who designed this Gothic masterpiece of a hotel in 1873, the restaurant has the splendour of a Grand Salon but the buzz of a busy brasserie. More significantly, the kitchen celebrates our culinary heritage by trumpeting both our native produce and regional specialities. In amongst the Eccles cakes, Manchester tart, Cullen skink and Glamorgan sausages are also dishes like 'soles in coffins' and 'Tweed kettle' that prove someone's done some research.

Ⓝ Shrimpy's

H2

St Pancras
The King's Cross Filling Station,
Goods Way ✉ N1C 4UR
☎ (020) 8880 6111 – **www**.shrimpys.co.uk

⊖ **King's Cross St. Pancras**
Closed 24 and 26 December –
booking essential

Carte £28/46

The capital's restaurant scene is fast moving, thrilling, witty and ephemeral, and if anywhere represents the zeitgeist it must be this old petrol station in the huge regeneration project behind St Pancras and King's Cross stations. The site is shrouded in a fibreglass hoarding, there are no signs and in a couple of years it will have turned into flats. Until then, the old garage shop has 14 tables squeezed into it; they are clad, ironically, in linen and staff wear crisp white jackets. The menu is California meets Latin America; chipotle, chicharrón, chimuichurri and ceviche all feature and there's plenty of deep frying going on. The soft shell crab burger is the speciality; the cocktails are terrific and the whole thing is enormous fun.

Bradley's ☻

G2

Swiss Cottage
25 Winchester Rd. ✉ NW3 3NR
☎ (020) 7722 3457
www.bradleysnw3.co.uk

⊖ **Swiss Cottage**
Closed Saturday lunch
and Sunday dinner

Menu £18/25 – Carte £32/40

Simon Bradley has been steadily going about his business for nigh on 20 years and has engendered such loyalty in his regulars that many of them wouldn't countenance a visit to a competitor until it had been going for at least a couple of years. Whilst there is an appealing and nicely balanced à la carte, the real draw here are the very well priced set menus. This affordability is achieved by proper 'cheffing' such as braising beef and buying less fashionable and underused fish like ling to create dishes with clear, complementary flavours. Simon is also a proper neighbourhood restaurateur: he can often be found at the local farmers' market and is now also responsible for the catering at the splendid Hampstead Theatre around the corner.

Eriki

G2

Swiss Cottage
4-6 Northways Par, Finchley Rd
✉ NW3 5EN
✆ (020) 7722 0606 – **www**.eriki.co.uk

⊖ Swiss Cottage
Closed Saturday lunch

Menu £20 (dinner) – Carte £16/27

A/C

☼

VISA

M©

Eriki eschews tired old standards and instead offers a diverse and contrasting gastronomic tour around all parts of India, from Goan curries to Punjabi-style prawns, Hariyali scallops to Lucknowi lamb. The cooking is fresh and invigorating; vegetarians will be in clover and the breads are good. The cutlery is imported from Rajasthan and the carved tables and heavy chairs add a sense of permanence. The staff are a pleasant bunch, although this vibrantly coloured restaurant can go from quiet to full in a matter of moments so get your order in quickly. Eriki is so much more than your typical neighbourhood Indian restaurant, a fact not lost on its many regulars. The only negative is the less than inspiring view of drab old Finchley Road.

Singapore Garden

G2

Swiss Cottage
83 Fairfax Rd. ✉ NW6 4DY
✆ (020) 7328 5314
www.singaporegarden.co.uk

⊖ Swiss Cottage
Closed 24-28 December

Menu £30 (dinner) – Carte £21/52

A/C

☼

VISA

M©

AE

Avoid the more generic dishes on the menu at this long-standing Swiss Cottage favourite and head instead to the back page of Singaporean and Malaysian specialities or to the separate list of seasonal dishes such as the 'grandma pork belly'. Squid blachan with sugar snap peas and plenty of chilli is a fresh and fiery number; Chiew Yim soft shell crab is full of flavour and Daging curry of tender beef and coconut is satisfying and filling. The staff are a happy and helpful lot; its female members wear traditional costumes, their male counterparts, bow ties. The room is comfortable and the clientele are a smart and mature bunch. The moped-riders keeping warm outside testify to its popularity in the local home delivery market too.

Junction Tavern

modern

Tufnell Park

101 Fortess Rd ✉ NW5 1AG

✆ (020) 7485 9400

www.junctiontavern.co.uk

Carte £24/36

⊖ **Tufnell Park.**

Closed 24-26 December
and 1 January

Over the years, Tufnell Park has appealed to young urban professionals because, along with its pretty Victorian terraces, it has a belligerent edge to add a little credibility. The Junction Tavern fits in well. The menu changes daily and portion size has been slightly reduced to give more balance to the menu as a whole; the cooking remains unfussy and relies on good flavours. There's plenty of choice, from light summer dishes such as grilled sardines and seared tuna to the more robust rib-eye and pork belly. Staff are a chatty bunch who know their beers – they offer weekly changing guest ales and hold a popular beer festival; the 'pie and a pint' choice remains a favourite. Commendably, they also offer tap water without being prompted.

Sushi-Say

Japanese

Willesden Green

33B Walm Ln.

✉ NW2 5SH

✆ (020) 8459 2971

Menu £15/21 – Carte £18/48

⊖ **Willesden Green**

Closed 2 weeks August, 25-26 December,
1 January, Wednesday after bank holidays,
Monday and Tuesday – (dinner only and
lunch Saturday-Sunday)

One of the delights of Willesden Green must surely be this long-standing Japanese restaurant which has never looked back since being revamped in 2007 and which is nearly always full. As the name suggests, sushi is the reason why many come and a seat at the counter, watching owner Mr Shimizu's expertise with his knife, is the place to be; if you're tempted to supplement your selection with some creamy uni or rich, warmed unagi then just ask him and he'll oblige. If you prefer other styles of Japanese cookery then you'll find plenty of choice; it's often worth considering the monthly specials menu; the yakitori is particularly good and there's a well-priced selection of sake and shochu. Mrs Shimizu leads her team with alacrity and efficiency.

North-East London

If northwest London is renowned for its leafy acres, then the area to its immediate east has a more urban, brick-built appeal. Which has meant, over the last decade or so, a wholesale rebranding exercise for some of its traditionally shady localities. A generation ago it would have been beyond the remit of even the most inventive estate agent to sell the charms of Islington, Hackney or Bethnal Green. But then along came Damien Hirst, Tracey Emin et al, and before you could say 'cow in formaldehyde' the area's cachet had rocketed.

Shoreditch and **Hoxton** are the pivotal points of the region's hip makeover. Their cobbled brick streets and shabby industrial remnants were like heavenly manna to the artists and designers who started to colonise the old warehouses twenty years ago. A fashionable crowd soon followed in their footsteps, and nowadays the area around **Hoxton Square** positively teems with clubs, bars and galleries. Latest must-see space is Rivington Place, a terrific gallery that highlights visual arts from around the world. Nearby are Deluxe (digital installations), and Hales (galleries).

Before the area was ever trendy, there was the Geffrye Museum. A short stroll up Hoxton's **Kingsland Road,** it's a jewel of a place, set in elegant 18C almshouses, and depicting English middle-class interiors from 1600 to the present day. Right behind it is St. Mary's Secret Garden, a little oasis that manages to include much diversity including a separate woodland and herb area, all in less than an acre. At the southern end of the area, in Folgate Street, Dennis Severs' House is an original Huguenot home that recreates 18 and 19C life in an original way – cooking smells linger, hearth and candles burn, giving you the impression the owners have only just left the place. Upstairs the beds remain unmade: did a certain local artist pick up any ideas here?

When the Regent's Canal was built in the early 19C, **Islington's** fortunes nose-dived, for it was accompanied by the arrival of slums and over-crowding. But the once-idyllic village managed to hold onto its Georgian squares and handsome Victorian terraces through the rough times, and when these were gentrified a few years ago, the area ushered in a revival. **Camden Passage** has long been famed for its quirky antique emporiums, while the slinky Business Design Centre is a flagship of the modern Islington. Cultural icons established themselves around the Upper Street area and these have gone from strength to strength. The **Almeida** Theatre has a habit of hitting the production jackpot with its history of world premieres, while the King's Head has earned itself a reputation for raucous scene-stealing; set up in the seventies, it's also

C. Eymenier / MICHELIN

London's very first theatre-pub. Nearby, the Screen on the Green boasts a wonderful old-fashioned neon billboard.

Even in the 'bad old days', Islington drew in famous names, and at Regency smart **Canonbury Square** are the one-time homes of Evelyn Waugh (no.17A) and George Orwell (no.27). These days it houses the Estorick Collection of Modern Italian Art; come here to see fine futuristic paintings in a Georgian villa. To put the history of the area in a proper context, head to St. John Street, south of the City Road, where the Islington Museum's shiny new headquarters tells the story of a colourful and multi-layered past.

Further up the A10, you come to **Dalston,** a bit like the Islington of old but with the buzzy Ridley Road market and a vibrant all-night scene including the blistering Vortex Jazz Club just off Kingsland Road. A little further north is **Stoke Newington,** referred to, a bit unkindly, as the poor man's Islington. Its pride and joy is Church Street, which not only features some characterful bookshops and eye-catching boutiques, but also lays claim to Abney Park Cemetery, an enchanting old place with a wildlife-rich nature reserve.

Greater London:
North East
(Plan XVI)

J

K

The Roundway Lane

High Rd

TOTTENHAM HALE

Lordship
Wood Green Lane

Lordship

Lane

Walsmead Rd

A 1055

Way

HORNSEY

Westbury Ave

A 1080

High Rd

The Avenue

Road

Tottenham Hale

Turnpike Lane

Phillip Lane

Tottenham Hale

Cranley Gdns

Muswell Hill

Park Rd

High St

Wightman

Ferry Lane

Fore

1

CROUCH END

Ferme Park Rd

Tottenham La

A 105

Green St

West Green

Seven Sisters Rd

Green

Broad Lane

Blackho Road

Highgate ⊖

HARINGEY

Road

Ann's

Seven Sisters Rd

A 10

A 1

Hornsey Lane

Crouch Hill

STROUD GREEN

Lanes

Amhurst Park

Stamford

Upper Clapton Rd

A 107

Lea

Chatsworth

Archway ⊖

Holloway

Hornsey Rd

A 1201

Seven

FINSBURY PARK ⊖

Road

Manor House ⊖

STOKE NEWINGTON

Tufnell Park ⊖

Sisters

Finsbury Park

CLISSOLD PARK

SHACKLEWELL

Downs

A 10

A 102

Tollington Rd

Holloway

Arsenal ⊖

HIGHBURY

Au Lac ✕

Lanes

HOLLOWAY

Caledonian

Highbury Park

Road

KENTISH TOWN

Camden

York Way

BARNSBURY

Trullo ✕

Dalston Lane

Graham Rd

A 107

Mare Street

2

Kentish Town Rd

e in en

Roots at N1 ✕✕

Liverpool Rd

CANONBURY

Canonbury Kitchen ✕

Northgate 🏠

Queensbridge Rd

Prince Arthur 🏠

HACKNEY

Camden

Fig Bistro ✕

ISLINGTON

New North Road

Cat & Mutton ✕

Victoria

Empres

KING'S CROSS

Eversholt St.

Upper Essex

Fellow 🏠

HOXTON

Albany St

ST PANCRAS INTERNATIONAL

Pentonville Rd

City Rd

Lena ✕✕

Hackney Rd

Old

EUSTON 🚉

KING'S CROSS

Fifteen London ✕

A 501

Old Street

Tramshed ✕

Rivington Grill ✕

SHOREDITCH

M

Tottenham Court Road ⊖

Farringdon Rd

The Hoxton 🏠🏠

Hoxton Grill ✕✕

Great Eastern Dining Room ✕✕

Boundary ✕✕✕

Heath Rd

Mile E

Princess of Shoreditch 🏠

Eyre Brothers ✕✕

Commercial St

SPITALFIELDS

Theobald's Rd

High Holborn

L'Anima ✕✕✕

Commercial

A 13

Road

Strand

Embankment

Upper Thames St

Commercial

WHITECHAPEL

LIMEHOL

Tottenham Court Road

see "Central London"

Highway

ST KATHARINE'S DOCK

3

ST JAMES'S PARK

Victoria

Blackfriars Rd

A 201

Union St

Borough High St

Mansell St

WAPPING

River

Thames

Jamaica Road

Lower Rd

A 302

Victoria Street

WATERLOO 🚉

A 201

Elephant & Castle

A 3

St George's

New Kent Rd

Tower Bridge Rd

SOUTHWARK PARK

VICTORIA

⊖ Belgrave Rd

0   1 Km

0   1/2 Mile

Lambeth Rd

A 201

ELEPHANT AND CASTLE

J

K

324

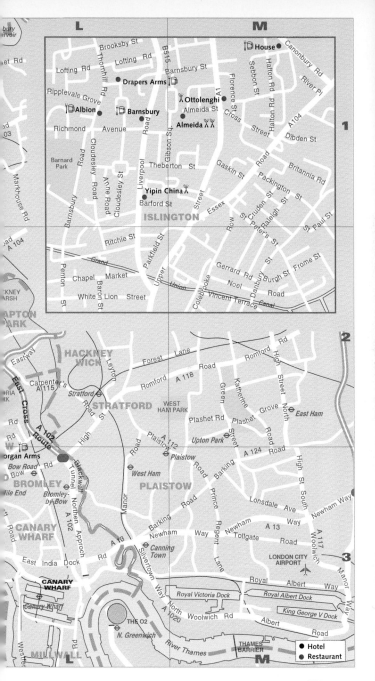

Fig Bistro

modern ✗

J2

Barnsbury
169 Hemingford Rd. ✉ N1 1DA
✆ (020) 7609 3009
www.figbistro.co.uk

⊖ **Caledonian Road**
Closed 22 December-3 January,
Sunday and Monday – (dinner only)

Carte £19/31

VISA
MC
DC

It's often the case that when a chef-owner opens a second restaurant he tries to give the impression that he's still also at the stove in his original premises. Owner-chef Christoffer Hruskova, now ensconced at North Road, is far too honest for such subterfuge and flagged up the simpler cooking style here by adding 'bistro' to the name. That being said, he may now be slightly underselling things here, as the flavoursome dishes still display a degree of polish in both execution and presentation. The compact, slightly frayed room may also lack the clutter and clamour of a bistro but it has definitely become more accessible – just check out the popularity of Sunday brunch. This welcoming, charmingly run little place deserves its success.

Roots at N1

Indian ✗✗

J2

Barnsbury
115 Hemingford Rd ✉ N1 1BZ
✆ (020) 7697 4488
www.rootsatn1.com

⊖ **Caledonian Road**
Closed 25-26 December and Monday
– booking essential – (dinner only)

Menu £20 – Carte £25/36

A/C
☼
VISA
MC
AE

Three friends from India came to London, worked at Benares for three years, then went their own ways. But they kept in touch and their shared dream came true when together they opened this restaurant in a converted Victorian pub in Barnsbury. The most startling and refreshing aspect of this warm, friendly operation is the unusually short menu, which changes every two months. Around a dozen dishes are offered, many of which are available in two sizes, along with a few vegetables dishes and four desserts. This means everything is prepared to order, and tastes accordingly. The tandoori lamb chops and the lamb shank Rogan Josh quickly established their own fan clubs, the breads are terrific and the refreshing kulfi provides a great finish.

Morgan Arms

British traditional

Bow

43 Morgan St ✉ E3 5AA

✆ (020) 8980 6389

www.capitalpubcompany.com/The-Morgan-Arms

⊖ Bow Road.
Closed 25 December

Carte £20/30

This former boozer's clever makeover respects its heritage while simultaneously bringing it up to date. The bar's always busy while the dining area is more subdued. You'll find the kitchen keeps its influences mostly within Europe but also understands just what sort of food works well in a pub. The daily changing menu usually features pasta in some form and staples like whitebait - which come devilled in this instance - assorted tarts and the perennial favourite, fishcakes accompanied by a poached egg. What's more, prices are kept at realistic levels which makes this pub appealing to those who live nearby and who like a little spontaneity in their lives. Look out for the occasional themed evening and charity auction.

Canonbury Kitchen

Italian

Canonbury

19 Canonbury Ln ✉ N1 2AS

✆ (0207) 2269 791

www.canonburykitchen.com

⊖ Highbury & Islington
Closed Monday –
(dinner only and lunch Saturday-Sunday)

Menu £10 – Carte £24/35

Inserting the word 'kitchen' into the name of one's restaurant is becoming more and more common as it instantly evokes images of simple food and unpretentious dining. That certainly applies to Canonbury Kitchen, which comes with an appropriately light, fresh look, thanks to its exposed brick walls, high ceiling and painted floorboards. With seating for just forty it also feels like the very epitome of a neighbourhood restaurant. Owner Max and his team provide gently reassuring service and the kitchen – on-view at the far end – sensibly keeps things simple. That includes an ever-popular fritto misto made with cuttlefish and octopus, pan-fried hake with herbs, and a lemon tiramisu with limoncello replacing the marsala.

House

 modern

Canonbury
63-69 Canonbury Rd ✉ N1 2DG
✆ (020) 7704 7410
www.thehouse.islington.com

⊖ Highbury & Islington.
Closed Monday
except bank holidays

Menu £10 (weekdays) – Carte £23/34

The front terrace is certainly an appealing feature in summer but, thanks to its warm atmosphere and candlelit tables, The House is just as welcoming on a winter's night. The regulars relaxing around the bar exude a general sense of localness and on the whole they prefer the sort of food that goes well with a pint; it's others who come looking for something a little special on the menu. The kitchen is intelligent enough to appreciate these two different markets in equal measure, so puts just as much effort into a shepherd's pie or a burger as it does with the sea bass or partridge. Weekends are busy, especially the breakfasts, but check first as The House often holds wedding receptions for those who've got hitched at Islington Town Hall.

Trullo

 Italian

Canonbury
300-302 St Paul's Rd ✉ N1 2LH
✆ (020) 7226 2733
www.trullorestaurant.com

⊖ Highbury & Islington
Closed Christmas-New year
and Sunday dinner – booking essential
– (dinner only and Sunday lunch)

Carte £24/34

The owners' CVs read like a checklist of eateries known for their relaxed atmospheres and uncomplicated cooking, including Moro, St John, and the River Café, so it is no surprise to find delicious Italian cooking here in this friendly restaurant, filled every day with noisily contented diners. The menu, small in size and content, changes daily so don't be surprised when something runs out. Expect great antipasti, such as pumpkin and chilli fritti, as well as flavoursome dishes cooked on the charcoal grill – and all at terrific prices. Trullo is named after the conical-shaped buildings of southern Italy, used primarily by farm workers for meeting and eating, which seems most appropriate for somewhere exuding such contentment.

Cat & Mutton

British traditional

Hackney
76 Broadway Mkt ⊠ E8 4QJ
☏ (020) 7254 5599
www.catandmutton.co.uk

⊖ **Bethnal Green.**
Closed 25-26 December

Menu £15 (dinner) – Carte £22/37

The Cat & Mutton has been a fixture here since the 1700s, when it was a drovers' inn quenching the thirst of farm workers bringing their livestock down from East Anglia. The streets round here might still frighten out-of-towners and the pub may now look a little frayed around the edges but step inside, look past the rough and ready character, and the young staff will make you feel reassuringly welcome. The open kitchen adds a little theatre to proceedings and the relatively concise menu changes often. The cooking is straightforward but is also undertaken with more care than you expect. Their beef is organic and in the evening steaks stand out amongst the more elaborate dishes. It's upstairs for quiz nights and art classes.

 **Empress** 🐶

Mediterranean

Hackney
130 Lauriston Rd., Victoria Park
⊠ E9 7LH
☏ (020) 8533 5123 – **www**.empresse9.com

⊖ **Mile End.**
Closed Monday lunch

Carte £22/29

The name of this 1850s pub was changed from the Empress of India as some customers arrived expecting chicken tikka – information which will dishearten history teachers everywhere. Queen Victoria has been demoted to the Empress of E9 but then everything is about being 'local' these days and that includes this re-launched pub. Sourdough comes from the baker down the road and their butcher and fishmonger are within walking distance; the menu is pleasingly seasonal and the cooking is several notches above usual pub fare. Dishes like risotto made with pearl barley and feta, or lamb's liver with lentils demonstrate that this is a kitchen with confidence and ability. Prices are kept in check and Sunday lunch is a very languid affair.

Lena

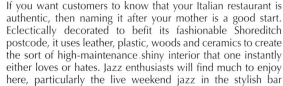

Italian 🍴🍴

Hackney
66 Great Eastern St. ✉ EC2A 3JT
📞 (020) 7739 5714
www.lenarestaurant.com

⊖ **Old Street**
Closed 25 December,
1 January and Sunday lunch

Menu £20 (weekday lunch)/45 – Carte £21/46

If you want customers to know that your Italian restaurant is authentic, then naming it after your mother is a good start. Eclectically decorated to befit its fashionable Shoreditch postcode, it uses leather, plastic, woods and ceramics to create the sort of high-maintenance shiny interior that one instantly either loves or hates. Jazz enthusiasts will find much to enjoy here, particularly the live weekend jazz in the stylish bar downstairs. The cooking looks to southerly regions of Italy for influences, especially around Naples and the Amalfi coast. Dishes have a bracing freshness to them, although the dessert selection is a little more predictable. Breads, pastas and ice creams are all homemade.

Prince Arthur

British modern 🍴🍺

Hackney
95 Forest Rd ✉ E8 3BH
📞 (020) 7249 9996
www.theprincearthurlondonfields.com

⊖ **Bethnal Green.**
Closed 25-26 December –
(dinner only and
lunch Saturday-Sunday)

Carte £21/43

Those who judge by first impressions will probably walk on by as this slightly scruffy corner pub would struggle to entice anyone on looks alone. To be honest, the inside isn't much keener on the eye, apart from the stuffed animals and the postcard collection, but then this isn't about appearances, more about good food and convivial company. Sit anywhere in the U-shaped room and the amiable staff will be quick to come over. The menu reads appealingly: smoked salmon, terrines, fish and chips, sausage and mash – but the cooking is done with unexpected care and more than a little skill; fish from Billingsgate is handled particularly deftly. Just thinking about the deep-fried jam or cherry sandwich for dessert will be enough to seal an artery.

Au Lac

Vietnamese ✗

Highbury
82 Highbury Park ✉ N5 2XE
✆ (020) 7704 9187
www.aulac.co.uk

Carte £10/23

⊖ **Arsenal**
Closed 24-26 December
and 1-2 January –
(dinner only and lunch Thursday-Friday)

It's unlikely to ever attract passers-by on its looks alone but fortunately enough people know about this longstanding Vietnamese restaurant, run by two brothers, to ensure that its phone rings red hot most nights. The comforts inside may also be fairly unremarkable but that just allows everyone to focus their attention on the lengthy menu, to which new dishes are added regularly. The pho noodle soup is a favourite but along with the traditional dishes there are plenty of more contemporary creations, all exhibiting the same freshness and lively flavours. The prices are kept honest, especially as the generous portion sizes mean that you don't have to order too many dishes to feel satisfied. They also do a roaring trade in takeaways.

Fifteen London

Italian ✗

Hoxton
15 Westland Pl. ✉ N1 7LP
✆ (020) 3375 1515
www.fifteen.net

Menu £24 (lunch) – Carte £31/48

⊖ **Old Street**
Closed 24-26 December and
1 January – booking essential

This is the original branch of Jamie Oliver's charitable 'Fifteen' restaurants and it's already on its ninth intake of trainees. Their programme lasts for 18 months and they receive schooling in all departments of the restaurant while being closely monitored by the experienced full-time staff. There are two operations here: the buzzy ground floor trattoria and a slightly more formal basement restaurant. The Italian cooking bears the unmistakeable signature of Jamie Oliver and the students are clearly being taught that most valuable of lessons: buy the best quality, seasonal ingredients and don't mess them about too much. This laudable project makes worrying about the occasional lapse seem somewhat mean-spirited.

Great Eastern Dining Room

Asian 🍴🍴

Hoxton ⊖ **Old Street**
54 Great Eastern St Closed Saturday lunch and Sunday
✉ EC2A 3QR
☎ (020) 7613 4545 – **www**.rickerrestaurants.com

Menu £24/38 – Carte £17/33

Will Ricker's flourishing group of hip restaurants came into its own here in Great Eastern Street and coincided with Hoxton's own emergence onto the fashion radar. The format here is similar to the others in the group: the bar, given equal billing as the restaurant, occupies most of the front section and it's usually so packed even a sardine would think twice. The noise spills into the restaurant, adding a lively vibe to the place. It's all great fun. The kitchen's influences spill across South East Asia, with dim sum, curries, roasts and tempura all carefully prepared. Helpfully, the reverse of the menu carries a glossary of Asian culinary terms. The serving team are a sassy and well-informed bunch.

Hoxton Grill

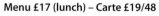

North-American 🍴

Hoxton ⊖ **Old Street**
81 Great Eastern St. ✉ EC2A 3HU
☎ (020) 7550 1014
www.hoxtongrill.com

Menu £17 (lunch) – Carte £19/48

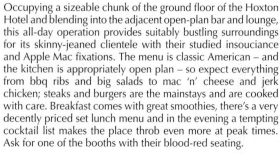

Occupying a sizeable chunk of the ground floor of the Hoxton Hotel and blending into the adjacent open-plan bar and lounge, this all-day operation provides suitably bustling surroundings for its skinny-jeaned clientele with their studied insouciance and Apple Mac fixations. The menu is classic American – and the kitchen is appropriately open plan – so expect everything from bbq ribs and big salads to mac 'n' cheese and jerk chicken; steaks and burgers are the mainstays and are cooked with care. Breakfast comes with great smoothies, there's a very decently priced set lunch menu and in the evening a tempting cocktail list makes the place throb even more at peak times. Ask for one of the booths with their blood-red seating.

 **Albion**

British traditional

Islington   ⊖ Highbury & Islington.

10 Thornhill Rd ⊠ N1 1HW
✆ (020) 7607 7450
www.the-albion.co.uk

Carte £21/42

This Georgian jewel couldn't be better named and it's not just the wisteria-covered façade or the comfortably worn-in look with its sofas and log fire that bring a patriotic tear to the eye. The menu also has a distinctive British feel with grills and rare breeds taking centre stage; Dexter, Belted Galloway and Longhorn beef all feature, along with Tamworth pork and Romney Salt Marsh lamb. For Sunday lunch expect a whole host of roast meats, and if you have 9 friends and the ability to plan ahead then consider pre-ordering the whole suckling pig. You can eat or drink anywhere – the bar has slightly more buzz than the restaurant. In summer everyone moves out into the walled garden at the back and barbeques become a regular feature.

Almeida

French ✗✗

Islington   ⊖ Angel

30 Almeida St. ⊠ N1 1AD   Closed 1-2 January,
✆ (020) 7354 4777   Sunday dinner and Monday lunch
www.almeida-restaurant.com

Menu £19 (lunch and early dinner) – Carte £20/49

If you're not here for a pre-theatre bite before going to the Almeida theatre opposite then try not to arrive around 7-7.30pm as you'll find yourself in the midst of an almighty exodus which leaves the restaurant in a degree of disarray and the waiters looking shell-shocked. They then dim the lights and take a deep breath but it's usually a while before the atmosphere builds again. Prices at this crisply decorated restaurant are more realistic these days, especially at lunch when the room really benefits from the two large windows. The menu's French influence is a little less pronounced but dishes still use intelligent combinations, like venison with pumpkin and lamb with artichoke. Look out for some interesting regional French wines.

Barnsbury

British traditional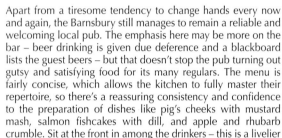

Islington

209-211 Liverpool Rd ✉ N1 1LX

✆ (020) 7607 5519

www.thebarnsbury.co.uk

⊖ Highbury & Islington.
(dinner only
and lunch Friday-Sunday)

Carte £17/30

Apart from a tiresome tendency to change hands every now and again, the Barnsbury still manages to remain a reliable and welcoming local pub. The emphasis here may be more on the bar – beer drinking is given due deference and a blackboard lists the guest beers – but that doesn't stop the pub turning out gutsy and satisfying food for its many regulars. The menu is fairly concise, which allows the kitchen to fully master their repertoire, so there's a reassuring consistency and confidence to the preparation of dishes like pig's cheeks with mustard mash, salmon fishcakes with dill, and apple and rhubarb crumble. Sit at the front in among the drinkers – this is a livelier spot than the small dining area at the back.

Drapers Arms

British modern

Islington

44 Barnsbury St ✉ N1 1ER

✆ (020) 7619 0348

www.thedrapersarms.com

⊖ Highbury & Islington.
Bookings advisable at dinner

Menu £16 (lunch) – Carte £25/32

Unless meeting the in-laws, your best bet is to stay on the ground floor of this handsome Georgian pub, as the more demure surroundings of the upstairs dining room, with its powder blue walls and flickering candlelight, are slightly at odds with the muscular nature of the cooking. This is the sort of food that prompts the rolling up of sleeves and the generous pouring of wine. Snail and chorizo soup, game terrine, Barnsley chop and onglet: flavours here pack a veritable punch and the kitchen recognises a decent ingredient when it sees one. The owners never forget that this is a pub and so prices are kept at sensible levels. Even the wine list plays its part by offering most of its largely French and Spanish selection for under £30.

Northgate

 Mediterranean

Islington
113 Southgate Rd ✉ N1 3JS
☏ (020) 7359 7392
www.thenorthgaten1.com

Dalston Kingsland (Rail)
Closed 25-26 December
and 1 January –
(dinner only and lunch Saturday-Sunday)

Carte £21/35

The Northgate is decked out in the usual gastropub aesthetic of mismatched furniture and local artists' work for sale on the walls; at the back you'll find tables laid up for dining and an open kitchen. You'll also find an extraction fan that's so strong you can feel its tug. Staff are pretty laid back, at times almost to the point of somnolence; go with a similarly relaxed frame of mind to avoid irritation. Where the pub scores is in the food: there's a strong Mediterranean influence on the vast blackboard. You'll find merguez and chorizo sausages, assorted pastas, a bit of Greek and some French – all in generously sized portions with the emphasis on flavour. Finish with something a little closer to home like treacle tart.

Ottolenghi

Mediterranean

Islington
287 Upper St. ✉ N1 2TZ
☏ (020) 7288 1454
www.ottolenghi.co.uk

Highbury & Islington
Closed 25-26 December,
dinner Sunday and bank holidays –
booking essential

Carte £25/30

Coming with friends and sharing is the key at Ottolenghi. It's primarily a deli, with tempting salads and piles of meringues in its window, but morphs into a little restaurant at night, with communal tables, speedy but sociable service and a fun atmosphere. Dishes come either 'from the counter', where a waitress will go and dish up for you – so be nice – or 'from the kitchen' which involves some heating up. The menu changes daily and influences come from all parts of the wider Mediterranean: this is all about good fresh ingredients yielding plenty of flavour – and Veggies will be in clover. Three dishes per person are too many, yet two are not enough, so sharing is the key. The desserts are especially good and if you think you know salad, think again.

Yipin China

Chinese ✕

L1

Islington
70-72 Liverpool Rd ✉ N1 0QD
☏ (020) 7354 3388
www.yipinchina.co.uk

⊖ **Angel**
Closed 25 December

Carte £16/30

A/C

Don't be put off by the flashing fairy lights or the pink and cream colour scheme, otherwise you'll miss out on some very appealing cooking. The menu at this modest little spot features Hunanese, Cantonese and Sichuanese specialities, but it is the spicy, chilli-based dishes from Hunan province that use techniques like smoking and curing that really stand out. Dry-wok dishes are a speciality here, as are the spicy pig's intestines and offal slices. Chairman Mao red-braised pork (he came from Hunan) is a fragrant, glossy stew and the sea bass with comes with an enormous number of salted chillies is exhilaratingly fresh tasting. The staff may seem a little shy at first but will make recommendations if prompted.

VISA

ⓜⓒ

Fellow

modern

J2

King's Cross
24 York Way ✉ N1 9AA
☏ (020) 7833 4395
www.thefellow.co.uk

⊖ **King's Cross St Pancras.**
Closed 25-26 December and 3 June

Carte £20/34

A/C

It was just a matter of time before a few decent pubs opened around the rapidly developing area of King's Cross. The Fellow is one of the busiest, attracting a youthful and local clientele; it also manages to give the impression it's been here for years. Eating happens on the dark and atmospheric ground floor, with drinkers heading upstairs to the even more boisterous cocktail bar. The menu is quite a sophisticated little number but the kitchen is up to the task. Start with ham hock terrine or potted crab, followed by roast rump of lamb or grilled haddock with champ. Desserts such as apple tart display a lightness of touch. The serving team are a bright, capable bunch. There is an outdoor terrace but you'll be surrounded by smokers.

VISA

ⓜⓒ

AE

NORTH-EAST ▶ PLAN XVI

L' Anima

Italian 𝕏𝕏𝕏

K3

Shoreditch

1 Snowden St. ✉ EC2A 2DQ
✆ (0207) 4227 000
www.lanima.co.uk

⊖ Liverpool Street
Closed 25 December, Saturday lunch,
Sunday and bank holidays –
booking essential

Menu £25 (weekday lunch)/29 – Carte £35/70

L'Anima is an extremely handsome restaurant that looks as though it should be located somewhere slightly more glamorous than the edge of The City. A glass wall separates the bar from the restaurant, where you find limestone walls, impeccably laid tables, white leather chairs and clever lighting; ask for one of the tables on the raised section at the back. The mood is sophisticated and the look smart and stylish. The chef may come from Calabria but his team have arrived from all parts of Italy. His menu is appealing and balanced, offering a mix of classic and less familiar dishes; and there's a helpful glossary of terms for the unfamiliar. The emphasis is on flavour and most dishes deliver that in spades. Service is smooth but also personable.

Boundary

French 𝕏𝕏𝕏

K3

Shoreditch

2-4 Boundary St ✉ E2 7DD
✆ (020) 7729 1051
www.theboundary.co.uk

⊖ Old Street

Menu £20 (lunch and early dinner) – Carte £34/65

When the management team took over his restaurant group, many thought Sir Terence Conran's days of opening restaurants were over. Not a bit of it, because he was soon back with a bang with Boundary. As is his way, he has taken an interesting building, in this case a large warehouse and former printworks, and turned it into a veritable house of fun. From the top, you have a roof terrace with an open fire; Albion is a ground floor 'caff' alongside a shop and bakery, and Boundary is the French-inspired 'main' restaurant below. The room is stylish, good-looking and works well, while the kitchen serves up reassuringly familiar cross-Channel treats, including fruits de mer. The fourth part of the equation are the comfy, individually designed bedrooms.

Eyre Brothers

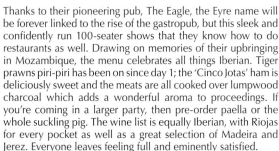

Thanks to their pioneering pub, The Eagle, the Eyre name will be forever linked to the rise of the gastropub, but this sleek and confidently run 100-seater shows that they know how to do restaurants as well. Drawing on memories of their upbringing in Mozambique, the menu celebrates all things Iberian. Tiger prawns piri-piri has been on since day 1; the 'Cinco Jotas' ham is deliciously sweet and the meats are all cooked over lumpwood charcoal which adds a wonderful aroma to proceedings. If you're coming in a larger party, then pre-order paella or the whole suckling pig. The wine list is equally Iberian, with Riojas for every pocket as well as a great selection of Madeira and Jerez. Everyone leaves feeling full and eminently satisfied.

Princess of Shoreditch

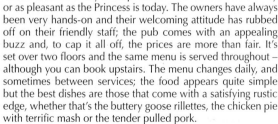

Apparently there has been a pub on this corner site since 1742 but it is doubtful many of the previous incarnations were as busy or as pleasant as the Princess is today. The owners have always been very hands-on and their welcoming attitude has rubbed off on their friendly staff; the pub comes with an appealing buzz and, to cap it all off, the prices are more than fair. It's set over two floors and the same menu is served throughout – although you can book upstairs. The menu changes daily, and sometimes between services; the food appears quite simple but the best dishes are those that come with a satisfying rustic edge, whether that's the buttery goose rillettes, the chicken pie with terrific mash or the tender pulled pork.

338

Rivington Grill

K3

Shoreditch
28-30 Rivington St ✉ EC2A 3DZ
☎ (020) 7729 7053
www.rivingtonshoreditch.co.uk

⊖ **Old Street**
Closed 25-26 December

Carte £26/56

A/C

A converted warehouse surrounded by design studios, galleries and printing premises means not only that this place is popular with artistically inclined types but that it also shows work itself, including a Tracey Emin neon "Life without you, never". However, it is also close to The City so head left when you enter as larger groups tend to occupy the tables on the right. The British menu will fill you with patriotic fervour – if this was what John Major had meant when he referred to 'back-to-basics' there wouldn't have been such derision. There's a section 'on toast' and oysters are a speciality; there are pies, chops and faggots, even fish fingers and bubble and squeak. There are also plenty of bottles under £30 and special offers for weekend lunches.

VISA

MC

AE

DC

Ⓝ Tramshed

K3

Shoreditch
32 Rivington St ✉ EC2A 3LX
☎ (020) 7749 0478
www.chickenandsteak.co.uk

⊖ **Old Street**
Closed 25-26 December

Carte £26/55

A/C

A striking Grade II warehouse, designed by Vincent Harris in 1905 to house the generators for the trams, is the setting for this stunning brasserie from Mark Hix. The vast industrial room is dominated by a piece of work from his mate Damien Hirst and this tank with a Hereford cow and a cockerel in formaldehyde reflects what's on the menu. The choice of main course is simply chicken or beef: a whole Woolley Park Farm free-range chicken (they come head down on a spike, claws and all) or marbled sirloin steak by the 250g, dry aged in the Himalayan salt chamber and ionised for extra sweetness. Come with two friends as starters, which include chicken livers in a Yorkshire pud, come in sets of three and one chicken feeds three.

VISA

MC

AE

DC

South-East London

Once considered not only the wrong side of the tracks, but also most definitely the wrong side of the river, London's southeastern chunk has thrived in recent times courtesy of the Docklands Effect. As the gleaming glass peninsula of **Canary Wharf** (ironically, just north of the Thames) sprouted a personality of its own – with bars, restaurants, slinky bridges and an enviable view, not to mention moneyed residents actually putting down roots – the city's bottom right hand zone began to achieve destination status on a par with other parts of London. You only have to stroll around the glossy and quite vast **Limehouse Basin** – a slick marina that was once a hard-grafting East End dock – to really see what's happened here.

Not that the area hasn't always boasted some true gems in the capital's treasure chest. **Greenwich,** with fabulous views across the water to the docklands from its delightfully sloping park, has long been a favourite of kings and queens: Henry VIII and Elizabeth I resided here. The village itself bustles along with its market and plush picturehouse, but most visitors make their way to the standout attractions, of which there are many. The **Royal Observatory** and the Meridian Line draw stargazers and hemisphere striders in equal number, while the palatial Old Royal Naval College is a star turn for lovers of Wren, who designed it as London's answer to Versailles. On the northern edge of Greenwich Park, the **National Maritime Museum** has three floors of sea-faring wonders; down by the pier, the real thing exists in the shape of the **Cutty Sark**. Up on the peninsula, the O2 Arena's distinctive shape has become an unmistakable landmark, but if you fancy a contrast to all things watery, the Fan Museum on Crooms Hill has more hand-held fans (over 3,000 of them) than anywhere else on earth. Strolling south from Greenwich park you reach **Blackheath,** an alluring suburban village, whose most striking feature is the towering All Saints' Church, standing proud away from the chic shops and restaurants.

Of slightly less spectacular charms, but a real crowd-pleaser nevertheless, is **Dulwich Village,** hidden deeper in the southeastern enclaves. It's a leafy oasis in this part of the world, with a delightful park that boasts at its western end, next to the original buildings of the old public school, the Dulwich Picture Gallery. This will soon reach its 200th birthday, and its pedigree is evident in works by the likes of Rembrandt, Rubens, Van Dyck and Canaletto. Half an hour's walk away across the park is the brilliant Horniman Museum, full of natural history and world culture delights – as well as a massive aquarium that seems to take up much of southeast London.

C. Eymenier / MICHELIN

A bit further east along the South Circular, there's the unexpected gem of Eltham Palace, originally the childhood home of Henry VIII with a magnificent (and still visible) Great Hall. What makes it unique is the adjacent Art Deco mansion built for millionaires in the 1930s in Ocean Liner style. It's the closest you'll ever get to a setting fit for hog roast and champagne. Heading back towards London, a lifestyle of bubbly and banquets has never really been **Peckham**'s thing, but it boasts a couple of corkers in the shape of the South London Gallery with its zeitgeist-setting art shows, and the Peckham Library, a giant inverted 'L' that after a decade still looks like a lot of fun to go into.

Back in the luxury flat-lands of the **Docklands, Wapping** has become an interesting port of call, its new-build architecture mixing in with a still Dickensian feel, in the shape of glowering Victorian warehouses and Wapping New Stairs, where the bodies of pirates were hanged from a gibbet until seven tides had showered their limp bodies. You can catch a fascinating history of the whole area in the nearby Museum in Docklands.

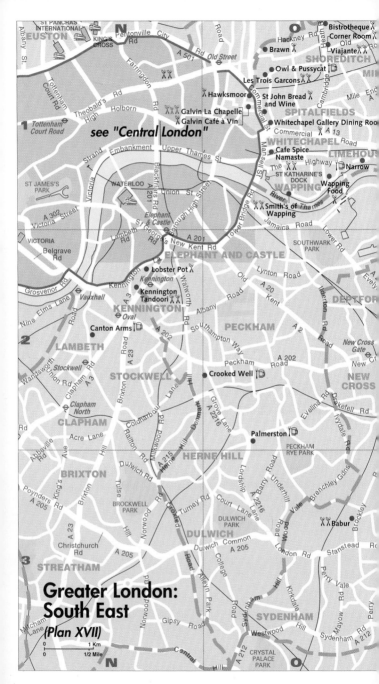

Greater London: South East

(Plan XVII)

0 ——— 1 Km
0 ——— 1/2 Mile

see "Central London"

EUSTON
ST PANCRAS INTERNATIONAL
KING'S CROSS
SHOREDITCH
SPITALFIELDS
WHITECHAPEL
LIMEHOUSE
WAPPING
ST KATHARINE'S DOCK
ELEPHANT AND CASTLE
KENNINGTON
LAMBETH
STOCKWELL
CLAPHAM
PECKHAM
NEW CROSS
DEPTFORD
HERNE HILL
BRIXTON
DULWICH
STREATHAM
SYDENHAM

Bistrotheque
Corner Room
Viajante
Brawn
Owl & Pussycat
Les Trois Garcons
Hawksmoor
St John Bread and Wine
Galvin La Chapelle
Galvin Café à Vin
Whitechapel Gallery Dining Room
Cafe Spice Namaste
Narrow
Wapping Food
Smith's of Wapping
Lobster Pot
Kennington Tandoori
Canton Arms
Crooked Well
Palmerston
Babur

ST JAMES'S PARK
VICTORIA
VAUXHALL
WATERLOO
BROCKWELL PARK
DULWICH PARK
PECKHAM RYE PARK
SOUTHWARK PARK
CRYSTAL PALACE PARK

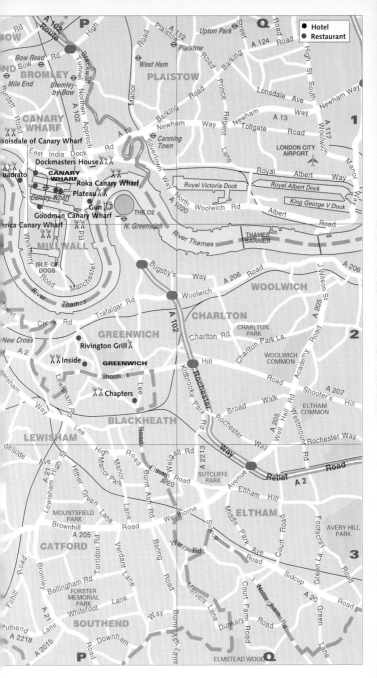

ⓝ Bistrotheque

modern ✗

01

Bethnal Green
23-27 Wadeson St ✉ E2 9DR
✆ (020) 8983 7900
www.bistrotheque.com

⊖ Bethnal Green
Closed 24 and 26 December
and lunch Monday to Friday –
booking advisable

Carte £24/44

When a restaurant has an exterior as irredeemably bleak as this, it can only mean one thing: it's going to be painfully cool inside. Converted from an old sweat shop, the owners purposely left the exterior bereft of any sign of gastronomic life – just head past the anguished graffiti and take the stairs in the courtyard up to the 1st floor. Here you'll find a warmly run, wonderfully bustling industrial-looking space, with beams and girders, ducting and concrete. It's all great fun, especially as the restaurant rubs shoulders with the cabaret. The menu is predominantly French bistro in style with some British classics thrown in. A good value set menu is offered early and late in the evening and weekend brunch comes with live music.

Brawn

Mediterranean ✗

01

Bethnal Green
49 Columbia Rd. ✉ E2 7RG
✆ (020) 7729 5692
www.brawn.co

⊖ Bethnal Green
▶ **Plan XVI**
Closed Sunday dinner and bank holidays
– (dinner only and lunch Thursday-Sunday)

Carte £21/30

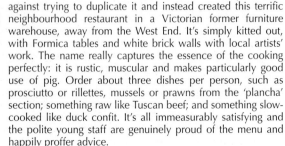

After the success of Terroirs, the owners wisely decided against trying to duplicate it and instead created this terrific neighbourhood restaurant in a Victorian former furniture warehouse, away from the West End. It's simply kitted out, with Formica tables and white brick walls with local artists' work. The name really captures the essence of the cooking perfectly: it is rustic, muscular and makes particularly good use of pig. Order about three dishes per person, such as prosciutto or rillettes, mussels or prawns from the 'plancha' section; something raw like Tuscan beef; and something slow-cooked like duck confit. It's all immeasurably satisfying and the polite young staff are genuinely proud of the menu and happily proffer advice.

Corner Room 😊

innovative ✗

01

Bethnal Green
Town Hall Hotel,
Patriot Sq ✉ E2 9NF
✆ (020) 7871 0461 – **www**.cornerroom.co.uk

⊖ Bethnal Green
(bookings not accepted at dinner)

Menu £19/21 – Carte £24/33

[AC] [☼] [VISA] [MC] [AE]

Corner Room is Nuno Mendes' more accessible addendum to his Viajante restaurant and is secreted upstairs in the old town hall. You'll find cooking that is equally innovative and undertaken with the same care, but by using slightly lesser cuts and fewer luxury ingredients, the prices are far more down to earth. Dishes such as sea bass ceviche with edamame, Iberico pork with Portuguese bread pudding or dark chocolate with peanut butter ice cream are as tasty as they are attractive. It's open all day so just pitch up and, if they haven't got a table, simply give them your name and wander down to the bar. A backdrop of hanging lamps adds character to the simply furnished and quite small room, which has just 13 tables.

Chapters

modern ✗✗

P2

Blackheath
43-45 Montpelier Vale ✉ SE3 0TJ
✆ (020) 8333 2666
www.chaptersrestaurants.com

Closed 2-3 January

Carte £21/30

[AC] [☼] [VISA] [MC] [AE] [①]

Down at Chapters it appears to be the '80s all over again: the champagne flows, the cocktails are shaken and everyone knows everyone else. If ever there was a change of concept that worked it was here: out went the serious, in came just the sort of place you'd want to come to after a hard day's work. The bar is always packed; the restaurant has an ersatz industrial feel and the menu is reassuringly familiar with a roll-call of classics that include fish and chips and belly of pork. The most expensive dishes are also the most popular – the assorted meats cooked over charcoal in the Josper oven. It's an all-day operation and they take as much care with breakfast as they do with dinner, while service is ably performed by a nimble team.

SOUTH-EAST ▶ PLAN XVI

345

Viajante ✿

01

innovative 𝖷𝖸

Bethnal Green
Town Hall Hotel,
Patriot Sq. (entrance on
Cambridge Heath Rd) ✉ E2 9NF
☏ (020) 7871 0461
www.viajante.co.uk

Menu £35/65

⊖ Bethnal Green
Closed bank holidays –
booking essential –
(dinner only and
lunch Friday-Sunday)

Viajante

Portuguese chef Nuno Mendes finds the inspiration for his innovative cuisine from his travels, so it is fitting that he opened his restaurant in Bethnal Green, one of London's most culturally diverse districts. You'll find this two-roomed restaurant inside the old town hall, where a subtle scent of civic functionality still permeates. The open kitchen is an integral part of the setup but don't arrive expecting blasts of heat and drama – this is a sleek, controlled environment that's more about sous-vide than stockpots. Choose 6, 9 or, if pre-booked, 12 courses, which is not as daunting a prospect as it sounds: even though considerable work has gone into the dishes, they are perfectly balanced and the combinations of flavours and textures have been thoroughly considered. Delicate, diminutive dishes like scallops with carrots or lobster with duck egg provide pleasingly familiar flavours, while other dishes such as pickled and raw cucumber with milk sorbet or beetroot with dark chocolate offer more challenging yet still highly enjoyable combinations.

First Course

- Razor clams, frozen pine nut and squid.
- Crab with egg yolk and rhubarb.

Main Course

- Iberico pluma with goat's curd and black quinoa.
- Turbot with spring vegetables and mussels.

Dessert

- Cucumber with reduced milk and sorrel.
- Jerusalem artichokes, chocolate soil and orange.

Boisdale of Canary Wharf

regional ✗✗

Canary Wharf

Cabot Pl ⊠ E14 4QT
☎ (020) 7715 5818
www.boisdale.co.uk

⊖ Canary Wharf
Booking advisable

Menu £20 – Carte £32/84

This is two operations under one roof: get out of the lift on the 1st floor for the art deco inspired Oyster bar: a richly decorated, tartan room centred around a marble topped bar. Here it's about relaxed dining, with an impressive selection of crustacea along with burgers and steaks. It has a lovely terrace overlooking Cabot Square and a walk-in humidor with an impressive selection of Cuban cigars. Climb out on the 2nd floor and three things hit you: the fabulous bay window, a stage and a remarkable wall of whiskies. Things here are grander and more comfortable and there's live jazz for which a charge in made. In amongst the caviar, steaks and assorted dishes of Scottish persuasion is the more moderately priced Jacobite menu.

Dockmaster's House

Indian ✗✗✗

Canary Wharf

1 Hertsmere Rd ⊠ E14 8JJ
☎ (020) 7345 0345
www.dockmastershouse.com

⊖ Canary Wharf
Closed 25 December-1 January,
bank holidays, Saturday lunch
and Sunday – booking advisable

Menu £20 (lunch and early dinner) – Carte £28/46

On the edge of Canary Wharf and in the shadow of its skyscrapers sits this striking three-storey Georgian house which has been given a contemporary overhaul. There are two contrasting dining rooms: one in the original part of the house with all the period features; the other more modern and shiny and encased in a glass extension. There's a funky basement bar, plus rooms upstairs and a garden for private parties. The Indian food adds modern twists to its conventional foundations. The menu is more seasonally based than many but it is also more expensive. The saffron prawns are good, the grilled section is worth exploring and there are interesting teas; but a little less pretentiousness all round wouldn't be a bad thing.

Goodman Canary Wharf

meats and grills ✕✕

P1

Canary Wharf Discovery Dock East, 3 South Quay ✉ E14 9RU
☎ (020) 7531 0300
www.goodmanrestaurants.com

⊖ South Quay (DLR)
Closed 25-26 December, 1 January and Sunday – booking advisable

Carte £40/90

No one likes their meat more than those who business is business, so Canary Wharf was the logical next location for this growing group. Whether you're thinking corn or grass fed Scottish fillet, rib on the bone or US strip loin, the delightful staff will show you what's on offer and explain the maturation process. It can be wet and vac-packed from the US or dry hung from Scotland and Ireland; even the Aussies get in on the act with their Wagyu. You then decide on the cut and the weight, which depends on the relative sizes of your appetite and wallet. The quality of the beef is excellent, as are the side dishes like truffle chips. The lively brasserie style room, with semi-private booths, offers great waterfront views.

Gun

British traditional

P1

Canary Wharf
27 Coldharbour ✉ E14 9NS
☎ (020) 7515 5222
www.thegundocklands.com

⊖ Blackwall (DLR).
Closed 25-26 December

Carte £26/47

The 18C Gun may have had a 21C makeover but that doesn't mean it has forgotten its roots: its association with Admiral Lord Nelson, links to smugglers and ties to the river are all celebrated in its oil paintings and collection of assorted weaponry. The dining room and the style of service are both fairly smart and ceremonial, yet The Gun is a pub where this level of formality seems appropriate. Dockers have now been replaced by bankers, the majority of whom rarely venture beyond the 35-day aged steak. This is a shame as the menu cleverly combines relatively ambitious dishes such as game or John Dory with more traditional local specialities like eel and oysters. Even the dessert menu offers a mix, from soufflés to stewed plums.

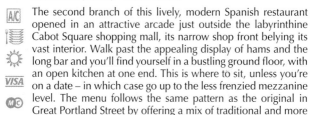

Iberica Canary Wharf

Spanish ❌❌

Canary Wharf

⊖ Canary Wharf

Cabot Sq ✉ E14 4QQ
☏ (020) 7636 8650
www.ibericalondon.co.uk

Menu £15 (lunch) – Carte £17/27

A/C 🕯 ☀ VISA MC AE ①

The second branch of this lively, modern Spanish restaurant opened in an attractive arcade just outside the labyrinthine Cabot Square shopping mall, its narrow shop front belying its vast interior. Walk past the appealing display of hams and the long bar and you'll find yourself in a bustling ground floor, with an open kitchen at one end. This is where to sit, unless you're on a date – in which case go up to the less frenzied mezzanine level. The menu follows the same pattern as the original in Great Portland Street by offering a mix of traditional and more contemporary tapas to share. Must tries are asparagus on toast with Manchego, grilled prawns with chilli and garlic, and the scrambled eggs with caramelised onions.

Plateau

modern ❌❌

Canary Wharf

⊖ Canary Wharf

Canada Place (4th floor), Canada Square
✉ E14 5ER
☏ (020) 7715 7100 – **www.**plateaurestaurant.co.uk

Closed 25 December,
1 January and Sunday

Menu £22 – Carte £29/57

🏠 A/C 🖵 VISA MC AE ①

In a building that wouldn't look out of place in Manhattan is a restaurant that harks back to a time when bankers ruled the world. This striking room, with its subtle 1950s design influences, is an impressive open-plan space and its dramatic glass walls and ceilings make the surrounding monolithic office blocks seem strangely appealing, for some reason. There are two choices: the Grill where, as the name suggests, the choice is from rotisserie meats and classic grilled dishes, or the formal restaurant beyond it, which comes with more comfortable surroundings. Here, the range is more eclectic and dishes are constructed with more global influences. They also come in ample sizes, though, so ignore the enthusiastic selling of the side dishes.

Quadrato

P1

Canary WharfFour Seasons Hotel,   ⊖ Canary Wharf
Westferry Circus ✉ E14 8RS
✆ (020) 7510 1858
www.fourseasons.com/canarywharf

Carte £27/53

Grumbling that a restaurant within a Four Seasons Hotel in Canary Wharf is a little too corporate in its look is like protesting about all the grockles in a Torquay tea room. Granted, most customers are tied and jacketed, but it is still a comfortable, well run room whose size is made more manageable by its subdivision into four smaller sections – but do ask for a table either facing the exposed glass-fronted kitchen or overlooking the terrace and river. The kitchen helps itself to plenty of luxury ingredients and uses them in dishes that reflect styles and flavours from all parts of Italy; portions are generous and clearly much care goes into the preparation. Sunday brunches draw in the crowds from an easterly direction.

Roka Canary Wharf

P1

Canary Wharf   ⊖ Canary Wharf
4 Park Pavilion (1st Floor) ✉ E14 5FW   Closed 25 December –
✆ (020) 7636 5228   booking essential
www.rokarestaurant.com

Carte £20/89

London's second Roka restaurant sits in the shadow of Canary Wharf Tower, now the UK's second tallest building, and the first thing to hit you, once you've actually found the entrance, is a wall of sound. This is a big, open and perennially busy affair, with tightly packed tables which are usually occupied by large groups of City folk – and is not somewhere for a quiet dinner à deux. The menu follows the format of the Charlotte Street branch by offering a wide selection of mostly contemporary Japanese dishes. The easiest option is to head straight for one of the tasting menus which offer a balanced picture of what the food is all about. The robata grill is the centrepiece of the kitchen's operation – the lamb chops are particularly good.

Palmerston

East Dulwich   ⊖ East Dulwich (Rail)
91 Lordship Ln ✉ SE22 8EP
✆ (020) 8693 1629
www.thepalmerston.net

Menu £14 (weekday lunch) – Carte £24/53

It's not just for the locals – those passing through for a visit to the Horniman Museum or Dulwich Picture Gallery must also be pleased to have somewhere so welcoming in which to extend their stay in SE22. You can sit anywhere, although there is a section at the back with wood panelling and a mosaic floor which they call 'the dining room'. The menus tend to evolve on a monthly basis, with influences ranging from the Med to Asia. The bread is good, which usually augurs well and, refreshingly, the dishes come with just the ingredients described on the menu. Add a well-priced weekday menu and a host of engaging young staff and it's little wonder the pub attracts such a wide range of ages, which in turn creates a pleasant atmosphere.

Inside

Greenwich   ⊖ Greenwich (DLR)
19 Greenwich South St. ✉ SE10 8NW   Closed 24-28 December,
✆ (020) 8265 5060   Sunday dinner and Monday
www.insiderestaurant.co.uk

Menu £18 (weekday lunch)/25 – Carte £25/35

The advantage of having an unremarkable façade is that it dampens unrealistic expectations. Indeed, 'Inside' was so named because the chef and his fellow owners had very little money when they opened, so wisely concentrated on the interior. With seating for just under forty, the room is tidy, comfortable and uncluttered, although it does take a few diners to generate an atmosphere. On offer is an appealingly priced set menu, elements of which change every fortnight. Dishes are attractively presented, relatively elaborate in their makeup and clearly prepared with care; most of the influences come from within Europe but staples do include the chicken and coriander spring rolls. There's also a decent choice of wine for under £25.

Rivington Grill

P2

Greenwich

178 Greenwich High Rd. ✉ SE10 8NN
✆ (020) 8293 9270
www.rivingtongreenwich.co.uk

⊖ Greenwich (DLR)
Closed 25-26 December,
Monday and
lunch Tuesday-Wednesday

Carte £25/39

It's open from breakfast until late and the menu changes every two weeks so they can introduce seasonal specials; the 'on toast' section is a local favourite and includes Welsh rarebit or devilled kidneys. Steaks are from Scotland; the prosperous can upgrade their fish and chips to lobster and chips; the puds are satisfyingly rich. The wine list is sensibly priced and includes beers and Somerset brandies. It's spread over two floors, with the ground floor being the more casual; it attracts a younger, hipper crowd than the Shoreditch branch and has a more local feel; it also gets swamped with look-alikes whenever there's a pop siren playing the O2 arena. Tables of up to four people can get a discount at the next door cinema.

Kennington Tandoori

N2

Kennington

313 Kennington Rd ✉ SE11 4QE
✆ (020) 7735 9247
www.kenningtontandoori.com

⊖ Kennington
Closed 25 December –
booking advisable

Menu £15/28 – Carte £17/29

Known affectionately as KT, the Hoque family's long-standing Indian restaurant was reinvigorated a couple of years ago when their son Kowsar took over. He brought the look up-to-date and then set about raising the standards all round. The result is that he now has a very pleasant neighbourhood restaurant that is clearly a cut above the norm. The menu is made up of recognisable classics and old favourites but the kitchen's skill is evident in the execution. Vegetarian dishes stand out and everything is made from scratch, from the chutneys to the kulfi. Mind you, many of the regulars, who make up the vast majority of customers – and include plenty of cricket fans and politicians – don't even bother with the menu and just ask for their 'usual'.

Lobster Pot

French 🍴

Kennington

3 Kennington Ln. ✉ SE11 4RG
📞 (020) 7582 5556
www.lobsterpotrestaurant.co.uk

⊖ **Kennington**
Closed 1 week Christmas,
Sunday and Monday

Carte £38/54

A/C
VISA
MC
AE

Ignore the fairly shabby exterior, dive straight in and you'll think you've stumbled onto a French film set. Fish tanks, portholes, the cries of seagulls and the hoots of ferries…the place has the lot and it's hard to avoid getting caught up in the exuberance of it all. It's no surprise that it's also all about fish. The chef-owner, from Vannes in Brittany, goes to Billingsgate each morning and he knows what he's doing: his menu is classical and appetising, with fruits de mer, plenty of oysters, a lobster section and daily specials on the blackboard. Be sure to make room for the crêpes, which are great. It's not cheap but it is an experience. Underlining the family nature of the business, the son has opened a brasserie next door.

ⓝ Babur

Indian 🍴🍴

Lewisham

119 Brockley Rise ✉ SE23 1JP
📞 (020) 8291 2400
www.babur.info

Closed 25-26 December

Carte £25/31

A/C
☀
VISA
MC
AE
⓪

It's not just its good looks and innovative cooking that set Babur apart – this long-standing Indian restaurant is also run with great passion and enthusiasm. Regular customers are invited to tastings and can even have an input on the quarterly changing menus – and the makeup of each dish is fully explained when dishes are presented at the table. The south and north west of India feature most predominantly on the menu but there are also Western-influenced dishes available, like crab claws with asparagus and saffron. Seafood is certainly a highlight, so look out for the periods of the year when the separate 'Treasures of the Sea' menu appears. You'll find suggested wine pairings for each dish, along with some inventive cocktails.

Narrow

B r i t i s h   m o d e r n

Limehouse

44 Narrow St ✉ E14 8DP
𝒫 (020) 7592 7950
www.gordonramsay.com

⊖ Limehouse (DLR).
Booking essential

Menu £22 (lunch and early dinner) – Carte £21/42

There can't be many London pubs with better views than The Narrow and Gordon Ramsay's group have made the most of the Thames-side location by wrapping a conservatory around this Grade II listed former dockmaster's house. The place has a real buzz, thanks largely to the many regulars at the bar, the occasional live music and the large number of diners which include plenty of tourists. The menu gives them an opportunity to discover our more traditional dishes such as Scotch egg, cottage pie, toad in the hole and the ubiquitous fish and chips. Dishes on the whole hit the mark although the kitchen can be a little heavy-handed at times. Look out for the good value set menu, available at all times except after 7pm on Fridays and Saturdays.

Galvin Café a Vin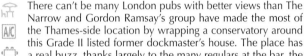

F r e n c h

Spitalfields

35 Spital Sq. (entrance on Bishops Sq.)
✉ E1 6DY
𝒫 (020) 7299 0404 **www**.galvinrestaurants.com

⊖ Liverpool Street
Closed 24-26 December

Menu £15 – Carte £23/34

In the same building as La Chapelle, but with a separate entrance around the corner, is this simpler but no less professionally run operation from the Galvin brothers. The room may not have the grandeur of next door but what it does offer is classic French bistro food at very appealing prices. Snails, confit of duck and rum baba are all here — tasty and satisfying dishes to evoke memories of French holidays and have you reaching for the Gauloises. So, if you want the fillet or the loin, go next door; if you're happy with the leg or bavette then come here. The place is loud, fun and friendly, and the atmosphere is helped along by a cheerful team and a thoughtfully compiled wine list which is also well-priced.

Galvin La Chapelle ✿

French XXX

Spitalfields
35 Spital Sq. ✉ E1 6DY
✆ (020) 7299 0400
www.galvinrestaurants.com

⊖ Liverpool Street
Closed dinner 24-26 December
and 1 January

Menu £25 (lunch)/30 – Carte £32/56

Galvin La Chapelle

These days, it is rare to walk into a restaurant in London and be taken back with the grandeur and sheer scale of a room. However, this venture from the Galvin Brothers, who have already proved themselves expert restaurateurs, is one that will dazzle the most jaded of diner. The Victorian splendour of St Botolph's Hall, with its vaulted ceiling, arched windows and marble pillars, lends itself effortlessly to its role as a glamorous restaurant. There are tables in booths, in the wings or in the middle of the action and those who like some comfort with their food will not be disappointed. It is also a fitting backdrop to the cooking, which is, in essence, bourgeois French but with a sophisticated edge, which means it is immensely satisfying. There are no unnecessary fripperies, just three courses of reassuringly familiar combinations with the emphasis on bold, clear flavours. Add in a service team who are a well-drilled, well-versed outfit and you have somewhere that will be part of the restaurant landscape for years to come.

First Course	*Main Course*	*Dessert*
• Lasagne of Dorset crab, velouté of girolles.	• Tagine of Bresse pigeon, couscous, aubergine purée, harissa sauce.	• Chilled Valrhona chocolate fondant, banana and yoghurt ice cream.
• Ballotine of Landaise foie gras, peaches and pain d'épice.	• Pavé of sea trout, risotto of tomatoes and broad beans.	• Toasted hazelnut parfait, lime confiture.

Hawksmoor

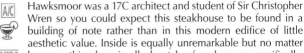

meats and grills ✗

01

Spitalfields
157 Commercial St. ✉ E1 6BJ
✆ (020) 7426 4850
www.thehawksmoor.com

⊖ **Shoreditch**
Closed 1 week Christmas
and Sunday dinner – booking essential

Carte £39/62

Hawksmoor was a 17C architect and student of Sir Christopher Wren so you could expect this steakhouse to be found in a building of note rather than in this modern edifice of little aesthetic value. Inside is equally unremarkable but no matter because this place is all about beef and, more specifically, British beef which has been hung for 35 days. It comes from Longhorn cattle raised by the Ginger Pig Co in the heart of the North Yorkshire Moors and the quality and depth of flavour is exceptional. Just choose your preferred weight – go for 400g if you're hungry. Starters and puds don't come close in quality but again, no matter, because when you've got some fantastic red meat in front of you, all you need is a mate and a bottle of red wine.

Owl & Pussycat

British traditional

01

Spitalfields
34 Redchurch St ✉ E2 7DP
✆ (020) 3487 0088
www.owlandpussycatshoreditch.com

⊖ **Shoreditch.**
▶ **Plan XVI**
Closed 25-26 December, 1 January and
bank holidays

Carte £20/33

As they did with The Fellow in King's Cross, the owners like to open pubs at the embryonic stage of a neighbourhood's gentrification. This was a run down East End boozer called The Crown which now has a raggedly modish look, with ironic touches of Victoriana to match the Edward Lear name. The ground floor is for drinkers and snackers; dining is done upstairs, where a concise but constantly changing and appealingly stout British menu is offered in the evening. Pork terrines, a crayfish cocktail or even oysters and Guinness may be followed by a Barnsley chop or a proper pie. Their puds, like lavender rice pudding and rhubarb crumble, are the kind that should be compulsory in all pubs. Bread and filtered water are provided gratis.

St John Bread and Wine

British traditional ✗

 01

Spitalfields
94-96 Commercial St ✉ **E1 6LZ**
☏ (020) 3301 8069
www.stjohnbreadandwine.com

⊖ **Shoreditch**
Closed Christmas-New Year and
August bank holiday

Carte £20/33

Less famous but by no means less loved than its sibling, this English version of a classic comptoir is the sort of place we would all like to have at the end of our road. Just the aroma as you enter is enough to get the appetite going. As the name suggests, this is a wine shop and a bakery but also a local restaurant. The menu changes twice a day and depends on what's in season; the Britishness of its ingredients and its promotion of forgotten recipes will enthuse everyone, not just culinary genealogists. But it's not all man-food like roast pig spleen or 'raw Angus'; there are lighter dishes such as plaice with samphire; and the Eccles cakes are a must. From breakfast to supper, certain dishes are only ready at certain times, so do check first.

Les Trois Garcons

French ✗✗

01

Spitalfields
1 Club Row ✉ **E1 6JX**
☏ (020) 7613 1924
www.lestroisgarcons.com

⊖ **Shoreditch**
Closed 23 December-3 January,
Saturday lunch, Sunday dinner
and bank holidays

Menu £23/47

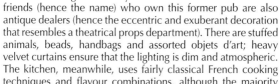

The surrounding streets may be somewhat drab but the three friends (hence the name) who own this former pub are also antique dealers (hence the eccentric and exuberant decoration that resembles a theatrical props department). There are stuffed animals, beads, handbags and assorted objets d'art; heavy velvet curtains ensure that the lighting is dim and atmospheric. The kitchen, meanwhile, uses fairly classical French cooking techniques and flavour combinations, although the majority of ingredients are British. Menus change seasonally and presentation on the plate is neat and appetising. The early-in-the-week set menu is good value; the à la carte somewhat expensive. Service can occasionally veer from the efficient to the over-confident.

Canton Arms

British modern

177 South Lambeth Rd ⊠ SW8 1XP

℘ (020) 7582 8710

www.cantonarms.com

⊖ Stockwell.
Closed Christmas-New Year,
Monday lunch, Sunday dinner
and bank holidays

Carte £19/31

VISA

Its appreciative audience prove that the demand for fresh, honest, seasonal food is not just limited to smart squares in Chelsea or Islington. The oval-shaped bar dominates the room, with the front half busy with drinkers and the back laid up for diners, although it's all very relaxed and you can eat where you want. The kitchen's experience in places like the Anchor & Hope and Great Queen Street is obvious on their menu which features rustic, earthy British food, of the sort that suits this environment so well. Lunch could be a kipper or tripe and chips; even a reinvented toasted sandwich. Dinner sees a short, no-nonsense menu offering perhaps braised venison or grilled haddock, with daily specials like steak and kidney pie for two.

Smith's of Wapping

fish and seafood

22 Wapping High St ⊠ E1W 1NJ

℘ (020) 7488 3456

www.smithsbrasserie.com

⊖ Wapping
Closed Sunday dinner –
booking advisable

Menu £20/30 – Carte £29/58

VISA

Having been providing seafood to the burghers of Essex for over 50 years, the Smith family have finally got around to opening a second branch. In 2011 they joined forces with a local restaurateur to open this large, contemporary brasserie looking out over the bobbing houseboats on the river and providing great views of Tower Bridge. The menu is a lengthy but appealing read and the kitchen is unapologetically traditional in its approach. Subsequently the best dishes are old favourites like deep-fried calamari from Cornwall, whole dressed Scottish crab or Dover sole meunière, served on or off the bone. Lobster thermidor is proving equally popular and they'll cook your fish however you wish. They also do a decent pudding.

Wapping Food

modern ✗

O1

Wapping
Wapping Wall ✉ E1W 3SG
✆ (020) 7680 2080
www.thewappingproject.com

⊖ **Wapping**
Closed 24 December-3 January,
Sunday dinner and bank holidays

Menu £38/54 – Carte £27/45

VISA
MC
AE

What does a former theatre director with a passion for food do when looking for a change? She buys a disused Victorian former hydraulic power station, spends two years doing it up and then opens it as the Wapping Project, a bringing together of a restaurant and an art gallery. The two functions marry perfectly: you sit among the old turbines and enjoy robust dishes fashioned from what suppliers have brought in that day. This could be mackerel with fennel, a ham hock terrine, Brecon lamb shank or panna cotta; all served by an enthusiastic team who know their onions. To make the most of your visit, be sure to take in the artwork before or after your meal; it could take the form of an installation, an exhibition or a performance.

Cafe Spice Namaste ☺

Indian ✗✗

O1

Whitechapel
16 Prescot St. ✉ E1 8AZ
✆ (020) 7488 9242
www.cafespice.co.uk

⊖ **Tower Hill**
Closed 25 December-2 January, Saturday
lunch, Sunday and bank holidays

Menu £35 – Carte £24/37

A/C
VISA
MC
AE
①

Cyrus Todiwala's contribution to Indian cuisine and the hospitality industry was recognised in 2010 when he was appointed an OBE. Café Spice Namaste opened back in 1995 and was where the dining public first became aware of his ability. The bright decoration of this former magistrate's court may not be quite so effervescent these days but the food remains just as fresh and vibrant. Many of the ingredients used are from within the British Isles and the cooking influences are spread across India; the Parsee specialities are particularly memorable. There's a plethora of menus to look through but don't hesitate to ask Cyrus' wife Pervin for guidance; she's a charming hostess who runs a tight ship and keeps an eye on everything.

Whitechapel Gallery Dining Room

Italian 🍴

01

Whitechapel
77-82 Whitechapel High st. ✉ E1 7QX
✆ (020) 7522 7896
www.whitechapelgallery.org/dining-room
Menu £22/28 – Carte £21/34

⊖ Aldgate East
Closed Christmas-New Year,
Monday and dinner Sunday
and Tuesday –
booking advisable

A/C
📱
📋
VISA
MC
AE

Angela Hartnett oversees things here in her role as a consultant chef and she's made some positive changes. Out went the set menu and in came greater flexibility that is far more appropriate to an informal gallery setting. The menu is divided into 'nibbles', 'small plates' and 'bigger plates' and most of the dishes are of European provenance, with the Med supplying plenty of influences, in dishes like rump of lamb with Niçoise salad. The Whitechapel Gallery was founded in 1901 and is best known for exhibiting Picasso's 'Guernica'. It underwent a major refit in 2009, when it expanded into the former library next door and created this very sweet restaurant. It's a bright, well-lit room, with tightly packed tables.

Somewhere for breakfast?
Look for the 🛏 !

Royal
Observatory
Greenwich

SHEPHERD PATENTEE
53 LEADENHALL ST LONDON
GALVANO-MAGNETIC CLOCK

South-West London

Meandering like a silver snake, **The Thames** coils serenely through south-west London, adding definition to the area's much-heralded middle-class enclaves and leafy suburbs. It's the focal point to the annual **university boat race** from **Putney** to **Mortlake,** and it serves as the giant glass pond attractively backing countless bank-side pubs. This area has long been regarded as the cosy bourgeois side of town, though within its postcode prowls the lively and eclectic **Brixton,** whose buzzing street markets and lauded music venues add an urban lustre and vibrant edge.

In most people's minds, though, south-west London finds its true colours in the beautiful terrace view from the top of **Richmond Hill,** as the river bends majestically through the meadows below. Or in the smart **Wimbledon Village,** its independent boutiques ranged prettily along its own hill, with the open spaces of the Common for a back garden. Or, again, in the Italianate architecture that makes **Chiswick House** and grounds a little corner of the Mediterranean close to the Great West Road.

Green space is almost as prolific in this zone as the streets of Victorian and Edwardian villas. **Richmond Park** is the largest royal park in the whole of London and teems with kite flyers, cyclists and deer – though not necessarily in that order. From here, round a southerly bend in the river, delightful grounds surround **Ham House,** which celebrated its 400th birthday in 2010, although not so excessively as during the seventeenth century when it was home to Restoration court life. Head slightly north to **Kew Gardens** and its world famous 300 acres can now be viewed from above – the treetop walkway, takes you 60 feet up to offer some breath-taking views. Just across the river from here is another from the historical hit-list: **Syon Park,** which boasts water meadows still grazed by cattle, giving it a distinctly rural aspect. Syon House is considered one of architect Robert Adam's finest works; it certainly appealed to Queen Victoria, who spent much of her young life here. Up the road in bourgeoning Brentford, two unique museums bring in hordes of the curious: the Musical Museum includes a huge Wurlitzer theatre organ (get lucky and watch it being played), while almost next door, the Kew Bridge Steam Museum shows off all things steamy on a grand scale, including massive beam engines which pumped London's water for over a century.

Hammersmith may be known for its bustling Broadway and flyover, but five minutes' walk from here is the Upper Mall, which has iconic riverside pubs and Kelmscott House, the last home of artistic visionary William Morris: down in the basement and coach house are impressive memorabilia related to

D. Chapuis / MICHELIN

his life plus changing exhibitions of designs and drawings. From here, it's just a quick jaunt across **Hammersmith Bridge** and down the arrow-straight Castelnau to the Wetland Centre in Barnes, which for ten years has lured wildlife to within screeching distance of the West End. **Barnes** has always revelled in its village-like identity – it juts up like an isolated peninsula into the Thames and boasts yummy boutiques and well-known restaurants. The Bulls Head pub in Lonsdale Road has featured some of the best jazz in London for half a century.

In a more easterly direction, the urbanised areas of **Clapham** and **Battersea** have re-established themselves as desirable places to live over the last decade. **Clapham Common** is considered prime southwest London turf, to the extent that its summer music festivals are highly prized. It's ringed by good pubs and restaurants, too. Battersea used to be famous for its funfair, but now the peace pagoda in the park lends it a more serene light. And if you're after serenity on a hot day, then a cool dip in the wondrous **Tooting** Lido is just the thing.

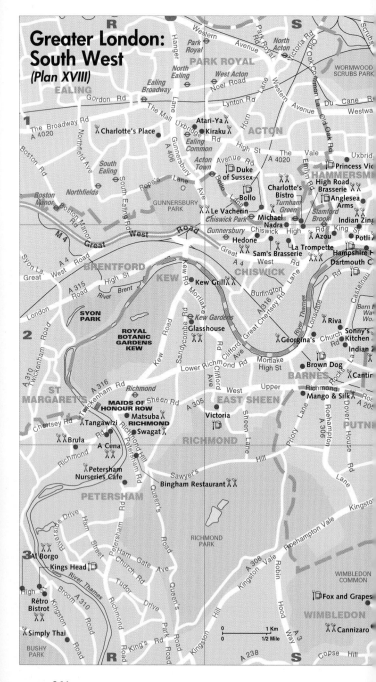

Greater London: South West
(Plan XVIII)

R

Scrubs

S

Western Avenue

Park Royal

North Acton

WORMWOOD SCRUBS PARK

Hanger Lane

Park Royal Rd

Victoria Rd

Old Oak Common Lane

Oak Rd

Du Cane Rd

Westwa

PARK ROYAL

EALING

North Ealing

West Acton

Noel Road

Western Avenue

Ealing Broadway

Gordon Rd

The Broadway Rd A 4020

The Mall

Uxbridge Rd

Lynton Rd

High St

The Vale A 4020

Uxbrid

Northfield Ave

Boston Rd

South Ealing

Charlotte's Place ✗

Atari-Ya ✗
Kiraku ✗

ACTON

Emlyn Rd

🏠 Princess Vic

HAMMERSM

Boston Manor Rd

Northfields

Ealing Common

Acton Town

Gunnersbury Ave

Rope's Lane

Bollo Lane

🏠 Duke of Sussex

Charlotte's Bistro

High Road Brasserie ✗✗

✗✗

Boston Manor Rd

M 4

GUNNERSBURY PARK

✗ Le Vacherin

🏠 Bollo

Chiswick Park

Turnham Green

Michael Nadra ●

Stamford Brook

🏠 Anglesea Arms

Gunnersbury

Chiswick High

Rd

Azou ●

Indian Zing

Potli

Great West Road

Great West Rd A 4

Hedone ●

Sam's Brasserie ✗✗

● La Trompette ✗✗✗

King's Rd

Hampshire H

Dartmouth C 🏠

BRENTFORD

High St

KEW

Kew Rd

Mortlake Rd

● Kew Grill ✗✗

Burlington A316

Great Chertsey Rd

Lonsdale

River Thames

CHISWICK

Castelnau

Bern Wa Wo

A 315

Syon La

Great West Rd

London Rd

A 310 Twickenham Road

Brent River

SYON PARK

ROYAL BOTANIC GARDENS KEW

Kew Road

Sandycombe Rd

Kew Gardens

Glasshouse ✗✗

Clifford Ave

Lower Richmond Rd

Clifford Ave

Great Chertsey Rd

Georgina's ✗

Mortlake High St

● Brown Dog

✗ Riva

Church Rd

Sonny's Kitchen ✗

Indian Z ✗

BARNES

Rocks

✗ Cantir

ST MARGARET'S

Twickenham Rd

Richmond

Sheen Rd

A 316

West

Upper Richmond

A 305

Sheen Lane

EAST SHEEN

Mango & Silk ✗

Roehampton Rd

Dover House Rd

PUTN

A 306

A 20

Chertsey Rd

✗ Tangawizi ●

MAIDS OF HONOUR ROW

RICHMOND

Matsuba ✗

Swagat ✗

Victoria 🏠

RICHMOND

Priory Lane

Roehampton

✗✗ Brula

Richmond Rd

A Cena ✗✗

Richmond Hill

Richmond

Petersham Rd

Petersham Nurseries Café ✗ ●

Sawyers

Bingham Restaurant ✗✗

RICHMOND PARK

Kingsto

PETERSHAM

Queen's

Ham Gate Ave

Ham Common

Kingston Vale

Roehampton Vale

Petersham Rd

Ham Church Rd

A 308

Kingston Vale

Robin

Hood

A 3

WIMBLEDON COMMON

River Thames

✗✗ Al Borgo

Kings Head 🏠

RIVER Drive

Ham Street

Petersham Rd

Broom Rd

A 310

Tudor Drive

Richmond Rd

Queen's Road

Park Road

King's Rd

Kingston Road

Hood Lane

🏠 Fox and Grapes

WIMBLEDON

High

Rétro Bistrot ✗✗

✗ Simply Thai

BUSHY PARK

R

A 238

Kingston Hill

Copse Hill

✗✗ Cannizaro

0   1 Km
0   1/2 Mile

A 3

S

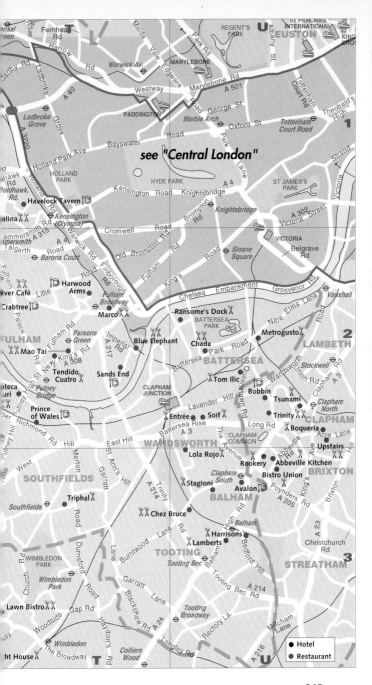

see "Central London"

Fernhead Rd
Harrow Rd
REGENT'S PARK
ST PANCRAS INTERNATIONAL
EUSTON
KING'S CROSS
Albany St.

Maida Vale
Warwick Av.
Edgware Road
Park Rd
MARYLEBONE
Tottenham Court Rd
Theobald's
High

Westway
A 40
Marylebone Rd
A 501
George St.

PADDINGTON
Marble Arch
Oxford St
Tottenham Court Road

Ladbroke Grove
A 3220
Bayswater Road
Park Lane
HYDE PARK
A 4
Kensington Road
Knightsbridge

HOLLAND PARK
ST JAMES'S PARK
VICTORIA
Belgrave Rd
Strand

Havelock Tavern
Kensington (Olympia)
Hammersmith Rd
A 315
Talgarth Road
Cromwell Road
Old Brompton Road
Brompton Rd
Knightsbridge
A 302
Victoria Street

Barons Court
Finborough Road
Fulham Road
King's Road
Sloane Square
Grosvenor Rd
Vauxhall

River Café
Crabtree
Harwood Arms
Fulham Broadway
Chelsea Embankment
Nine Elms Lane

Marco
Ransome's Dock
BATTERSEA PARK
Metrogusto
LAMBETH

FULHAM
Parsons Green
Blue Elephant
Chada
BATTERSEA
Stockwell
Union Rd

Mao Tai
Imperial Road
A 217
Battersea Park Road
Tom Ilic
Queenstown Rd
Wandsworth Road
A 3

Tendido Cuatro
Sands End
CLAPHAM JUNCTION
Lavender Hill
Bobbin
Tsunami
Clapham North

Boteca
Putney Bridge
Prince of Wales
Battersea Rise
Entrée
Soif
Long Rd
Trinity
CLAPHAM

Richmond Rd
East Hill
WANDSWORTH
A 3
CLAPHAM COMMON
The Avenue
Boqueria
Acre Lane
Upstairs

SOUTHFIELDS
Garratt Lane
St Ann's Hill
Lola Rojo
Rookery
Abbeville Kitchen
BRIXTON

Southfields
Triphal
Merton Road
Trinity Road
A 214
Stagioni
Clapham South
Bistro Union
Avalon
Poynders Rd
A 205
Brixton

Chez Bruce
BALHAM
Balham High Rd

WIMBLEDON PARK
Burntwood Lane
Harrisons
Lamberts
A 23
Christchurch Rd

Wimbledon Park Road
Garratt Lane
TOOTING
Tooting Bec
Bedford Hill
STREATHAM

Lawn Bistro
Gap Rd
Blackshaw Rd
A 24
Tooting Broadway
Tooting Bec Rd
A 214
Mitcham Lane

Wimbledon
The Broadway
Light House
Colliers Wood
Longley Rd
Rectory La.
A 216

● Hotel
● Restaurant

365

Bollo

Mediterranean

S1

Acton Green   ⊖ Chiswick Park.

13-15 Bollo Ln ✉ W4 5LR

☎ (020) 8994 6037

www.thebollohouse.co.uk

Carte £20/30

The Bollo is a large, handsome Victorian pub whose glass cupola and oak panelling give it some substance and personality in this age of the generic pub makeover. Tables and sofas are scattered around in a relaxed, sit-where-you-want way and the menu changes as ingredients come and go. The kitchen appeals to its core voters by always including a sufficient number of pub classics like the Bollo Burger, the haddock or fishcakes. But there is also a discernible southern Mediterranean influence to the menu, with regular appearances from the likes of chorizo, tzatziki, bruschetta and hummus. This is a pub where there's always either a promotion or an activity, whether that's the '50% off a main course' Monday or the Wednesday quiz nights.

Duke of Sussex

Mediterranean

S1

Acton Green   ⊖ Chiswick Park.

75 South Par ✉ W4 5LF   Closed dinner 25 December

☎ (020) 8742 8801   and lunch 26 December

www.realpubs.co.uk

Carte £21/30

Perhaps it's part of the plan but the Duke of Sussex seems like a typical London pub, even from the front bar, but step through into the dining room and you'll be in what was once a variety theatre from the time when this was a classic gin palace, complete with proscenium arch, glass ceiling and chandeliers. If that wasn't unusual enough, you could then find yourself eating cured meats or fabada, as the menu has a strong Spanish influence. Traditionalists can still get their steak pies and treacle tart but it's worth being more adventurous and trying the sardines, the paella and the crema Catalana. This is a fun, enthusiastically run and bustling pub and the kitchen's enthusiasm is palpable. On Mondays it's BYO; Sunday is quiz night.

Le Vacherin

S1

Acton Green
76-77 South Par. ✉ W4 5LF
✆ (020) 8742 2121
www.levacherin.com

⊖ Chiswick Park
Closed 25 December and Sunday dinner
– (dinner only and lunch Saturday-Sunday)

Menu £19 (weekday lunch)/25 – Carte £30/44

[A/C]
[VISA]
[MC]
[AE]

Le Vacherin calls itself a bistro but, with its brown leather banquette seating, mirrors and belle époque prints, it feels more like a brasserie, and quite a smart one at that. The most important element of the operation is the appealing menu of French classics which rarely changes, largely because they don't need to but also because the regulars wouldn't allow it. The checklist includes oeufs en cocotte, escargots, confit of duck and crème brûlée. Beef is something of a speciality, whether that's the côte de boeuf, the rib-eye or the chateaubriand. Portions are sensible, flavours distinct and ingredients good. The only thing missing in terms of authenticity are some insouciant French staff and a little Piaf playing in the background.

Avalon

U3

Balham
16 Balham Hill ✉ SW12 9EB
✆ (020) 8675 8613
www.theavalonlondon.com

⊖ Clapham South.
Closed 25-26 December –
booking advisable

Carte £22/34

[icons]
[A/C]
[icon]
[icon]
[VISA]
[MC]
[AE]

So Avalon really does exist…and it comes in the shape of a huge, atmospheric pub topped with an illuminated sign that makes it hard to miss on Balham Hill. Sir Edward Coley Burne-Jones prints add a suitably mythical edge to the aesthetic of the long bar and here you can order the sort of snacks that go well with a pint. Head through to the tiled and characterful rear dining room for their seasonal menu which is of the sort to appeal to a broad constituency. You'll find everything from a pie of the day and steaks to dishes of a more Mediterranean persuasion like whole grilled bream with caponata or gnocchi with porcini mushrooms. Once the team warm up, service is pleasant and the large summer terrace at the back is a great feature.

Harrison's

Mediterranean 🍴

Balham
⊖ Balham

15-19 Bedford Hill ✉ SW12 9EX
Closed 24-28 December
✆ (020) 8675 6900
www.harrisonsbalham.co.uk

Menu £14/28 – Carte £21/38

Sam Harrison's Balham brasserie may not occupy quite as impressive a building as his place in Chiswick but it does emit a welcoming glow to passers-by and is just as popular with the locals. It's cleverly laid out with drinkers and diners around the central bar and kitchen which results in a lively buzz, helped along further by an appealing cocktail list. Cooking is fresh, simple and unfussy and dishes arrive with a polite smile and in good time; 'Harrison's burgers' are top sellers as is the fish and chips. The midweek set menus are very good value, BYO Mondays are popular and so are weekend lunches when the basement bar is transformed into a kid's play area/holding pen, giving parents the chance to grab a peaceful meal.

Lamberts

British traditional 🍴

Balham
⊖ Balham

2 Station Par. ✉ SW12 9AZ
Closed 24-26 December,
✆ (020) 8675 2233
1 January , Sunday dinner and Monday
www.lambertsrestaurant.com

Menu £15/30

Mr Lambert and his eponymous restaurant have succeeded by offering the locals exactly what they want: relaxed surroundings, hospitable service and tasty, seasonal food. The menu is updated each month and small suppliers have been sought out. The cooking is quite British in style and has a satisfying wholesomeness to it; Sunday's ribs of Galloway beef or legs of Salt Marsh lamb are hugely popular. Equal thought and passion have gone into the commendably priced wine list, which includes some favourites offered in 300ml decanters. Other nice touches include filtered water delivered gratis and velvety truffles brought with the coffee. The owner's enthusiasm has rubbed off on his team, for whom nothing is too much trouble.

Brown Dog

S2

Barnes
28 Cross St ✉ SW13 0AP
✆ (020) 8392 2200
www.thebrowndog.co.uk

⊖ **Barnes Bridge (Rail)**
Closed 25 December

Carte £21/32

VISA
MC
AE

Thankfully, changes of ownership don't appear to mean much here – perhaps you really can't teach an old dog new tricks – because The Brown Dog remains a terrific neighbourhood pub and the locals clearly love it just the way it is. Mind you, this pretty Victorian pub is so well hidden in the maze of residential streets that it's a wonder any new customers ever find it anyway. The look fuses the traditional with the modern and service is bubbly and enthusiastic. Jugs of iced water arrive without prompting and the cleverly concise menu changes regularly. A lightly spiced crab salad or pint of prawns could be followed by a succulent rump of lamb, while puddings like sticky toffee date pudding or gooseberry cheesecake are also commendably priced.

Georgina's

S2

Barnes
56 Barnes High St ✉ SW13 9LF
✆ (020) 8166 5559
www.georginasrestaurants.com

Closed Sunday dinner

Carte £15/41

A/C
VISA
MC
AE

Dubbed 'Superwoman' by the tabloids for juggling motherhood with a successful City career, Nicola Horlick has now turned her hand to the restaurant business by opening this bright, modern eatery which appears to be a perfect fit for Barnes. It certainly ticks all the on-trend boxes, from the clean white furnishings to the counter of artisan breads, salads and pastas – it resembles more of a smart café during the day and an informal restaurant by night. The cooking is simple, unadorned, easy to eat and comes with occasional Middle Eastern hints. They also do a weekend brunch and a take home service for the salads, cakes and breads. Service can be a little too serious at times but this is an undeniably pleasant spot.

Indian Zilla

Indian XX

Barnes

2-3 Rocks Ln. ✉ SW13 0DB

☎ (020) 8878 3989

www.indianzilla.co.uk

Closed 25 December –
(dinner only and lunch Saturday-Sunday)

Menu £15/27 – Carte £20/36

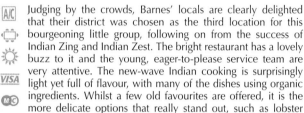

A/C

Judging by the crowds, Barnes' locals are clearly delighted that their district was chosen as the third location for this bourgeoning little group, following on from the success of Indian Zing and Indian Zest. The bright restaurant has a lovely buzz to it and the young, eager-to-please service team are very attentive. The new-wave Indian cooking is surprisingly light yet full of flavour, with many of the dishes using organic ingredients. Whilst a few old favourites are offered, it is the more delicate options that really stand out, such as lobster Balchao and specialities from the owner's home province of Maharashtra, like vegetable Bhanavla. The breads are super as is the lemon and ginger rice, and be sure to end with the Tandoori figs.

Riva

Italian X

Barnes

169 Church Rd. ✉ SW13 9HR

☎ (020) 8748 0434

Closed 3 weeks August,
10 days Christmas-New Year,
Saturday lunch and bank holidays

Carte £29/52

Customer loyalty is the sine qua non of any successful restaurant; those seeking guidance on how to build it should get down to Barnes and learn from Andrea Riva. His secret is to shower so much attention on his regulars that all other diners sit imagining the day when they will be treated in the same way – when he will tell them what he's going to cook especially for them. That could be some milk-fed lamb, game, suckling pig or risotto; all expertly rendered using tip-top, seasonal ingredients. While you wait for graduation, you'll be served by a friendly young female team and still get to enjoy some gutsy, flavoursome food. Andrea is also a keen wine collector so if you can talk oenology it could improve your chances of joining the club.

Sonny's Kitchen

modern 𝄪

S2

Barnes
94 Church Rd ⊠ SW13 0DQ
☎ (020) 8748 0393
www.sonnyskitchen.co.uk

Carte £26/39

When restaurants try to be all things to all people, they usually come a cropper, but Sonny's has successfully managed the task of being a deli, bar-café and restaurant and, as such, has firmly established itself as a much valued local landmark. It has also reinvested regularly over the years so that its upkeep is unimpeachable; and the owner's private art collection has added to its personality. The restaurant menu is full of seasonal goodness, like pot-roasted pheasant to warm the bones in winter or tortellini of crab for lighter months. This being Not-the-West-End means portions are generously sized and there's a very smartly priced set menu for midweek. Meanwhile, staff display a warmth and confidence that belie their youthful looks.

Chada

Thai 𝄪

U2

Battersea
208-210 Battersea Park Rd. ⊠ SW11 4ND
☎ (020) 7622 2209
www.chadathai.com

Closed Sunday
and bank holidays –
(dinner only)

Carte £17/36

Chada, whose positively resplendent façade marks it out on Battersea Park Road, is still going strong after 20 years, although it doesn't face huge competition. A striking carved Buddha dominates the simply dressed room but check out the owner's gilded headdress, displayed in a cabinet, which she uses for festivals. This may never be the busiest restaurant around but the welcome is always warm, the service polite and endearing and the Thai cooking satisfying and keenly priced. The menu is still a very long affair but it's easy to navigate through and the seafood selection is an undoubted highlight. Several dishes can be made with a choice of chicken, duck, prawn or vegetables; portions are generous and presentation is appealing.

Entrée

U2

Battersea
2 Battersea Rise ✉ SW11 1ED
✆ (020) 7223 5147
www.entreebattersea.co.uk

Closed 24-28 December –
(dinner only and Sunday lunch)

Menu £20 – Carte £25/42

The name doesn't quite fit as it implies a devotion to all things French and a degree of pretentiousness that is thankfully absent. In reality they have gone more for a casual bistro look which, along with an intimate basement bar and weekend pianist, appears to have hit the right note with the locals. The style of food is a little harder to categorise: the attractively priced menu offers a selection of French classics together with dishes of a more modern European persuasion, as well as other choices that could be considered as being more from the '80s. It is this third section which actually provides some of the highlights, such as the scallop and crab lasagne. Haunch of venison and the ubiquitous pork belly are also popular choices.

Lola Rojo

U3

Battersea
78 Northcote Rd ✉ SW11 6QL
✆ (020) 7350 2262
www.lolarojo.net

Closed 25-26 December –
booking essential

Menu £9 (weekday lunch)/15 – Carte £17/27

Northcote Road hosts a plethora of restaurants but few are as fun as this lively Spanish eatery. There's no denying the layout is a little cramped but the all-white look, dotted with splashes of red, makes it feel fresh. The owner-chef comes from Valencia so paella is a sure thing but other Catalan specialities are worth seeking out, such as the tomato bread, the creamy spinach with pine nuts, various salt-cod and shellfish dishes and, to finish, crema Catalana. Despite the volume of customers the kitchen delivers dishes promptly and consistently while the serving team just about keep up; 3 or 4 tapas per person should do it and there's an affordable wine list to lift the mood even more. It's little wonder the locals can't get enough.

Metrogusto

U2

Battersea
153 Battersea Park Rd. ✉ SW8 4BX
✆ (020) 7720 0204
www.metrogusto.co.uk

Closed 25-26 December,
Easter and Sunday dinner

Menu £12 (weekdays) – Carte £19/31

A/C

VISA

M©

AE

Ambro Ianeselli is one of London's most affable restaurateurs and his move from Islington back to his original Battersea base resulted in moans in the north and cheers in the south. This was once a pub and he's kept it uncluttered, although Metrogusto followers will recognise some of his modern art collection. They will also notice he's gone back to basics: the menu starts with 'morsels' such as delicious sweet and sour Sicilian aubergines, which can be followed by goat's cheese ravioli with a great walnut sauce or a generous helping of pappardelle with veal ragout and a decent panna cotta to finish. The food is simple and satisfying, matched with a fair range of wines from his homeland and his never-ending hospitality.

Ransome's Dock

U2

Battersea
35-37 Parkgate Rd. ✉ SW11 4NP
✆ (020) 7223 1611
www.ransomesdock.co.uk

Closed Christmas, August bank
holiday and Sunday dinner

Menu £16 (weekday lunch)/23 – Carte £23/46

VISA

M©

AE

①

It's not just honest cooking and a great wine list that are responsible for the impending 20 year anniversary: owners Martin and Vanessa Lam's passion and palpable enjoyment have also contributed to the success. Their menu is underpinned by seasonality and careful sourcing: duck is from Devon; lamb from Elwy Valley; beef from Cornwall and fish from Essex day boats. They also know their butchery and have most beasts delivered whole, so you may find gutsy dishes like braised shin on the lunch menu. Martin is equally passionate about wine; not only is his wine list far-reaching and well-priced but he also hosts winemaker dinners. The converted warehouse has a relaxed feel and the terrace overlooking the canal is a great spot in summer.

Soif

French

U2

Battersea
27 Battersea Rise ✉ SW11 1HG
☏ (020) 7233 1112
www.soif.co

Closed bank holidays and Monday-
Wednesday lunch
– booking essential at dinner

Menu £25 – Carte £23/33

A/C

Eminently satisfying food, an appealingly louche look and a thoughtfully compiled wine list – yes, it's another terrific eaterie from the team behind the hugely successful Terroirs and Brawn. This busy bistro-cum-wine bar has a predominantly French list which includes plenty of 'natural' wines. The food menu is compiled daily and the cooking is gloriously no-nonsense and comes with bags of flavour. All things piggy are done particularly well – the charcuterie is well worth ordering; there's Lardo di Colonnata to spread on the great sourdough and the Montbéliard sausage will satisfy most hungers. Add in fair prices, a great atmosphere and delightfully natural service and it's no surprise they have another hit on their hands.

VISA

MC

AE

Tom Ilić

other world kitchens

U2

Battersea
123 Queenstown Rd. ✉ SW8 3RH
☏ (020) 7622 0555
www.tomilic.com

Closed Christmas, 1 week summer,
Monday, Sunday dinner
and Tuesday lunch –
booking essential

Menu £13/20 – Carte £32/44

A/C

Serbian Tom Ilić came to the UK 20 years ago, took a job as a dish washer before a planned career in engineering, developed an interest in food and now has his own restaurant. He chose the site formerly occupied by The Food Room and turned it into an unpretentious, neighbourly place with closely set tables and a semi-open kitchen. It's also in an area of Battersea that's played host to a few famous restaurants in its day. His menu is written in a refreshingly straightforward way. There's plenty of offal featured as well as lots of pork, something of a beloved national dish for Serbs. Flavours are far from shy but his cooking also displays a certain graft and clear respect for the ingredients; prices are kept realistic.

VISA

MC

AE

Boqueria

Brixton

192 Acre Ln. ✉ SW2 5UL
✆ (020) 7733 4408
www.boqueriatapas

⊖ **Clapham North**
Closed Monday-Friday lunch

Carte approx. £30

Named after – and inspired by – Barcelona's famous food market, this contemporary tapas bar is a welcome addition to the neighbourhood and has quickly established a local fan-base. The menu doubles as a place mat and is a mix of recognisable classics and more adventurous offerings; it is also supplemented by specials on the blackboard. As everyone involved appears to hail from Andalucía, it makes sense to kick off with their notable gazpacho. The Ibérico hams are in excellent order, the lamb medallions are full of flavour and be sure to save room for a particularly good Crema Catalana. It's worth sitting at the counter as the main dining area at the back lacks a little personality. Their café next door serves coffee and churros.

Upstairs

Brixton

89b Acre Ln. ✉ SW2 5TN
✆ (020) 7733 8855
www.upstairslondon.com

⊖ **Clapham North**
Closed 23 December-8 January,
14 March-2 April, 18 August-3 September,
Sunday and Monday –
(dinner only)

Menu £28/39

At the risk of upsetting the locals - who clearly like the idea of having a hard-to-find, and thus almost secret, restaurant in their neighbourhood - you'll need to look for the buzzer on the side door next to the Opus coffee shop if you want to go Upstairs. You'll still be a little unsure as you climb the dark staircase, at least until you're greeted by the hospitable manager who'll offer you a drink in the bar; dining is then done on the next floor up. The set menu is a short but nicely balanced affair, with just three choices per course plus the occasional special; its also represents unquestionably decent value for money. The food is prepared with understanding and seasonal relevance; it is easy to eat, uncomplicated and flavoursome.

Charlotte's Bistro

modern ✗✗

S1

Chiswick
6 Turnham Green Terr ✉ W4 1QP
☎ (020) 8742 3590
www.charlottes.co.uk

⊖ **Turnham Green**
Booking advisable

Menu £18/30

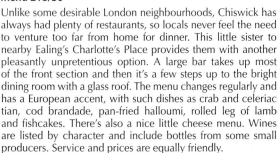

Unlike some desirable London neighbourhoods, Chiswick has always had plenty of restaurants, so locals never feel the need to venture too far from home for dinner. This little sister to nearby Ealing's Charlotte's Place provides them with another pleasantly unpretentious option. A large bar takes up most of the front section and then it's a few steps up to the bright dining room with a glass roof. The menu changes regularly and has a European accent, with such dishes as crab and celeriac tian, cod brandade, pan-fried halloumi, rolled leg of lamb and fishcakes. There's also a nice little cheese menu. Wines are listed by character and include bottles from some small producers. Service and prices are equally friendly.

High Road Brasserie

French ✗

S2

Chiswick
High Road House Hotel,
162 Chiswick High Rd. ✉ W4 1PR
☎ (020) 8742 7474 – **www**.highroadhouse.co.uk

⊖ **Turnham Green**
Booking essential

Menu £16 (lunch) – Carte £20/30

It's usually so busy you'll have trouble getting in the door – quite literally sometimes, as the entrance is often crowded with evening drinkers or lunchtime pushchairs. This modern take on the brasserie certainly has the look, with its mirrors, panelling and art deco lighting; turn right for the more comfy seating. Staff are used to being busy and get the job done, although without much time for pleasantries. What is surprising is that, despite the volume of customers, the kitchen is able to deliver a good standard of accurately cooked classics including steak frites, duck confit, grilled lobster or whole sea bass, along with salads and sandwiches. The bill can rise quickly as sides are required, but there's a good value daytime menu.

Hedone ✿

modern XX

S2

Chiswick
301-303 Chiswick High Rd
✉ W4 4HH
✆ (020) 8747 0377
www.hedonerestaurant.com

Menu £30/50

⊖ Chiswick Park
Closed 23 December-9 January,
13-27 August, Sunday and Monday
– (dinner only and lunch Friday-
Saturday)

A/C

VISA

MC

AE

Michelin

Swedish chef-owner Mikael Jonsson, an enthusiastic food blogger and former lawyer, put his money where his mouth is and his reputation on the line by opening his own restaurant. It didn't take long for Hedone, which is Greek for 'pleasure', to prove that gamble had paid off. The refreshingly unfussy food, from a small and daily changing menu, relies primarily on the superlative quality of the ingredients and, by cooking them carefully and sympathetically, Mikael ensures that their natural flavours are allowed to shine. This is food that is exceptionally easy to eat and, while you can choose four or five courses from the main menu, taking the 7 course Tasting Menu is a far from daunting prospect. His passion is palpable and is evident in every aspect of the restaurant, especially in the enthusiasm of his charming service team. The kitchen forms part of the room by being very open plan, with the counter proving particularly popular with various bands of foodies; others should ask for the seats along the wall where the back-rest cushions hang from poles.

First Course

- Cévennes onions, parmesan foam and pear shavings.
- Poached rock oysters, Granny Smith, pickled shallots.

Main Course

- Smoked pigeon salad with braised radicchio.
- Pan-fried seabass, whelks, sea aster, asparagus, vin jaune emulsion.

Dessert

- Apple millefeuille with caramel ice cream.
- Lemon variation.

Michael Nadra

modern ✗✗

Chiswick
6-8 Elliott Rd. ✉ W4 1PE
✆ (020) 8742 0766
www.restaurant-michaelnadra.co.uk

⊖ **Turnham Green**
Closed 24-26 December,
1 January and Sunday dinner

Menu £20/49

Tucked away from the more excitable restaurants on the High Street, Michael Nadra has been quietly and steadily going about the business of creating a very good restaurant. The result is that there are enough regulars now appreciating his cooking for him to have the confidence to finally put his own name above the door. Seafood remains an important part of his repertoire – crab tempura and monkfish with salmon mousse remain perennial favourites – but he now offers more meat dishes and there's a greater degree of sophistication to his cooking. Along with the fixed price menu is a very reasonable 7 course tasting menu, with suggested wine pairings. The restaurant has an intimate, local feel which is helped along by friendly staff.

Sam's Brasserie

Mediterranean ✗

Chiswick
11 Barley Mow Passage ✉ W4 4PH
✆ (020) 8987 0555
www.samsbrasserie.co.uk

⊖ **Turnham Green**
Closed 23-28 December

Menu £17 (weekdays) – Carte £25/43

The building was once a Sanderson wallpaper mill and the industrial feel works well in this bustling brasserie environment. An added helping of hipness comes courtesy of the artwork from local resident, and occasional diner here, Sir Peter Blake. Look out too for the regular Soul and Jazz evenings. Dining is on two levels; the mezzanine is the quieter one, while the larger room looks into the kitchen and has plenty of bustle. The modern brasserie food is prepared with more care and expertise that one expects when one considers the size of the operation and, with a wine list offering over half its bottles for under £30, it's no surprise that the place gets busy. Service is efficient but could be a little more communicative.

La Trompette ♔

Chiswick
5-7 Devonshire Rd
✉ W4 2EU
📞 (020) 8747 1836
www.latrompette.co.uk

Menu £28/43

⊖ **Turnham Green**
Closed 24-26 December –
booking essential

La Trompette

These days you need to do more than merely live in a nice part of town to make your friends envious – if you really want to see what resentment looks like you'll need a great neighbourhood restaurant too. La Trompette is the real McCoy, which is probably why many of the residents of Chiswick always look so pleased with themselves. The staff here are delightful, the room is comfortable without being fussy or stuffy and the cooking is undertaken with obvious care and attention. The daily menu avoids unnecessary showiness and sticks to tried-and-tested combinations of seasonal ingredients so, in spring for example, the corn-fed chicken supreme comes with morels and Jersey Royals, and the asparagus is accompanied by crab mayonnaise. The wine list is thoughtfully compiled and the sommelier will come up with some unexpected suggestions. Those in the know tend to either come for lunch or arrive before 7.30 in the evening to take advantage of the great value set menu; the best seats are those along the walls.

First Course

- Lasagne of braised rabbit and cepes.
- Shellfish bisque with a black olive and salt cod crouton.

Main Course

- Pan-fried skate wing with smoked anchovy and shrimp beurre noisette.
- Rump of lamb with spring vegetables, garlic and rosemary jus.

Dessert

- Hot chocolate fondant with vanilla ice cream.
- Warm stem ginger cake with pineapple, crème fraîche and lime.

Abbeville Kitchen

✗

U3

Clapham Common

47 Abbeville Rd ✉ SW4 9JX
✆ (020) 8772 1110
www.abbevillekitchen.co.uk

⊖ Clapham Common
Closed Monday lunch – bookings
advisable at dinner

Carte £20/30

The owner has a small boulangerie on this road where his customers would buy their baguettes and bemoan the lack of a decent local restaurant. Moved by their plight, he subsequently found an empty shop, recruited a chef – and his bistro was born. The narrow room has a simple yet homely feel, with the kitchen visible at the far end. The food is gutsy and wholesome and the daily changing menu offers the option of ordering small tasting plates or a more traditional three-courser. The choice is varied – it's not often one sees empanadas and braised goat on the same menu – and the prices are fair. The charcuterie boards stand out, as do those dishes involving slow cooking such as the shoulder of lamb for two. The bread is pretty good too.

Bistro Union 😊

✗

U3

Clapham Common

40 Abbeville Rd ✉ SW4 9NG
✆ (020) 7042 6400
www.bistrounion.co.uk

⊖ Clapham Common
Closed Sunday dinner –
booking advisable

Carte £16/27

'Comforting' is the word that comes to mind at Bistro Union, chef Adam Byatt's affordable and bustling offspring of his Trinity restaurant. Whether it's the menus written in old school exercise books or the rolled sheet of brown paper listing the day's snacks, there is something reassuring and familiar about everything at this fun neighbourhood spot. The food is hearteningly British and manages to evoke feelings of nostalgia while simultaneously being bang on-trend. Start with some snacks like the fish finger sarnie, beef with dripping toast or pickled quail eggs. Then share a spit-roast chicken, or try the Toad in the Hole or the cottage pie along with one of their great ales – and finish off with their homemade Eccles cake ice cream.

Bobbin

Mediterranean 🍺

U2

Clapham Common
1-3 Lillieshall Rd ✉ SW4 0LN
☎ (020) 7738 8953
www.thebobbinclapham.com

⊖ **Clapham Common.**
Closed 25 December –
(dinner only and lunch Friday-Sunday)

Menu £15 – Carte £21/30

You'll find the Bobbin in a quiet residential street which, combined with its warm service, cosy bar and the Wednesday Quiz night, makes it feel like a proper local. You can eat in the bar or in the conservatory, from a menu which changes every six weeks and offers a choice of five starters and five mains. The charcuterie boards are great for sharing but vegetarians are also looked after, with the likes of leek, nettle and artichoke cannelloni. The kitchen sticks to using what's in season and, refreshingly, they don't feel they have to name-check every supplier to prove it. This pub may never set the world on fire yet that's part of its charm: they seem to have got everything right and are just, well, bobbin' along nicely.

 Rookery

British traditional 🍴

U3

Clapham Common
69 Clapham Common South Side
✉ SW4 9DA
☎ (020) 8673 9162 – **www**.therookeryclapham.co.uk

⊖ **Clapham Common**
Closed 25-26 December
and Monday lunch

Carte £19/27

The on-trend Rookery shows that Soho doesn't have a monopoly on ersatz Brooklyn speakeasies. It was set up by a former Guardian journalist who regularly lunched at The Eagle, and he has stayed true to his principles by naming it after the colloquial term for a city slum. Downstairs is dominated by the bar, which comes with an impressive selection of artisan beers, but if you don't want to jostle for space with the drinkers then try the upstairs – and in summer head for the large outdoor terrace. Food is an important part of the operation; the menu may be short but usually includes a soup, a salad, a pasta dish, some charcuterie or offal, and a daily pie for sharing. The kitchen doesn't muck around and delivers some punchy flavours.

Trinity

innovative XX

U2

Clapham Common
4 The Polygon ⊠ SW4 0JG
☎ (020) 7622 1199
www.trinityrestaurant.co.uk

⊖ Clapham Common
Closed 24-30 December,
Monday lunch and Sunday dinner

Carte £29/58

Trinity is smarter and a little more formal than your average neighbourhood restaurant and residents of Clapham Old Town have clearly taken to it, especially as it means they don't have to schlep up to the West End for a 'proper' night out. The cooking is suitably sophisticated, with the kitchen adding some innovative combinations to what is a fairly classical base. Offal dishes are often the highlight and the pig's trotter on toasted sourdough has become a signature dish. The lunch menu is simpler in style and content but is priced very appealingly. To underline its neighbourhood credentials, the restaurant also offers cookery classes. In summer, ask for a table by the windows, which open up to add a little continental colour.

Tsunami

Japanese X

U2

Clapham Common
Unit 3, 5-7 Voltaire Rd ⊠ SW4 6DQ
☎ (020) 7978 1610
www.tsunamirestaurant.co.uk

⊖ Clapham North
Closed 24-26 December –
(dinner only and
lunch Saturday-Sunday)

Carte £17/43

As fun, noisy and as lively as ever, particularly at weekends when it stays open until 2am, Tsunami continues to pull in plenty of Clapham locals, many of whom make the effort to scrub up nicely for this good looking Japanese restaurant with its popular club-like bar. The menu's focus is on modern fusion food but there is also an extensive selection of nigiri, sashimi and sushi rolls. Sharing is actively encouraged which is wise as some of the dishes are really quite substantial. Tempura is suitably light and allows the ingredient to shine, while steamed fish dishes such as the sea bass are often the highlight. Desserts are light and refreshing and presentation is appealing. There is another branch in Charlotte Street.

Atari-ya

Ealing
1 Station Par, Uxbridge Rd ✉ W5 3LD
☎ (020) 8896 3175
www.atariya.co.uk

⊖ **Ealing Common**
Closed 25-26 December,
1 January and Monday

Menu £20/25 – Carte £20/35

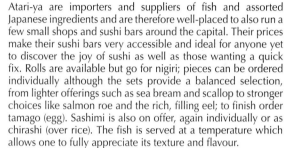

Atari-ya are importers and suppliers of fish and assorted Japanese ingredients and are therefore well-placed to also run a few small shops and sushi bars around the capital. Their prices make their sushi bars very accessible and ideal for anyone yet to discover the joy of sushi as well as those wanting a quick fix. Rolls are available but go for nigiri; pieces can be ordered individually although the sets provide a balanced selection, from lighter offerings such as sea bream and scallop to stronger choices like salmon roe and the rich, filling eel; to finish order tamago (egg). Sashimi is also on offer, again individually or as chirashi (over rice). The fish is served at a temperature which allows one to fully appreciate its texture and flavour.

Charlotte's Place

Ealing
16 St Matthew's Rd. ✉ W5 3JT
☎ (020) 8567 7541
www.charlottes.co.uk

⊖ **Ealing Common**
Closed 26 December-4 January

Menu £15 (weekday lunch), £25/30

It's been a sweet shop, a transport café and a private club but really found its niche as an honest and warmly run local restaurant. The ground floor offers views over the Common so is more popular at lunch; downstairs is ideal for couples who only have eyes for each other. The à la carte offers ample choice and the cooking is largely British, with smoked fish, traditional Sunday lunches and homely puddings done well; there are also one or two Mediterranean influences and the beef onglet enjoys a constant presence. There is a small cover charge but it does cover bread and unlimited amounts of filtered water rather than being an accountant's wheeze for squeezing more money out of the customers.

Kiraku

Japanese

Ealing

8 Station Par., Uxbridge Rd. ⊠ W5 3LD

✆ (020) 8992 2848

www.kiraku.co.uk

⊖ **Ealing Common**

Closed Christmas-New Year,
10 days August, Monday and
Tuesday following bank holidays

Menu £10 (lunch) – Carte £11/36

Ayumi and Erica became so frustrated with the lack of a decent local Japanese restaurant that they decided to open one themselves; and now it is not just the bourgeoning Japanese community who flock to this cute little place. It's modestly styled and enthusiastically lit, but service is very charming. Look out for the blackboard menu and its daily changing dishes. Zensai, or starters, include the popular Agedashi dofu; these can then be followed by assorted skewers, noodles and rice dishes. Fish is purchased daily and their sushi now displays a more modern touch; Bara Chirashi is the house speciality. Be sure to end with matcha ice cream or green tea sponge cake. The restaurant's name means 'relax and enjoy' and it's hard not to.

Mango & Silk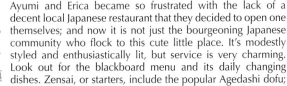

Indian

East Sheen

199 Upper Richmond Rd. West

⊠ SW14 8 QT

✆ (020) 8876 6220 – **www**.mangoandsilk.com

Closed 25-27 December and Monday
– (dinner only and buffet lunch Sunday)

Carte approx. £21

Mango and Silk was opened by the late Udit Sarkhel who did so much to change the image of Indian restaurants in the UK. His culinary philosophy lives on in the cooking from the young North Indian chef, who ensures that the spicing of the dishes remains sufficiently pronounced but subtle enough to add to the flavour of the ingredients, instead of dominating them. The kitchen also uses very little fat and oil which adds to their fresh, healthy taste. The daily changing specials board is where you'll find the more interesting seasonal dishes like tandoori squid; the house favourite is Saag Gosht, a Punjabi dish which uses tender pieces of lamb; and the kulfi is rich and creamy – a world away from what's offered in many Indian restaurants.

Victoria

S2 British modern 🍺

East Sheen

⊖ Mortlake (Rail).

10 West Temple Sheen ✉ SW14 7RT
📞 (020) 8876 4238
www.thevictoria.net

Menu £13 – Carte £19/37

Many pubs claim to be genuine locals – The Victoria is the real deal: it sponsors local clubs and the chef is patron of the local food festival; he also holds cookery workshops at the school next door. This is a beautifully decorated pub, with a restored bar with a wood burning stove and plenty of nooks and crannies; a few steps down and you're in the more formal conservatory overlooking the terrace. The cooking is modern British with the odd international note. Warm homemade bread could be followed by Scotch egg with roast beetroot, cod with a white bean stew and, to finish, blood oranges with rhubarb sorbet. Produce is local where possible: veg is from Surrey and honey from Richmond. Service is engaging and there are bedrooms available.

Ⓝ Blue Elephant

T2 Thai ✕✕

Fulham

Closed 1 January,
25-26 December –
booking advisable

The Boulevard, Imperial Wharf ✉ SW6 2UB
📞 (020) 7751 3111
www.blueelephant.com

Menu £14/38 – Carte £27/54

The Blue Elephant was a Fulham Road landmark for so long that everyone was taken by surprise when it packed its trunk and relocated. Fortunately for its followers, it didn't wander too far and these swankier premises within the large development that is Imperial Wharf have given it a new lease of life. Spread over two floors, the decoration is as exotic as one expects – except that instead of the koi ponds you have the Thames outside, along with two terrific terraces; even the golden dragon made the journey from the old address but can now be found in a different guise at the bar. The appealing menu traverses Thailand and in amongst the classic dishes are a few more contemporary offerings; the curries here are always worth ordering.

Harwood Arms

British modern

Fulham
Walham Grove ✉ SW6 1QP
✆ (020) 7386 1847
www.harwoodarms.com

⊖ Fulham Broadway.
Closed 24-28 December,
1 January and Monday lunch
– booking essential

Carte approx. £34

Michelin

Its reputation may have spread around London like wildfire but what many visitors find most reassuring is how unaffected the Harwood Arms has remained. This is still a proper local pub, just one that happens to serve really good food; Tuesday is quiz night and it's packed when Chelsea are playing at home. The reason for its success is largely down to the shared passion of the three owners. Accordingly, it comes as no surprise that, despite the change in the kitchen in 2011, there has been no discernible deviation in the standard of the food. The cooking remains very seasonal and properly British; faggots, nettle soup, beef cheeks and Hampshire lamb all make regular appearances. There is obvious skill in the cooking but none of the dishes ever seem out of place in this relaxed environment – it's cooking that's all about carefully matched ingredients and great flavours, and not about technique and ego. The wine list has clearly been complied by someone who knows their food and the bar snacks are pretty good too.

First Course	Main Course	Dessert
• Salad of chicken leg, cauliflower, hazelnuts and marjoram.	• Pork belly and root vegetable broth with ginger beer glazed ribs.	• Baked lavender custard with honeycomb ice cream and biscuits.
• Grilled monkfish cheeks with fennel, radish and fairy ring mushrooms.	• Halibut with cauliflower, shrimp, potato and samphire.	• Brown sugar doughnuts with sea buckthorn curd and sour cream.

Mao Tai

 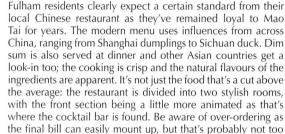
Fulham
58 New Kings Rd, Parsons Grn
✉ SW6 4LS
✆ (020) 7731 2520 – **www**.maotai.co.uk

⊖ Parsons Green
Closed 25-27 December –
(dinner only and Sunday lunch)

Carte £32/65

Fulham residents clearly expect a certain standard from their local Chinese restaurant as they've remained loyal to Mao Tai for years. The modern menu uses influences from across China, ranging from Shanghai dumplings to Sichuan duck. Dim sum is also served at dinner and other Asian countries get a look-in too; the cooking is crisp and the natural flavours of the ingredients are apparent. It's not just the food that's a cut above the average: the restaurant is divided into two stylish rooms, with the front section being a little more animated as that's where the cocktail bar is found. Be aware of over-ordering as the final bill can easily mount up, but that's probably not too much of a concern for the locals.

SOUTH-WEST ▶ PLAN XVIII

Sands End

British modern

Fulham
135-137 Stephendale Rd ✉ SW6 2PR
✆ (020) 7731 7823
www.thesandsend.co.uk

⊖ Fulham Broadway.
Closed 25-26 December –
booking advisable

Menu £14 (weekday lunch)/33 – Carte £22/43

Sands End is probably not the best known part of London, or indeed Fulham, but no doubt its residents prefer it that way so they can keep their eponymous pub to themselves. It's a cosy, warm and welcoming one, with a central bar offering some nifty homemade snacks, but try resisting because the main menu – which changes every few days – is pretty appealing itself. There's a distinct British bias which amounts to more than merely name-checking the birthplace of the ingredients. Winter dishes like braised lamb neck or roast partridge with Savoy cabbage are particularly pleasing and West Mersea oysters a good way of starting things off. There's a well-chosen and equally equitably priced wine list that sticks mostly to the Old World.

Tendido Cuatro

T2

Fulham ⊖ Parsons Green
108-110 New Kings Rd ✉ SW6 4LY
✆ (020) 7371 5147
www.cambiodetercio.co.uk

Menu £30 – Carte £16/29

A/C

VISA
MC
AE
①

Any resemblance to their other restaurants in Old Brompton Road is entirely intentional: here too the front panels burst open in summer to reveal a warm interior where vivid colours are used with wild abandon. The main difference is that, along with tapas, the speciality is the Valencian classic, paella. Using bomba rice, the choice varies from seafood to quail and chorizo; cuttlefish ink to vegetarian. They are designed for two but that assumes a more than eager appetite, especially if you've had a couple of small dishes as a run-up. The tapas is nicely varied, from refreshing baby anchovies to crisp pigs ears. Service is spirited and the room comes alive later in the evening as the locals return from work and wander over.

Anglesea Arms

S1

Hammersmith ⊖ Ravenscourt Park.
35 Wingate Rd ✉ W6 0UR   Closed 25-27 December –
✆ (020) 8749 1291   bookings not accepted
www.anglesea-arms.com

Carte £20/52

A/C

VISA
MC

While the menu here changes daily and is largely governed by what its suppliers bring, some aspects remain constant: there's always pig's head terrine, prawns, a tart and a seasonal salad. Fish and game are handled well and dishes are pleasingly robust – try the delicious Orb of Joy: braised onion which comes with roast partridge. The treacle tart has a cult following but the ice creams and sorbets are delicious too. The pub has a cluttered, very lived-in look and gets properly crowded but has a refreshing honesty, with staff providing thoughtful advice. Look for its windows etched with the inviting words 'Pies and Hams' and 'Stout and Oysters'. Above the door is 'Mon Mam Cymru', Mother of Wales, as the Isle of Anglesey is known.

Azou 🐸

North-African ✗

Hammersmith
375 King St. ✉ W6 9NJ
✆ (020) 8563 7266
www.azou.co.uk

⊖ Stamford Brook
Closed 1 January, 25 December –
booking essential – (dinner only and lunch
Saturday-Sunday)

Carte £18/37

A/C
☼
VISA
MC
AE
◑

You'll probably walk past the first time and not notice this unassuming little place but, once visited, you won't walk past again. Inside is all silks, lanterns and rugs but it is also very personally run; the owner will often pop out from his kitchen to offer guidance – and his advice is well worth listening to. The cooking skips across North African countries – order some Algerian olives while you choose from the wide choice of main courses. Understandably, most of the regulars come here for a tagine, especially the Constantine with its tender lamb and triple-steamed couscous. Highlights to start include the terrific baba ganoush with homemade bread and fresh briouat. It's the perfect food to share as the dishes come in large portions.

Crabtree

modern

Hammersmith
4 Rainville Rd ✉ W6 9HA
✆ (020) 7385 3929
www.thecrabtreeW6.co.uk

⊖ Barons Court.

Carte £24/34

☂
A/C
☼
VISA
MC
AE
◑

On a sunny day few things in life beat being by the river in a London pub and The Crabtree certainly makes the most of its location. Its beer garden, with its barbeque-style menu, can hold up to 200, while the dining room boasts its own terrace overlooking the river – and if you haven't yet booked for lunch on Boat Race day then you're probably already too late. A variety of ploys are used to fill the equally large interior of this Victorian beauty, from BYO Mondays to quiz nights on Tuesdays. For lunch the selection varies from ciabatta sarnies to shepherd's pie; the evening menu is more adventurous. The kitchen does things properly – parfaits and terrines are highlights and fish is perfectly timed – but vegetarians are also looked after.

SOUTH-WEST ▶ PLAN XVIII

389

Dartmouth Castle

Mediterranean

S1

Hammersmith
26 Glenthorne Rd ✉ W6 0LS
✆ (020) 8748 3614
www.thedartmouthcastle.co.uk

⊖ Hammersmith.
Closed 24 December-2 January and
Saturday lunch

Carte £19/31

Plenty of locals pop into this Victorian pub just for a drink so
you may find one of them has nabbed your table. It's worth
biding your time though, as it's better than decamping to the
upstairs room as the atmosphere up there isn't a patch on the
bustling ground floor with its worn-in look and etched mirrors.
Simply hand over your credit card and order at the bar to enjoy
dishes from the well-priced and quite lengthy Mediterranean-
influenced menu which is the same lunch and dinner. The
antipasti platter for two is a winner and pasta dishes appear
to come in two sizes – big or even bigger. The blackboard
wine list is also a cut above your average pub list and uses the
reliable Italian orientated merchant Liberty.

Hampshire Hog

British modern

S2

Hammersmith
227 King St ✉ W6 9JT
✆ (020) 8748 3391
www.thehampshirehog.com

⊖ Ravenscourt Park.
Closed 25-26 December and Sunday dinner

Carte £23/37

For many years the owners ran The Engineer, a much loved pub
in Primrose Hill, before their lease ran out. They subsequently
moved west, took over what was the Ruby Grand, did it up and
gave it back its original name. The Hampshire Hog is a big old
place and calls itself a 'pub and pantry' – the pantry is open for
breakfast, tea and cakes and doubles as a private party room;
the bright bar serves cocktails and snacks like Scotch quail
eggs and pork boards; and the large dining room focuses on
freshness and seasonality. So, in spring, that means asparagus
or broad bean risotto; a choice of daily salads and popular
main courses like marinated leg of lamb. Like The Engineer,
The 'Hog' comes with a terrific terrace and garden.

Havelock Tavern

T1

Hammersmith
57 Masbro Rd, Brook Grn ⊠ W14 0LS
✆ (020) 7603 5374
www.havelocktavern.com

⊖ **Kensington Olympia.**
Closed 25-26 December –
bookings not accepted

SOUTH-WEST ▶ PLAN XVIII

Carte £19/35 s

The word 'gastropub' was first coined in the early '90s to describe pubs that offered great food while remaining true to their roots – and was never about pubs masquerading as restaurants. The warm and friendly Havelock Tavern was at the vanguard of this movement and little about its lived-in look has changed here over the years, which is probably why it's as busy as ever. Put your name down for a table at the bar, order a drink and then place your order from the blackboard menu which changes with each service and reflects the seasons. The food is comforting and prices fair while the freshness is underlined by the fact that dishes often run out; there could be a grilled mackerel or goujons of coley alongside a tagine or roast pork belly.

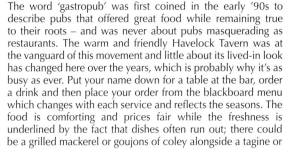

Indian Zing

S1/2

Hammersmith
236 King St. ⊠ W6 0RF
✆ (020) 8748 5959
www.indianzing.co.uk

⊖ **Ravenscourt Park**
Closed dinner 25 December

Menu £15/27 – Carte £20/35

Despite opening a couple more restaurants, none of the zing appears to have gone out of this keenly run Indian neighbourhood favourite. Chef-owner Manoj Vasaikar flits between them and remains committed to seeing his customers satisfied, so much so that he has been known to send out an extra dish on the house if he feels an order is not sufficiently balanced. While he is from Bombay, his cooking seeks inspiration from all over India; from sweet fish dishes to drier North Indian dishes or spicier Madras specialities. Effort is also made to match wines with the food and the list even offers a couple of choices from India. The restaurant is colourfully decorated while the serving team are keen if a little disorganised at times.

Potli

N

S2

Indian XX

Hammersmith
319-321 King St ⊠ W6 9NH
✆ (020) 8741 4328
www.potli.co.uk

⊖ Ravenscourt Park

Menu £13/16 – Carte £17/24

A/C
☀
VISA
MC
AE
①

Potli is the latest Indian restaurant to try its luck on King Street. The two close friends behind it spent their formative years training with the Oberoi hotel group and they have created a smart and warmly run restaurant. It's named after a sort of spiced version of a bouquet garni which is apt as spicing plays a huge part here: the spices are ground – and the pastes made – in house. The classically trained kitchen uses food markets from across India as their inspiration; some dishes are smaller-sized and inspired by street food while others are more traditional. 'Chicken 65' – spiced breast with black pepper – has quickly become a firm favourite, while the rich curries are often a highlight. Be sure to order a freshly made lassi.

Kew Grill

R2

meats and grills XX

Kew
10b Kew Grn. ⊠ TW9 3BH
✆ (020) 8948 4433
www.awtrestaurants.com/kewgrill

⊖ Kew Gardens
Closed 25 December-4 January,
6-19 August and bank holidays –
booking essential

Menu £12 (weekday lunch) – Carte £24/49

A/C
☀
VISA
MC
AE

Busy, relaxed and fun are the hallmarks of this neighbourhood joint which specialises in meats. Top quality steaks come with a choice of a sauce or butter; there are daily specials like shepherd's pie or duck confit and even a section dedicated to pork. There are seasonal dishes like haunch of venison but fish-eaters and Veggies are also catered for and children aren't forgotten either. The cooking is heart-warming and unfussy, the aged beef really is excellent and the nursery puds will finish you off. The concise wine list offers a good selection by the carafe. It's all done in quite a narrow room with something of a country feel; the friendly staff help the atmosphere along nicely.

River Café ☦

Italian ✗✗

Hammersmith
Thames Wharf, Rainville Rd
✉ W6 9HA
✆ (020) 7386 4200
www.rivercafe.co.uk

⊖ **Barons Court**
Closed 24 December-1 January,
Sunday dinner and bank holidays
– booking essential

Carte £49/78

VISA

River Café

They should run a shuttle service from local catering colleges to the River Café so that the students can learn the secret of good cooking: good ingredients. There's a vigour and honesty to the kitchen and, with the chefs all on view as they go about their work, there seems to be more of a relationship here between cook and customer than is found in most restaurants. The big wood-fired oven really catches the eye and the restaurant seems to attract a wonderfully mixed bunch of customers, united in their appreciation of what makes a restaurant tick. That includes charming service: on looks alone, the team can rival those in glossier and glitzier restaurants but they break ranks here by actually smiling and caring about their customers. The menu is still written twice a day and head chef Sian Wyn Owen brings an added sparkle to the cooking. Things taste just the way you want them to taste. Ordering a pasta dish ought to be made compulsory and the Chocolate Nemesis dessert should be a recognised treatment for depression.

First Course

- Risotto Amarone.
- Beaten salt cod with grilled polenta and black olives.

Main Course

- Gran bollito misto.
- Char-grilled sea bass with artichoke trifolati and Castelluccio lentils.

Dessert

- Chocolate Nemesis.
- Panna cotta with grappa and champagne rhubarb.

The Glasshouse ✿

modern ✗✗

Kew   ⊖ Kew Gardens
14 Station Par.   Closed 24-26 December and 1 January
✉ TW9 3PZ
✆ (020) 8940 6777
www.glasshouserestaurant.co.uk

Menu £28/43

The Glasshouse

There are some restaurants where the style of food matches the setting perfectly and The Glasshouse is one such example. Despite opening on the eve of the new millennium, the bright and open interior still feels fresh and contemporary. Meanwhile, the seasonally informed cooking is as crisp and vibrant as ever. A seamless change of head chef has seen no drop in the general standard and the flavours are allowed to shine on each dish. The menu is a lesson in balance and the cooking is predominantly modern European but the kitchen is not averse to slipping in a few tastes of the East. Offal remains something of a highlight and wines are shrewdly recommended and graciously served. The service team are imbued with an unflappable confidence which, in turn, relaxes the room, although most of the customers appear to already have the imperturbable demeanour of those who know their food and recognise a decent restaurant when they see one. Reservations for weekends, when lunches are largely family affairs, need to be made about a month in advance.

First Course

- Seared scallop with ponzu dressing and wasabi.
- Quail and wild mushroom tortellini with quail consommé.

Main Course

- Roast wood pigeon with pommes Sarladaise and poached pears.
- Sea bass with brown shrimps and a vermouth velouté.

Dessert

- Valrhona chocolate mousse with milk ice cream and nougatine.
- Piña colada rum baba with crème Chantilly.

Cantinetta

Italian 𝕏

S2

Putney
162-164 Lower Richmond Rd
(Entrance on Pentlow St) ✉ SW15 1LY
✆ (020) 8780 3131 – **www**.cantinetta.co.uk

Menu £13/19 – Carte £17/33

⊖ **Putney Bridge**
Closed Sunday dinner
and Monday –
(dinner only and lunch
Saturday-Sunday)

The Phoenix occupied this spot for many years until it finally burnt itself out. A series of pop-up restaurants then followed until seasoned restaurateur Rebecca Mascarenhas opened this relaxed, modern day trattoria. The bright room opens onto a much sought-after terrace and the bar is a great spot for a light bite at lunch. The menu represents decent value and the cooking delivers on flavour, whether that's the deep-fried anchovies with carpione dressing, the Ligurian classic 'trofie al pesto' or market fresh fish with lentils. The bread basket is worth its price and includes wonderfully light focaccia. Add a well chosen wine list with lesser known grape varieties and some spirited service and you have a very appealing local spot.

Enoteca Turi

Italian 𝕏𝕏

T2

Putney
28 Putney High St. ✉ SW15 1SQ
✆ (020) 8785 4449
www.enotecaturi.com

⊖ **Putney Bridge**
Closed 25-26 December,
1 January, Sunday and lunch bank
holiday Mondays

Carte £27/45

He may originally be from Puglia, but Giuseppe Turi has been Putney's favourite Italian restaurateur for over 20 years. In that time hardly a day has gone by without his restaurant bursting with chat and buzz – this is a local institution. He began life in London as a sommelier in the city's grandest hotels and so the grape plays an important role here: the menu matches wines with the dishes, the list has over 300 bins, he hosts regular food and wine evenings and the cellar hosts larger parties. The cooking is undertaken with a clear passion and the flavours pack a punch, which points to more northerly influences; dishes are satisfying and authentic. The restaurant is divided into three - the roomier front section is the best place to sit.

Prince of Wales

B r i t i s h   m o d e r n

T2

Putney
138 Upper Richmond Rd ✉ SW15 2SP
✆ (020) 8788 1552
www.princeofwalesputney.co.uk

⊖ **East Putney.**
Closed 23 December-
1 January and Monday lunch
except bank holidays

Carte £23/36

Idiosyncratic decoration and good food make this substantial Victorian pub stand out. Its deep green walls are lined with tankards and its ceiling is covered in playing cards; head further in and you'll find the dining room in the old billiard room. Here lights are fashioned from antlers and its walls are decorated with vintage farming photos and a little taxidermy; mind you, it's so dimly lit you'll be pushed see anything. The kitchen is out to impress and its daily changing menu reads well, ranging from rabbit and pork terrine to Cornish sardines and even a plate of Spanish delicacies. Although the ingredients are top-notch, the plates are sometimes a little too busy which perhaps explains the popularity of the simpler bar menu.

Bingham Restaurant

m o d e r n ✕✕

R3

Richmond
Bingham Hotel,
61-63 Petersham Rd. ✉ TW1O 6UT
✆ (020) 8940 0902 – **www**.thebingham.co.uk

⊖ **Richmond**
Closed first week January
and Sunday dinner

Menu £16/60 – Carte approx. £45

The Bingham always feels part of the local community and has lots of supporters in the neighbourhood who use it for a variety of different occasions. Perhaps its location, within a relatively unremarkable looking building, does it a favour as the restaurant has something of a 'hidden jewel' feel about it and the décor is surprisingly swish and comfortable. Come on a warm summer's day and you could find yourself having lunch on the balcony terrace, looking out over a garden and the Thames – and you don't get that everywhere. The cooking is contemporary and displays some original touches, however, dishes don't always deliver the flavours promised by the impressive presentation.

Matsuba

Richmond
10 Red Lion St
✉ TW9 1RW
☎ (020) 8605 3513

⊖ Richmond
Closed 25-26 December,
1 January and Sunday

Carte £40/45

A/C
VISA
MC
AE

Matsuba is a small, family-run place that is so understated it's easy to miss – look out for the softly lit sign above the narrow façade. The interior is equally compact and low-key, with just a dozen or so tables along with a small counter at the back with room for four more. In fact the biggest thing in the room is the menu, which offers a comprehensive tour through most recognisable points in Japanese cooking. The owners are Korean so you can also expect to see bulgogi, the Korean barbecue dish of marinated meat that comes on a sizzling plate. All the food is fresh and the ingredients are good; lunch sees some very good value set menus. The service is well-meaning and it's hard not to come away thinking kind thoughts.

Swagat

Indian ✗

Richmond
86 Hill Rise ✉ TW10 6UB
☎ (0208) 9407 557
www.swagatindiancuisine.co.uk

⊖ Richmond
Closed 25-26 December, 1 January and
Sunday – (dinner only)

Menu £30/35 – Carte £18/29

A/C
VISA
MC

Richmond's nascent restaurant scene was given a boost by the arrival of Swagat, which translates as 'welcome'. With just 14 tables, it's best to book otherwise you'll find yourself in a queue with the locals. Its popularity is down to the attentive, very well-meaning service and the likeable menu, which aims to promote healthy eating by using less oil and more subtle spicing. You'll find plenty of classics but try the less recognisable dishes, like chicken Chettinad from southern India. Fortnightly changing specials add further interest, as do the moist breads, fresh chillies and the complimentary poppadoms and chutneys. Prices are also appealing and allow vegetarian dishes to be ordered as main courses or accompaniments.

SOUTH-WEST ▶ PLAN XVIII

Petersham Nurseries Café ✿

Mediterranean ✗

Richmond
Church Ln (off Petersham Rd)
✉ TW10 7AG
✆ (020) 8940 5230
www.petershamnurseries.com

Closed 24-29 December and Monday
– booking advisable – (lunch only)

Carte £32/50

Michelin

The celebrated chef Greg Malouf closed his MoMo restaurant in Melbourne to take over the reins here at Petersham Nurseries in 2012 and he appears to be a perfect fit for this idyllic lunch spot. Born in Australia to Lebanese parents, his relatively unique style of cooking combines great produce and subtle Middle Eastern flavours to produce surprisingly refined yet enormously satisfying and healthy tasting dishes. From a terrific baba ganoush to the delicate Egyptian spices accompanying the chicken liver terrine or the delicious rose petal panna cotta, his food comes with an appealing vitality and freshness which chimes perfectly with the café's ethos of seasonality and sustainability. The café itself is as charming as ever, whether you're eating on the terrace in the sun or in the greenhouse with its wobbly tables and soil underfoot. The staff remain engaging and welcoming and only the hard-hearted could fail to be charmed by it all. Buy into the whole thing by making time to wander around the nursery before lunch.

First Course	*Main Course*	*Dessert*
● Mackerel with Jersey Royal potato, chilli relish and brik pastry.	● Duck Bistayeea.	● Crème fraîche and rosewater ice cream with fig Ma'amoula biscuits.
● Quail with Turkish chilli, chickpeas and chorizo salad.	● Halibut with borlotti beans, datterini, broad beans and grains.	● White peach and orange blossom sorbet with almond water.

Malina

Polish ☓☓

Shepherd's Bush
166 Shepherd's Bush Rd ✉ W6 7PB
✆ (020) 7603 8881
www.malinarestaurant.com

⊖ Shepherd's Bush

Menu £15 – Carte £17/29

AC

VISA

MC

AE

Malina was born because a group of Polish friends decided that the only way to get decent food from their homeland was to do it themselves. It's easy to be charmed by this pretty little spot, where the service is endearingly sweet and the food is pleasingly heartening. Fans of beetroot should kick off with a large bowl of soup and the very hungry should try the 'Bigos' stew, but the undoubted highlight of anyone's meal will be pierogi: these little dumplings of delight are from their mothers' recipes and have fillings ranging from buckwheat and chicken liver to blueberries and so can be enjoyed as a savoury or sweet course. A nice touch is the shot glass of homemade raspberry vodka delivered with the bill (malina means raspberry).

Princess Victoria

British traditional ⏐⏐🍺

Shepherd's Bush
217 Uxbridge Rd ✉ W12 9DH
✆ (020) 8749 5886
www.princessvictoria.co.uk

⊖ Shepherd's Bush.
Closed 24-28 December

Menu £13 (lunch) – Carte £21/35

AC

VISA

MC

London has a wealth of fine Victorian gin palaces but few are as grand as The Princess Victoria. From the friezes to the etched glass, the portraits to the parquet floor, the last restoration created a terrific pub. Mind you, that's not all that impresses: there's a superb, wide-ranging wine list, with carafes and glasses providing flexibility; enticing bar snacks ranging from quail eggs to salt cod croquettes; a great menu that could include roasted skate wing or homemade pork and herb sausages; and, most importantly, cooking that's executed with no little skill. Those with proclivities for all things porcine will find much to savour – charcuterie is a passion here and the board may well include pig's cheeks and rillettes.

Triphal 🎭

Indian ✗

T3

Southfields
201 Replingham Rd ✉ SW18 5LY
✆ (020) 8870 0188
www.triphalindianrestaurant.com

⊖ Southfields
Closed 25-26 December,
1 January and Monday

Carte approx. £16

A/C
☼
VISA
M©
D

When the Indian restaurant Sarkhel's closed a few years back, it left a big hole in this neighbourhood, but those still mourning its passing should be delighted that a worthy successor has been found in the form of Triphal. Created on a shoestring by three partners, two of whom are chefs with some impressive addresses on their CVs, this is a sweet little place making real efforts. The decoration may have been largely inherited from the previous occupants but the cooking is fresh and full of vitality. The menu is concise and includes a broad palate of regional Indian dishes, although, as both chefs are from Goa, the fish curries are often a highlight. In further echoes of Sarkhel's, the prices represent excellent value.

Al Borgo

Italian ✗✗

R3

Teddington
3 Church Rd. ✉ TW11 8PF
✆ (020) 8943 4456
www.alborgo.co.uk

Closed Sunday and bank holidays

Menu £17 (weekday dinner) – Carte £25/47

VISA
M©
AE

Aside from being home to Ted, love rival to Ernie the Fastest Milkman in the West, Teddington has rarely featured in the national consciousness – but a few more restaurants like Al Borgo may start to change people's perceptions. This refreshingly unpretentious Italian eatery, owned and keenly run by Brescia born Marco and his partner Nikola, exudes warmth and bonhomie in the way that only a true neighbourhood restaurant can. The menu cleverly appeals to both traditionalists and those a little more adventurous. The focaccia is homemade, as is the pasta; try the tagliolini with scallops or the pumpkin tortelli with sage. Special seasonal offerings such as a black truffle menu prove popular and there's a great value lunch menu too.

King's Head

m o d e r n

R3

Teddington
123 High St ✉ TW11 8HG
✆ (020) 3166 2900
www.whitebrasserie.com

⊖ Teddington (Rail)

Menu £12 – Carte £20/67

Britain has its pubs and France its brasseries; The King's Head does its bit for the entente cordiale by combining both. Raymond Blanc's team has given this Victorian pub a tidy makeover and, although there might not be much character left, they have created a suitably warm environment. The brasserie at the back is run by a pleasant, enthusiastic team and the menus offer all comers plenty of choice. Classic brasserie dishes such as Toulouse sausages and beef stroganoff come with a satisfyingly rustic edge, while the dual-nationality element is maintained through the inclusion of a ploughman's board alongside the charcuterie. Steaks on the charcoal grill are popular and families are lured in by the decent kiddies menu.

Rétro Bistrot

F r e n c h

R3

Teddington
114-116 High St ✉ TW11 8JB
✆ (0208) 9772 239
www.retrobistrot.co.uk

Closed first 2 weeks August,
first 10 days January,
Sunday dinner and Monday

Menu £11/23 – Carte £26/47

There's substance as well as style to this classic French bistrot. The kitchen brigade were once teammates at the much missed Monsieur Max, so they know their way around a French menu. Moules marinière, coq au vin, foie de veau and crème brûlée – all the classics of bourgeois cuisine are here and all are prepared with innate skill and understanding. Lunch and early evening menus are a steal, and the service team display equal commitment to the cause as cheeks are kissed and cries of "bon appétit" ring out. The mix of fabrics, exposed brick walls, simple tables and art for sale creates a very genial environment. The best seats are in the room at the back with the partially open kitchen, which adds aroma and a little more noise.

Simply Thai

Thai ✗

R3

Teddington
196 Kingston Rd. ✉ **TW11 9JD**
℘ (020) 8943 9747
www.simplythai-restaurant.co.uk

Closed 25-26 December
and Sunday – (dinner only)

Carte £21/28

A/C
VISA
MC

The delightful owner, Patria Weerapan, made her television debut on Gordon Ramsay's 'The F Word'. Her restaurant wasn't exactly quiet beforehand, but now her long term future here seems assured. Decoratively it's as modest inside as the unassuming façade suggests but everyone comes here for the food and forgives the occasional delay. She cooks everything fresh, from a bewilderingly large menu; dishes themselves are quite small so order one dish more than you think you need, which shouldn't be too difficult as the prices are far from high. Along with the new creations that are often being added to the menu are the favourites like spicy sweet pork, fishcakes, a refreshing trout salad and crisp deep-fried soft shell crab.

A Cena

Italian ✗✗

R2

Twickenham
418 Richmond Rd. ✉ **TW1 2EB**
℘ (020) 8288 0108
www.acena.co.uk

⊖ **Richmond**
Closed 25-26 December,
1 January, Good Friday, Easter Sunday,
4 June, 27 August, bank holidays, Sunday
dinner and Monday lunch

Carte £18/46

A/C
VISA
MC
AE
①

A Cena is a little unusual for an Italian restaurant insofar as the owners and the chef are all Brits, but their passion for all things Italian is palpable. More relevantly, they have wholeheartedly embraced the Italian ethos of using fresh produce, cooked carefully, in simply presented dishes. The menu, written in both languages, is constantly evolving. Not all dishes exude the appropriate zing but pasta dishes are usually a highlight. The place looks a little deceptive from the outside as it's not as small as it appears: avoid the tables at the front and head for the more open-plan rear area from where you can see what's going on. The restaurant's local popularity had led to the opening of a nearby foodstore and bakery.

Brula

French ✗✗

Twickenham
43 Crown Rd., St Margarets ✉ TW1 3EJ
☎ (020) 8892 0602
www.brula.co.uk

Closed 26 December
and Sunday dinner –
booking essential

Menu £15/25 – Carte £24/49

Brula is already well past its tenth birthday and this relative longevity can be put down to a combination of reliable cooking, sensible prices and personable service. This pretty Victorian building has been both a pub and a butcher's shop in the past but now thoroughly suits its role as an authentic looking bistro. France remains at the heart of the cooking but over the past couple of years influences from Spain and Italy have started to appear on the menu, which is priced per dish rather than per course as it once was. Cooking is also more exact in its execution. The cheeses and the thoughtfully arranged wine list remain exclusively French. The friendly and helpful service also extends to those using one of the private rooms.

Tangawizi

Indian ✗

Twickenham
406 Richmond Rd., Richmond Bridge
✉ TW1 2EB
☎ (020) 8891 3737 – www.tangawizi.co.uk

⊖ Richmond
Closed 25-26 December
and 1 January –
(dinner only)

Carte £15/31

Rich in colour and vitality, Tangawizi - meaning 'ginger' in Swahili – is another in the new breed of Indian restaurants. That means thoughtful design with clever use of silks and saris, attentive and elegant staff but, above all, cooking that is original, fresh and carefully prepared. North India provides much of the influence and although the à la carte menu offers plenty of 'safe' options, there are gems such as the roasted then stir-fried 'liptey' chicken. Diners should, however, head for the 'specials' section where the ambition of the kitchen is more evident. Lamb is another house speciality and is marinated to ensure it arrives extremely tender. For cooking this good, the prices are more than fair.

SOUTH-WEST ▶ PLAN XVIII

R3

R2

Chez Bruce ✿

French 🍴

Wandsworth
2 Bellevue Rd
✉ SW17 7EG
📞 (020) 8672 0114
www.chezbruce.co.uk

⊖ **Tooting Bec**
Closed 24-26 December
and 1 January – booking essential

Menu £28/45

Chez Bruce

Not only did Chez Bruce weather the choppy waters of recession better than most but it finally expanded into the old deli next door. What this meant for its merry band of dependable followers was nothing more than 'business as usual', as Chez Bruce has had a successful formula for years. That means flavoursome and uncomplicated food, sprightly service, sensible prices and an easy-going atmosphere. Matthew Christmas is the head man in the kitchen, having worked closely with Bruce Poole for over 10 years. His cooking provides an object lesson in the importance of flavours and balance: dishes are never too crowded and natural flavours are to the fore. The base is largely classical French but comes with Mediterranean tones, so expect words like parfait, pastilla, brandade and confit. The menu offers an even-handed selection, with a choice of around seven dishes per course. Cheese is always worth exploring and coffee comes with shortbread at lunch and terrific palmiers at dinner.

First Course	Main Course	Dessert
• Foie gras and chicken liver parfait with toasted brioche.	• Roast cod with olive oil mash and gremolata.	• Hot chocolate pudding with praline parfait.
• Turbot with a blanquette of coco beans, bacon and chestnuts.	• Grouse with port-glazed pears, bread sauce and green peppercorns.	• Warm Cognac-soaked coffee cake with walnut ice cream.

 Stagioni

U3

Italian ✗

Wandsworth

95 Nightingale Ln ✉ SW12 8NX
☎ (020) 8675 1010
www.lestagioni.co.uk

⊖ Clapham South
Closed 25-26 December –
(dinner only and lunch
Friday-Sunday)

Carte £24/41

A/C
☀
VISA
MC
AE

The owners of this unpretentious Italian in an area known as 'Twixt the commons' had originally earmarked it as a coffee shop to go with those they run in town but in the end felt the space would lend itself better to being a local restaurant. They subsequently gathered a team of chefs from across Italy and devised a simple but effective menu. The pasta is homemade and certainly worth trying; there are usually a couple of daily fish specials and dishes are confidently prepared and eminently satisfying. The other thing they got right is the service: it's all smiles from a warm and welcoming team. The chunky wooden tables give the restaurant an unpretentious look; ask for one by the window rather than in the room at the back.

Cannizaro House

S3

modern ✗✗

Wimbledon

Cannizaro House Hotel,
West Side, Wimbledon Common ✉ SW19 4UE
☎ (020) 8879 1464 – www.cannizarohouse.com

⊖ Wimbledon

Menu £25 – Carte £32/44

A/C
☀
VISA
MC
AE
①

London can offer the curious diner a vast number of dining options and, with Cannizaro House, that now includes a part-Georgian mansion in 34 acres of parkland. There is a choice to be made once you're here: you can sit in the elegant and classically dressed main room or the more intimate, glass fronted Loggia overlooking the Italian sunken garden. The daily changing set menu offers a range of carefully prepared and quite simple modern British dishes. The à la carte deals with more elaborate, but never overcomplicated, constructions; flavours and textures work well together and presentation is appealing. A preponderance of business types can sometimes lend too much of a corporate feel to proceedings but staff keep things light and relaxed.

Fox and Grapes

S3

British modern 🍺

Wimbledon
9 Camp Rd ✉ SW19 4UN
✆ (020) 8619 1300
www.foxandgrapeswimbledon.co.uk

⊖ Wimbledon.
Closed 25 December –
booking advisable

Menu £20 (lunch and early dinner) – Carte £24/38

AC

☼

VISA

MC

Claude Bosi first made his mark in Ludlow where, along with his Hibiscus restaurant, he also had a pub. When he moved to London the plan was to open a pub again once his restaurant was established and this he duly did in 2011. Cedric, his brother, runs the show and one look at the menu confirms their credentials as honorary Brits: this is proper pub food. Their prawn cocktail is hugely popular, as is the Cumberland sausage with mash, the ale battered hake and Angus sirloin. Scotch egg is made with wild boar, and junket makes an appearance, which makes you forgive their sneaking in the odd Gallic touch like snails and some of the over-formality. Thankfully, the pub's bigger than it looks as it's very popular. It also has three cosy bedrooms.

Ⓝ Lawn Bistro

T3

modern 🍴🍴

Wimbledon
67 High St. ✉ SW19 5EE
✆ (020) 8947 8278
www.thelawnbistro.co.uk

⊖ Wimbledon
Closed 25-26 December.
1 January and Sunday dinner

Menu £23/35

AC

⊡

VISA

MC

AE

Those disheartened by the homogenised look of most UK high streets will be cheered by the prominent position of Lawn Bistro in Wimbledon Village. This attractive room is comfortable and relaxed, with leather seating down one side facing the well-stocked bar. A personable Frenchman is at the helm in the kitchen and those who know their south London restaurants will recognise the signs of a previous engagement at La Trompette: his menu is an appealing mix of modern European dishes and his cooking is clean and well-defined. The kitchen does its own butchery and uses ingredients wisely: lunchtimes' saddle of rabbit with offal becomes a rabbit and ale casserole at dinner; similarly, it's leg of guinea fowl leg for lunch, breast for dinner.

Light House

Mediterranean ✗

T3

Wimbledon
75-77 Ridgway ✉ SW19 4ST
✆ (020) 8944 6338
www.lighthousewimbledon.com

Menu £14/24 – Carte £22/37

VISA

MC

AE

The façade may have been smartened up but one's first impression is of being in a branded operation. Fortunately, that notion is quickly dispelled by the quality of the food. While they still have the odd Thai dish, it is in Italy where the majority of the menu and the kitchen's strength lie, with a roll call of favourites that include tagliatelle, gnocchi, saltimbocca and panna cotta. The food is wholesome and confident, with plenty of bold flavours and prices at lunch and early evening are attractive, which ensures that it is often very busy. The result is that the young team can sometimes struggle to keep up, but they remain admirably calm and cheery. As this was once a shop selling lights and fittings, it is fittingly well lit.

SOUTH-WEST ▶ PLAN XVIII

Good food without
spending a fortune?
Look for the Bib
Gourmand .

Where to **stay**

▶ *These 50 recommended hotels are extracted from the Great Britain & Ireland 2013 guide, where you'll find a larger choice of hotels selected by our team of inspectors.*

Thierry Burot/Fotolia.com

Andaz Liverpool Street

M2

40 Liverpool St. — ⊖ Liverpool Street
✉ EC2M 7QN
✆ (020) 7961 1234
www.andazdining.com

264 rm – 🚹£105/330 🚹🚹£135/360, ☕ £24 – 3 suites

1901 and Catch *(See restaurant listing)*

Andaz Liverpool Street

The 'Andaz' brand (which apparently means "personal style" in Hindi) belongs to Hyatt, and this former railway hotel, which once went by the less ambiguous name of the Great Eastern, was the London prototype before its export to New York and L.A. The idea is to create luxury hotels with a less structured and more informal feel. In practical terms this mostly means that instead of a reception desk you have staff wandering around the nearest thing they have to a lobby, armed with laptops. The hotel may not be quite as hip as they imagine but it does provide a comfortable and contemporary environment that has a palpable sense of individualism. The crisply dressed bedrooms use a slick red, white and black palette and mod cons are comprehensive and largely concealed. Those wanting to be fed and watered will find themselves almost overwhelmed by the choice: there's the traditional George pub, a cosy Japanese, a lively brasserie, a stylish seafood bar and the eye-catching 1901 restaurant.

Arch

F2

50 Great Cumberland Pl — ⊖ Marble Arch
✉ W1H 7FD
✆ (020) 7724 4700
www.thearchlondon.com

80 rm – †£246/360 ††£246/360, ☕ £22 – 2 suites

The Arch

If God is in the detail, then The Arch shows touches of the divine. Fashioned out of a row of seven terraced houses and a couple of mews cottages, the hotel has been thoughtfully put together by people who have clearly stayed in a lot of places and who know what it takes to make them comfortable. For starters, the bedrooms offer an impressive list of extras such as HD TVs and internet radios; beds have oversized duvets so there's no nocturnal wrestling required to secure one's half; there are complimentary soft drinks and coffee; and some of the larger rooms not only have a TV in the bathroom but also have a pillow in the tub to make the watching of it more comfortable. The public areas are relatively compact but are smartly designed. The restaurant, which doubles as a champagne bar and is named after the dialling code from the '50s, has an easy-going menu, with a kitchen that makes good use of its wood fired oven. The Martini bar has discreet call buttons to summon service and interesting pieces of art are scattered liberally around the hotel.

Aster House

E6

3 Sumner Pl.
✉ SW7 3EE
☎ (020) 7581 5888
www.asterhouse.com

⊖ South Kensington

13 rm ☕ – †£108/150 ††£162/324

If you made a mathematical calculation to find the best location for a tourist in London, then chances are the X would mark a spot somewhere near Aster House on Sumner Place. You've got all the best museums within strolling distance; Hyde Park mere minutes away; all the famous shops and, above all, you're staying in a charming Victorian house in a typical Kensington street where people actually live rather than in a faceless hotel district. Mr and Mrs Tan keep the house commendably shipshape and are enthusiastic hosts. The bedrooms at the front of the house benefit from larger windows while those at the back are quieter and overlook the garden, but all boast fairly high ceilings and room to breathe. Wi-fi is available without charge in all the rooms, while L'Orangerie, a first floor conservatory looking down over Sumner Place, doubles as the breakfast room and guests' sitting room. Prices are also kept within the parameters of decency so bookings need to be made plenty of time in advance.

Athenaeum

116 Piccadilly ⊖ Hyde Park Corner
✉ W1J 7BJ
☏ (020) 7499 3464
www.athenaeumhotel.com

153 rm – ♟£390/480 ♟♟£390/480, ☲ £27.50 – 11 suites

Athenaeum

The Athenaeum has such a high number of regular guests who treat it as a home from home, that before the hotel undertook its latest refurbishment, it conducted a lengthy survey to find out what they wanted. Gone is the country house style of old and in its place has come a refreshing new look which blends all the latest mod cons with pastel shades and floor to ceiling windows. In these days of hidden charges, it's refreshing to find a hotel where the price of the room includes wi-fi, soft drinks from the mini-bar and a daily paper. The restaurant menu is appealingly down-to-earth and offers a decent selection of easy-to-eat classics with an English bent and the bar holds over 270 whiskies from around the world. Another striking feature of the hotel is its 'Living Wall', which is basically a vertical garden; this can be admired from the lounge, which does a brisk trade in afternoon tea. There are apartments for longer stays and those with children will appreciate the Kids' Concierge who will organise relevant activities.

MAYFAIR ▶ PLAN II

Berkeley

G4

Wilton Pl.   ⊖ Knightsbridge
✉ SW1X 7RL
✆ (020) 7235 6000
www.the-berkeley.co.uk

189 rm – ♦£310/660 ♦♦£378/900, ☲ £29 – 25 suites

🍴○ **Marcus Wareing at The Berkeley and Koffmann's**
(See restaurant listing)

The Berkeley

You'd have thought that having Marcus Wareing's luxury restaurant on one side of the hotel would be enough, but the hotel then coaxed Pierre Koffmann out of retirement and his restaurant now provides the bookend on the other side. In the middle you have the Blue Bar which is as cool as the name suggests and, on the other side of the lobby, the Caramel Room whose target audience is obvious when you consider that tea is called "Prêt-à-Portea" and the biscuits look like mini handbags. The most unique area of the hotel must be the 7th floor, with its rooftop pool, treatment rooms and personal training services to satisfy the most slavishly health-conscious traveller. By using a number of different designers, bedrooms have been given both personality and a sense of individualism; the most recent have softer, calmer colours and a lighter, more contemporary feel while the classic rooms feel richer, thanks to their deeper, more intense colours. All the rooms are immaculately kept and several of the suites have their own balcony.

Blakes

D6

33 Roland Gdns ⊖ Gloucester Road
✉ SW7 3PF
✆ (020) 7370 6701
www.blakeshotels.com

33 rm – ♼£209/309 ♼♼£249/369, ☕ **£22.50 – 8 suites**

Blakes

To see Blakes at its best, one needs to up the financial ante and go for one of the stylish deluxe rooms with their towers of cushions, flowing drapes and luxury bathrooms. Room 5 comes all in white, which means it occupies the housekeeping department more than any other; Room 7 covers such an impressive acreage that entry-level bedrooms can suffer by comparison. The hotel was created by Anouska Hempel in the early '80s and remains a favoured pit-stop for those riding the celebrity circuit. All mod cons are there in the rooms but are just camouflaged and concealed – Anouska was clearly not too fond of TVs and other electronic paraphernalia as they must have got in the way of the overall design effect. Downstairs is a slick and stylish affair, from the dark and mysterious Chinese Room and bar to the intimate restaurant with its Asian-influenced menu. There's a charming courtyard at the back and since these days the hotel is a little more welcoming to those who aren't staying, it now offers afternoon tea.

Brown's

H3

Albemarle St   ⊖ Green Park
✉ W1S 4BP
✆ (020) 7493 6020
www.roccofortehotels.com

105 rm – ♥£318/1,080 ♥♥£318/1,080,   ☲ £30 – 12 suites

🍴 **HIX at The Albemarle** *(See restaurant listing)*

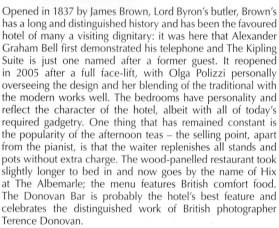

Brown's

Opened in 1837 by James Brown, Lord Byron's butler, Brown's has a long and distinguished history and has been the favoured hotel of many a visiting dignitary: it was here that Alexander Graham Bell first demonstrated his telephone and The Kipling Suite is just one named after a former guest. It reopened in 2005 after a full face-lift, with Olga Polizzi personally overseeing the design and her blending of the traditional with the modern works well. The bedrooms have personality and reflect the character of the hotel, albeit with all of today's required gadgetry. One thing that has remained constant is the popularity of the afternoon teas – the selling point, apart from the pianist, is that the waiter replenishes all stands and pots without extra charge. The wood-panelled restaurant took slightly longer to bed in and now goes by the name of Hix at The Albemarle; the menu features British comfort food. The Donovan Bar is probably the hotel's best feature and celebrates the distinguished work of British photographer Terence Donovan.

Bulgari

171 Knightsbridge   ⊖ Knightsbridge
✉ SW7 1DW
☎ (020) 7151 1010
www.bulgarihotels.com

78 rm – ∮£612/828 ∮∮£612/828, ☕ £32 – 7 suites

Bulgari

Having wowed them in Milan, Bulgari waited until they'd found the perfect location before creating this London jewel. This is a hotel that shouts style, with silver its underlying theme in homage to the brand's silversmith origins. Actually, it is so cool, so impeccably tailored, it wouldn't possibly be caught shouting anything. The dark lobby, with its camouflaged staff, sets the tone of restrained elegance and leads into the sleek bar. From there it is down a sweeping staircase to the restaurant, where the influences run from Nice to Tuscany, with a few other classics thrown in. The hotel is on 15 floors but six of those are underground and used for a state-of-the-art spa, a ballroom and a terrific cinema. The bedrooms are stunning and all about sensual curves, polished mahogany, silks and black marble; the bathrooms are worth the price of admission alone and there are some delightful touches, such as minibars hidden within upright trunks. Unlike other fashion-led hotels, there is real substance behind the style here and an emphasis on comfort.

HYDE PARK ▶ PLAN XII

417

The Capital

F5

22-24 Basil St.
✉ SW3 1AT
☎ (020) 7589 5171
www.capitalhotel.co.uk

⊖ Knightsbridge

49 rm – †£240/318 ††£300/600, ☕ **£20 – 1 suite**

🍴 **The Capital Restaurant** *(See restaurant listing)*

(See restaurant listing)

The Capital is one of London's most enduringly discreet and comfortable hotels and is thoroughly British in its feel. It is owned by David Levin, who opened it in 1971, and it is this continuity which has lead directly to there only being five head chefs in over 40 years. The restaurant is as elegant as ever, with a menu filled with classic British dishes and an extensive wine list that includes selections from the Levins' own winery in the Loire. Bedrooms remain classically chic and the contemporary embellishments are restrained and in keeping with the general atmosphere. Each floor is slightly different and uses designs from the likes of Mulberry, Ralph Lauren and Nina Campbell. What has always raised The Capital to greater heights than similarly styled hotels has been the depth and detail of the service. No one can walk through the small lobby without being greeted and the concierge is old-school in the best sense of the word and can arrange anything for anyone.

CHELSEA ▶ PLAN XI

Charlotte Street

12

15 Charlotte St
W1T 1RJ
(020) 7806 2000
www.charlottestreethotel.co.uk

⊖ Goodge Street

48 rm – †£300 ††£372, £20 – 4 suites

Firmdale

Expect the lobby and bar to be full of men with man-bags and horn-rimmed specs, for Charlotte Street is the hotel of choice for those in the advertising industry. But even if you've never pitched, promoted or placed a product and are just after a stylish, contemporary hotel in a street thronged with bars and restaurants then get on the mailing list here. Oscar is the busy bar and restaurant that spills out onto the street in summer; its sunny contemporary European menu and vivid mural brighten it in winter. Film Club is on Sunday evening: dinner followed by a film in the downstairs screening room. Those after some quiet can nab one of the sofas in the Drawing room or Library. The bedrooms are, as with all hotels in the Firmdale group, exceptionally well looked after. Every year, three or four are fully refurbished and one thing you'll never see is a bit of dodgy grouting or a scuff mark. They are all decorated in an English style but there is nothing chintzy or twee about them. Bathrooms are equally immaculate and the baths face little flat screen TVs.

Claridge's

Brook St   ⊖ Bond Street
✉ W1K 4HR
✆ (020) 7629 8860
www.claridges.co.uk

143 rm – ♦£792/936 ♦♦£792/936, ☕ £32 – 60 suites

Claridge's

Stand in the lobby looking bewildered and, before you know it, a liveried member of staff will appear promptly before you to enquire after your well being; Claridge's may have a long and very illustrious history but it recognises that reputations are forged because of service rather than longevity. That being said, no modern, purpose-built hotel could afford the extravagance of having such wide corridors or such ornate decoration. The art deco is perhaps the hotel's most striking decorative feature and it's kept suitably fresh and buffed. Despite its long and glittery past, Claridge's has never been in danger of being a museum piece; the David Collins designed bar attracts a more youthful crowd and The Foyer, with its eye-catching light sculpture, proves that afternoon tea need not be a stuffy or quaint affair. The Gordon Ramsay restaurant continues to pull in the punters and the people-watchers. Further bedrooms and other guest facilities are to be added over the next few years and the challenge will be to make this extension as seamless as possible.

Connaught

G3

Carlos Pl.   ⊖ Bond Street
✉ W1K 2AL
✆ (020) 7499 7070
www.the-connaught.co.uk

95 rm – ♛£888 ♛♛£888/936, ☕ £30 – 26 suites

🍴 **Hélène Darroze at The Connaught**
(See restaurant listing)

The Connaught

The restored, refurbished and rejuvenated Connaught still retains a sense of effortless serenity and exclusivity – but has now been discovered by a new generation. These sprightlier guests should take the stairs up to their room, that way they'll see the largest mahogany staircase in the country. The bedrooms are now more contemporary in style; they have wooden floors, leather worked into the soft furnishings and come with larger marble bathrooms; some overlook a small oriental garden, others peer down on mews houses. All rooms have full butler service, use linen specially woven in Milan and toiletries from Daylesford. The Coburg Bar honours the hotel's original name and its seats are so deep it's a wonder anyone ever leaves. In contrast, the Connaught Bar attracts a more youthful clientele. Hélène Darroze oversees the restaurant with her refined French cooking and Espelette is an all-day venue just off the lobby that offers a weekly changing list of classic French and British dishes. If you need anything, just ask one of the hotel's 300 members of staff.

MAYFAIR ▶ PLAN II

Covent Garden

13

10 Monmouth St.
✉ WC2H 9HB
✆ (020) 7806 1000
www.firmdalehotels.com

⊖ Covent Garden

56 rm – ♦£312 ♦♦£384, ☕ £20 – 2 suites

🍴 **Brasserie Max** *(See restaurant listing)*

Firmdale

The Covent Garden Hotel has always been hugely popular with those of a theatrical bent, whether cast or audience member, not least because of its central location, a mere saunter away from the majority of playhouses and productions. The hotel was once a French hospital – the words 'Nouvel hopital et dispensaire francais' are still etched into the brickwork – but the style is essentially British. Mannequins, soft fabrics and antique furniture are juxtaposed with crisp lines and contemporary colours to create a very stylish and comfortable environment. The first floor residents-only wood-panelled sitting room is a delight and so is occasionally used by a visiting grandee for a backdrop to an interview; the presence of an honesty bar adds further to the appeal. The Screening Room holds weekend dinner-and-a-film nights, while Brasserie Max feels much more like a proper restaurant than a mere addendum; its menu is appealingly accessible and afternoon tea is a popular event.

Dorchester

🏛🏛🏛

Park Ln.   ⊖ Hyde Park Corner
⊠ W1K 1QA
📞 (020) 7629 8888
www.thedorchester.com

200 rm – ♦£282/618 ♦♦£318/834, ⊑ £26 – 50 suites

🍽 **Alain Ducasse at The Dorchester and China Tang and The Grill** *(See restaurant listing)*

The Dorchester

The focus here recently has been on improving still further the quality of service and this is most apparent in The Promenade: it may look as though it is an extension of the lobby but try walking through and you won't get far without being welcomed enthusiastically by a member of staff. Afternoon tea here remains a huge draw but they also now offer more of an evening service, to the accompaniment of a jazz trio who replace the day-shift pianist. Suites are always snapped up quickly and it is easy to see why: all have their own personality, from the three elegant rooftop suites which have their own outside terraces, to the Lionel Messel suite on the 7th floor, which has seemingly hosted virtually every visiting idol and has now been listed. There's an impressive choice of restaurant, after you've had a Martini in the bar: they've added more grilled dishes to the menu in The Grill, which seems logical; China Tang sets the standard for stylish dining in a Chinese restaurant and Alain Ducasse provides luxury surroundings to match the food.

MAYFAIR ▶ PLAN II

Dukes

35 St James's Pl.   ⊖ Green Park
✉ SW1A 1NY
✆ (020) 7491 4840
www.dukeshotel.com

84 rm – 🛉£270/444 🛉🛉£270/444, ☕ £24 – 6 suites

Dukes

Every hotel needs a little reinvention now and again and Dukes has been steadily changing its image over the last few years. It has enjoyed a constant presence in St James's for over a century and traditionally had a clubby, very British feel but this has given way to a brighter, fresher look which seems to suit it equally well. What hasn't been lost is the discreet atmosphere which is largely down to the very central, yet surprisingly quiet, location. The basement restaurant, which looks out at street level thanks to the vagaries of local topography, now offers an ambitious, modern menu with dishes that are original in look and elaborate in construction. The comfortable sitting rooms still do a brisk trade in afternoon tea but there is now also an outside cigar lounge. The bar is something of a London landmark (and was reputedly one of Ian Fleming's old haunts). Bedrooms are devoid of chintz and come in warm, calming colours; they have smart marble bathrooms and are decently proportioned.

Egerton House

17-19 Egerton Terr
✉ SW3 2BX
☏ (020) 7589 2412
www.egertonhousehotel.com

27 rm – ♦£276/432 ♦♦£276/432, ☕ £29 – 1 suite

⊖ South Kensington

Egerton House

In challenging economic times hotels can either panic and cut staff and slash rates – a course of action which usually ends in ruin – or they can hold their nerve and provide greater value for their guests. Anyone wondering what more a hotel can do should get along to Egerton House. This is a townhouse whose decorative style is at the lavish end of the scale; the fabrics are of the highest order and the colours neatly coordinated. The ground floor Victoria and Albert Suite comes with its own little decked terrace and a row of filled decanters for company. All the rooms are slightly different; the marble bathrooms are very neat and the hotel has made the best use of limited space – ask for one of the quieter rooms at the back overlooking the little garden. What really makes this little place stand out, though, is the service and the eager attitude of the staff. Lots of hotels spout tosh about being 'a home from home' but here they do make a genuine effort to make their guests feel part of things by, for example, arranging complimentary admission to events at the V&A.

CHELSEA ▶ PLAN XI

45 Park Lane

G4

45 Park Ln   ⊖ Hyde Park Corner
⊠ W1K 1PN
✆ (020) 7493 4545
www.45parklane.com

35 rm – ♦£474/834 ♦♦£474/834, ☕ £30 – 10 suites

⫯○ **Cut** *(See restaurant listing)*

45 Park Lane

It was the original site of the Playboy Club and has also been a car showroom but now 45 Park Lane has been reborn as The Dorchester's little sister and, lit up at night, her art deco façade makes her look rather cute. The style is certainly different from her famous sibling but the quality and depth of service come from the same top drawer. On each floor you'll find the work of a different contemporary British artist as well as a couple of hosts to take care of everything from unpacking your bags to booking you a restaurant. The bedrooms, which all have views over Hyde Park, are wonderfully sensual, with velvet walls, leather-wrapped doors and warm, heavy fabrics and the marble bathrooms are beautiful. Suites take up great positions on the corners of the building and have the best views, while the penthouse occupies the entire top floor. The red leather makes the cocktail bar on the mezzanine level a very sexy spot, while on the ground floor sits Wolfgang Puck's glamorous restaurant Cut which specialises in steaks.

Four Seasons

Hamilton Pl, Park Ln ⊖ Hyde Park Corner
✉ W1J 7DR
☎ (020) 7499 0888
www.fourseasons.com/london/

148 rm – ♦£594/750 ♦♦£594/750, ☕ £30 – 45 suites

⫯○ **Amaranto** (See restaurant listing)

Four Seasons

These days competition is pretty fierce at the luxury end of the
hotel market so, to stay ahead of the game, contenders need to
do more than just tinker with the cosmetics. The Four Seasons,
which was the group's first hotel outside the US, closed for a
couple of years and in that time was stripped right back, before
being put together again. The result is that Park Lane now has
a hotel that's really raised the bar in the comfort stakes. The
bedrooms, trimmed with plenty of walnut, sycamore, marble
and shiny steel, are particularly striking and come with all
the latest wizardry like self-regulating ambient heating. They
also occupy impressive square footage, as do the suites, the
number of which has been greatly increased. Dining is a
flexible feast – Amaranto is divided into a three areas: a bar,
restaurant and lounge and you can eat what you want, where
you want it, and that includes on the secluded outdoor terrace.
The stunning top-floor spa, with its fantastic views, caps off
this hotel's dazzling renaissance.

MAYFAIR ▶ PLAN II

The Gore

D5

190 Queen's Gate
✉ SW7 5EX
✆ (020) 7584 6601
www.gorehotel.com

⊖ Gloucester Road

50 rm – 🛉£204/360 🛉🛉£204/360, ☕ £15

The Gore

Being the nearest hotel to the Royal Albert Hall makes The Gore a popular choice for performers as well as attendees and the bright, casual bistro is always busier early and late in the evening than it ever is at 8pm. The hotel clearly stands out at the top of Queen's Gate with its fluttering Union flag and gleaming brass plaque and who needs a fitness room when you've got Kensington gardens just yards away. If you were in any doubt that this is the part of London most closely associated with Queen Victoria, then just step through the door because the walls are covered with pictures and paintings relating to her reign. But, despite the plethora of antiques and all that Victoriana, this is a hip little hotel with a large element of fun attached. Rooms like Miss Fanny and Miss Ada are as camp as they sound; the Tudor Room has a secret bathroom and minstrel's gallery, and many of the bathrooms give meaning to the expression 'sitting on the throne'. Bend down in the rooms and you might find a card saying "Look, we've cleaned here too".

Goring

H5

15 Beeston Pl, Grosvenor Gdns   ⊖ Victoria
✉ SW1W 0JW
✆ (020) 7396 9000
www.thegoring.com

62 rm – ♦£528 ♦♦£606, ⬭ **£30 – 7 suites**

 Goring *(See restaurant listing)*

The Goring

Not only has The Goring celebrated its centenary, but it is still owned by the family who built it. Jeremy Goring, the great-grandson of the founder, is now at the helm and this lineage is clearly welcomed by the staff – many of whom have been working at the hotel for years – as well as being appreciated by regular guests, who benefit from the excellent service. The hotel still has a pervading sense of Britishness, which designers like Nina Campbell fully respected when they were asked to update its look. There has been a clever introduction of new technology, from the TVs that rise from the desk to the touch panels that control everything but, reassuringly for those less familiar or enamoured with the modern world, one can still get a proper key with which to open one's bedroom door. The ground floor restaurant is a bright, discreet and comfortable affair and its menu celebrates Britain's own culinary heritage; the bar is colonial in its feel and the veranda overlooks the hotel's surprisingly large back garden.

VICTORIA

Halkin

G5

5 Halkin St
✉ SW1X 7DJ
☏ (020) 7333 1000
www.halkin.como.bz

35 rm – ▾£336/552 ▾▾£336/552, ☕ **£30 – 6 suites**

🍽 **Nahm** *(See restaurant listing)*

⊖ Hyde Park Corner

Halkin

The Halkin is still looking pretty sharp considering it opened just over 20 years ago as one of London's first boutique hotels. It's certainly more discreet than its sibling, The Metropolitan, which attracts a livelier and feistier crowd, although guests here can use its spa. Apart from the relatively recent addition of a small gym, there is not much in the way of public areas, save for the small but perfectly formed bar area next to the lobby, and Nahm, the hotel's acclaimed and inventive Thai restaurant. The hotel is really all about the bedrooms, which are neatly set out and cleverly thought through. The touch pad operation makes everything seem so effortless but the technology never reaches baffling proportions. All rooms have silk covered walls and marble bathrooms with lots of natural minerals and the Nahm menu is also available as room service. Staff are in abundance and appear to stay for a long time, which improves standards of service no end and pleases the regulars. They also all wear Armani, so no pressure there, then.

Hart House

51 Gloucester Pl   ⊖ Marble Arch
✉ W1U 8JF
✆ (020) 7935 2288
www.harthouse.co.uk

15 rm ⌂ – ♙£95/130 ♙♙£135/175

Michelin

Hart House has been in the same family for nearly 40 years and while the owner may not spend as much time in the hotel as he used to, he's got enough friendly staff running the place in his absence. Equally importantly, he's also still writing the occasional cheque, as the recent introduction of new LCD TVs would testify. The hotel wouldn't win any design awards but what you get, for a fair price, is clean and tidy accommodation in a late Georgian terrace house that's in a useful central location: it's just a short walk from Oxford Street and Hyde Park and less than a ten minute cab ride from Paddington for those who've taken the Heathrow Express. Gloucester Place may be a fairly busy thoroughfare but the bedrooms on the front have sufficient double glazing; there are family rooms available as well as rooms on the ground floor. Ceilings get lower the higher you climb, reflecting the time when the house's staff had their quarters at the top of the house. The only public area is the small, basement breakfast room but the hotel still manages to have a sociable, international atmosphere.

Haymarket

14

1 Suffolk Pl. ⊖ Piccadilly Circus
✉ SW1Y 4HX
✆ (020) 7470 4000
www.haymarkethotel.com

47 rm – ♥£318 ♥♥£372, ⊊ £20 – 3 suites

🍴 **Brumus** *(See restaurant listing)*

Firmdale

It's hard to believe that The Haymarket hotel opened back in 2007 – you would think it no more than a few months ago, which is testament to its housekeeping department. The hotel is a stylish, hip place, fashioned out of a grand John Nash Regency building that had been a gentleman's club and office before being gutted by a fire. Art and an eclectic collection of furniture now run through it; the lobby, conservatory and library are immaculately decorated and set the tone. No two rooms are the same but all come with dressed mannequins – the motif of the Kemp's hotels – and custom-made furniture. Those on the front could be used to advertise double-glazing but for extra quiet, ask to overlook the inner decked courtyard. The location couldn't be better: theatre-land is literally just outside – indeed, the hotel adjoins the Haymarket Theatre – and all that London offers is a short stroll away. If that isn't enough, there's a very swish swimming pool downstairs, just for residents. Brumus is the spacious restaurant serving easy, Italian food.

Hazlitt's

6 Frith St ⊖ Tottenham Court Road
✉ W1D 3JA
☎ (020) 7434 1771
www.hazlittshotel.com

27 rm – ♥£198/222 ♥♥£227/282, ☕ £12 – 3 suites

Hazlitt's

Along with its central Soho location, one of the best features of Hazlitt's has always been its intimate and chummy atmosphere, which even the addition of eight rooms in 2009 failed to disrupt. The building dates from 1718 and was named after the essayist and critic William Hazlitt, whose home it was. Appropriately, it still attracts plenty of writers today, but while there is much character to be found in all the bedrooms - from the wood panelling and busts to the antique beds and Victorian fixtures - you do also get free wi-fi. Duke of Monmouth is the most striking of the newer rooms: it's spread over two floors and has its own terrace with a retractable roof. Madam Dafloz, named after another of Soho's former roguish residents, is also appealing, with a sultry, indulgent feel. The Library, with its 24/7 honesty bar, is the hotel's only communal area and was slightly enlarged when the newer rooms were added. This is also one of the few hotels where breakfast in bed really is the only option – and who is going to object to that?

SOHO ▶ PLAN II

The Hempel

D3

31-35 Craven Hill Gdns.
✉ W2 3EA
☎ (020) 7298 9000
www.the-hempel.co.uk

⊖ Queensway
Closed 24-27 December

44 rm ☕ – ♦£170/300 ♦♦£200/350 – 6 suites

The Hempel

It's no surprise that The Hempel stands out in this part of town – on any given day you can walk past tourists with faces that tell of the disappointment and distress caused by staying in one of the terrible local hotels. This hotel remains true to the principles of its original designer, Anouska Hempel, who, in the late '90s, created a crisp, minimalist environment in a blizzard of white; the maintenance man must get through gallons of white emulsion to keep it looking fresh. Room 107 boasts one of the highest ceilings in London; there's a suspended bed in 110 and those who prefer black should ask for 405. As newer design-led hotels have sprouted up, so everyone has had to raise their game – The Hempel is no exception and these days is not quite so self-satisfied which, in turn, makes it feel more welcoming. The restaurant was moved to the ground floor and the menu changed to a more British affair. Its former space downstairs is now used as an art gallery and for private parties.

The Hoxton

K3

81 Great Eastern St.
✉ EC2A 3HU
✆ (020) 7550 1000
www.hoxtonhotels.com

⊖ Old Street

208 rm ☕ – †£69/259 ††£69/259

⑩ **Hoxton Grill** *(See restaurant listing)*

The Hoxton

A hotel run for the convenience of its guests rather than the management is a concept not as prevalent as one would think, but The Hoxton is one with an inherent understanding of what paying customers want. For a start they offer plenty of freebies, from newspapers and internet access on Apple Macs to 'Pret Lite' breakfasts and even an hour's free phone calls per day. Then there's the convenience of the rakish and relaxed Hoxton Grill, where all-day dining is positively encouraged; you can get a bacon sandwich for breakfast or a burger and a smoothie late at night. The young, good-looking, Converse-wearing staff may look indistinguishable from the customers but are a very helpful and refreshingly cheerful bunch. Bedrooms are quite compact – this isn't the sort of place where you tuck yourself away in your room anyway – but there are some nice touches, like the natty credit-card sized booklet which gives relevant information on the local area. The 'no rip-off' mantra even extends to a twice yearly auction when bedrooms are sold at crazy prices.

K + K George

C6

1-15 Templeton Pl
✉ SW5 9NB
☎ (020) 7598 8700
www.kkhotels.com

⊖ Earl's Court

154 rm 🛏 – ♦£130/220 ♦♦£150/240

K&K Hotels

Providing a model lesson on the importance of keeping on top of your product, The K+K hotel spent time during the recent economic turndown refurbishing all its bedrooms; they now boast fast internet, 320 thread count linen, American cherry wood panelling, flat screen TVs, full minibars, and under-floor heating in the bathroom; and the hotel is reaping the rewards. It occupies seven houses of a stucco fronted terrace; its interior in contrast to the period façade, is colourful and contemporary and fresh flowers and bowls of fruit are scattered around the lobby. The unexpectedly large rear garden, for which most hotels would give their eye teeth, has won local horticultural prizes and hosts breakfast on warm summer days. A simple menu is served in the bar but most guests take advantage of the central location and go out to eat. The hotel may be part of an international chain but there are plenty of staff on hand to add a personal touch and it also manages to feel part of the local community.

Knightsbridge

10 Beaufort Gdns ⊖ Knightsbridge
✉ SW3 1PT
℘ (020) 7584 6300
www.knightsbridgehotel.com

44 rm – ♦£195 ♦♦£235/285, ☕ £20

Firmdale

Firmdale Hotels all seem so quintessentially British that it'll be interesting to see what New Yorkers make of them now they have one of their own. The Knightsbridge, converted from a row of Victorian terrace houses in an attractive square, is another typical example of what they do so well: it proves style and comfort are not mutually exclusive and that a hotel can be fashionable without being fuzzy. The work of British artists, such as Carol Sinclair's slate stack and Peter Clark's dog collages sets the tone and the bedrooms are constantly being refreshed and rearranged. Those facing the square on the first floor benefit from floor to ceiling windows, while the Knightsbridge Suite stretches from the front to the back of the building. All rooms are so impeccably tidy and colour coordinated it'll make you question your own dress sense. The Library Room differs from many similarly named hotel sitting rooms by actually containing books, along with an honesty bar which holds everything from fruit and snacks to champagne and ice cream.

CHELSEA ▶ PLAN XI

Lanesborough

G4

Hyde Park Corner
✉ SW1X 7TA
✆ (020) 7259 5599
www.lanesborough.com

⊖ Hyde Park Corner

83 rm – †£474/546 ††£630, ☕ £35 – 10 suites

🍴 **Apsleys** *(See restaurant listing)*

The Lanesborough

Many of London's luxury hotels boast long and illustrious histories and have names that are recognised the world over. Having opened relatively recently in 1991, The Lanesborough still feels like something of a newcomer, but there is no doubt that it deserves its place among the top tier of London hotels. Constructed in 1733 as Viscount Lanesborough's country house, the building was perhaps better known as a hospital before it was converted into a hotel. The series of drawing rooms are smartly kitted out; the clubby library bar offers a vast selection of whiskies and cognacs and the Garden Room provides a hugely popular sanctuary for cigar smokers. Apsleys is their lavishly dressed Italian restaurant with superlative cooking. Bedrooms come in a rich and decorative Regency style and boast a host of extras, including laptops. There's a butler on each floor, on call 24 hours a day, and rooms are tripled-glazed. Ask for a room facing Hyde Park – you may not hear anything of the outside world but you can enjoy some pretty terrific views.

Langham

H2

1c Portland Pl., Regent St.
✉ W1B 1JA
✆ (020) 7636 1000
www.langhamhotels.com

⊖ Oxford Circus

355 rm – ✚£258/1,056 ✚✚£258/1,056, ☕ **£30 – 21 suites**

🍴 **Roux at the Landau** *(See restaurant listing)*

Langham

The Langham was one of Europe's first purpose-built Grand hotels when it opened in 1865. Since then it has been owned by all sorts, including at one stage the BBC – they used it as their library and was where 'The Goon Show' was recorded. In 2009 it emerged from an extensive refurbishment programme that didn't provide much change from £80 million and it is now competing with the big boys once again. Pride of place must be the Palm Court, a twinkling ersatz art deco space, which serves light meals and afternoon teas. The Artesian bar is a stylish affair and does interesting things with gin; there's a small courtyard terrace named in honour of a BBC radio gardener and the striking restaurant is under the aegis of the Roux organisation. The bedrooms have personality and, for a change, the furniture is free-standing rather than fitted; the boldly decorated Club rooms are particularly distinctive. The health and fitness club is impressively kitted out and includes a swimming pool in what was once a bank vault.

The Levin

F5

28 Basil St.
✉ SW3 1AS
✆ (020) 7589 6286
www.thelevinhotel.co.uk

Ө Knightsbridge

12 rm 🖵 – ♥£282/360 ♥♥£282/600

The Levin

Its bigger sister, The Capital, is a few strides down the road and may be better known, but The Levin still does the (Levin) family proud. Here you'll find a different decorative style but still the same level of care and enthusiasm in the service. The eye-catching fibre optic chandelier dominates the staircase, while the collection of Penguin paperbacks reminds you that this is a fundamentally British hotel. All 12 bedrooms are light and fresh-feeling; there are subtle nods in the direction of art deco in the styling but these are combined with a cleverly contemporary look which blends in well with the building. The best room is the top floor open-plan suite. Mini-bars are stocked exclusively with champagne - along with some helpful hints on how to prepare an assortment of champagne cocktails. In the basement you'll find Le Metro which provides an appealing, all-day menu with everything from quiche and salads to shepherd's pie and sausage and mash, along with selections from the family estate in the Loire.

Mandarin Oriental Hyde Park

F4

66 Knightsbridge   ⊖ Knightsbridge
✉ SW1X 7LA
✆ (020) 7235 2000
www.mandarinoriental.com/london

173 rm – ♦£354/900 ♦♦£354/900, ☕ £32 – 25 suites

🍴 **Bar Boulud and Dinner by Heston Blumenthal**
(See restaurant listing)

Mandarin Oriental Hyde Park

When the bewilderingly expensive new apartments next door went on sale things could finally quieten down in this part of town for a while. That said, during their construction there was also plenty of work being done on the hotel too. Bar Boulud, celebrated New York based chef Daniel Boulud's first European venture, occupies what was previously the hotel's housekeeping storeroom and proved a hit from day one. But that was nothing compared to the frenzy caused by Heston Blumenthal's enigmatically named restaurant with its thrilling menu of rediscovered and re-imagined British dishes. Meanwhile, the hotel continues to constantly upgrade and redecorate its bedrooms which all offer every imaginable luxury and extra. They are decorated in a classic English country house style and come in either beige and blue or red and gold – although the TVs do seem to be incongruously large. If evidence were still needed that the hotel is keen to remain one of the most luxurious in the capital, it comes in the fact that it recently spent a mere £1 million just on doing up its Royal Suite.

Mayflower

C6

26-28 Trebovir Rd.
✉ SW5 9NJ
☎ (020) 7370 0991
www.mayflowerhotel.co.uk

⊖ Earl's Court

43 rm ⌷ – 🛉£109/149 🛉🛉£149/299 – 4 suites

Mayflower

The Mayflower shares the same ownership as Twenty Nevern Square just around the corner and it too offers good value accommodation. It is also twice the size so the chances of actually getting a room are somewhat greater. Some of those rooms can be a little tight on space but this is also reflected in the room rates. Rooms 11, 17 and 18 are the best in the house and the general decoration is a blend of the contemporary with some Asian influence; some of the rooms have jet showers and others balconies. But what makes the hotel stand out is that the owner is nearly always on the property and his enthusiasm has been passed to his staff. This may not be a glitzy West End hotel but they really do make an effort to get to know their guests and help in anyway they can. There is no restaurant, but then it doesn't need one: there are plenty of places in which to eat that are no more than a vigorous stroll away. A plentiful breakfast is provided and, on summer days, can even be taken on the small terrace.

Metropolitan

G4

Old Park Ln   ⊖ Hyde Park Corner
✉ W1K 1LB
☏ (020) 7447 1000
www.metropolitan.como.bz

144 rm – ♦£299/479 ♦♦£335/515, ☕ £22 – 3 suites

○ **Nobu** *(See restaurant listing)*

Metropolitan

The Metropolitan is inextricably linked to its über-cool hang-out, The Met Bar. If you've never managed to blag your way past the doorman at night you can now secure entry by grabbing yourself some 'Afternoon Delight': a healthy version of afternoon tea with low-fat cakes and breadless sandwiches. The Metropolitan Hotel is well over a decade old now; in design terms, there may be more contemporary competitors around but it continues to hold its own in the fashion stakes by letting its guests create their own atmosphere. The bedrooms are neutral in colour and gadgets are discreetly integrated; all get regular licks of paint or, following an overnight stay from the occasional wannabe rock star, a full redecoration. Plenty of rooms overlook the park but the more interesting views are those facing east over the rooftops. The spa promises plenty of holistic treatments while London's original Nobu on the first floor ensures a further sprinkling of stardust. Even better, the staff now provide good service instead of just standing at an angle, looking cool.

The Milestone

D4

1-2 Kensington Ct.
W8 5DL
(020) 7917 1000
www.milestonehotel.com

High Street Kensington

56 rm – ♀£444/600 ♀♀£444/600, £25 – 6 suites

The Milestone

VISA

AE

The Milestone proves that it is the service, not the space, which makes a hotel. With 100 members of staff for 56 bedrooms, it's odds-on you'll be well looked after; the hotel prides itself on keeping records of the whims and preferences of their regulars. Plenty of thought has gone into the design and decoration of the bedrooms which are undergoing a refurbishment. It's in the detail where you notice the extra effort: there's a little gift with the turn-down service and the bathrobes are seasonally adjusted so one gets a lighter robe in summer. The suites display greater levels of whimsy than the standard rooms – just check out the art deco inspired Mistinguett Suite, named in honour of the celebrated music hall entertainer, while Johnny Weissmuller would feel more at home in The Safari Suite. The sitting room is a comfy place, with a jaunty looking Noel Coward hanging above the fireplace. The Jockey bar is so named as this was where the horses were stabled in the days when this Victorian building was a private house. The dining room is an intimate, wood-panelled affair.

Number Sixteen

16 Sumner Pl. ⊖ South Kensington
✉ SW7 3EG
☏ (020) 7589 5232
www.numbersixteenhotel.co.uk

41 rm – †£168 ††£222, ☕ £20

Firmdale

Number Sixteen opened back in 2001 and was the first one in Tim and Kit Kemp's Firmdale Group of hotels not to have its own restaurant. This actually suits it because it feels more like a private house than the others and, with repeat business standing at around 55%, they've clearly got it right. Attention to detail underpins the operation, whether in the individual styling of the bedrooms or the twice-daily housekeeping service. Breakfast is in the conservatory overlooking the little garden – don't miss the smoothie of the day – and is served until midday: welcome acknowledgement that not every guest has an early morning meeting. Firmdale also operates its own laundry service which explains how the bed linen retains such crispness. Rooms 2 and 7 have their own private patio terrace and all the first floor rooms benefit from large windows and balconies. The drawing room, with its plump sofa cushions and pretty butterfly theme, is a very charming spot and there's the added bonus of a nearby honesty bar.

One Aldwych

J3

1 Aldwych
WC2B 4RH
(020) 7300 1000
www.onealdwych.com

Temple

93 rm – †£288/498 ††£288/498, £26 – 12 suites

Axis *(See restaurant listing)*

One Aldwych

VISA MC AE

Things have gone all green down at One Aldwych. The hotel is hoping to take a lead within the hospitality industry on matters environmental (without, of course, neglecting its duties as a luxury hotel) and has appointed a 'green team' to oversee and coordinate procedures. The swimming pool is chemical and chlorine free; bath products are organic; and the chocolate on your pillow has been replaced by a book called 'Change the World'. As far as guests are concerned though, it's business as usual, which means extremely comfortable bedrooms and plenty of polished staff. Fruit and flowers are changed daily in the rooms, which are awash with Bang & Olufsen toys and also come with Frette linen; deluxe rooms and corner suites are particularly desirable. There's a choice of restaurant: the first floor Indigo offers a light, easy menu while Axis boasts more personality and greater ambition in its cooking. The lobby of the hotel is perhaps its most well-known feature; not only does it double as a bar surprisingly successfully but it also changes its look according to the seasons.

The Pelham

15 Cromwell Pl   ⊖ South Kensington
✉ SW7 2LA
✆ (020) 7589 8288
www.thepelhamhotel.co.uk

51 rm – ♦£228/276 ♦♦£288/354, ☕ £18 – 1 suite

The Pelham

It may no longer be part of the Firmdale group – it is owned by the people who have The Gore in Queensgate – but The Pelham retains that stylish look which comes from juxtaposing the feel of a classic English country house with the contemporary look of a city townhouse. Originally three houses, the hotel has a pleasing lack of conformity in its layout. Bold pastel colours, fine fabrics and a housekeeping department that could satisfy Howard Hughes combine to create bedrooms that are pristine, warm and comfortable. Spend too long in the panelled sitting room or library, with all those cushions, an honesty bar and a fridge full of ice cream and the world outside will seem positively frenzied. Downstairs you'll find Bistro Fifteen, a relaxed all-day affair which becomes a cosy and romantic dinner spot. Its menu is mostly centred on Europe with an extra Gallic element – a nod to the high number of French émigrés in the neighbourhood. There's a genuine helpfulness and an eagerness to please amongst the staff.

Ritz

 H4

150 Piccadilly
✉ W1J 9BR
✆ (020) 7493 8181
www.theritzlondon.com

⊖ Green Park

113 rm – †£282/768 ††£282/768, ☕ **£28 – 21 suites**

🍽 **Ritz Restaurant** *(See restaurant listing)*

🍽
♨
🛗
A/C
📶
🍴
VISA
MC
AE
O

The Ritz

Henry James considered that, "There are few hours in life more agreeable than the hour dedicated to the ceremony known as afternoon tea". Such is the popularity of Tea at the Ritz, which is served daily in the grand surroundings of the Palm Court, that the ceremony begins at 11.30 am – an hour before lunch is served in their restaurant – and doesn't cease until 7.30pm. Meanwhile, the rest of the hotel, built in 1906 in the style of a French chateau, remains in fine form thanks to constant re-investment by its owners, the Barclay Brothers. The William Kent Room must be the most ornate private dining room in London and the bedrooms are all immaculately kept. The Royal and Prince of Wales Suites both have enormous square footage and are often booked for long stays by those for whom the credit crunch is no more than a mild irritant. The Ritz Restaurant, with its dinner dances, lavish surroundings and brigades of staff, evokes images of a more formal but more glamorous age and the art deco Rivoli bar remains a veritable jewel.

St James's ▶ Plan II

448

The Rockwell

181-183 Cromwell Rd.　　　　　　　　　　⊖ Earl's Court
✉ SW5 0SF
☎ (020) 7244 2000
www.therockwell.com

40 rm – ♦£110/150 ♦♦£160/250, ☕ £10

The Rockwell

The Rockwell is steadily establishing itself on the London hotel scene and is building up quite a loyal client base. They certainly get a lot of things right: the reception is manned 24/7 and staff are imbued with sufficient self-confidence to make eye-contact with their guests and offer help when needed; the housekeeping department also do an evening service of all the rooms. The lobby is a comfortable space, with its fireplace and generous scattering of newspapers. The hotel is made up of two Victorian houses; the best two rooms are the split level 104 and 105 and those on the lower ground floor have their own private patios. All rooms have showers rather than baths, and come with top-brand toiletries, mini bars and free internet – you can even borrow a laptop. Meals are relaxed affairs with plenty of favourites and decent cocktails. Freshly baked croissants and homemade breads are a feature of breakfast; sometimes served on the south-facing garden terrace which is the hotel's most appealing feature.

SOUTH KENSINGTON ▶ PLAN XI

The Rookery

L2

12 Peters Ln, Cowcross St
✉ EC1M 6DS
✆ (020) 7336 0931
www.rookeryhotel.com

⊖ Barbican
Closed 24-26 December

32 rm – †**£210/282** ††**£282/472,** ☕ **£12 – 1 suite**

The Rookery

The mere fact that the original opening of the hotel was delayed because the owner couldn't find quite the right chimney pots tells you that authenticity is high on the agenda here. Named after the colloquial term for the local area from a time when it had an unruly reputation, the hotel is made up of a series of Georgian houses whose former residents are honoured in the naming of the bedrooms. Its decoration remains true to these Georgian roots, not only in the antique furniture and period features but also in the colours used; all the bedrooms have either half-testers or four-poster beds and bathrooms have roll-top baths. Rook's Nest, the largest room, is often used for fashion shoots. However, with the addition of flat screen TVs and wireless internet access, there is no danger of the hotel becoming a twee museum piece. Breakfast is served in the bedrooms and there is just one small sitting room which leads out onto a little terrace - its mural of the owner herding some cows goes some way towards blocking out the surrounding sights of the 21C.

St James's Hotel and Club

7-8 Park Pl. ⊖ Green Park
✉ SW1A 1LS
✆ (020) 7316 1600
www.stjameshotelandclub.com

55 rm – ♦£300/474 ♦♦£300/474, ☕ £22 – 10 suites

🍽 **Seven Park Place** (See restaurant listing)

St James's Hotel & Club

Dating from 1892, this building was a private club for many years and the hotel manages to retain something of that clubby spirit. It certainly feels as though it is run for the benefit of its guests rather than a balance sheet, and staff make genuine efforts to get to know the guests and their individual peculiarities. While the public areas are quite compact, the interior has been sympathetically modernised and features over 200 pieces of art, most of which are German works from the 1930s and '40s. Bedrooms are well-equipped and have smart, marble bathrooms; a few have small terraces and the Presidential Suite comes with an enormous one that can host up to 60 people. The restaurant is intimate and the cooking and service are undertaken with considerable expertise. The hotel's other great bonus is its location: this is the centre of central London but Park Place is also a cul-de-sac so it's quiet to boot. There's also a cut-through to Green Park where you'll find a pile of towels and water, placed there by the hotel for those who insist on running round it.

ST JAMES'S ▶ PLAN II

451

St Martins Lane

13

45 St Martin's Ln
✉ WC2N 3HX
✆ (020) 7300 5500
www.stmartinslane.com

⊖ Charing Cross

202 rm – 🚹£294/438 🚹🚹£318/462, ☕ £25 – 2 suites

🍴 **Asia de Cuba** *(See restaurant listing)*

St Martin's Lane

If you're uncomfortable with the idea of hotel staff calling you by your first name or have never considered working out in a gym wearing a pair of stilettos then St Martins Lane is probably not the hotel for you; nor you the right guest for them. Philippe Starck's design of the modern juxtaposed with the baroque creates an eye-catching lobby. The bedrooms are decorated in a blizzard of white, although you can change the lighting according to your mood. The views get better the higher you go but all have floor to ceiling windows. Thanks to the paparazzi, readers of the more excitable magazines will be familiar with Bungalow 8: Anne Sacco's London outpost of her hip New York club is a favoured hang-out for the already-famous, the would-be-famous and the related-to-someone-famous-famous. Asia de Cuba is Scarface meets Dr No: fiery Floridian Cuban mixed with teasing influence from across Asia – dishes are designed for sharing. The Light Bar is sufficiently hip and the Gymbox is a branded gym with a nightclub vibe – what else?

Sanderson

50 Berners St
⌧ W1T 3NG
☎ (020) 7300 1400
www.morganshotelgroup.com

150 rm – **♟£318/474 ♟♟£342/486**, ☕ **£25**

⫶○ **Suka** *(See restaurant listing)*

Sanderson

When the doorman greets you with a "how ya doing?" you know this is not a hotel that stands on ceremony. The staff do now smile here, something that was all too rare in the early days when they were mostly recruited from model agencies and had a somewhat disdainful attitude towards the whole concept of service. The Sanderson has always worn its exclusivity with confidence but now there's some substance to it. The Philippe Starck designed bedrooms still impress, with their celestial whiteness, sleigh beds in the middle of the room and idiosyncrasies such as the framed print hung on the ceiling – its actually the same print in all the rooms, is called 'Pathway to Heaven' and is designed to encourage heavenly thoughts before sleep. Some bedrooms have their own treadmills while others boast small terraces; the top two suites have their own lifts. On the ground floor the Purple Bar has over 75 different vodkas, miniature chairs and a selective door policy; the Long Bar is more accessible and leads into Suka, their modern Malaysian restaurant.

Savoy

Strand   ⊖ Charing Cross
✉ WC2R 0EU
✆ (020) 7836 4343
www.fairmont.com/savoy

221 rm – �£678 ♦♦£750, ☕ £30 – 30 suites

🍽 **Savoy Grill and River Restaurant** *(See restaurant listing)*

The Savoy

It took longer than anyone expected, but finally, in late 2010, the grande dame of London hotels made her long-awaited entrance. The careful restoration took nearly three years but the best news for the hotel's legions of regulars was that many of the familiar Edwardian and art deco features were retained. There is no longer a front desk – just numerous staff waiting to greet you as soon as you enter. Afternoon tea is served in the Thames Foyer, which remains at the heart of the operation – although it now has a steel gazebo beneath a glass dome. Just off the Foyer is a new bar to complement the world famous American Bar: The Beaufort Bar occupies the space from where the BBC once broadcast, with a champagne bar on the original stage. The River Room's art deco splendour has been given a contemporary makeover and its windows looking out over the river open fully in summer. The luxurious bedrooms remain true to the hotel's origins and are split between Edwardian or art deco styles.

STRAND AND COVENT GARDEN ▶ PLAN III

454

Soho

J3

4 Richmond Mews ⊖ Tottenham Court Road
✉ W1D 3DH
✆ (020) 7559 3000
www.sohohotel.com

85 rm – 🚹£354 🚹🚹£402, ☕ £20 – 2 suites

🍴 **Refuel** *(See restaurant listing)*

Firmdale

It's almost as if they wanted to keep it secret. The hotel is on a relatively quiet mews – not something one readily associates with Soho – and, even as you approach, it gives little away. But inside one soon realises that, if it was a secret, it wasn't very well kept as it's always buzzing with people. Their guests' every dietary whim or food mood should find fulfilment in 'Refuel', the restaurant with its own bar as a backdrop. Whether your diet is gluten-free, vegetarian, vegan, carnivorous or organic you'll discover something worth ordering and, if you're off out, you'll find the early dinner menu a steal. It's also worth checking out the Film Club for a meal and a movie in the screening room. Upstairs and the bedrooms are almost celestial in their cleanliness. From jazzy orange to bright lime green, from crimsons to bold stripes, the rooms are vibrant in style and immaculate in layout; those on the top floor have balconies and terraces. Add infectiously enthusiastic service and it's little wonder the hotel has so many returning guests. And to think this was once an NCP car park.

Stafford

16-18 St James's Pl.
✉ SW1A 1NJ
☎ (020) 7493 0111
www.kempinski.com/london

⊖ Green Park

105 rm – ♦£260/360 ♦♦£400/600, ☕ £25 – 8 suites

The Stafford has, for a few years, been a mix of the new and the more traditional. Recently, the owners have been busy injecting considerable amounts of money into its refurbishment; something which no doubt terrifies many of its loyal and longstanding guests who appear to like things just the way they are. Thanks to some judicious lighting, the lobby and lounge appear brighter and more inviting. The dining room now opens out more into the drawing room and has changed its name to the Lyttleton, after a family who once lived here, but it has wisely kept its traditional British menu. The relatively recently created suites in the Mews House, a converted office block in the rear courtyard of the hotel, are the most impressive of all the bedrooms. What will never change at The Stafford is the celebrated American Bar, which is festooned with an impressive collection of assorted ties, helmets and pictures and is one of the best in London for those who like their bars with chairs and without music.

Twenty Nevern Square

20 Nevern Sq.   ⊖ Earl's Court
✉ SW5 9PD
✆ (020) 7565 9555
www.twentynevernsquare.co.uk

20 rm ☕ – ♥£84/360 ♥♥£96/480

Michelin

Booking well in advance is the key here, as this small but friendly hotel, with its quiet and leafy location in the typically Victorian Nevern Square, represents good value for money and gets booked up pretty quickly. The two best rooms are the Pasha and the more recently added Ottoman Suite and both have their own terrace, but all rooms are well looked after and given regular refits. Ten of the rooms overlook the gardens opposite but try to get one of the rooms on the top floor as these have more space. Hand-carved Indonesian furniture is found throughout and, together with the elaborately draped curtains, adds a hint of exoticism. You'll find gratis tea, coffee, water and a pile of daily newspapers laid on in the pleasant lounge beside the lovebirds, Mary and Joseph. Continental breakfast comes included in the room rate; it can be taken in the bedroom or the bright conservatory. The hotel's other great selling point is the genuine sense of neighbourhood one feels. Its sister hotel, the Mayflower, is around the corner.

Westbury

🏨🏨🏨

Bond St
✉ W1S 2YF
☎ (020) 7629 7755
www.westburymayfair.com

⊖ Bond Street

233 rm – 🛏£275/469 🛏🛏£275/469, ☕ **£26 – 13 suites**

🍴 **Alyn Williams at the Westbury** *(See restaurant listing)*

🍴
💪
🛗
♿
A/C
📶
🍴
VISA
MC
AE
◑

The Westbury opened in the 1950s and caused quite a commotion with its New York sensibilities. Over recent years, considerable funds have been spent restoring it to its former glory with the result that this is now one of Mayfair's more comfortable hotels. It is traditional without being staid and discreet without appearing previous; the staff are suitably enthusiastic and clearly proud of their hotel. There is no doubt that its location is also a huge draw: there are enough exclusive designer brands just outside the front door to satisfy even the most committed disciple of Edina and Patsy. The bedrooms are sleek and comfy and each floor is decorated with photos from the corresponding decade (so 1960s style icons adorn the 6th floor). The suites are particularly smart, especially those with art deco styling. The iconic Polo bar is elegantly dressed in Gucci and Fendi and its celebrated cocktail list ensures it's busy at night. Along with a sushi bar the hotel now offers sublime dining courtesy of chef Alyn Williams' creative and elaborate cuisine.

Zetter

K1

St John's Sq., 86-88 Clerkenwell Rd. ⊖ Farringdon
EC1M 5RJ
(020) 7324 4444
www.thezetter.com

72 rm – †£222 ††£222, £14

Bistrot Bruno Loubet *(See restaurant listing)*

The Zetter

The Zetter ticks all the boxes for a contemporary hotel - it's a converted Victorian warehouse in a hitherto neglected area of the city that's now having its time and is environmentally aware, with spring water bottled from its building's own well. Its restaurant, thanks to the reputation of chef Bruno Loubet, is busy pulling in the crowds; it has understated bedrooms offering everything from a huge array of music tracks to classic Penguin paperbacks and, to appreciate all these things, it attracts a clientele who know their wiis from their wi-fis. But what makes the place more than just another hip hotel is its friendly and hospitable staff who understand that the principles of hospitality remain the same, regardless of whether the hotel is trendy or traditional, and that coolness need not equate to aloofness. Across St. John's Square you'll find the more idiosyncratically decorated Zetter Townhouse, fashioned from two Georgian houses. Despite a very busy cocktail lounge, this is sadly used more as an overflow than a hotel in its own right.

The Michelin Adventure

It all started with rubber balls! This was the product made by a small company based in Clermont-Ferrand that André and Edouard Michelin inherited, back in 1880. The brothers quickly saw the potential for a new means of transport and their first success was the invention of detachable pneumatic tyres for bicycles. However, the automobile was to provide the greatest scope for their creative talents. Throughout the 20th century, Michelin never ceased developing and creating ever more reliable and high-performance tyres, not only for vehicles ranging from trucks to F1 but also for underground transit systems and aeroplanes.

From early on, Michelin provided its customers with tools and services to facilitate mobility and make travelling a more pleasurable and more frequent experience. As early as 1900, the Michelin Guide supplied motorists with a host of useful information related to vehicle maintenance, accommodation and restaurants, and was to become a benchmark for good food. At the same time, the Travel Information Bureau offered travellers personalised tips and itineraries.

The publication of the first collection of roadmaps, in 1910, was an instant hit! In 1926, the first regional guide to France was published, devoted to the principal sites of Brittany, and before long each region of France had its own Green Guide. The collection was later extended to more far-flung destinations, including New York in 1968 and Taiwan in 2011.

In the 21st century, with the growth of digital technology, the challenge for Michelin maps and guides is to continue to develop alongside the company's tyre activities. Now, as before, Michelin is committed to improving the mobility of travellers.

MICHELIN TODAY

WORLD NUMBER ONE TYRE MANUFACTURER
- 69 production sites in 18 countries
- 115,000 employees from all cultures and on every continent
- 6,000 people employed in research and development

Moving
for a world

Moving forward means developing tyres with better road grip and shorter braking distances, whatever the state of the road.

CORRECT TYRE PRESSURE

RIGHT PRESSURE

- Safety
- Longevity
- Optimum fuel consumption

-0,5 bar

- Durability reduced by 20% (- 8,000 km)

-1 bar

- Risk of blowouts
- Increased fuel consumption
- Longer braking distances on wet surfaces

forward together
where mobility is safer

It also involves helping motorists take care of their safety and their tyres. To do so, Michelin organises "Fill Up With Air" campaigns all over the world to remind us that correct tyre pressure is vital.

WEAR

DETECTING TYRE WEAR

MICHELIN tyres are equipped with tread wear indicators, which are small blocks of rubber molded into the base of the main grooves at a height of 1.6 mm. When tread depth is the same level as indicators, the tyres are worn and need replacing.

Tyres are the only point of contact between vehicle and the road, a worn tyre can be dangerous on wet surfaces.

NEW TYRE

WORN TYRE
(1,6 mm tread)

The photo shows the actual contact zone on wet surfaces.

Moving forward
means sustainable mobility

By 2050, Michelin aims to cut the quantity of raw materials used in its tyre manufacturing process by half and to have developed renewable energy in its facilities. The design of MICHELIN tyres has already saved billions of litres of fuel and, by extension, billions of tonnes of CO2.

Similarly, Michelin prints its maps and guides on paper produced from sustainably managed forests and is diversifying its publishing media by offering digital solutions to make travelling easier, more fuel efficient and more enjoyable!

The group's whole-hearted commitment to eco-design on a daily basis is demonstrated by ISO 14001 certification.

Like you, Michelin is committed to preserving our planet.

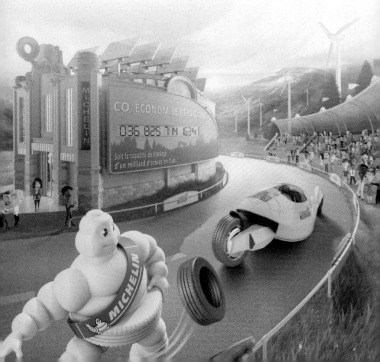

Chat with Bibendum

Go to
www.michelin.com/corporate/fr
Find out more about Michelin's
history and the latest news.

QUIZ

Michelin develops tyres for all types of vehicles. See if you can match the right tyre with the right vehicle…

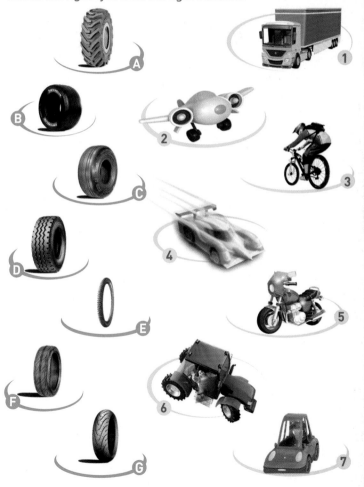

Solution : A-6 / B-4 / C-2 / D-1 / E-3 / F-7 / G-5

Notes

Index of maps

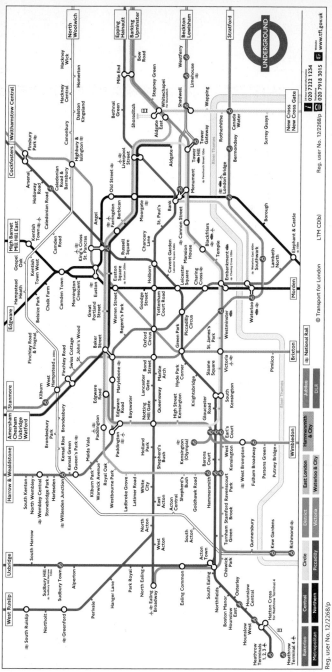

Index & Maps

UNDERGROUND

www.tfl.gov.uk

24 hour travel information
020 7222 1234
020 7918 3015

Reg. user No. 12/2268/p

LTM CDIb

© Transport for London

National Rail

Bakerloo   Central   District   East London   Jubilee   Metropolitan

Circle   Hammersmith & City   Victoria   Northern   Waterloo & City   Piccadilly   DLR

Great Britain: Based on Ordnance Survey of Great Britain with the permission of the Controller of Her Majesty's Stationery Office, © Crown Copyright 100000247.

Cover photography : Pollen Street Social

Michelin Travel Partner

Société par actions simplifiées au capital de 11 629 590 EUR
27 Cours de l'Ile Seguin - 92100 Boulogne Billancourt (France)
R.C.S. Nanterre 433 677 721

© Michelin, Propriétaires-éditeurs

Dépot légal octobre 2012
Printed in Italy : 09-2012
Printed on paper from sustainably managed forests
Compogravure : NORD COMPO à Villeneuve-d'Ascq (France)
Impression et brochage : LA TIPOGRAFICA VARESE, Varese (Italie)

No part of this publication may be reproduced in any form
without the prior permission of the publisher